Making Good

Making Good

Creation, Creativity, and Artistry

Trevor Hart

BAYLOR UNIVERSITY PRESS

Scripture quotations from the New Revised Standard Version Bible are copyright 1989, Division of Christian Education of the National Council of the Churches of Christ in the United States of America. Used by permission. All rights reserved.

Cover design by John Barnett, 4 Eyes Design
Cover art: St. Joseph Portrayed as a Medieval Carpenter from the Merode Altarpiece c. 1425 (oil on panel), Master of Flemalle (Robert Campin) (1375/8–1444) / Metropolitan Museum of Art, New York, USA / The Bridgeman Art Library

Library of Congress Cataloging-in-Publication Data
Hart, Trevor A.
  Making good : creation, creativity, and artistry / Trevor Hart.
  380 pages cm
  Includes bibliographical references and index.
  ISBN 978-1-60258-988-9 (hardback : alk. paper)
1. Christianity and art. 2. Creation (Literary, artistic, etc.)—Religious aspects—Christianity. 3. Imagination—Religious aspects—Christianity. 4. Creationism. I. Title.
  BR115.A8H38 2014
  261.5'7—dc23
                        2014010727

Printed in the United States of America on acid-free paper with a minimum of 30% post-consumer waste recycled content.

For the staff and students of
St Mary's College, University of St Andrews, 1995–2013,
the congregation of Saint Andrew's
Episcopal Church, St Andrews,
and the clergy and people of the Diocese of
St Andrews, Dunkeld and Dunblane
Oremus pro invicem

Yours Lord is the greatness, the power,
the glory, the splendor and the majesty;
for everything in heaven and earth is yours.
All things come from you,
and of your own do we give you.

Contents

Preface

Books are odd things. Some take far longer to write than others or find themselves shunted temporarily into a siding to permit other projects to overtake them. This book brings to a head scholarly work conducted gradually over a period of eight years, its origins lying in a period of research leave taken during the academic session 2005–2006. It was always conceived as the first of three volumes, and work on the other two has continued alongside it and will hopefully follow it into publication duly.

I have entitled the larger project A Poetics of Redemption, because the whole will reflect the shape of the Trinitarian drama of God's engagement with the world as Christians understand it (following the "moments," as they are sometimes called, of creation, incarnation, and the outpouring of the Holy Spirit), and because the project's particular concern is with the significance and impact of various acts of human *poesis* in shaping both our appreciation of and our participation in that drama. Thus, this first volume is not a full-orbed doctrine of creation as such, but an attempt to situate accounts of human "creativity"—in the arts and more broadly—within the theological context provided by a Christian account of God's identity as Creator of heaven and earth. In it I shall argue that, despite some perfectly proper and theologically astute concerns about the metaphorical appropriation of the verb *creō* and its cognates to refer to human aspiration and achievements, in the final analysis such appropriation need not be mischievous but may properly be redeemed in a manner that, by looking forward already to the horizons of Christology and eschatological fulfillment, both maintains the vital distinctions between God and the creature and reckons fully with the implications of our humanity having been drawn fully and permanently into the dynamics of God's triune *operationes ad extra* in the enfleshing of the Son. Volume 2 (already drafted in significant part) will concentrate on aspects of the relationship between the material and the nonmaterial dimensions of the human world as these manifest themselves in the arts, seeking clarity and a framework of interpretation from classic christological paradigms and in turn exploring ways in which Christology and our understanding of the redemptive import of the incarnation have themselves been expressed in and shaped by human artistry of one sort or another. Finally, volume 3 will offer a more comprehensive and systematic treatment of the imaginative in human experience and action and will explore the possibility that it is through the captivity, regeneration, and transfiguration of the human imaginary (personal, social, cosmic) that the Holy Spirit lays hold of our humanity as a whole and transforms it redemptively from within.

Readers who are allergic to the suggestion that the imaginative might have anything properly to do with Christian theology or the life of faith would be advised to put this book down now, before a nasty adverse reaction is triggered. I have argued the contrary case carefully and at length elsewhere[1] and feel no particular need to add extra pages to what is already a bulky volume by repeating the exercise here. I would, of course, commend that same argument to those as yet unpersuaded but willing to consider the matter in a spirit of generous conversation. Those undeterred, intrigued, or even attracted by the suggestion may, I hope, include both theologians (whether scholars, students, or interested lay readers) and others whose work compels them to reckon seriously with the workings of human imagination, in the arts or elsewhere. The book is written from a theological standpoint, and it begins and ends, therefore, with material of an unashamedly and explicitly biblical and theological sort. Chapters 5 to 13, though, are an attempt to participate precisely in an interdisciplinary conversation to which Christian theology contributes only one voice among others and which seeks deliberately to allow other voices to speak more prominently and on their own terms before responding in its turn. So, readers with philosophical, art-historical, or other theoretical interests and concerns may—as long as they are willing to tolerate the inevitable (and hopefully worthwhile) reflections and interjections that a Christian theologian cannot help himself but indulge in as this conversation proceeds—find much else to engage with besides in the larger part of the book. The work does, though, seek finally to argue a theological case (one addressed not to those outside the discipline so

---

[1] See Trevor Hart, *Between the Image and the Word: Theological Engagements with Imagination, Language and Literature* (Farnham, U.K.: Ashgate, 2013), chap. 1.

much as to those within it); and this is most apparent in the opening and closing chapters, though it breaks the surface for air repeatedly throughout.

An author is generally most conscious of what ought to go into a book only as he or she runs out of time and space, and if I had more of either (which, thankfully, I do not), I might have sought to expand the space given in this book to questions pertaining to evil and its surd appearance in a creation understood as the gift of God's grace and the object of his promise. By way of mitigation, I will say only that I have sought to acknowledge the issue at various key junctures and to provide a framework within which cheery optimism about human "creative" capacities finds no necessary place. My preferred emphasis here, though, has been on the essential continuity between God's work in creation and that other work necessitated by sin and evil, which Christians call the economy of redemption. Concentration on this redemptive dynamic itself will be more apparent in the perspective adopted by the two companion volumes, and I can ask only that readers and reviewers bear in mind the sense in which the present work, therefore, points identifiably beyond itself for its own completion.

A book with so long a period of gestation inevitably cross-fertilizes with other projects that the author is involved in concomitantly, and this one is no exception. In particular, readers will discover some overlap both of concerns and of expression here and there with passages in *Between the Image and the Word*, a volume based on a series of shorter pieces written during the years 1997–2013. Thanks are due to Ashgate Publishing Ltd for kind permission to reproduce the relevant handful of short passages in the current, larger work on the themes in question, within the horizons of which they have their natural (and originally intended) home. Thanks are also due to my colleagues and students in the University of St Andrews, especially its Institute for Theology, Imagination and the Arts, whose collegiality, encouragement, and insight over those same years have helped to shape the project since its inception. I am grateful too to the University of New South Wales for inviting me to deliver the New College Lectures in September 2008 and to Biola University in California who generously hosted me as their Visionary in Residence in November 2013. It was in Sydney that the key ideas for this book were given their first tentative outing in public and among friends (academics and practitioners in the arts) in Los Angeles that some of them received their final honing and testing. Of course, I could and should have learned much more from the contributions and criticisms of others, and any perceived shortfalls or errors in the pages that follow bear witness to that fact.

The completion of this book straddles two distinct phases in my ministry as a Christian theologian and as a priest in the Scottish Episcopal Church. The work was conceived of, and most of the research and writing undertaken, during my tenure as Professor of Divinity and Director of the Institute for Theology, Imagination and the Arts in the University of St Andrews. By the time that the final couple of chapters were drafted, though, I had already moved from the position of professional theologian within the academy to take up a full-time liturgical and pastoral role as Rector of Saint Andrew's Episcopal Church in the town of St Andrews. The final stages of writing this book accompanied that transition step by step. I am grateful to the University of St Andrews for affording me plentiful opportunities over the past nineteen years to participate in the sort of theological engagement demanded by the research library, the lecture hall, and the seminar room, and for permitting me even yet to retain such involvement in scholarship and in the supervision of its research students as the demands of pastoral ministry will permit. I am grateful, too, to the Vestry of Saint Andrew's Episcopal Church and to the Bishop and the Diocese of St Andrews, Dunkeld and Dunblane for recognizing and endorsing God's call to me to return to the coalface, so allowing me to engage in theology in a rather different and more down-to-earth mode. I have therefore dedicated the book to these two distinct communities of faith and practice.

Trevor Hart
St Andrews
Candlemas
February 2014

1

Grammars of Creation

My chief concern in this book will be with what George Steiner has described helpfully as "grammars of creation,"[1] some arising within the provinces of Christian theology and others situated identifiably beyond its borders. If we take the current state of the English language as our starting point (as in some sense we are bound to), we find that talk of "creation" and "creativity" crops up nowadays in a range of quite different semantic fields. Some of these uses are by now well established, while others still bear the marks of relatively recent linguistic innovation. The effective democratization of such terms that has occurred during the past fifty years in particular, some would argue, entails a metaphorical redeployment more profligate than profound. Writing in the 1960s, the art historian Erwin Panofsky already noted with implicit disdain the then modish talk of "creative hairstyles," "creative play" for small children, and undergraduate modules purporting to teach students the skills of "creative writing."[2] By the second decade of the twenty-first century, things have, of course, progressed further in the same direction, the epithet "creative" having successfully colonized (or been dragooned into service by) the self-descriptions of a wide range of economic, cultural, and media industries, one famous motor manufacturer proudly proclaiming itself (its tongue only half lodged in its cheek in doing so)

---

[1] George Steiner, *Grammars of Creation* (London: Faber & Faber, 2001).

[2] Erwin Panofsky, *Renaissance and Renascences in Western Art* (New York: Harper & Row, 1972), 187n3.

"Créateur d'automobiles."[3] Much of this certainly seems to be very far removed from the territories of concern with which talk of "creation" and "creativity" has more traditionally (and, some would insist, more properly) been associated—namely, religious and theological accounts of God's primal *actiones ad extra*, and, by way of presumed analogy, those aesthetic discourses having to do with the processes and significance of certain creaturely acts of artistic making. In recent decades it has been those passionately concerned for the integrity of the latter as distinct from the former use, perhaps, who have complained most loudly about what they perceive as a debasing of linguistic coinage by ill-judged and prodigal use.[4] Ironically, though, the transplanting of *creare*, *creator*, and *creatio* from the hallowed ground of Christian liturgy and doctrine (which hitherto had been their sole preserve) onto the soils of art-historical and art-theoretical description in the sixteenth century was itself a deliberate act of semantic transgression, and one resisted by many at the time as sacrilegious in its presumption. Whether it desecrated anything or not, the new use eventually took root and grew, and as it did so it not only expressed but also effected subtle but profound shifts in the prevalent vision of human artistry and its capacities, some of which turned out to be less than wholly felicitous in religious and theological terms. The semantic fields of "creation," Steiner notes, overlap and interfere,[5] and those who borrow and try the term on for size in whatever human context situate themselves and their actions of "making," whether knowingly or not, in relation to divine precedent.

What, from a theological perspective, are we to make of this "presumption of affinity"?[6] That is the question to which my investigation in this book will be directed. In asking it, in the first instance at least, my point will not be to inquire whether some sorts of human activities are more warranted in such linguistic presumption than others and on what grounds. Instead, I want to begin by posing the larger and more basic question alluded to above and thrown up at once by any serious engagement with the Christian doctrine of God as "Créateur du monde." Is "creating," in fact, an activity that anyone other than God himself may reasonably be supposed capable of? Or, put differently, should the vocabulary of "creation" and "creativity" properly be reserved in the theologically informed lexicon to denote something that God alone does and is capable of doing? We cannot, of course, put the lexical genie back in the bottle; but some

---

[3] See Rob Pope, *Creativity: Theory, History, Practice* (London: Routledge, 2005), xix.

[4] See, e.g., John Tusa, *On Creativity: Interviews Exploring the Process* (London: Methuen, 1994), 5–12.

[5] Steiner, *Grammars of Creation*, 17.

[6] Steiner, *Grammars of Creation*, 18.

have certainly suggested that Christians ought,[7] nonetheless, to pursue a strategy of countercultural resistance, refusing in principle to sanction use of the term "creation" for anything other than a particular sort of "act of God" and its outputs, or at least interjecting whenever occasion permits (and we remember to do so) that, in the strict and proper sense, "finite agents do not create"[8] (they merely "make" or "invent" or whatever). What ought we to make of this suggestion?

Such unilateral retrenchment might seem to be warranted if not actually demanded by significant currents in the Christian doctrine of creation across the ages, a doctrine linked closely to the apprehension of God's radical otherness and uniqueness, and defining of many attempts to articulate that. God, it has commonly been insisted, is absolutely distinct in ontological terms from that which he has created—Scripture's "the heavens and the earth," the creed's "all things, visible and invisible"—an otherness conveniently summed up simply by appeal to the corresponding negative. God himself is "uncreated"; nothing else is or ever could be. The categories of the doctrine of creation naturally cross-fertilize, therefore, with those of classical Trinitarian and incarnational theologies, the Nicene insistence that the Son of God was Creator rather than creature ("begotten, not made") being a clinching argument in the fourth-century assertion of his hypostatic identity as God.[9] Richard Bauckham has recently argued that something directly parallel may be observed in the rather different conceptual world of the New Testament, where in terms of the categories proper to Second Temple Jewish monotheism, the preexistent Christ is spoken of as participating directly in the creation of the cosmos (e.g., Col 1:15-16) and thereby understood to be included (in Bauckham's terms) within the "unique identity of the God of Israel."[10] In each case, the relevant theological premise taken for granted is that God alone is uncreated and God alone creates. Not only is God radically and incomparably other than the world; it is precisely his act of creating the cosmos that, more obviously than anything else, marks him out as such. "Tautologically, only God creates."[11] Viewed thus, the language of creation itself seems to smolder with

---

[7] See, e.g., Calvin Seerveld, *Rainbows for the Fallen World: Aesthetic Life and Artistic Task* (Toronto: Tuppence Press, 1980).

[8] Colin Gunton, *The Triune Creator: A Historical and Systematic Study* (Grand Rapids: Eerdmans, 1998), 1n2.

[9] See Thomas F. Torrance, *The Trinitarian Faith: An Evangelical Theology of the Ancient Catholic Church* (Edinburgh: T&T Clark, 1988), 76–109.

[10] Richard Bauckham, *Jesus and the God of Israel: God Crucified and Other Studies on the New Testament's Christology of Divine Identity* (Grand Rapids: Eerdmans, 2008), 18, cf. 26–27.

[11] Steiner, *Grammars of Creation*, 20.

holiness and might reasonably be supposed best left well alone rather than toyed with or borrowed without explicit divine permission.

What is this thing, then, that only God has done and is capable of doing? What is it to "create" in this sense? Most fundamentally, the term refers to the divine donation of existence as such where otherwise there was neither scope nor possibility for it, an act of absolute origination necessarily unparalleled within the realm of the created order itself.[12] Here, the philosopher's "interrogation of the ontological"[13]—"Why is there not nothing?"—finds a response reaching beyond the categories of philosophical ontology alone and drawing explicitly on the resources of a theology of grace. There is "not nothing" because God freely grants something *esse* alongside himself and invites it to "be with him"; in doing so, furthermore, God establishes a "primordial plenitude"[14] of meaning and possibility, an orderly habitation fit for human (and other sentient creaturely) indwelling and flourishing. All this, of course, bespeaks the radical transcendence of God with respect to the cosmos and its concomitant dependence on him not just for its inception but for its continuing moment-to-moment existence. What distinguishes "creation proper" though, Colin Gunton argues, is its status as something done and dusted "in the beginning," the necessary presupposition of historical existence rather than a feature of it. What remains, he insists, is not "more creation, but simply what creator and creature alike and together make of what has been made."[15]

These are important theological emphases to be sure, and ones central to classical articulations of the doctrine; but there is more yet to be said. As Gunton himself admits, if divine "creating" is indeed an action situated properly within the grammar of the perfect tense (God always *has* created), there is nonetheless a vital sense in which "creation" itself (the output of that action)[16] remains incomplete and a work very much still in progress.[17] In the Genesis narrative, the advent of the seventh day certainly

[12] So, for Aquinas, "God's proper effect in creating is . . . existence *tout court.*" St. Thomas Aquinas, *Summa Theologiae,* vol. 8, *Creation, Variety, and Evil* (1a. 44–49), ed. Thomas Gilby, O.P. (London: Blackfriars in conjunction with Eyre & Spottiswoode, 1967), 1a.45.4 (p. 47).

[13] Steiner, *Grammars of Creation,* 32.

[14] I owe this helpful phrase to Michael Northcott.

[15] Gunton, *Triune Creator,* 89. Gunton draws directly here on the account of Oliver O'Donovan, *Resurrection and Moral Order: An Outline for Evangelical Ethics* (Leicester, U.K.: InterVarsity, 1986), chaps. 2–3.

[16] Gunton reminds us that the term "creation," whether applied to God or human agents, tends to be used in a dual sense, to refer both to the action of "creating" and to the thing duly "created." Gunton, *Triune Creator,* 1.

[17] Gunton, *Triune Creator,* 88–89.

seems to mark a firebreak in the characterization of divine action, a point in time by which certain things are already established and "given" and beyond which they need not be repeated or modified. The world is now "finished" (Gen 2:1) inasmuch as it is ready for immediate occupation, and after this, Wolfhart Pannenberg suggests, in a fundamental sense, God "does not bring forth any new creatures."[18] Wherever in prehistory we imagine this point in time to have arisen, though (in the text it is only with the appearance on the scene of human beings), it is clear that in another equally fundamental sense all this is only the beginning of "God's project,"[19] not its divinely intended end. The divine expression of aesthetic satisfaction in Genesis 1:31 is thus, Karl Barth insists, not a valediction but a prolepsis, an evaluation made with the divine gaze fixed precisely and firmly on what can and will yet be made of what has been made.[20] The fulfillment of God's "creative" labors, shaping and reshaping a world fit for human and divine cohabitation (the "external basis of the covenant" as Barth has it),[21] must therefore be traced not in protology but in an eschatology christologically and soteriologically determined and oriented. The creation is "very good," but from this perspective the divine declaration that "it is finished" must await utterance on another occasion altogether.[22] While we may still wish to insist upon reserving talk of "creation proper" for a particular set of precise and technical uses, therefore, it is nonetheless clear that the term has a penumbra already gesturing toward wider and extended ("improper"?) use, even within the grammar of theology itself.

The shape of the biblical witness to creation is, as Terence Fretheim observes, entirely consonant with this semantic overspill.[23] Hebrew possesses no single term covering the range of meanings of the English "creation," and while the Hebrew poets certainly take trouble to demarcate some lexical holy ground which must never be trespassed upon (the singular verb *bārā'* being set apart from the wider imaginative field to name a unique and nontransferable activity of "creation proper"[24]), their witness

[18] Wolfhart Pannenberg, *Systematic Theology* (Edinburgh: T&T Clark, 1994), 2:36. Cf. Karl Barth, *Church Dogmatics III/1* (Edinburgh: T&T Clark, 1958), 182.

[19] Gunton, *Triune Creator*, 202.

[20] Barth, *Church Dogmatics III/1*.

[21] Barth, *Church Dogmatics III/1*, 94–228.

[22] John 19:30.

[23] "Creation is not simply past; it is not just associated with 'the beginning.' God does not cease to be the Creator when the work of Genesis 1–2 has been completed nor is God thereafter reduced to the role of creative manager." Terence Fretheim, *God and World in the Old Testament: A Relational Theology of Creation* (Nashville: Abingdon, 2005), 7.

[24] So Walter Brueggemann, *Theology of the Old Testament: Testimony, Dispute, Advocacy* (Minneapolis: Fortress, 1997), 148–49.

to God's primordial performance equally resists reduction to any "single or simple articulation" of the matter.[25] Instead, the writers deploy a string of verbal images inevitably and deliberately suggestive of human analogy to some, at least, of what occurs "creatively" during the first six days. Indeed, recent studies by William P. Brown, Michael Welker, and others have insisted, if we are faithful to the imaginative logic of the biblical text here, we find arising within it quite naturally the suggestion that there are aspects of God's "fashioning" of a cosmos not only analogous to but actually enlisting and, via some presumed kenotic self-accommodation, *requiring* the participation of creaturely forces and agencies as such.[26] This, Brown suggests provocatively, is a God whose creative work is ultimately achieved *per collaborationi.*[27] Such poetic suggestion concurs, of course, with what we now understand of the shaping of the material cosmos, an understanding no longer tolerating imaginative confinement of it to a single working week situated "in the beginning." Whatever we may suppose about the temporal status of the primal act of incipience, granting *esse* charged with meaning and potential to all things (including, Augustine reminds us, time itself),[28] several centuries of learning in physics, geology, and biology serve to assure us that the work of forming a physical world fit for human indwelling is one which, precisely insofar as it harnesses and involves the created capacities of the cosmos itself, cannot be hurried but takes a long time. Again, wherever we locate the advent of creation's seventh day, to the best of our knowledge those same creaturely forces and processes are ones that rumble on beyond it, possessed of an abiding remit, a temporal future as well as a murky prehistoric past. Correspondingly, many of the biblical images used to picture God's ancient fashioning of the cosmos are extended perfectly naturally to picture his hand still at work, shaping the world's history and moving it toward its promised future.

If Brown's further argument that, in the "creation traditions" of Scripture itself, God's activity of generating and ordering a physical *cosmos* is understood to be of a piece with—and not properly separable from—his calling forth an accompanying *ethos* to render an integral

---

[25] Brueggemann, *Theology of the Old Testament*, 149.

[26] See William P. Brown, *The Ethos of the Cosmos: The Genesis of Moral Imagination in the Bible* (Grand Rapids: Eerdmans, 1999), 36–52; Michael Welker, *Creation and Reality* (Minneapolis: Fortress, 1999), 6–20. Brueggemann, too, refers to a "transactional" quality in the OT's description of the relationship between Creator and creation. See Brueggemann, *Theology of the Old Testament*, 528.

[27] David Brown, *Tradition and Imagination: Revelation and Change* (Oxford: Oxford University Press, 1999), 41.

[28] Augustine, *City of God* 11.6.

material-spiritual-social "world,"[29] then acknowledgment of the *enhypo-static* inclusion of creaturely agency in the relevant processes by which this same world is "made" becomes inevitable (there can be no cultivation or culture without human activity), as does the concomitant insistence that its making continues beyond the threshold of the day of divine rest. Of course Adam's divinely mandated naming of the animals must be situated on a wholly different plane from God's own earlier "creative" speech acts; but, if Brown's appeal to a biblical "cosmopolis"[30] is correct, as a symbol of the birth and flowering of human "culture," Adam's act of linguistic *poesis* is nonetheless part and parcel of God's project to *establish* a world (which in this sense comes "unfinished" from his hand) and not merely con-cerned with preserving or yet (since it arises in the narrative prior to sin's appearance) with redeeming one. Currents in the psychology of percep-tion ever since Kant, and others in contemporary cultural theory, point to the likelihood that categories such as "object" and "subject," and "nature" and "culture" (cosmos and ethos), are themselves more closely entangled than we typically suppose, the boundaries between them being perme-able rather than absolute; however much may stand authoritatively over against us as something already divinely "given," therefore, it seems that the reality of the "human world" (the world as experienced humanly)[31] is in any case always one mediated by some relevant human activity of making—whether individual or social, explicit or occult. "The world," Iris Murdoch insists, "is not given to us 'on a plate,' it is given to us as a creative task. . . . We *work*, . . . and 'make something of it.' We help it to be."[32] If so, Steiner avers, the hermeneutics of "reception theory" offers us a vital aesthetic analogue for the creation of a "world" that comes to us thus deliberately (and wonderfully) "incomplete" and full of promise, impli-cating us directly and dynamically in the processes by which the "work" takes shape, realizing (and doing so only gradually) some if not all of the plenitude of potential meaning invested in it by the divine artist.[33]

Again, therefore, while for perfectly good theological reasons we may still wish to reserve talk of "creation proper" for something that God and God alone does, and does during creation's first "six days" alone, it seems artificial and perhaps even theologically unhelpful to draw the relevant

[29] William Brown, *Ethos of the Cosmos*, 1–33 passim.

[30] See William Brown, *Ethos of the Cosmos*, 13–14.

[31] See Anthony O'Hear, *The Element of Fire: Science, Art and the Human World* (London: Routledge, 1988).

[32] Iris Murdoch, *Metaphysics as a Guide to Morals* (London: Vintage, 2003), 215 (emphasis in original).

[33] Steiner, *Grammars of Creation*, 53.

lines with too thick a pencil. The biblical texts associated naturally with a doctrine of "creation," it seems, flag continuities as well as discontinuities both between patterns of divine and creaturely action and between what precedes and follows the divine "Sabbath" on the seventh day. Taken together with other considerations drawn from theological and "nontheological" sources, this suggests that "what creator and creature alike and together make of what has been made"[34] might even yet helpfully be viewed under the aegis of a "creation theology," rather than being subsumed rigorously and without further ado instead under the alternative rubrics afforded by doctrines of "preservation," "providence," or "redemption."

This will be the suggestion I shall pursue in what follows. Whether we regret and resist the de facto semantic slippage of "creation" or view it largely as *adiaphora*, the interference generated between the fields of the word's use draws attention in a helpful manner to the need to situate acts of human making theologically, relating them to a purported divine precedent and intent. Viewing creation as a project divinely begun and established, yet one that is handed over to us with "more to be made of it yet" and inviting our responsible participation in the making, affords a fruitful perspective on the matter. Having acknowledged and underlined the uniqueness and incomparability attaching properly to God's role as "Creator," we may nonetheless understand certain acts of human *poesis* (including but not restricted to those we habitually identify as "artistic") as contributing directly to the fulfillment of this project, adding to the sum of things extant in the world in ways consonant with the pattern of God's own creative vision for it, drawing on an excess of value and meaning invested in it by God in the beginning, but deliberately left for creaturely discovery, unpacking, and realization. As a habitus intended finally not just for human habitation but for the dwelling of God and humankind together, the world is not and cannot be "given" all at once; its inner reality "unfolds in time,"[35] shaped and reshaped by what Creator and creature together make of it, human acts of response and re-presentation being integral not just to the process but to the very nature of the outcome itself (a "covenanted way of existence"). Ultimately, I shall suggest later, this dynamic of "making together" finds due fulfillment only in the flesh taking and self-substitution of God himself for us in Christ, the one in the very depths of whose personal being the trajectories of all divine and human action and reaction come to a head and take proper shape. Acts of genuine human *poesis* must therefore finally be grounded and participant in the once-for-all

[34] Gunton, *Triune Creator*, 89.
[35] Rowan Williams, *Grace and Necessity: Reflections on Art and Love* (Harrisburg, Pa.: Morehouse, 2005), 139.

priestly and *theopoetic* humanity of Christ and viewed from the perspectives afforded by the doctrines of Trinity and redemption. Equally importantly, though, precisely as such (and not otherwise) they can and must be seen as a creaturely sharing in the furtherance of God's ancient purposes in and for creation, falling naturally within the gravitational field of the doctrine of creation itself. In the next three chapters, I shall pursue this claim further by attending more closely to dominant strands in the Bible's highly imaginative presentation of God's activity as "Maker of all things," concentrating in particular on the image of God as artist/craftsman, an image in whose own capacity for engendering semantic interference the genesis of contemporary grammars of creation may to some extent be traced.

2

Creation, Imagination, and Artistry

Theology as Imaginative Response

Theology is a human activity in which the quotient of imagination is set extraordinarily and necessarily high. Despite the misunderstandings that may and do quickly accrue in the wake of such a statement, it is important to make it, if only to clear some of them away. I have argued the case more fully elsewhere, but I reiterate it here.[1] Christian theology, by virtue of the nature of its proper and primary object (the God made known in Jesus Christ) and its own nature as an activity of response shaped and determined by that same object, is closely and necessarily wedded to certain capacities and acts of imaginative *poesis*.

According to Aquinas' classic discussion of the matter, God is "more distant from any creature than any two creatures are from each other," and univocal predication (a particular word or phrase used more than once and bearing exactly the same sense on each occasion) is unavailable for theological use.[2] If we are to avoid the hermeneutic emptiness of utter

---

[1] For a more developed engagement with the issues addressed in this chapter, see Trevor Hart, *Between the Image and the Word: Theological Engagements with Imagination, Language and Literature* (Farnham, U.K.: Ashgate, 2013), 13–42.

[2] St. Thomas Aquinas, *Summa Theologiae*, vol. 3, *Knowing and Naming God (1a. 12–13)*, ed. Herbert McCabe, O.P. (London: Blackfriars in conjunction with Eyre and Spottiswoode, 1964), 1a.13.5 (p. 63). This observation arises in one of the arguments *in contrarium*, but Aquinas's reply endorses it as the proper basis for rejecting univocity.

equivocation, therefore, we are bound in all talk about God to rely on the power of imaginative modeling, either in the explicit comparisons of simile or via the stretching, breaking, and remaking of our terms themselves to bridge the gap. The *logos* concerning *Theos*, that is to say, will necessarily be a word that "takes flesh" and in doing so becomes for us also a fitting "image" of its object.

According to classical Christian theology, such stretching occurs first and foremost in an act of gracious divine self-accommodation whereby God places himself within the semantic range and patterns of our language, giving himself to be known and responded to concretely. Central to this economy of self-giving is the action in which the eternal Word himself assumes our creaturely "flesh" in order to break and remake it, thereby situating himself once for all and with transfiguring impact amidst "the order of signs."[3] Theology, on this understanding, is thus finally contingent on an act of divine rather than merely human *poesis*, but one that duly demands and enables (rather than prohibiting or proscribing) highly imaginative acts of reception and response from the human side. Despite the unfortunate intellectual hangover caused by Feuerbach's notorious use of the term in the middle of the nineteenth century,[4] therefore, we must insist that an appeal to the importance of acts of imagination *as such* in theology involves no conflict whatever with an equally robust appeal to the dynamics of revelation.[5]

[3] See David Jones, *Epoch and Artist* (London: Faber & Faber, 1959), 179. Jones' appropriation of this phrase from Maurice de la Taille pertains to the dominical institution of the Eucharist, but the phrase itself seems to apply more fundamentally still to what occurs in the act of incarnation itself.

[4] Ludwig Feuerbach, *The Essence of Christianity*, trans. George Eliot (New York: Harper & Row, 1957). For Feuerbach the God of religious and theological utterance is a sheer construct of human imagination, an imaginary *son et lumiere* projection onto the clouds from below rather than a genuine apprehension or glimpse of objective reality breaking in from beyond them. The same dichotomy between the respective logics of revelation and imagination is developed in Gordon D. Kaufman, *The Theological Imagination: Constructing the Concept of God* (Philadelphia: Westminster, 1981), esp. 21–57, 263–79.

[5] See, e.g., Bruce McCormack, "Divine Revelation and Human Imagination: Must We Choose between the Two?" *Scottish Journal of Theology* 37, no. 4 (1984): 431–55; Tony Clark, *Divine Revelation and Human Practice: Responsive and Imaginative Participation* (Eugene, Ore.: Cascade, 2008). Being *imaginative* is essential to our day-to-day dealings with realities of all sorts, not least those hard-edged dealings that we typically privilege with the description "scientific" (see, e.g., Ian G. Barbour, *Myths, Models and Paradigms: The Nature of Scientific and Religious Language* [London: SCM Press, 1974]; Garrett Green, *Imagining God: Theology and the Religious Imagination* [San Francisco: Harper & Row, 1989], 41–60), and we ought not to allow ourselves to be misled by the

As Karl Barth notes, that God gives himself to be known by appropriating human activities and outputs of a highly imaginative (as well as ones of a relatively unimaginative) sort is a straightforward enough observation if our account of revelation is linked closely to the particular literary forms which Christian Scripture takes and the styles of reading that much of it most naturally demands of us.[6] Our claim here, though, is a more fundamental one—namely, that appeal to our imaginative capacities as such would seem to be an epistemic prescription of our circumstance as creatures indwelling a world with a mode of being radically distinct from God's own, and hence indigenous rather than incidental to the forms which God's self-revealing takes.[7] If "poetic" forms are fundamental to our meaningful speech about many realities *within* that world, they are more essential yet to our utterance concerning what transcends its finite threshold. Such things cannot be known or experienced in any ordinary sense of the word, and the ordinary sense of our words itself, therefore, is not fitted to speak of them but must be broken open and made anew in the venture. It follows too, of course, that appeals to "revelation" themselves afford no immunity from the peculiar challenges and demands of working with a "poetic logic." Whether we attend to the divinely furnished images of Scripture, the concrete self-imaging of God in the flesh, or the myriad ways in which these have been taken up and responded to in the patterns of Christian tradition across the centuries, theology is an intellectual practice in which the logic of the poetic imagination is and must be kept constantly and identifiably in play.

Mystery, Realism, and the Instability of the Sign

It is a commonplace of contemporary semiotics to remind us that meaning is a rather more fragile and fluid thing than we have sometimes supposed. Cultural signs do not remain static but shift, albeit sometimes imperceptibly, from one time and place to another. The "order of signs," therefore, is by nature an unstable rather than a rigid order, and even our most prosaic, literal, and precise uses of words have a charge of mystery and humility

---

culturally pervasive but wholly erroneous identification of the scope and epistemic force of the imaginative with that of the merely *imaginary*.

[6] See, e.g., his discussion of the "non-historical" genre of saga in the biblical creation accounts. Karl Barth, *Church Dogmatics III/1* (Edinburgh: T&T Clark, 1958), 80–94. On the wider point, see G. B. Caird, *The Language and Imagery of the Bible* (London: Duckworth, 1980).

[7] Cf. Sallie McFague, *Metaphorical Theology: Models of God in Religious Language* (Philadelphia: Fortress, 1982), 14.

attaching to them. Insofar as they have to do with reality, not remaining trapped within self-reinforcing and tautological systems of meaning but pointing to and suggesting a world that transcends and resists capture or containment by them, our acts of utterance and inscription always experience what may be construed as either a shortfall or a surplus in semantic terms, haunted in some measure by an inability to speak the world fully into presence for us. The quotient of mystery is more pronounced, though, in the case of words self-consciously stretched and destabilized by their users, as in the poet's imaginative resort to analogies and metaphors, where words are obliged to operate in new ways, sometimes well beyond the limits of their established comfort zone. Such deliberate distention of meaning relies upon some similitude that the poetic eye grasps in a relation characterized otherwise by nonidentity and dissimilarity, thereby disclosing the deep interconnectedness of things.[8] But the scale of similitude, of course, may vary significantly and with it the extent of the relevant imaginative stretch called for.

Metaphor in particular, it is generally supposed, demands more rather than less of us in this regard, putting its finger initially on what often appears to be the merest thread of similarity between two radically dissimilar objects or states of affairs.[9] Here as elsewhere, though, appearances can be deceptive, and the richest metaphors prove to be suggestive of opportunities for deeper and much more expansive imaginative modeling, occasioning not just fleeting comparisons but deeper epiphanies, permitting us to say "that which may be said in no other way"[10] and holding out the hope that more yet may duly be disclosed. Precisely because it speaks about one thing in terms suggestive of another,[11] though, metaphor effectively draws a veil over reality even in the act of unveiling it, affirming something to be the case yet simultaneously "refusing complete identification and closure."[12] In metaphor, David Brown suggests, "some sense of what is promised is grasped . . . but the mystery remains."[13] Sallie McFague draws on Paul Ricoeur's account of the trope to make the same basic point: metaphor, she insists, always contains the whisper "it is, *and it is not!*"[14] Metaphors, we might say, have by nature a pronounced apophatic

[8] See David Brown, *God and Mystery in Words: Experience through Metaphor and Drama* (Oxford: Oxford University Press, 2008), 46–55.

[9] McFague, *Metaphorical Theology*, 12, 15.

[10] Janet M. Soskice, *Metaphor and Religious Language* (Oxford: Clarendon, 1985), 43–53.

[11] Soskice, *Metaphor and Religious Language*, 49.

[12] Brown, *God and Mystery*, 22.

[13] Brown, *God and Mystery*, 8.

[14] McFague, *Metaphorical Theology*, 13 (emphasis in original).

impulse which shadows the illuminating claims that they make and so safeguards against the consequences of mistaken identity.

Aquinas observes that some human terms seem to apply to God more fully and "naturally" than others, so that there seems to be rather less of an imaginative stretch involved, for instance, in referring to God as good or wise than there is in calling him a shepherd or a king, let alone a rock or a lion. This, Aquinas suggests, is because the former constitute analogies, whereas the latter are instances of the more awkward and uncomfortable stretching involved in metaphor.[15] Whether we follow him in this explanation or not, though, the more fundamental consideration seems to be the one with mention of which Aquinas embarks upon his treatment of this whole subject—namely, the insistence that God is "more distant from any creature than any two creatures are from each other," a circumstance bound to place unique conditions and strains on the elastic functioning of our language. For if this is true, then a wholly unique and unprecedented scale of stretch will necessarily be involved in applying *any* human term meaningfully to God, one to which not even the most striking and surprising and penetrating of mundane metaphors can begin to aspire, and in the instant that likeness of any sort is dangled tantalizingly before us, it will properly be snatched away again, to be offset and qualified by the equal and opposite suggestion of an incomparable difference remaining utterly unscathed. Where God is concerned, it seems, the semantic shortfall in our language assumes a radical and unique aspect. Here more than anywhere, therefore, the whisper "and it is not" demands to be heard, precisely in order to remind us that we are dealing with the logic of images and so prevent the collapse of our theology into an inappropriate, impious, and finally idolatrous form of "conceptual rationalism."[16] Indeed, here as elsewhere—yet more vitally here than anywhere else—we stumble across a paradox: it is precisely and only as we acknowledge the inadequacy of our words, it seems, that their very brokenness promises to become a blessing rather than a curse, and their shortfall, confessed and owned rather than denied, the means to a profound semantic surplus.

[15] Aquinas, *Summa Theologiae* 1a.13.3, 1a.13.6.

[16] I.e., an approach to language that "attempts to find . . . privileged types of words and ways of discovery which give direct access to reality and are, at least in principle, immune from error." Colin Gunton, *The Actuality of Atonement: A Study of Metaphor, Rationality and the Christian Tradition* (Edinburgh: T&T Clark, 1988), 38. Gunton identifies such an approach in Hegel's bid to purge religious language of its attachment to images (*Vorstellungen*) in the pursuit of pure concepts (*Begriffen*).

Metaphor and Responsible Theological Imagination

This latter point is one made forcefully in the writings of T. F. Torrance. If any of the statements we make about God are to be "true" (i.e., refer to God appropriately and in ways that illuminate rather than obscure his uncreated reality), Torrance insists, our creaturely words are bound to possess and retain a fundamental density and resistance to precise determination, remaining fluid in their mode of signification. Torrance privileges spatial metaphors in his articulation of this point, picturing words as physical tools having a side that faces us as we handle and deploy them and another turned appropriately to make contact with the object. Theological statements, he acknowledges, must certainly "be closed on our side, for we have to formulate them as carefully and exactly as we can," but on God's side they must be broken, their sense remaining "open (and therefore apposite) to the infinite objectivity and inexhaustible reality of the divine Being."[17] Only thus can our words possess an appropriate transparency, encouraging and enabling us to look *through* them rather than *at* them. Theological language, he urges, is *paradeigmatic*, never precisely *descriptive*; it points beyond itself to God rather than attempting to picture him.[18] Because he tends to presume all images to be complicit in or naturally inclined toward such a "picturing" function, though, Torrance himself finally eschews the role of images in theology altogether, insisting that only "pure concepts" (in effect, images deliberately stripped of their imaginative content) will suffice.[19]

By a "picturing" relation, Torrance seems to intend one that aspires to mirror reality in fairly precise terms, offering as close an approximation to its shape and substance as the relevant medium will bear—in the case of certain sorts of "naturalistic" painting, for instance, seeking to transcribe three dimensions convincingly into two, and rendering a convenient trompe l'oeil surrogate for reality itself. In passing, we ought at least to note that not all visual images are wedded to aspirations of this sort, and "pictures" too, therefore, despite their solidity and opacity as objects in the world in their own right, may in principle retain a high degree of openness and (paradoxically) transparency of the sort that Torrance demands. More important for our purposes, though, is the observation that certain sorts of verbal image, in particular, contain an inbuilt resistance to being dragooned inappropriately into any such crude "picturing" role. Thus, as we have seen, it is part of the nature of metaphor to function obliquely

---

[17] Thomas F. Torrance, *God and Rationality* (London: Oxford University Press, 1971), 186–87.

[18] Thomas F. Torrance, *Theological Science* (London: Oxford University Press, 1969), 20.

[19] See, e.g., Torrance, *God and Rationality*, 23; Torrance, *Theological Science*, 20.

rather than directly, speaking of one thing in terms *suggestive of* another[20] but with a high quotient of "contra-indication" kept constantly in play[21] and a flickering interplay sustained between the tantalizing suggestion that "it is" and the sober and equally vital acknowledgment that "it is not." Such images, we might say, are already broken and chastened by nature and lend themselves well to further acts of imaginative asceticism where appropriate.

In theology, as elsewhere in our dealings with reality, it is precisely the broken or chastened image that, Gunton suggests, opens us to the world and permits the world in its turn to enforce changes in the meanings that our words bear.[22] We should notice that the deliberate activity of stripping and breaking the "visible" form and content of any image in the interests of such epistemic transparency and fluidity is itself one of a highly imaginative sort. If one (widely acknowledged) function of imagination is to set us free from the given constraints of the empirical, it is certainly another of its functions (though much less widely recognized) to liberate us from pictures by which we might otherwise, as Ludwig Wittgenstein puts it in a closely related discussion, be "held captive" in inappropriate and damaging ways.[23] So, instead of urging the purgation or abandonment of imagination in the interest of a putative conceptual purity, we would be better advised to think in terms of the need for acts of *responsible theological imagining*, ones in which the logic of images itself is first taken fully seriously on its own terms and images are then duly modified, broken open, and (if we prefer) "purified" in accordance with the demands of the particular epistemic circumstance.

Whatever else it may properly be and involve, therefore, Christian theology is in large part bound to be a matter of the responsible exploration of the "logic" of such images (what Lakoff and Johnson refer to help- fully as the proper "entailments" of an image),[24] unpacking them, ordering them in relation to one another, extrapolating imaginatively on the basis

[20] Soskice, *Metaphor and Religious Language*, 15.

[21] Nelson Goodman, *Languages of Art: An Approach to a Theory of Symbols* (London: Oxford University Press, 1969), 69.

[22] See, e.g., Gunton, *Actuality of Atonement*, 45–47.

[23] Ludwig Wittgenstein, *Philosophical Investigations: The German Text with a Revised English Translation*, trans. G. E. M. Anscombe, 3rd ed. (Oxford: Blackwell, 2001), 1, §115. Wittgenstein has in mind one particularly unhelpful "picture" of how language itself is related to reality—i.e., precisely that which treats it as though it in its turn in some sense *pictured* the things its speaks of.

[24] See George Lakoff and Mark Johnson, *Metaphors We Live By*, 2nd ed. (Chicago: University of Chicago Press, 2003), 147–53.

of them,[25] and, crucially, "chastening" and remaking them so that they remain transparent mediators of our knowing of God rather than hardening and becoming effective obstacles to it. If, as I have suggested, all this occurs within the context of a divine action of self-unveiling, at one level it is clearly a matter of grasping and receiving something given, something originating in God rather than in our own creative impulses alone and revelatory only as and when God accompanies and undergirds it with his personal presence and activity. But it will be a constant theme of this book that, in Christian understanding, divine giving is generally the occasion for more rather than less human activity; God gives us something *to work with* and both expects and calls forth from us responses of a genuinely "creative" sort rather than a passive disposition or strategies of mere conservation. As more widely, so too here in the context of God's giving of himself to be known this same rule applies, and theology of any sort must be acknowledged to be a matter of responsible human *doing and making* immediately we have insisted that it is first (and remains) a matter of God's doing and making too. Acknowledgment of the intrinsically imaginative aspect of theological activity (both receiving and self-consciously "working with" what is given by God) reinforces the point, since, as Mark Johnson notes, in the wider sphere of our imaginative engagements with the world the most revelatory/heuristic moments are generally those demanding of us the highest levels of creative/poetic response, rather than positivistic passivism, in the face of a reality that impresses its shape upon us relentlessly and asks merely that we sit up and take note of it.[26]

Imagining Creation

The radical distinction between God and the world that, I have argued, places all our thought and speech about God finally in the domain of the imaginative and the poetic is, Barth reminds us, not an a priori truth for Christian theology but rather an a posteriori entailment of the event of

---

[25] This, I take it, is exactly what is happening when the church allows canonical metaphors of the atonement, for instance, to be augmented and supplemented by extra-biblical ones which it judges to be faithful to the basic pattern of biblical thinking, or when the threefold narrative pattern of talk about God as Father, incarnate Son, and Holy Spirit is worked up into a more precise conceptuality of God as Trinity, and so on.

[26] See Mark Johnson, *The Body in the Mind: The Bodily Basis of Meaning, Imagination and Reason* (Chicago: University of Chicago Press, 1987), 98, 157, et passim. The point (and the comparison) holds good at the level of the *structure* of our knowing, despite the fact that the language of "discovery" does not really fit the theological case. Cf., though, Torrance's appeal to Polanyi in a similar vein.

revelation itself,[27] the fact of it, the forms that it takes, and the substance of what is actually revealed about God in and through it. The doctrine with which we shall be most fully and directly concerned in this book is the doctrine of creation (and of God as Creator), and it is one of the features and functions of this doctrine in both its biblical and its later more conceptually precise forms to hold in tension the twin claims that God is wholly other than the finite cosmos and yet radically involved not just in its primordial origination but in its continuing history. Thus the fact of "creation," too, in its distinctly Christian sense is not a truth human beings could ever procure for themselves through empirical or logical processes, nor merely a peculiarly "religious" response to Leibniz's question "Why is there not nothing?" (though it does, of course, offer an answer to this question), but precisely an *article of faith* derived from God's own witness to himself in revelation.[28] To speak of "creation" is thus already to presuppose and to speak of the character and the larger purposes and promises of the God who creates,[29] and the scope of the doctrine is not limited to an affirmation of God's radical transcendence with respect to the world and the world's reciprocal absolute dependence on God, though again this is integral to it. It is also true, of course, that in what it has to say about God and the nature of God's dealings with the world as Creator, and especially those primordial acts of origination that we tend to associate most immediately with the language of creation, the doctrine is compelled to speak of things the reality of which lies by definition (on both the vertical and the horizontal axis) beyond the limits of the world and its history and thus is unavailable for human observation or accounting. If we are to hear of such things at all, or speak and think of them for ourselves, therefore, we can only do so under forms in which the quotient of imagination is necessarily set extraordinarily high.

This is not just true of the revealed doctrine articulated by Christian faith, of course, but of all other religious traditions too, insofar as they have things to say concerning the world's ultimate origins, and, let us not forget, equally to those "scientific" accounts of penultimate cosmic beginnings which trespass boldly beyond the domain of nature's regular processes and what may properly be claimed with confidence on the basis of observation and experiment directed toward them. Thus, whether we are reckoning with images of a world hatching from a cosmic egg, the dismembered corpse of a giant dragon, the bubbling over and spilling of

[27] See Barth, *Church Dogmatics III/1*, 3.

[28] See the critical response to David Burrell in Michael Welker, *Creation and Reality* (Minneapolis: Fortress, 1999), 2.

[29] Gerhard von Rad, *Genesis: A Commentary*, trans. John H. Marks, 2nd ed. (London: SCM Press, 1963), 43–44; Wolfhart Pannenberg, *Systematic Theology* (Edinburgh: T&T Clark, 1994), 2:9.

eternal divine matter, a spectacular "big bang," or a gale howling blindly across the surface of a raging sea, cosmogonies of one sort or another are all compelled to operate under imaginative conditions, even though the entailments or connotations of the images they work with and offer to us may differ vastly from one case to another. Christian claims concerning revelation, as we have already noted, cannot circumvent this situation but must reckon fully with it and embrace it, coming to terms with and owning gladly the fact that God has given and gives himself and his purposes to be known here and elsewhere through events and forms that capture and shape and constantly reshape our imagination just as surely as any other facet of our humanity. Thus Barth rightly insists that Christian theology must resist to the very last the peculiar habit of the modern Western mind that itself suffers above all from a chronic lack of imagination[30] and is consequently unable to trust or find worth (let alone "revealed" truth) in any engagement trespassing beyond the reach of what is empirically or logically verifiable. Where the "history" (*Geschichte*) of the world's creation is concerned,[31] Barth insists, in dealing with what are strictly speaking "non-historical" (*unhistorische*)—because "pre-historical"—realities, the saying or telling (*sagend*) of them by the biblical writers is properly and necessarily achieved through the poetic device of tale or story (*Sage*). That this imaginative depiction of how things stood in the beginning between God and the world is, as such, *revelatory* Barth does not for one moment doubt.[32] What matters, though, he urges, is that we acknowledge, respect, weigh, and take it seriously on its own poetic terms and not some others of our own choosing.

---

[30] "*krankhaften Phantasielosigkeit*." See Karl Barth, *Die kirchliche Dogmatik III/1* (Zollikon-Zürich: Evangelischer Verlag, 1945), 87.

[31] Barth insists that "[n]ot all history is 'historical'"; indeed, "in its immediacy to God every history is in fact 'non-historical,' i.e. it cannot be deduced and compared and therefore perceived and comprehended. But this does not mean that it ceases to be genuine history." Barth, *Church Dogmatics III/1*, 80. No account of God's involvement in the world's history, let alone one that extends to what occurs before the creation of time itself, could possibly be "historical" in the sense of conforming to the established conventions and demands presumed by the professional historian. Yet, Barth reminds us, "in genuine history the 'historical' and the 'non-historical' accompany each other and belong together" (81).

[32] "We are no less truly summoned to listen to what the Bible has to say here in the form of saga than to what it has to say in other places in the form of history, and elsewhere in the form of address, doctrine, meditation, law, epigram, epic and lyric." Barth, *Church Dogmatics III/1*, 83.

The Divine Craftsman

In his illuminating treatment of the subject, Terence Fretheim suggests the availability of some twenty different images of God's role as Creator to be discerned in Genesis 1–2 alone.[33] Among these, those that have dominated the Christian imagination are perhaps God as King or Sovereign Lord and God as laborer, either commanding or himself effecting the various stages of the creative process. In the next chapter, I shall argue that when we turn to consider what the biblical poets have to offer us in this regard, we discover at the heart of their vision the image of God himself as an artist and the cosmos as the "work" issuing forth creatively, as it were, from his divine studio or workshop. The suggestion itself is not a new one, but less notice has been taken of this image than one might naturally expect, resulting in its virtual eclipse by others. In part this may be due to prevalent habits of interpretation whereby the activity of the first six "days" of creation is viewed as preparatory to the "rest" enjoyed by God on the seventh day. Of course there is nothing wrong with doing this, which seems more or less to be demanded by Genesis 2:2-3. The danger here, though, is that of reading a poor theology of leisure and the Sabbath back into this text and what precedes it. Imagining God's "work" only in terms of the sort of hard graft that must necessarily be punctuated by regular periods of inactivity (a pattern familiar enough to us from the structure of our own working lives in a world driven by instrumentalist economies), we fail to recognize in the "rest" of Sabbath the spirit of joy, festival, and celebration, projecting instead our own exhausted weekly collapse onto the divine circumstance.[34] Another factor is likely to be the anachronism involved in reading back into the biblical text the sort of associations that cling stubbornly to the vocabulary of "art" and "artistry" in the modern period (not least their habitual association with the world of leisure and play rather than that of useful work), but that are in principle detachable from it and largely foreign to the outlook of the biblical writers. So, some clarification is in order.

At the risk of caricature, then, let me cobble together some of the associations I have in mind. In the modern imagination (which, despite the strong currents of postmodernity, has not really kept apace with the latest in aesthetic theory), the true artist is a one in a million figure, set apart identifiably from and elevated above the crowd of ordinary men and women by the possession of some remarkable gift or talent, an individual creative genius who, in moments of profound inspiration and

[33] Images of creation are to be found elsewhere in Scripture too, of course. See Terence Fretheim, *God and World in the Old Testament: A Relational Theology of Creation* (Nashville: Abingdon, 2005), 36.

[34] I shall have more to say about this in chap. 12.

self-expression, wrestles autonomously with form and matter to bring forth "works" unique both in their originality and in their power to enchant and bewitch others, and which are duly celebrated and, in their turn, set apart from the mass of everyday artifacts to be contemplated and enjoyed for their own sake. While this familiar construct has roots in the classical cultures of antiquity and while there have doubtless always been individuals whose personality, prowess, and aspirations were suggestive of it, as we shall see later it was not until the European Renaissance that the role of "the artist" in this peculiar sense finally emerged to find widespread public acceptance.[35] Thereafter it quickly became securely embedded in cultural institutions and was eventually afforded intellectual warrant by theorists eager to disentangle the products of "Art" from wider patterns of human making and cultivation. Significantly, though, the idea has little place in biblical culture and seemingly found little purchase in either the patristic or medieval eras of Christian history. For pre-Renaissance Christian thought, therefore, terms properly rendered in English as "artist" are also translatable (and perhaps less misleadingly so in light of subsequent developments) as "craftsman"—no mere manual laborer to be sure[36] nor yet the tortured individual genius struggling in his garret to create something of which the world has never so far quite seen or heard the like.

Since it is in this earlier model of artistry or "craftsmanship," as a human activity of skilled making or forming, that the biblical saga traces an analogy fit to speak of aspects of God's own creative working, it seems appropriate at this juncture to take time briefly to consider the phenomenon as it appears across different epochs and cultures. These are described helpfully in authoritative studies of the theme such as those by Edward Lucie-Smith and Richard Sennett, on whose work I draw gratefully and

---

[35] For an overview of the emergence of the idea, see Margot Wittkower and Rudolf Wittkower, *Born under Saturn: The Character and Conduct of Artists; A Documented History from Antiquity to the French Revolution* (New York: New York Review Books, 2007).

[36] Thus Plato (*Symposium* 205b–c) insists that craftsmen (*demiergoi*) are properly called "poets" (*poetai*) since they in their turn, like their literary counterparts, bring new things into existence through acts of skilled composition (*poesis*). See W. R. M. Lamb, ed., *Plato: Lysis, Symposium, Gorgias*, Loeb Classical Library (Cambridge, Mass.: Harvard University Press, 1925), 186–87. Aristotle (*Metaphysics* 981a30–b10), meanwhile, differentiates sharply between those who are master workers/artists (*architectonas/technites*) in each craft and those who are no more than manual workers (*cheirotechnoi*), the latter working from mere habit and without wisdom or the proper appreciation of principles and reasons operative in their trade. See Hugh Tredennick, ed., *Aristotle: The Metaphysics*, Loeb Classical Library (Cambridge, Mass.: Harvard University Press, 1933), 6–9. See further Richard Sennett, *The Craftsman* (London: Penguin, 2008), 21–24.

directly in what follows.[37] For the sake of convenience, the pattern may be treated here under three headings.

CRAFT AS HANDWORK

Mention of the craftsman summons an image immediately to mind. "Peering through a window in to a carpenter's shop, you see inside an elderly man surrounded by his apprentices and his tools. Order reigns within, parts of chairs are clamped neatly together, the fresh smell of wood shavings fills the room, the carpenter bends over his bench to make a fine incision for marquetry. The shop is menaced by a furniture factory down the road."[38] While, as Sennett insists, the notion of craftsmanship is only "poorly understood" if we limit it to manual engagement of this sort (there is "craft" in a proper and an important sense, he insists, in the ways in which, for instance, the doctor, the orchestral conductor, the diplomat, the writer, and software designers do what they do when they do it well)[39] and while we must certainly see beyond the sometimes unduly romanticized visions of the notion conjured up by John Ruskin and his followers as part of the nineteenth-century backlash against rampant industrialization,[40] it remains true that the primary association of the language of "craft" has to do with a way of working fairly immediately with the material world, using the hands (and tools held in the hands) to fashion matter into some significant and valuable form. The craftsman fashions artifacts, and the "value" of these artifacts is in fact linked directly to their intended and perceived contribution to the common good.[41] Craft is not, then, a mode of "making" linked primarily to the realization or gratification of an artist's burning individual vision or his or her need to express some inner emotional excess (though it need not exclude these entirely), but it is rather a fundamentally *social* phenomenon. The craftsman is, in Lucie-Smith's phrase, by definition a "social animal," one whose role is to make useful things designed and produced for the benefit of the wider community, even though her craftsmanship exceeds considerations of utility alone.[42]

The latter point is a very important one, though, and while in a wider sense *all* human making prior to the early modern period might be concluded technically under the category of "craft" (being some form of

<hr/>

[37] Edward Lucie-Smith, *The Story of Craft: The Craftsman's Role in Society* (Oxford: Phaidon, 1981); Sennett, *Craftsman.*

[38] Sennett, *Craftsman,* 19.

[39] Sennett, *Craftsman,* 20.

[40] See Lucie-Smith, *Story of Craft,* 14.

[41] Sennett notes that the ancient Greek term *demiergos* reflects precisely this, a compound between the public (*demios*) and the productive (*ergon*). Sennett, *Craftsman,* 22.

[42] Lucie-Smith, *Story of Craft,* 7.

making "by hand"),[43] the language of craftsmanship generally connotes something much more than "manual labour" alone. The craftsman is one who possesses a special skill and knowledge, developed in the case of the master craftsman in particular to a very high degree indeed[44] and reflected in a particular way of handling the world. As Sennett puts it, the craftsman is, through his training and experience, thoroughly "anchored in tangible reality,"[45] able to work closely, as it were, "with the grain" of his materials, understanding and respecting their potential, their various capacities and incapacities, and therefore able to draw from them their best, enhancing and adding perceived value to their "raw" and uncrafted manifestation.

CRAFT AND GRATUITY

Thus, while craft is a means of social production and one in which the value (social usefulness) of what is made is an essential rather than an incidental consideration, craftsmanship is, if never less, nonetheless always much more than the means to some other end. It is perceived to be a good in its own right, and one deserving the expenditure of an effort and care that far outstrip any merely utilitarian demands.[46] In Sennett's phrase, craft is

[43] Lucie-Smith observes that until the time of the Renaissance (when a putative theoretical distinction between "craft" and "art" began to emerge) and the Industrial Revolution (when the advent of machines displaced many long-established manual practices in order to maximize "efficiency" in productivity and thus economic gain) this category covered most productive activity that was, in a fairly direct sense, conducted "by hand." See Lucie-Smith, *Story of Craft*, 11.

[44] Sennett, *Craftsman*, 20.

[45] Sennett, *Craftsman*, 21. Sennett bewails the tendency in many modern modes of design and production to separate head and hand, and for design thus to run aground on some material intransigency or impracticality arising from the designer's lack of familiarity with material realities. See Sennett, *Craftsman*, 38–39. Lucie-Smith draws attention, though, to something analogous in examples of ancient Roman sculpture forced to resort to clumsy (and aesthetically demeaning) strategies of reinforcement due to "a disregard for the true nature of the material." Lucie-Smith, *Story of Craft*, 58–59.

[46] This is what Ruskin identifies as the "spirit of sacrifice" characteristic of artistry, which "prompts us to the offering of precious things, merely because they are precious, not because they are useful or necessary" (e.g., in the case of architecture), "taking up and admitting, as conditions of its working, the necessities and common uses of the building, impresses on its form certain characteristics venerable or beautiful, but otherwise unnecessary," striving always to produce the best work that can be produced within the constraints of a given circumstance. See John Ruskin, *The Seven Lamps of Architecture*, vol. 8 of *The Complete Works of John Ruskin*, ed. E. T. Cook and Alexander Wedderburn (London: George Allen, 1903), 28, 30, 43–45. Typically, Ruskin sets this within an explicitly religious and theological context, the "sacrifice" in question being offered consciously by the craftsman to God. I shall argue later in this volume that while "Eucharist" is certainly a

fundamentally a "quality-driven" practice,[47] one in which a clear standard of excellence operates, in which the artist is dedicated to "good work" for its own sake, aspiring always to do the best he or she can do rather than making do with what will suffice for practical purposes and taking a pride in the finished product. The "craft aesthetic," Lucie-Smith observes, thus involves a peculiar fusion of utility with gratuity, the practical with the psychologically satisfying.[48] Craftsmanship, at its most authentic, is not tied to an overbearing sense of short-term economic "efficiency," involving what may well, when measured by such considerations, appear to be forms of extravagant waste but which, on another way of viewing things, are of the very essence of the sort of constructive engagement with the world that artistry properly is. It is a fact, Lucie-Smith points out, that "the most elaborate and beautiful flint objects of all were not produced until after the introduction of metal," whose properties were, in practical terms, far more efficient in practical and economic terms. "Apparently," he concludes, "they were made simply as artistic *tours de force*," considerations of utility tackled head-on but not permitted to dominate.[49] Again, the elaborate decoration of pots in some ancient societies is interesting and unexpected, because "it seems to take precedence over the desire to make a pot useful and functional. . . . Slipping and burnishing techniques have an extremely practical result— they make a pot more waterproof. Nevertheless, archaeological investigation has made it clear that these additional processes were first developed for purely aesthetic reasons, to make the pot more pleasing to the eye."[50] Such examples serve to reinforce the point: the work of the craftsman is found again and again to be one of committed supererogation, going beyond what is necessitated in practical terms to do the best that can be done and doing so because it seems good and right so to do. *Ars* is—in the poet, painter, and engraver David Jones' terms—a matter of *gratuity*, lavishly exceeding what merely suffices (the "utile"), in pursuit of a perceived (personal, moral, aesthetic, spiritual) good and doing so seemingly by way of response to a given reality (the world and the materials afforded by it) which is in its turn apprehended as *gratuitously rich* in potential and promise.

---

fitting theological category in terms of which to understand the gratuitousness of the artist's labors as response, this need neither entail nor be taken to imply any conscious religious motive. The sense of something "good" for which and to which thanks are properly due seems to prevail much more widely in the sphere of the arts even when no theological language is owned or appealed to in order to articulate or frame it.

[47] Sennett, *Craftsman*, 24.

[48] Lucie-Smith, *Story of Craft*, 22.

[49] Lucie-Smith, *Story of Craft*, 21–22.

[50] Lucie-Smith, *Story of Craft*, 28.

Craft and Collaboration

There is clearly much more that could be said about craftsmanship, and we shall have more yet to say about the putative distinction between art and craft in a later chapter. But the third and final point I wish to identify here is craft's nature as a *collective* practice. We have already noted that craft is bound up with a certain sort of social bond, having its sights clearly set on practices and outputs of making that will serve the common good rather than putting individual artistic vision or self-realization at the head of the agenda. There is a further level, though, at which the craftsman/artist across the centuries has experienced a social bond, and in relation to which considerations of artistic self-realization and personal self-denial are bound up inextricably together in a manner that renders some cherished assumptions attaching to later conceptions of the artist problematic.

In practice the craftsman only rarely works in anything approaching splendid isolation, and his or her work is always identifiably the product of a wider collective enterprise. Classically, this collective aspect of craft has been embodied in institutions such as the workshop or the guild and their equivalents, where the artist has "learned a trade," acquiring a set of practical skills and submitting to a set of socially endorsed norms with respect to how those skills might best be deployed. Indeed, the workshop was and remains a community within which "submission" has a proper and vital role to play, a "productive space in which people deal face-to-face with issues of authority."[51] Learning here means a lengthy training, and training consists from the first in forms of willing subordination by some to others, recognizing "the legitimacy of command" and "the dignity of obedience."[52] A significant proportion of craft knowledge, Sennett reminds us, is tacit in nature, an embodied knowledge embedded in established traditions of *practice* in which master, journeyman, and apprentice alike must all participate at their respective, unequal levels of attainment;[53] and the process of knowledge transfer whereby such traditions are transmitted from one generation to the next is at its lower levels essentially and necessarily an *imitative* one, learning being conducted by following example and under close supervision.[54] This, then, is not an environment in which

[51] Sennett, *Craftsman*, 54. For a wider account of the "workshop" structure, see pp. 53–80.

[52] Sennett, *Craftsman*, 54.

[53] On the nature of the tacit dimension and its contributions in various spheres of human knowing and practice, see more fully Michael Polanyi, *Personal Knowledge: Towards a Post-critical Philosophy* (London: Routledge & Kegan Paul, 1958), 69–202; Michael Polanyi, *The Tacit Dimension* (London: Routledge & Kegan Paul, 1967), passim.

[54] Sennett refers to "the absorption into tacit knowledge, unspoken and uncodified

much scope exists to encourage or accommodate the pretensions of the artistic prima donna or where the notion of artistic autonomy makes a great deal of sense.[55] Even the master craftsman—one who has undertaken the relevant training and long since attained a high level of skill and wisdom in his art so that he possesses considerable authority and may in turn induct others into the secrets of such things—continues to respect and to work broadly within the limits laid down by the wisdom of those who have preceded him, rather than kicking over the traces of the collective past in the interests of some putative individual "freedom" and "creativity." Freedom, creativity, and even a legitimate form of "originality" there may well yet be in the world of craft;[56] but it is not of this sort, and the authority to exercise the more relevant sorts is hard earned. Furthermore, as Lucie-Smith illustrates,[57] the workshop has from the earliest examples known to us often been marked by a deliberate and structured division of labor; the master craftsman's vision and judgments may shape and inform all that happens there, but very often the production of the larger work is no masterpiece crafted by the master (or, indeed, by some apprentice) from first to last in splendid isolation but instead relies heavily on the active collaboration and contribution of the whole community together.

In suggesting that the biblical writers imagine God as an artist, therefore, it is artistry of this sort, rather than modern variations on the theme, that we should have in our sights. Otherwise, we certainly shall not find what we are looking for. And while, as we shall see duly, Scripture bears clear witness to an understanding that "no analogy drawn from the human sphere can exhaust the meaning of God's creative activity,"[58] my argument in chapter 3 will be that, mutatis mutandis, it also encourages the

---

in words, that occurred there and became a matter of habit, the thousand little everyday moves that add up in sum to a practice." Sennett, *Craftsman*, 77. It is precisely the unspecifiable nature of a practice, its inability to be captured in words (and so held on to for perpetuity) that results in the effective "loss" (forgetting) of some skill through the death of the last person possessing its secret.

[55] Sennett, *Craftsman*, 54.

[56] Sennett observes that the great masters (e.g., Stradivari in the world of early eighteenth-century Italian violin making) often evinced "originality" precisely in the ways in which they maintained and enhanced the traditions and standards of practice that they had in their turn received. Such originality was clearly a personal contribution to the art, but it had nothing to do with a bid for individual "autonomy" in the field. See Sennett, *Craftsman*, 74–80.

[57] See Lucie-Smith, *Story of Craft*, 13–14.

[58] Fretheim, *God and World*, 37. Cf. Jon D. Levenson, *Creation and the Persistence of Evil: The Jewish Drama of Divine Omnipotence*, 2nd ed. (Princeton, N.J.: Princeton University Press, 1994), 117.

supposition that certain modes or aspects of God's creative work not only bear proper comparison to human activities (including those of skilled productivity and "creativity") but actually solicit and draw these into the dynamics of what Gunton refers to as God's creative "project."[59]

From *Deus Artifex* to *Divino Artista*

We have not quite finished yet, though, with the somewhat troubled figure of the "Artist" in modern and postmodern imagining, or fathomed the complexity of his or her relationship to the divine Creator of scriptural testimony. The distinction between this figure and her premodern forebear is an important one to draw not because the modern notion has nothing at all to do with ways in which Scripture and Christian tradition envisage God as relating to the world as its Creator, but precisely because it turns out to have rather a lot to do with these, and in what is in part at least a questionable and theologically problematic manner. Thus, Margot and Rudolf Wittkower argue that the notion of the artist that emerged at the Renaissance had in fact a complex heritage, marrying ancient Hellenistic sources and examples with an established tradition of Christian talk of God as artist—the divine architect and master craftsman responsible for fashioning the cosmos.[60] In the process, I shall argue in a later chapter, something odd happened to the way in which the relevant biblical image functioned. First, the directional flow of the imaginative relation was deliberately reversed, so that human artistry was pictured now in terms of God's artistry rather than vice versa. In and of itself, such a hermeneutical process is fair enough; sometimes, indeed, it performs a vital theological task, though it always needs to be handled with care.[61] In this case, though, the requisite care was lacking, and certain prerogatives and qualities which the biblical imagining of creation carefully and consistently ascribes to God and God alone (and that lie, therefore, wholly outside the proper terms of reference of the image of God as artist/craftsman) were, by virtue of their proximity and close association in the text, sucked incautiously over the threshold into the domain of that

[59] Colin Gunton, *The Triune Creator: A Historical and Systematic Study* (Grand Rapids: Eerdmans, 1998), 202.

[60] See Wittkower and Wittkower, *Born under Saturn*, 98.

[61] One thinks, for instance, of the way in which human power relations are (or ought to be) challenged and reconstructed by the modifications entailed in speaking of God as King or as Father. The particular way in which, within the patterns of biblical narration of his character, God models these roles effects shifts in our understanding of the relevant human terms themselves. These are important theological instances of the wider poetic phenomenon in which the use of metaphor typically modifies our understanding of both terms in the relevant relation. See C. Day Lewis, *The Poetic Image* (London: Jonathan Cape, 1947), 35–36.

image and thence back down the line to transform the wider understanding and expectations attaching to human "artistry" too.

By the careless elision of such distinctions (poetic and theological), the notion of the "otherness" of the artist grew up to provide a curious parody of the uncreated otherness of the Creator God,[62] and from the biblically sanctioned image of a *deus artifex* was born the potentially problematic notion of the *divino artista*, one who might even be considered (transgressively if somewhat tongue in cheek) an *alter deus*—another god.[63] We shall explore and unpack some of the implications of all this more fully later. Next, though, we return to the biblical image of God as artist/craftsman itself and consider some of the elements and entailments of its actual use.

[62] Wittkower and Wittkower, *Born under Saturn*, xxix.

[63] Leon Battista Alberti, *On Painting*, trans. John R. Spencer (London: Routledge & Kegan Paul, 1956), 64. Alberti's technical and programmatic treatise was published in 1436. Grayson's alternative translation (based on the Latin rather than the Italian text) renders the relevant phrase: "(masters of painting) . . . feel themselves to be almost like the Creator." This slight paraphrase jumps the gun somewhat but gets the relevant theological inference correct. See Leon Battista Alberti, *On Painting*, trans. Cecil Grayson (London: Penguin, 1991), 61. Such suggestions may, as Martin Kemp suggests, be merely the first thin cracks in a dam that otherwise held for the time being (and we should not underestimate the force of that carefully measured "almost"), but they are significant nonetheless as intimations of the direction in which things would eventually develop. See Martin Kemp, "From 'Mimesis' to 'Fantasia': The Quattrocento Vocabulary of Creation, Inspiration and Genius in the Visual Arts," *Viator: Medieval and Renaissance Studies* 8 (1977): 393.

3

Comparability and the Conscription of the Creaturely

God the Master Craftsman

At the heart of the saga of primeval history, the biblical poet pictures God getting his hands dirty, forming human beings out of lumps of clay,[1] before breathing the breath of life into their nostrils and, later in the same passage, repeating the same skilled technique to fashion in turn both the animals and the birds. The relevant Hebrew verb, *yatsar* (LXX *plassein*) and its cognate forms are used of God elsewhere in the Old Testament too, perhaps most familiarly in the preexilic prophets where God is again imagined in the guise of a cosmic potter (*yotser*) who molds the earth into shape with his own hands[2] and in whose hands the destiny of Israel and the nations alike are placed like so much clay to be shaped and, where necessary, reshaped in accordance with his divine design.[3] In these particular biblical texts, where it is clear that it is clay that is the material of divine choice, *yotser* is

---

[1] Speiser suggests that "clods in the soil" is a better rendering of Gen 2:7 than the traditional "dust of the earth." See E. A. Speiser, *Genesis*, ed. William Foxwell Albright and David Noel Freedman, The Anchor Bible (New York: Doubleday, 1964), 14–16. This alternative translation certainly evokes the relevant image more vividly.

[2] Isa 45:18; Jer 33:2.

[3] See Isa 29:16; 45:9-10; 64:8; Jer 18:1-11; cf. also Job 10:8-9. McKane suggests that the poet of Gen 2 probably has in mind the same image of something fashioned in a potter's workshop. See William McKane, *A Critical and Exegetical Commentary on Jeremiah*, International Critical Commentary (Edinburgh: T&T Clark, 1986), 1:421–22.

appropriately enough translated "potter" (LXX *kerameus*); but the Hebrew term itself actually has a much wider range of application than this, including skilled workers in other available materials too (wood, metal, stone) and is thus more accurately rendered by the generic "craftsman"[4] or, if we take into account what we have already said about wider pre-Renaissance conceptions, "artist"—one skilled in devising and then shaping and constructing "artistic designs" (*machashabeth*) such as those found, for example, in the construction of the tabernacle.[5] Indeed, although the word *yotser* and its cognates make no appearance there, the tabernacle traditions in Exodus 25–31 and 35–39 are particularly interesting in connection both with the biblical image of God as craftsman and with the creation narrative of Genesis 1 in particular, and we shall return to consider precisely how below.

The presence of an image is not determined by the use of particular nouns alone, of course, but equally by verbal constructions in which certain sorts of actions are ascribed to the relevant subject. Thus, the relatively infrequent deployment of the term *yotser* itself (or equivalents to it) in the Old Testament to refer to God needs to be set against the backdrop of a much wider pattern of description—in the prophets and Wisdom literature as well as the poetic accounts of creation in Genesis 1–2—depicting God as one who, in his *actiones ad extra*, does precisely those sorts of things most naturally associated with a master craftsman/artist. Again, the imagery of one who works skillfully with his hands is central to this: God forms the dry land and stretches the heavens into position with his hands (Ps 95:5; Isa 45:12), crafting the intricate jeweled splendor of the starry night sky with his fingers (Ps 8:3; cf. 102:25); the creation as a whole (cf. the formulaic "heaven and earth" [Isa 66:2; Ps 92:4]) and human beings at the heart of it (Gen 2:7; Job 10:8-9; Isa 29:23; 64:8) are explicitly referred to as divine handiwork, works wrought by God with his bare hands from the material at his disposal. Other texts take God's hands (and any other presumed tools of his trade) for granted, directing our attention instead to the actions of design and construction performed with them: laying the foundations on which the earth itself rests (Job 38:4; Ps 102:25); measuring, prescribing, and establishing bounds sufficient to keep the sky, sea, and dry land in their respective places (Job 38:5; 38:8-11; Isa 40:12;

---

[4] See, e.g., Jack R. Lundbom, *Jeremiah 1–20*, The Anchor Bible (New York: Doubleday, 1999), 813; B. Otzen, "Yatsar," in *Theological Dictionary of the Old Testament*, vol. 6, ed. G. Johannes Botterweck and Helmer Ringgren (Grand Rapids: Eerdmans, 1990), 258–59.

[5] Cf. Exod 35:32. According to Brueggemann the term *yotser* "bespeaks active material engagement with the stuff of creation, in an artistic endeavour." Walter Brueggemann, *Theology of the Old Testament: Testimony, Dispute, Advocacy* (Minneapolis: Fortress, 1997), 147.

Gen 1:6-10); irrigating the land to enable fertile growth (Job 38:25-27; Ps 74:15); installing efficient systems of lighting and heating, regulated precisely so as to sustain organic life, the regular cycles of day and night, and the seasons of summer and winter (Ps 74:16-17). And, whether we are transported in our mind's eye into the privacy of the artist's studio/ workshop or out onto a public building site where a grand cosmic design is taking shape before our eyes, judgments of quality are essential to all this: everything the divine craftsman/master builder forms or assembles is "fearfully and wonderfully made" (Ps 139:14), something deserving of admiration and praise (Ps 92:4); it issues forth from a depth of wisdom and understanding as well as manual and technical skill (Jer 10:12), is a job done to a high standard and fit for purpose rather than botched (Isa 45:18), and is one that, when it is finished, the artist himself can stand back and look at and be satisfied with, declaring it "very good" and taking time out from his industry to enjoy it (Gen 1:31–2:2).[6]

Von Rad observes that the relevant phrase in Genesis 1:31 might equally be translated "completely perfect" and "rightly refers more to the wonderful properness and harmony than to the beauty of the entire cosmos." Such "perfection" is thus, he insists, a matter of prelapsarian divine perspective rather than something immediately available to human appreciation and indeed lies beyond human grasp (and must thus be a matter of faith) in a world "full of innumerable troubles."[7] In his discussion of the passage, Barth suggests that the divine judgment is tied inexorably to the relationship between creation and covenant: namely, it is with respect to creation's eschatological orientation toward (as the "external basis of") the covenant between God and humankind that it can and must be judged "very good," though it is not yet "perfect" in any absolute sense (even at the point of its creation, before the entry of sin and death into the world). If this relationship between creation and covenant falls into the background, then creation's nature as blessing and "benefit" is wholly inexplicable. But it is precisely this relationship that God himself has in view and that leads him, once his creative work is completed, to rest and to take time to enjoy his work, rejoicing that it is so good.[8] These points are important and well made, but we should not underestimate the extent to which the eye of faith perceives a wider pattern of abiding primal goodness and beauty in

[6] See Claus Westermann, *Genesis 1–11: A Commentary*, trans. John J. Scullion, S.J. (London: SPCK, 1984), 113.

[7] See Gerhard von Rad, *Genesis: A Commentary*, trans. John H. Marks, 2nd ed. (London: SCM Press, 1963), 59.

[8] See Karl Barth, *Church Dogmatics III/1* (Edinburgh: T&T Clark, 1958), 97, 213–14, 330–31.

the world which is entirely relevant to its own sense of the work of God's hands as something "good" and deserving of praise and which it expects the unbelieving eye to be able to grasp as such even if it anticipates no discernible apologetic benefit arising from this fact.

Creation, Craft, and Covenant

Barth's linking of the primal goodness of creation proleptically to the purposes of covenant accords well, though, with the larger canonical pattern of allusions to God as artist/craftsman, within an overall creation theology in which, as Fretheim observes, "God does not cease to be the Creator when the work of Genesis 1–2 has been completed nor is God thereafter reduced to the role of creative manager."[9] The artist who begins his work in the beginning continues with it, keeps it securely within his hands, fashioning it ever more fully into the likeness of his artistic vision that, as Barth suggests, while from every historical perspective it stretches all the way to a state of "completeness" and perfection lying as yet hidden in the promise of God for the world's eschatological future, nonetheless reaches a decisive and irreversible state of realization in the coming of the God-man, the one in whom the covenant with Israel is for the first time fulfilled from both sides, in whom God and the creature dwell together at-one and as one, and in whom God (both hypostatically and by virtue of the indwelling of his Spirit within the life of the Christos) is "all in all." If God and Israel dwelling together in peace and joy is the heart of the covenant hope ("You shall be my people and I shall be your God"), so too God and humankind dwelling together in peace and joy is the heart of that wider creation theology within which and for which the specificity of covenant and election are understood to take their place. And the "place" where this is envisaged as happening or is expected to happen or is concretely anticipated is variously the world God has made (both in its empirical and its promised "regenerate" eschatological form), the tabernacle and temple (which, as we shall see, assumes particular significance in relation to the image of God as artist), and the humanity of Christ himself, the particular "space" in the space-time of creation that God makes and takes for his personal dwelling among us.[10] Inasmuch as this is the heart of God's "artistic" vision for his work, the primal judgment of "goodness" in Genesis 1:31, whatever it may tell us about the state of the prehistoric world must also be an ordination and not

---

[9] Terence Fretheim, *God and World in the Old Testament: A Relational Theology of Creation* (Nashville: Abingdon, 2005), 7.

[10] See Trevor Hart, "Complicating Presence: Interdisciplinary Perspectives on a Theological Question," in *Divine Presence and Absence in Exilic and Post-exilic Judaism*, ed. Nathan MacDonald and Izaak J. de Hulster (Tübingen: Mohr Siebeck, 2013), 11–15.

a valediction, because the world, God's "project," remains unfinished and God has much more work yet to do in and with and through it before it becomes the place wherein he makes his dwelling alongside us. Its "goodness" as he stands back to consider it and enjoy it at this primeval stage of things, therefore, certainly includes its fitness for what he has yet (and has promised) to do with it.

If the image of the divine artist arises in the context of covenant theology as well as that of creation, we might properly expect to find it reflected in that part of the canon concerned directly with the fulfillment of promise and the appearance of the Messiah. If, though, the New Testament writers have relatively less to say about God as artist, it is because they mostly presuppose the Old Testament witness as the given context for understanding their own message. Nonetheless, they too, at points, make direct appeal to the image or elaborate further upon it. Perhaps the most familiar instance of this is Paul's appeal to the divine *yotser* in Romans 9:20-24, picking up on a theme from Wisdom 15:7 and developing it metaphorically for his own ends, citing the LXX text of Isaiah 29:16 verbatim to clinch his argument.[11] The context, again, is precisely that of God's creative engagement with the world and the sovereign purposes guiding it. God is the potter (*kerameus*) who takes the same lump of clay and from it is able skillfully to fashion (*plassein*) objects intended for quite different ends, in fact sets out quite deliberately to do so. Such variety of production is essential to his craft, and it is no good artifacts intended for more menial tasks complaining about this. As both Cranfield and Dunn note, the way in which this text has sometimes been deployed in Christian exegesis over the centuries rather misses its main point, which is not an assertion of God's sovereign right to decide capriciously and absolutely but precisely an appeal to the sort of authority associated with the master craftsman as he handles his materials with skill and wisdom and, consonant with his larger artistic purpose (here "to make known the riches of his glory"), disposes them within his overall range of products for different particular purposes.[12] Naked caprice, in other words, has nothing whatever to do with the authority of the artist (is incompatible with, it in fact) and is alien to Paul's thought at this point.[13] No doubt, too, the phrase "out of

---

[11] See C. E. B. Cranfield, *A Critical and Exegetical Commentary on the Epistle to the Romans*, International Critical Commentary (Edinburgh: T&T Clark, 1979), 2:491.

[12] Cf. Wisdom 15:7. "A potter kneads the soft earth and laboriously moulds each vessel for our service, fashioning out of the same clay both the vessels that serve clean uses and those for contrary uses, making all alike; but which shall be the use of each of them the worker in clay decides."

[13] See Cranfield, *Epistle to the Romans*, 2:491; James D. G. Dunn, *Romans 9–16*, Word Biblical Commentary (Dallas: Word Books, 1988).

the same lump," as well as being a direct echo of Wisdom 15:7, is intended to evoke the clay of Genesis 2:7 from which all humankind was fashioned in the beginning by the hands of the divine *yotser*.[14] Again, following Old Testament usage, Paul has in mind a God who, unlike the deities of the Greek world, has no qualms at all about getting his own hands dirty in the earth of creation.[15]

In his study of the history of craft, Lucie-Smith notes that under the Roman Empire the artist/craftsman's public standing had on the whole declined (being too closely associated with the institution of slavery).[16] Yet one field of craftsmanship in which Roman genius made genuine and revolutionary advances (and which thus perhaps constituted something of an exception in terms of public acclaim and recognition), he suggests, was building and architecture.[17] It is significant to note, therefore, that the New Testament's most consistent and sustained way of imaging God as craftsman is drawn precisely from the vocabulary of architecture and the building trade,[18] picking up directly on Old Testament precedent to be sure but singling out and developing this metaphor in particular from among a cluster of cognate images to be found there. Thus the author of the Epistle

---

[14] The only other instance of *plassein* in the New Testament is in 1 Tim 2:13, where Paul alludes precisely to the primordial fashioning of Adam from the earth.

[15] *Theological Dictionary of the New Testament* notes that whereas *plassein* (often rendering *yatsar*) is used in LXX thirty-six times of God, in the Greek world the verb is used only of the activity of lesser deities or "created creators" whose acts of fashioning are restricted to material *plasmata* (bodies, the physical cosmos). The true God does not touch matter directly but deals only in the creation of souls. This dualism is quite foreign to the biblical imagination, which pictures God fashioning all things, visible and invisible, with his bare hands. See Herbert Braun, "Plasso, Plasma," in *Theological Dictionary of the New Testament*, vol. 6, ed. Gerhard Friedrich (Grand Rapids: Eerdmans, 1968), 255, 257.

[16] In the system inherited by Rome from Greece, he notes, "[i]n the craft workshops free men and slaves worked side by side, and the rate of pay for all was equal. . . . Because so many skilled craftsmen were, if not slaves, then freedmen, and still bore in Roman eyes the mark of slavery, there developed a prejudice against artisans in general." Edward Lucie-Smith, *The Story of Craft: The Craftsman's Role in Society* (Oxford: Phaidon, 1981), 43.

[17] So, e.g., with the invention and use of concrete from the second century B.C. onward, "[w]alls and ceilings could now be moulded in any way the builder wished, and space itself became a plastic element." Attitudes toward the builder's craft were transformed, and there was a gradual disentangling of the craft of skilled design from that of skilled construction. The architect—"the man who drew plans, measured, calculated stresses—became a different person from the builder, who carried someone else's ideas into effect." Lucie-Smith, *Story of Craft*, 58.

[18] Cf. P. C. Trossen, "Erbauen," *Theologie und Glaube* 6 (1914), 804ff. Cited in Otto Michel, "Oikos, Oikodomos, Oikodomeo Etc.," in *Theological Dictionary of the New Testament*, vol. 5, ed. Gerhard Friedrich (Grand Rapids: Eerdmans, 1967), 144.

to the Hebrews echoes the Old Testament's insistence that, as Creator, God himself is "the builder of all things" (Heb 3:4), the one who fashions a world fit for human habitation.[19] More commonly, though, the New Testament's concern in deploying this metaphor is with a divine building project distinct from that of creation as such—namely, the construction of an *oikos* or habitation suitable for God's own dwelling in the world's midst, drawing on the imagery and theology of the Old Testament's tabernacle and temple traditions and applying them now (in a further metaphorical shift) to the church, the eschatological people of God. Again, here, it is God who is identified as the one who does the relevant building and apart from whose skilled and authoritative craftsmanship, as we shall see duly, things quickly go awry.

Nonetheless, the testimony of Scripture does not sideline or seek to proscribe human artistry. On the contrary, it seems that, at various key points in the story of God's creative fashioning of a world fit for his own indwelling with us, divine artistry actively solicits a corresponding creaturely creativity, apart from which the project cannot and will not come to fruition. Biblical scholars such as William P. Brown, Walter Brueggemann, Terence Fretheim, and Jon Levenson and systematic theologians such as Jürgen Moltmann and Michael Welker have all drawn attention to the presence in the relevant biblical texts (not least the creation saga itself) of what Fretheim refers to as "a more relational model of creation than has traditionally been presented";[20] in short, one in which from first to last the divine project of creation evinces modes or aspects in which God's own creative activity is mediated through creaturely processes and agencies, in which "creation" therefore "takes place not from outside the created order but from within" and in which "[b]oth human and nonhuman creatures are called to participate in the creative activity initiated by God."[21] Of course, that is not the whole story, but it is a significant part of it that has often been underplayed. And, of course, it entails God placing himself voluntarily in an apparently vulnerable and risky circumstance, since now

---

[19] For the use of *kataskeuazein* in this sense, cf. Isa 45:7 LXX, glancing ahead to 45:19. See also 40:28, where "to the ends of the earth" resonates with "all things" here. As Lane points out, the author's argument at this point is a chiastic one based on an analogy of proportionality: "Jesus is worthy of more glory than Moses in the same measure as God has more honor than the universe he has created." In each case, the relationship is that of builder to thing built. William L. Lane, *Hebrews 1–8*, Word Biblical Commentary (Dallas: Word Books, 1991), 77.

[20] Fretheim, *God and World*, 36.

[21] Fretheim, *God and World*, 38. Cf., e.g., William P. Brown, *The Ethos of the Cosmos: The Genesis of Moral Imagination in the Bible* (Grand Rapids: Eerdmans, 1999), 36–52; Michael Welker, *Creation and Reality* (Minneapolis: Fortress, 1999), 6–20.

it is not just that God calls into existence something other than himself and thereby limits himself (the heart of Moltmann's claim that creation already involves a kenotic movement of God *ad extra*)[22] but that the ultimate success of his creative venture itself is rendered contingent upon the consequences of calling creatures to a responsible collaboration, while generously allowing them to be themselves.[23] If, as Brown suggests, the "world" that God proposes and promises as the goal of the whole creative enterprise—one in which God and the human creature may dwell peaceably together—is thus bound to be one consisting not merely of "cosmos" (the material environment) but also of "ethos" (the nonmaterial realm of meanings, values, and persons), then clearly a bilateral pattern of creative "making" (from the side of God and from the side of the creature) is essential. For while "nature" may be part of the given order of things confronting the human creature as gift, "culture" cannot meaningfully arise or take shape without human action, response, and involvement. A "world" in this sense is thus bound to be one into the successful construction of which acts of responsible human making are factored from the outset.

I will have much more to say about all this in subsequent chapters. For now we may return to our focus on artistry as a biblical analogate for God's activity as Creator and as a cultural phenomenon reflected here and there in the texts themselves. It is generally supposed that Scripture has relatively little place for the arts as a manifestation of human culture, being at best indifferent toward them and at worst suspicious and even, on occasion, hostile. I must beg the reader's patience for not responding more fully here to what I certainly take to be a misapprehension on the part of many biblical interpreters on this front, but to do so would take me too far beyond my precise concern.[24] I therefore limit myself to two succinct observations before proceeding.

The first regards the text to which discussions of the Bible and the arts typically turn sooner rather than later—namely, the Decalogue's apparent explicit prohibition on the production of images or likenesses of any creaturely form (Exod 20:4-6; cf. Deut 27:15).[25] As I have argued

---

[22] See Jürgen Moltmann, *God in Creation: An Ecological Doctrine of Creation*, trans. Margaret Kohl (London: SCM Press, 1985), 88–93.

[23] Fretheim, *God and World*, 38.

[24] For helpful, if partial, responses, see, e.g., Leland Ryken, *The Liberated Imagination: Thinking Christianly about the Arts* (Eugene, Ore.: Wipf & Stock, 2005); Alison Searle, '*The Eyes of Your Heart': Literary and Theological Trajectories of Imagining Biblically* (Milton Keynes, U.K.: Paternoster, 2008); Francis Schaeffer, *Art and the Bible*, 2nd ed. (Downers Grove, Ill.: InterVarsity, 2007).

[25] Aidan Nichols notes that the phraseology of the commandment deliberately and comprehensively covers "the three most basic habitats of creatures," viz., all that is distinct

elsewhere,[26] the exegesis of the opening verses of the Decalogue is far from straightforward, and the question of their interpretation in a specifically Christian context adds a further level of hermeneutic complexity. In his discussion of this text, Gerhard von Rad points out its specifically cultic situation and concern.[27] It is toward the production of images for a particular sort of religious practice rather than images as such that the prohibition is directed (hence NRSV's "idols"). Specifically, von Rad argues, it was directed against the propensity for idolatrous conflation (as distinct from confusion) of the image with its divine archetype and the supposition that Yahweh, like the gods of some of Israel's Canaanite neighbors, might be rendered present, directly influenced, or in any way given over into the hands of the worshipper through the cultic presentation and manipulation of the sign. Understood thus, the exclusion of images from Israel's cult testified to the elusiveness and utter freedom of the God of Sinai with respect to the creaturely and set her worship and theology starkly apart from the assumptions and expectations of the wider religious culture—assumptions and expectations which, hitherto, no doubt, most Israelites had shared. The prohibition is thus designed to drive home some of the radically new patterns of thought and speech which must be etched on Israel's imagination as she learns what it means to worship and to serve the elusive God of the covenant, the one whose holy name has only recently been disclosed in her midst. If this interpretation (effectively reading Exod 20:4-5a as a single commandment and as an extension of the range of the imperative contained in verse 3 ["you shall have no other gods before me"]) is correct, then, of course, the issue is not one about the absolute impropriety of imaging God (a suggestion rendered implausible by the way in which Scripture itself—even in these same texts—encourages and fuels an abundant and diverse poetic "imaging" of God on more or less every page, as king, shepherd, warrior, rock, lion, strength and shield, light, and so on),[28] nor even the absolute impossibility of creaturely forms serving as effective mediators of God's presence and activity in certain

---

from God himself—seemingly a comprehensive ban on representational figuration. See Aidan Nichols, *Redeeming Beauty: Soundings in Sacral Aesthetics*, Ashgate Studies in Theology, Imagination and the Arts (Aldershot, U.K.: Ashgate, 2007), 22.

[26] For what follows, see Trevor Hart, *Between the Image and the Word: Theological Engagements with Imagination, Language and Literature* (Farnham, U.K.: Ashgate, 2013), 39–42, 176–79.

[27] So, e.g., Gerhard von Rad, *Old Testament Theology*, vol. 1, *The Theology of Israel's Historical Traditions*, trans. D. M. G. Stalker (Edinburgh: Oliver & Boyd, 1962), 212–19.

[28] Cf. Tryggve N. D. Mettinger, *No Graven Image? Israelite Aniconism in Its Ancient Near Eastern Context* (Stockholm: Almqvist & Wiksell, 1995), 15.

contexts. And it certainly has nothing directly to do with the artistic fashioning of figurative likenesses per se.

If, though, the Old Testament has no particular interest in banishing the arts, statistically it cannot be gainsaid that there are relatively few mentions of human artistry in its pages or those of Scripture as a whole. Numbers alone, though, count for little and must always be offset by other relevant considerations such as the contexts within which instances arise. And this brings me to my second point, which can be stated briefly, since the next section will be dedicated to unpacking it in detail. For, while we are still in the proximity of the covenant and its founding events and charter, what is less often noticed is that it is precisely here, juxtaposed tantalizingly to the second commandment, that we find what is the first and arguably the only explicit and developed theological endorsement of human artistry as such. There have, to be sure, been anticipations of one sort or another. We shall have something to say later of Adam and his peculiar privilege, as the archetypal human, of naming the animals and so embarking on the project of human language. We ought not to forget the fleeting mention of patriarch Jubal Cain (Gen 4:21) whose distinctive gift was duly inherited by Israel's first true king (1 Sam 16:16-23) nor overlook the fact that Noah, as God's chosen participant in a scheme of ecological salvage (Gen 6:5–9:18), arrests the undoing of creation by chaos,[29] preserves the remnant of creation, and so carries forward the divine promise of redemption precisely as a master craftsman, one who skillfully builds an ark in accordance with a divinely given blueprint. The theme of human artistry as complicit in God's ways of working to bring the world to its completion is thus trailed early on in the biblical narration of history. But in Exodus 31 it assumes a wholly new prominence, and one that, given the context, seems unlikely ever to fade from view without profound misunderstanding arising. For here, too, in the account of the provenance of the tabernacle itself, we find that the skilled work of human hands is not only tolerated but actively commissioned and endorsed by the LORD in a manner that suggests that the finished product, if it is to be pleasing to him, is always going to be a matter of *creatio per collaborationi*—not between equal partners, of course, but collaboration nonetheless. But what is the tabernacle? Surely, it is the place where God commits himself to dwell in the midst of and together with his covenant people, and as such it is the symbol and the concrete anticipation in history's midst of that promised cohabitation of God with the creature, the provenance of which lies in creation itself. (And, as we shall see, the intertextual allusions between creation and tabernacle traditions are particularly strong. Here, the biblical

[29] Brown, *Ethos of the Cosmos*, 55.

writers wish to leave us in little doubt, we have to do with essentially the same thing.) In other words, at the very heart of the traditions concerning Israel's origins and the shape of her holy correspondence to God's own purposes and character, we find that God makes a space for himself to dwell in her midst and renders it pleasing to himself not by an act of divine fiat but in a manner that both celebrates human skill and creativity and commissions it into his service. "God with us," it seems, is a circumstance that solicits and demands and facilitates our full contribution, and not one that shuts us down or reduces us to passive observers or hushed consumers of divine spectacle. There can, we might say, be no God with us, without us. And the fact that it is artistry in particular, therefore, that receives prominence of profile in the midst of all this, is worth a thousand scattered references through the rest of the canon.

Artistry in the Tabernacle Traditions

The tabernacle traditions in the book of Exodus use the cognate terms *charash* and *chashab* to describe the roles of Bezalel and Oholiab, the human artists chiefly responsible for fashioning the ornate splendor of the tent of meeting.[30] These are men called by the LORD and equipped by him with wondrous skill (*chokmah*) in every kind of craftsmanship, working in precious metals, precious stones, wood, leather, and fabrics to furnish a dwelling place fit for the divine presence. The text leaves it unclear whether we should think here in terms of natural talent (i.e., a divine gift given at birth and developed through apprenticeship to others whose contribution is implied here but unnamed) or a sudden and unexpected pneumatic transformation of the men. Two things at least, though, serve to disentangle the situation identifiably from the Hellenic notion of the *poetes* as an individual genius possessed and driven by "divine mania," with which, otherwise, we might be inclined to link it.[31] First, the two men do not work alone. Having received their skills, they train others to work alongside them and under their supervision (Exod 35:34), suggesting that we are dealing here in effect with either the ongoing transmission or else the divine establishment of a tradition of craftsmanship (a "workshop") in which artistry is linked

[30] See Exod 31:1-11; 35:1-43.

[31] So, e.g., William H. C. Propp, *Exodus 19–40*, The Anchor Bible (New York: Doubleday, 2006), 487. Wittkower and Wittkower note that in fact this notion of "divinely inspired creativity" was associated with the visual and plastic arts only in later classical thought, being reserved earlier for the more "immaterial" outputs of poets and musicians. See Margot Wittkower and Rudolf Wittkower, *Born under Saturn: The Character and Conduct of Artists; A Documented History from Antiquity to the French Revolution* (New York: New York Review Books, 2007), 4–5.

decisively to the acquisition of skills through practices rooted in community, obedience, and imitation. Second, while Bezalel and Oholiab appear in this context in the guise of "master craftsmen" and while they receive their personal skills (by whatever process) directly from God himself, as Fretheim observes, the chapters recounting their artistic labors are marked by a peculiar repeated insistence on the fact that these are carried out under extensive, precise, and immediate divine instruction.[32] In other words, the true "master craftsman" in these traditions is clearly understood to be the LORD himself, the one who trains and instructs and oversees all that is done in his name.

The work of these cultic craftsmen, then, is in some proper sense an extension of God's own work and purposes in the world, just as the work done by the journeyman and the apprentice in a medieval workshop might be concluded within and identified as the work of the master after whom the workshop was named. In such a context, individual genius and autonomous vision are largely displaced, or at least relativized, by concentration on the concerns of a larger shared purpose and way of working.[33] What Bezalel receives at the LORD's hand to equip him for his share in this work is described in Exodus 31:3a in terms of a precise threefold formula: wisdom (*chokmah*), understanding (*tebunah*), and knowledge (*daath*). These qualities are explicitly linked to a bestowal of the *ruah elohim* ("divine spirit"), mention of which sets off allusive resonances with Genesis 1:2, pointing already to a link between the work of the human craftsman and the primordial fashioning of a world by the divine Creator. That such a link is not fanciful but illuminating is apparently confirmed by Proverbs 3:19-20, where the very same threefold description arises, ascribed now not to any human artisans but to God himself in his role as maker and sustainer of all things:

> [19]The LORD by wisdom founded the earth;
> by understanding he established the heavens;
> [20]by his knowledge the deeps broke open,
> and the clouds drop down the dew.

---

[32] See Terence Fretheim, *Exodus*, Interpretation (Louisville: John Knox, 1991), 313.

[33] This is not to suggest that medieval craftsmen were unanimously content with such self-effacing anonymity or that the more gifted among them did not crave a circumstance in which their individual contribution could be singled out and recognized. The point here is simply that the regulation provided by the professional and social structure of the "guilds" (*arti*) at that time did not for the most part foster such individualism. See Wittkower and Wittkower, *Born under Saturn*, 8–16; Richard Sennett, *The Craftsman* (London: Penguin, 2008), 53–80.

The suggestion is that the divine master craftsman, as it were, passes on the benefit of his own skill and experience, inculcating in those who work alongside him and under his close supervision precisely the same qualities he himself possesses in full measure. He establishes the design and both instructs and superintends those who undertake the work of executing it on his behalf. It is in a proper sense his work (undertaken in his name), even though their hands are on this occasion the ones getting dirty in the task.

If, therefore, what Yahweh does is to "create a visual model"[34] of the tabernacle for his human craftsmen to work with, what is striking about the model itself and the stages of its completion are the multiple direct correspondences it manifests with Yahweh's own creative acts of making "in the beginning." Cosmos and tabernacle, it seems, are consciously related as macro- and microcosm of one another, and those engaged in the construction of the latter are called to imitate in their manner of working the primordial making of heaven and earth itself.[35] In each case, what arises is a divinely initiated "form-filledness" that contradicts the claims of chaos and attracts divine approbation and enjoyment (Gen 1:31; Exod 39:43; 40:34-35).[36]

In the tabernacle traditions, the level of divine prescription governing the establishment of this "holy ecology"[37] in history's midst is therefore set higher rather than lower, specifying the precise measurements, color schemes, and materials to be used. This is an important job, and nothing must be left to chance! In general, as we have seen, the image of the craftsman and his workshop is one where the existence of certain established limits or boundaries is to the fore: there are considerations of authority and obedience to be observed, traditional ways of working with which faith must be kept, accepted standards of excellence to be acknowledged and pursued. Yet while this is indeed a very different set of emphases than those generally in the foreground of consideration when the term "artist" is used today, we should not overstate the contrasts in an unhelpful manner. In particular, we should be clear that the craftsman's workshop is not a place that wholly excludes the exercise of personal freedom and ingenuity but precisely one which trains and nurtures these, each being given a carefully circumscribed space and structure—but space nonetheless—within which to function. Freedom can only ever be exercised within certain given limits if it is to be anything other than meaningless caprice, and, in the arts as elsewhere, those who go on to exercise it most powerfully

[34] Brown, *Ethos of the Cosmos*, 83.
[35] For detailed unpacking of the textual parallels, see Brown, *Ethos of the Cosmos*, 73–89; Fretheim, *God and World*, 128–31; Fretheim, *Exodus*, 268–72.
[36] Brown, *Ethos of the Cosmos*, 84.
[37] Brown, *Ethos of the Cosmos*, 85.

and creatively have all first learned their craft through a painstaking and highly disciplined acquisition of skills and techniques learned at the feet of others. In human terms at least, every truly great master in the arts has first been an apprentice, and it is precisely the creativity of the master that typically calls forth and enables, rather than constraining or crushing, the emergent creativity of those working under his authority and direction.

This circumstance, too, is nicely captured in the tabernacle traditions. Thus, while Bezalel and Oholiab are clearly working with a divine blueprint in front of them and a watchful eye over their shoulders and while their gift includes, in Propp's phrase (with no pun apparently intended!), the conferring of "wondrous manual skill, the ability to actualize the divine intent,"[38] their craftsmanship is nonetheless never presented as a matter of manual dexterity alone. Rather, as Durham notes, the formula of Exodus 31:1 identifies Bezalel as one gifted with "the ideal combination of theoretical knowledge, problem-solving practicality, and planning capability who can bring artistic ideals to life with his own hands."[39] This is a craftsmanship that not only renders the vision of God's blueprint in material form but, mutatis mutandis, participates fully in the sort of wisdom and understanding out of which that vision is born. Bezalel and Oholiab's status as gifted craftsmen in their own right is manifest, as it were, precisely in a fundamental concurrence between their own artistic vision and ways of working, on the one hand, and those of the true master of the workshop, the LORD himself, on the other. Yet the concurrence is one in which a vital order of authority and subordination is preserved. Bezalel's name marks him out as one whose work, however expert and inspired it may be, is nonetheless always cast in the shade by God's own,[40] and if, as Propp suggests, the Bible regards the craftsman in Israel as "a kind of sage,"[41] his is properly a wisdom that consists precisely in humility, knowing its place to be penultimate rather than ultimate, its freedom exercised self-consciously within given constraints, and whatever authority it possesses, therefore, received from a higher authority before it is duly exercised over others. Craftsmanship, in the hands of the human master, is very much a matter of holding something in trust. The cultic artist in Israel is, it seems,

[38] Propp, *Exodus 19–40*, 487.

[39] John I. Durham, *Exodus*, Word Biblical Commentary (Waco, Tex.: Word Books, 1987), 410.

[40] *Bezalel* is literally rendered "in God's shade/shelter." See Propp, *Exodus 19–40*, 486.

[41] Propp, *Exodus 19–40*, 488. The term *chakam* (linked etymologically to the "spirit of *chokmah*" in Exod 31:3; 35:31-32, etc.) used on occasion to denote a "skilled craftsman" (e.g., 1 Chr 22:15; 2 Chr 2:7, 13-14; Jer 10:9) more commonly refers to a "wise person" (e.g., Exod 7:11; 2 Sam 14:2; Esth 1:13; Job 17:10; Ps 107:43; Prov 1:5, et passim).

like the king, one whose role both "images" and mediates that of a divine prototype. This demands high levels of responsibility, as human freedom, imaginative vision, and skill are all exercised to the full and with no loss of integrity but always within the dynamics of a logically prior divine action that both enables and establishes the parameters for their legitimate use. Human "creativity" is, in Tolkien's carefully judged phrase, a matter of creaturely "sub-creation"[42] and as such carefully to be differentiated from its divine source and counterpart in the very moment that they are held together for consideration.

Imagination, Creativity, and Idolatry

If, from one perspective, therefore, the role of craftsman in the tabernacle traditions may be said to have a certain esteem attaching to it (the artist functioning as both an image and an agent of God's own artistry in Israel's midst), the matter is nonetheless immediately complicated by connotations attaching to the Old Testament's wider use of some of the key terms. Thus, the basic term used to designate the role in Exodus 35:35, *charash* (translated variously as "craftsman," "artisan," "engraver"), arises elsewhere in connection with those who, instead of facilitating the proper worship of the LORD and providing a place fit for his indwelling,[43] spend their peculiar skill and energies doing precisely the opposite, fashioning idols that lead the people astray and alienate them from God. So, for instance, in Isaiah 40:19 it is precisely a *charash* who is responsible for casting and adorning the ornate cultic objects upon which the prophet heaps his scorn, in a context where it is exactly the incomparability of the LORD both as the only true God and, we should notice, as the one true Craftsman (who, in his divine wisdom, "has measured the waters in the hollow of his hand and marked off the heavens with a span," etc. [v. 12]) that is under consideration.[44] Again, in Jeremiah 10:9 it is a *charash* and a *chakam*—one possessing the spirit of *chokmah* ("wisdom" or "skill")—who compromises the uniqueness of the LORD by fashioning the objects of a false religious devotion, and here the prophet seems to play deliberately with the textual resonances, echoing not just the terms used in Exodus 35 to describe Bezalel and Oholiab but also some of the materials and colors most closely associated with that description (gold, blue, and purple fabric). Again the parallel with the role of king,

---

[42] See further chap. 14 below.

[43] N.b., the same term is used in 1 Kgs 7:14 to describe Hiram of Tyre, the artist entrusted by Solomon with the commission for the construction of the Jerusalem Temple and for whom Bezalel is in effect the scriptural type. Hiram too, it should be noted, is described as sharing in the three "divine" qualities of "skill, intelligence and knowledge."

[44] Cf. Isa 44:11: "the artisans [*charashim*] . . . are merely human."

if limited, nonetheless proves helpful rather than fanciful: precisely because of the esteem and importance of the office and its close association with the Lord's own agency, any breach of trust in the exercise of it leads quickly and inexorably to corruption and disaster, distorting the pattern of covenant life just as surely as faithful remittance of the task blesses it. The workers may be the same, the materials and color scheme the same, but, once removed from the oversight and direction of the divine master craftsman himself, even the most skilled human artistry goes awry and generates the very opposite of an earthly *habitus* fit for divine indwelling and the inculcation of communion between God and his people.

It is thus no coincidence that the texts concerning the divine design of the tabernacle and the commissioning of artists to work on it (Exod 25:1–31:11) and those giving an account of the satisfactory completion of that work (Exod 35:4–39:43) are rudely interrupted by an account of Israel's first serious lapse into apostasy. This adventure is focused on a singular act of impulsive and misplaced human *poesis*, the casting of the "golden calf" (whatever we may make of it in specifically religious terms) affording a convenient parody of the genuine artistry described in what immediately precedes and follows. The people make their offering of base materials (cf. Exod 25:2-7; 35:5-9), and the craftsman's skill duly transfigures these into something aesthetically significant; but all this is done outside the context of divine lawgiving and results in a serious breach of the Sinai covenant that must thereafter be renewed. Of course, the specifically cultic context is vital here, but in a context where the post-Renaissance division between sacred and secular was wholly unknown, a wider point is surely relevant: acts of human design and making, taking the raw materials of the world and transforming them in ways which modify not just their physical form but also, in some identifiable sense, their value (aesthetic, religious, practical, economic, and whatever other sort may pertain), is hereby acknowledged as a worthwhile and even a religiously important concern; but it is one that must always be pursued concurrent with and within the parameters of a larger divine design and purpose, and not autonomously or in direct contradiction of these.

The other key term used to describe the role to which Bezalel and Oholiab are duly called is *chashab*, one who devises and then executes "skilful designs," for example in the intricate working of motifs of cherubim into the weave of the curtains from which the tabernacle itself is to be constructed (Exod 26:1, 31; cf. 36:8, 35) and the precise fashioning of cultic objects such as the ephod (28:3; cf. 39:3) and the "breastpiece of judgment" (28:15; cf. 39:8) that will be placed in it. Alongside this reference to specifically artistic design and craftsmanship, though, *chashab* has a wider application to "crafty"[45] human designs, most commonly ones falling outside the boundaries of God's own designs for his people and thus squarely in the domain of sin and evil. Thus the psalmist laments the various schemes "devised" by the wicked, precisely those whose every thought and action is carried on as if "[t]here is no God" (Ps 10:2, 4), while the word of the LORD through the prophet Zechariah urges the people not to "devise evil in [their] hearts" against one another (Zech 7:10; 8:17) but to live in accordance with the shape and direction of God's own purposes for them.[46] Again, we find that the very skills of human *poesis* called upon to establish a place for divine indwelling in history's midst are yoked awkwardly and suggestively in the lexicon with the capacities and sorts of behavior most likely to dismantle or defile it.

Perhaps the most striking instance of this, though, is found in the use of words belonging to the group derived from the Hebrew root *yzr*. The "allusive interplay"[47] between variants on this root points us repeatedly to a complex relationship between the best and the worst of human ways of dealing with God, the world, and one another. More significantly, it links God's own activity as Creator/Craftsman (and the reflection of this in the constitution of his human creatures in particular) with the very root of the primordial transgression that first spoils the world and sets humankind fundamentally at odds with God's own creative purpose. Again, the theme of "artistry" (God's artistry in fashioning the world and a creaturely impulse to fashion things by way of reciprocation) is at the heart of all this.

We have seen already that the basic meaning of the verb *yatsar* is "to form," "to fashion," or "to shape"; it is a word used freely to refer to God's "forming" of an orderly and meaningful world for human indwelling (Isa 45:18)[48] but equally of various human activities of forming too. The primary image is of a literal shaping or fashioning of matter with the hands—hence the privileging of the translation "potter" for the relevant

---

[45] On the etymology of the English "craft" and "crafty," see Lucie-Smith, *Story of Craft*, 12.

[46] For other uses of the term *chashab* in a similar vein, see, e.g., Ps 140:4; Jer 18:18, 48:2; Ezek 11:2; Mic 2:1. Jeremiah also uses the term of God's own "designs" or intentions to bring evil on Israel in punishment for her sins: see Jer 18:11; 26:3; 36:3. A more neutral use occurs in 2 Chr 26:15 where the *chashab* is one who invents the battlefield technology that secures King Uzziah victory over his enemies.

[47] Richard Kearney, *The Wake of Imagination: Toward a Postmodern Culture* (London: Routledge, 1988), 39.

[48] Cf. Gen 2:8, "the man whom he had formed"; Ps 95:5, "the dry land, which his hands have formed"; Isa 44:2, "the LORD . . . who formed you in the womb"; Amos 4:13, "the one who forms the mountains"; etc.

participle form (*yotser*) which, again as we have already seen, is a word applied most commonly in the Old Testament to God himself to picture the supreme craftsmanship involved in his act of world making. But *yatsar* has wider connotations too, picking up on the logically prior activity of "fashioning" that is such a vital part of the craftsman's work—forming an idea, a conception, or a vision in the mind's eye, a process that from first to last accompanies and informs his manual engagements with clay or wood or whatever material he finds to hand. So, the related term *yetser* refers not just to the artifacts produced by the craftsman's activity (see, e.g., Isa 29:16: "shall the yetser say of the yotser, 'He has no understanding'?")[49] but draws within its domain of meaning other outputs of human imagination too: a plan, a design, an intention—something framed and then held in the mind's eye, duly guiding and shaping any action we may take toward its realization in the world of empirical actuality.

These constructs, too, along with those called into being by the specifically artistic imagination, are products of what Richard Kearney refers to as "the human impulse to transcend what exists in the direction of what might exist."[50] As a category such *yetserim* (imaginings) and the capacity that generates them are morally and religiously neutral, but individual instances of course cannot be. It is here that Kearney, following Martin Buber's lead, traces a decisive yet mysterious link in Jewish thought between God's own handiwork in creation—the fashioning of human creatures possessed of "imaginative potential" and an impulse to "make" things from whatever they find to hand in the world—and the specific and singular act of imagining that led to their expulsion from the world as a place of unalloyed creaturely blessing and enjoyment.[51] In a real sense, as Buber notes, the "fall" entails a self-expulsion, since it arises precisely from the creature's attempt to supplant the "divine reality, which was allotted to him, . . . the good actuality of creation," with an alternative reality of his own devising and making.[52]

All this begins precisely with the created capacity to construct and entertain an imagined alterity, a playful and seeming harmless "as if," as yet apparently unharnessed to either the heart or the will. Thus in some sense, Kearney avers, God takes a calculated risk; the creatures are blessed with an imaginative impulse that, once morality comes into play (as sooner or later it must), furnishes the conditions for acts of genuine freedom, the

---

[49] Cf. Ps 103:14, where the "human frame" is the *yetser* produced by the divine artisan's work.

[50] Kearney, *Wake of Imagination*, 42.

[51] Kearney, *Wake of Imagination*, 39–40.

[52] Martin Buber, *Good and Evil* (Upper Saddle River, N.J.: Prentice Hall, 1997), 92.

ability first to project and then to choose between good and evil courses of action.[53] The line between the impulse to imagine and the impulse to pursue morally significant imaginaries (wedding imagination to the activities of the will) is a difficult one to draw in the breach of course, and Kearney realizes that this puts God squarely in the frame as sharing some level of responsibility for what follows. John Milton captures the ambiguity of the circumstance nicely when, in his account of the fall in *Paradise Lost*, he has Satan visit Eve first in a dream, an experience that both disturbs her with its lurid depictions of the possible and, despite Adam's confident assurances about the intrinsic nonculpability of anything merely dreamed about, clearly prepares the ground for her actual waking encounter the next day with the snake and the forbidden fruit, posing deep questions about the points at which temptation and sin respectively begin and about the inherent vulnerability of *Homo faber*, blessed at creation with the gift of imagination, to the subtle predations of evil.[54]

Wherever the lines of divine and human responsibility for what happens are understood to lie, though, having at first only imagined rebellion, Adam and Eve quickly discover what its actuality tastes like. Now in the uncomfortable position of "knowing" evil as well as good,[55] they are bewildered by the "infinite horizon of possibilities" confronting them[56] and find themselves unable to navigate a safe course through the chaos of images that variously entice and repel them, their moral compass having been seriously damaged in the fall from grace. Thus, more often than not, the "imagining of their hearts" (*yetser lev*) results in the proliferation of evil rather than good,[57] a fact that is cited first in justification of God's decision to purge the face of the earth with a flood and then, in the wake

---

[53] Thus, in later Jewish use, at the time of Ben Sira the term *yetser* mostly connotes precisely this capacity for imaginative projection that alone renders morally significant choice possible. According to Cohen Stuart's study of the Rabbinic concept of the *yetser hara* (an "evil *yetser*"), it was some time between 200 B.C. and A.D. 200 that the meaning shifted decisively to indicate an actual impulse (fusing such projection with desire) toward either good or evil. See G. H. Cohen Stuart, *The Struggle in Man between Good and Evil: An Inquiry into the Origin of the Rabbinic Concept of* Yeser Hara (Kampen: Uitgeversmaatschappij J. H. Kok, 1984), 81–145.

[54] See Hart, *Between the Image*, 149–59.

[55] As Kearney notes, God himself properly "knows" that which contradicts his creation precisely in his capacity as Creator (as that which he excludes from it), and such transcendent knowledge does not damage him; the human creature, though, can only "know" evil by personal participation in it, and it is this that engulfs it in the "alienating dialectic" that ensues. See Kearney, *Wake of Imagination*, 41.

[56] Kearney, *Wake of Imagination*, 42.

[57] Gen 6:5; cf. 8:21.

of that catastrophe, as motivating the covenant that commits him henceforth to forbearance. There is a palpable intertextual irony and tension here. God's own *yetser*, humankind, was a work of supreme craftsmanship, passing through quality control with a resounding positive judgment and stamp of approval (Gen 1:31). The human *yetser*, though (the *yetser* of the *yetser* as it were), is now found to be "evil continually" and grieves God when he looks upon it. As Paul Ricoeur observes, this evil *yetser* is the same one originally "implanted by the Creator in man; it is one of the things which God has made and of which he has said that they were 'very good.' "[58] Buber reminds us, astutely, that it is not of course the creaturely impulse toward or capacity for acts of imaginative projection and construction as such that is judged to be evil but the activities and outputs of this same capacity whenever it seeks to part company with—and thus distracts from—the framework of divinely purposed reality.[59] In a similar vein, Kearney suggests that "[t]he yetser is evil to the extent that man loses all sense of belonging or direction, living according to his own way rather than according to God's way."[60] Picking up on our earlier discussion, the evil in question arises (and arises inevitably) whenever the human impulse to be "creative" in any sphere of life in God's world is indulged in a manner that breaks faith with the vision of the divine master craftsman, becoming in effect a countercreative bid to displace God's authority, and to realize a different reality corresponding to the creature's own preferred design. Without the oversight and direction of God—without Torah in fact—the human *yetser*, far from being "free" in the sense it anticipates and craves, finds itself trapped in a vortex of unimagined arbitrariness, one ironically precisely of its own "making."

Of course the problematic status of the human *yetser* is much wider than the sphere of "artistry" or "craftsmanship" in any technical sense, but the latter is certainly included within its scope and no less constrained by the terms of Kearney's suggestion that the imagination in all its guises, despite initial appearances to the contrary, is a fundamentally ethical and theological conception, being bound up with deep questions about God's own character and creative intent for the world and with the teeming creaturely possibilities and potentialities he has buried deep within it for human exploration and realization. This compels reiteration of Buber's point about the *yetser*: far from being entirely evil, it is in fact the very thing that, when directed toward God rather than seeking autonomy from his direction and oversight, enables responsible human participation in

---

[58] Paul Ricoeur, *The Symbolism of Evil* (Boston: Beacon, 1967), 131.

[59] Buber, *Good and Evil*, 91.

[60] Kearney, *Wake of Imagination*, 43.

the project of creation and the realization of its rich potential.[61] Again, this observation obviously pertains to our many imaginative engagements with God's world outside the sphere of artistry as such, but it certainly has to do with artistry too and must undergird any theological account of the place of specifically artistic imagination in the life of the human creature.

The Ambiguous Work of Human Hands

The New Testament naturally inherits such uncertainty about the capacities and contribution of acts of human making, especially with respect to God's core purpose in creation and redemption, to fashion a habitation in creation's midst fit for his own indwelling together with his people.

A key passage here is Stephen's speech to the Sanhedrin in Acts 7. Accused, among other things, of speaking against the temple (6:13-14), Stephen moves his speech toward its climax by insisting that the Most High, whose own hands built the entire cosmos, does not himself dwell in "houses made by human hands" (*en cheiropoiētois*). In the context of early Christian apologetic, this might simply be taken to mean that, in the light of the new and fuller revelation of God in Jesus Christ, God can no longer be thought of as dwelling in any "manufactured" structure of bricks and mortar, the focus of the divine presence having shifted now, as it were, to another place altogether (the "tabernacle" of Christ's own flesh[62] and the messianic community of believers).[63] It is clear that Stephen believes precisely this, and this claim alone would of course suffice to scandalize the hearers and add fuel to the demand for the ritual stoning that follows.[64]

---

[61] Buber, *Good and Evil*, 93.

[62] In John 1:14, *eskēnosen* connotes "setting up a tent." See C. K. Barrett, *The Gospel according to St John: An Introduction with Commentary and Notes on the Greek Text* (Philadelphia: Westminster, 1978), 165.

[63] As well as direct citation from Isa 66:1-2, there is an interesting echo here, too, of Solomon's prayerful reflection in 1 Kgs 8:27: "[W]ill God indeed dwell on the earth? Even heaven and the highest heaven cannot contain you, much less this house that I have built!" Stephen's point, of course, is not to correct a mistaken notion of "containment" (surely no Jew could ever think God capable of such?) but to insist that the presumed focus of God's "dwelling" as expressed in the institutions of Judaism was no longer apposite. "The point is that the Temple was not intended, any more than the Tabernacle, to become a *permanent* institution, halting the advance of the divine plan for the people of God." William Manson, *The Epistle to the Hebrews: An Historical and Theological Reconsideration; The Baird Lecture, 1949* (London: Hodder & Stoughton, 1951), 34 (emphasis in original). The tabernacling God has moved on, Stephen insists, and those who mistakenly cling to the site of the physical temple will be left behind.

[64] The charge of blasphemy leading to stoning rests finally, of course, on Stephen's claim in verse 56 that he sees Jesus at the right hand of God in heaven.

But the term *cheiropoiētos* here is very likely a semitechnical one,[65] bearing more semantic freight than first meets the eye and having ramifications just as serious for the dispensations of the new covenant as they ever were for the old.

Stephen's brief narration of various building projects designed to domicile Israel's God (vv. 44-50) contains within it a clear value judgment, privileging the nomadic tabernacle ("tent of testimony") over the static and more substantial "house" with which the Davidic monarchy insisted on providing him.[66] To some extent this value judgment is already present in the relevant Old Testament texts themselves,[67] though Stephen sharpens it in the interest of his distinctly Christian polemic. The thing about the tabernacle, as Stephen observes, is that while it was certainly built by human hands in a literal sense, its construction was nonetheless, as we have seen, from first to last a matter of divine command, undertaken under close divine oversight and following a detailed divine blueprint (see v. 44). In a proper sense, then, this was first and foremost not Israel's but God's own project, and one in which God was himself involved as master builder.[68] The temple built by Solomon, by contrast, while well intentioned, was from the outset primarily a venture of human initiative and action, and one attracting initial divine reluctance and eventual permission and acquiescence. In this project (the idea for which springs not from God's but from David's *yetser*), Solomon himself does all the relevant conscripting, instructing, and overseeing. God himself interjects at best occasional words of caution and while certainly accepting and consecrating the finished product (which he describes, tellingly, as "this house that *you* have built")[69] as a place for his name to dwell, nonetheless issues a stern word of warning about its long-term sustainability, rather than the priestly

---

[65] Bruce notes, "The contrast between the terms 'made with human hands' and 'not made with human hands' is a prominent feature of the primitive catechesis about the new temple which runs throughout the NT and early Christian apologetic." F. F. Bruce, *Commentary on the Book of Acts* (London: Marshall, Morgan & Scott, 1965), 159. See further C. F. D. Moule, "Sanctuary and Sacrifice in the Church of the New Testament," *Journal of Theological Studies*, n.s. 1 (1950): 33–34.

[66] So Bruce: "The brevity with which Solomon's building is introduced and dismissed . . . expresses plain disapproval." Bruce, *Commentary on the Book of Acts*, 159. See also Marcel Simon, "St Stephen and the Jerusalem Temple," *Journal of Ecclesiastical History* 2, no. 1 (1951): 128–29.

[67] See in particular 2 Sam 7:5-6. Simon suggests that it is the beginning of this chapter and "God's refusal to have a house built for Him" that "provides the very foundation of Stephen's attitude towards the Temple." Simon, "St Stephen," 129.

[68] See above pp. 41–45.

[69] 1 Kgs 9:3. Cf. 8:27 for the corresponding phrase on Solomon's own lips.

word of blessing uttered by Moses (echoing the divine approbation of Gen 1:31) over the completed tabernacle in Exodus 39. For Stephen (and to some extent for the Old Testament that he cites here as his authority), the temple is thus an edifice "made with human hands" in a sense that was never true of the tabernacle;[70] planned on the basis of a vision originating in human impulse rather than divine command, constructed in relative independence (albeit not actual contradiction) of God's purposes and provision, it has in Israel's hands, in Stephen's eyes, become an obstacle to Israel's appropriation of God's promise rather than a manifestation of it, and the divine warning of 1 Kings 9:6-9 hangs over it in judgment. Here, *cheiropoiētos* carries with it at best the connotation of a seriously flawed project, something not built by divine hands and thus unlikely to remain upright for much longer (Ps 127:1). But even this does not identify the full force of the punch contained in Stephen's words. For in the background too, almost certainly, is the regular formulaic use of *cheiropoiētos* and close equivalents to it in LXX and by Hellenic Jews[71] as a circumlocution for acts of idolatry,[72] projects of human making and fashioning that not only willfully depart from the straight and narrow of God's purposes and promises but actually conflict with and contradict them. Stephen has only recently referred to the worshippers of the golden calf as "reveling in the works of their hands" (*tois ergois tōn cheirōn autōn* [v. 41]), and his choice of terms in verse 48 effectively tars the temple and its worshippers with the same brush. It would seem, therefore, that the charge of the "false witnesses" referred to in 6:13 was not entirely trumped up!

In such a semantic context, the insistence that something is "not made with hands"—or, positively put, that God himself is to be identified as the one who will build it[73]—potentially possesses both an ontological and a

---

[70] Cf., though, Heb 9:11 and 9:27 that, by implication, refer to the tabernacle too as "made with hands" in order to contrast it with the *heavenly* sanctuary entered by Christ as High Priest. On the difference between Stephen's view and that of Hebrews (and Philo), see Simon, "St Stephen," 134–35.

[71] It is not clear that Stephen himself was of the party of the Hellenes, but his name (together with that of Philip) suggests that he may well have been. See Bruce, *Commentary on the Book of Acts*, 129.

[72] For *cheiropoiētos* used in this connection in LXX to translate the Hebrew *'elil* (idol), see, e.g., Lev 26:1; Isa 2:18, 10:11, 19:1, 31:7. For related uses, see Lev 26:30; Jdt 8:18; Wis 14:8; Isa 16:12; 21:9, 46:6; Dan 5:4, 23; 6:28. For the "work of human hands" (*erga cheirōn anthrōpōn*) in a similar vein, see Deut 4:28; 2 Kgs 19:18; 2 Chr 32:19; Pss 115:4; 135:15; Isa 37:19; Wis 13:10. I am grateful to my colleague Grant Macaskill for drawing this pattern of use to my attention. The point is addressed briefly in Moule, "Sanctuary and Sacrifice," 34; Simon, "St Stephen," 133.

[73] The term *acheiropoiētos* itself occurs only three times in the NT. In Mark 14:58, it is placed on Jesus' lips in a statement referring obliquely to the temple of his resurrection body (cf. John 2:20), and Paul uses it in a related manner in 2 Cor 5:1 to refer to

moral force. That which is *ou cheiropoiētou* is, as Hebrews 9:11 reminds us, ultimately "not of this creation" either; namely, it has its provenance identifiably in God's own craftsmanship as the Creator, rather than springing from acts of human devising and construction. But accompanying this observation is the thought that the work of human hands (i.e., that which arises precisely from human pretension) is not just finite and fleeting but frequently sinful and finally idolatrous. The insistence that responsibility for certain building tasks belongs securely in God's hands is thus not always a statement of sheer ontological necessity in circumstances from which human agency is by definition excluded (those pertaining to aspects of either the primordial or the eschatological new creation as, e.g., in Heb 9:11 and 2 Cor 5:11) but may also be an articulation of divine judgment and grace in circumstances where human agency is ordinarily taken for granted but where matters are nonetheless taken finally out of human hands so as to redeem them from probable failure and its destructive consequences.

Where the furthering of God's redemptive purposes for humankind within history are concerned in particular—including the construction and ornamentation of a dwelling fit for divine habitation in the world's midst—relevant levels of human participation in the building process are fully acknowledged, but these are situated unambiguously on a building site where the master architect and builder (Heb 11:10) is identified as God himself. Thus, in another key speech from Acts, in chapter 15 the speech of James before the council at Jerusalem conflates material from LXX of Amos 9:11-12 with other Old Testament texts in a typically Jewish piece of creative exegesis,[74] in order to insist that Israel's God plans now

---

the eternal heavenly "habitation" that God will fashion for us. In neither of these cases, of course, could there be any question of the relevant building work being undertaken by anyone other than God himself. In the third instance (Col 2:11), the term refers to the "nonmanual" (i.e., spiritual) circumcision that believers are participant in by virtue of their union with Christ. Again, it is God's hands here that perform the operation, not human hands. Of the six instances of *cheiropoiētos* in the NT, though, four are qualified by the negative adjective *ou*: in addition to Acts 7:48, see also 17:24; Heb 9:11, 24. More broadly, of course, whenever the NT writers insist that it is God who builds, the relevant connotations of *acheiropoiētos* are properly evoked; while, as we shall see, human agency is not always entirely excluded, the thought is that God is in charge as master builder, and the responsibility for the project is securely in his hands.

[74] See esp. Acts 15:14-20. See on this Richard Bauckham, "James and the Jerusalem Church," in *The Book of Acts: Palestinian Setting*, ed. Richard Bauckham (Grand Rapids: Eerdmans, 1995). The MT of Amos 9:11-12 suggests the conquering and possession of the nations, whereas LXX suggests their inclusion within Israel's covenant status not as proselyte converts (who would need to be circumcised), but precisely as Gentiles. James

to "rebuild the dwelling of David which has fallen" and to build Gentiles (qua Gentiles) into it as an integral part. Of course, the Gentile mission will involve human laborers too, but the one ultimately responsible for the design and execution and success of the project is God himself. In other passages developing the image of the church as the eschatological and "spiritual" temple of God, the "divine passive"[75] is used in a manner that indicates that here, too, the one who does the really skilled work of building so vital to the project's satisfactory completion is God himself. In Ephesians 2:20-22 and 1 Peter 2:4-5, this point is made emphatically through the image of believers not as co-workers but as the materials ("living stones")[76] that the builder takes and must fit together (*sunoikodomeō*) into a structure suitable for God himself to move into. The emphasis is thus precisely on grace, on the master builder's superior craftsmanship rather than any inherent qualities of the supplies available to him.

Other texts, though, handle the imagery differently, drawing attention to the active involvement of human agents in the building work. Thus, whereas in Ephesians 2:20 the apostles and prophets are part of the foundation that God lays and on which he himself builds,[77] in 2 Corinthians 10:8, 12:19, and 13:10, Paul describes the work of an apostle as being from first to last one of building and, in 1 Corinthians 3:10, even pictures himself as a "skilled master builder" (*architectōn*) who lays foundations for others to build on in their turn. Yet, in these texts it remains clear throughout that such tasks are a matter of divine delegation, undertaken securely within the scope of God's grace and on the basis of a divine rather than merely human authority and instruction, and ones in which God himself thus remains fully involved. Likewise, where believers more widely are invoked to get their own hands dirty in the work of construction and restoration (as, e.g., in 1 Cor 14:3; 1 Thess 5:11; Jude 20), it is apparent from the wider theological context that building up and being built up are all part and parcel of the same package and that the presence and activity of the divine builder himself (in the person of the Holy Spirit) is presupposed throughout. These are, of course, instances of metaphorical "craft," but it seems reasonable to take them as indicative of theologically informed attitudes toward more literal counterparts.

---

here effectively treats LXX as "a legitimate way of reading the Hebrew text of that verse." Bauckham, "James and the Jerusalem Church," 456.

[75] "[I]n the NT a passive often contains the thought of a divine action." Cranfield, *Epistle to the Romans*, 495.

[76] This image (see 1 Pet 2:4-5) is clearly presupposed in Ephesians 2, even though the precise phrase is absent.

[77] Cf. Matt 16:18.

After the original fashioning of the cosmos itself in the beginning, the greatest act of divine craftsmanship alluded to in Scripture is the "preparation" of the New Jerusalem that John envisages descending from heaven to earth at the very heart of the new heaven and new earth (Rev 21:1-2). As Richard Bauckham notes,[78] this great city is also a temple, "the home of God . . . among mortals" where "he will dwell with them" (21:3) and thus in an identifiable sense the fulfillment of all the building work God has been doing in the history of his dealings with his covenant people. For now (i.e., in the present occupied by John and his readers), this promised artifact has an opposite as well as a forerunner in the midst of history: Babylon—a convenient symbol of human creativity, culture, and civilization at its apogee—has fallen to become a dwelling place fit not for God but only for demons (18:2), a "temple" for the spirit of all that is opposed to God and God's purposes. Here, Bauckham suggests, we find in effect the consummation of yet another failed building project recorded early in Scripture, the erection of the Tower of Babel in the midst of a city built on the very same site (Gen 11:1-9),[79] its architects and artisans concerned only to make a name for themselves and thus departing presumptuously and dangerously from the soil of divinely established order in a Promethean attempt to storm the heavens. Just as an act of divine judgment and grace intervened to bring their autonomous labors to nothing (thereby limiting the damage caused), so too in the Babylon of John's vision human craftsmanship and artistry has now ground to a halt, as any attempt to build in direct competition with the shape of God's own designs and the implementation of them must eventually do. So, John notes, what could have become a great cultural center has instead turned into a cultural wasteland, the absence of the sound of music from within its walls betokening the wider demise of art and craft of any sort whatsoever (18:22). By contrast, though, Bauckham suggests, the New Jerusalem, even as it comes down identifiably from heaven as a work of consummate divine craftsmanship, does not displace or exclude the flourishing of human culture but accommodates, redeems, and fulfills it, taking it up into itself as the consummation of all "human history and culture insofar as these have been dedicated to God." It comes from above in the sense that "all good comes from God, and all that is humanly good is best when acknowledged to come from God."[80] But it is precisely a city/temple, a place of ethos

[78] Richard Bauckham, *The Theology of the Book of Revelation*, New Testament Theology (Cambridge: Cambridge University Press, 1993), 132.

[79] On the Babel incident and its significance for human creativity, see further below pp. 123–51.

[80] Bauckham, *Theology of the Book of Revelation*, 135.

and culture, and designed, therefore, for God and humankind to dwell together and to coexist in mutual flourishing. What is purged from it, therefore, is not human participation in its fashioning or enhancement (genuine human culture and community) but those overweening bids for artistic autonomy which inevitably clash with and distort the master craftsman's vision, rather than lending themselves directly and deliberately to its realization and further development. And, insofar as it manifests this, the New Jerusalem, the eschatological temple or tabernacle of God, comes simultaneously from above and from below, creaturely creativity responding to and meeting that of the Creator himself in a union made in heaven to be sure but realized only under the conditions of earth and the creaturely freedoms bestowed upon earth at its own making.

What we have seen in this chapter, then, is first that at the heart of Scripture's imagining of God's own role as Creator of the heavens and the earth lies the image of God himself as an artist or craftsman who fashions a cosmos as the master craftsman fashions a work in his workshop, bearing all the hallmarks of skill, wisdom, and imaginative power. We have seen, furthermore, that this goes further than the mere suggestion of appropriate analogy between aspects of God's creative role and certain human practices; human artistry or skilled craft is itself actively called for and solicited by the divine master craftsman in contexts pregnant with symbolic significance both with respect to God's primordial creation of the cosmos and the fulfillment of his creative project, perfecting a world fit for his own indwelling together with us. If, in the meanwhile, the creative "work of human hands" enjoys a decidedly ambiguous status, its potential toxicity is in direct proportion to its vital role in bringing this project to completion. Thus, rather than the creative work of human hands being excluded from consideration, it remains central—albeit in need of redemption—to the creative scheme of things, which involves a relational dynamic simultaneously from above and from below. Later I shall argue that in order to make sense of this, without embracing what I take to be unhelpful models of a "synergism" or "co-creation," a christological hermeneutic is required—namely, a reading of the circumstance which acknowledges to the full that this same bilateral movement, from Creator to creature and reciprocally from creature toward Creator, has its objective basis and its abiding source in the once-for-all incarnation of the eternal Son, a reality pictured by the apostolic writers as, among other things, the fulfillment of the tabernacle/temple traditions and thus of the peculiar poetic and constructive responsibilities invested by Yahweh in Adam, Noah, Bezalel son of Uri, and, we may suppose, many, many others.[81] First, though, we turn in the next chapter to reckon with something directly relevant to modern ways of thinking about the place and prowess of the human artist but in a manner that compels some careful reconsideration and adjustment of those expectations: the incomparable work of God as the one who alone is the sovereign Creator of all things, visible and invisible.

---

[81] On the links between Noah's ark, creation, covenant, and tabernacle, see Brown, *Ethos of the Cosmos*, 58–61; Fretheim, *God and World*, 129.

4

Creation, Incomparability, and Otherness

Irenaeus and the Two Hands of God

The biblical image of God as the divine *artifex* who gets his hands dirty in the hard work of fashioning a world is picked up and developed at various points in the tradition, and never more fully or more fruitfully than in the late second-century theology of Irenaeus of Lyons (c. A.D. 130–200). As well as resonating powerfully with the sorts of theological concerns and emphases we have already seen at work in the biblical texts, Irenaeus' particular way of handling this image—variously fusing and counterpoising it with others and so modifying its force—draws attention helpfully to another, theologically vital, element within the pattern of biblical and Christian imagining of God's role and activity as Creator, the one who alone is "Maker of all things, visible and invisible."

As Eric Osborn notes, it is characteristic of Irenaeus' modus operandi in his major work *Against Heresies*[1] to explore and deploy the peculiar logic of images (mostly, though not uniquely, biblical ones) in pursuing

---

[1] Written c. A.D. 175–185. References to the text in English in what follows are taken from J. Donaldson and A. Roberts, eds., *Ante Nicene Fathers: Translations of the Writings of the Fathers down to AD 325* (Buffalo, N.Y., 1885). Corresponding originals are cited from the critical edition of Adelin Rousseau et al., eds., *Irénée de Lyon Contre Les Hérésies*, in the relevant volumes of *Sources Chrétiennes* (Paris: Les Éditions du Cerf, 1965–1982).

a rigorously argued theological case against his opponents.[2] Responding to various strands of Gnosticism, Irenaeus was no doubt driven to
this self-consciously "poetic" line of approach both by his own sense of
the need to remain close to the nature and content of his biblical source
materials and by the strategy of his opponents themselves who frequently
fused argument and imagination.[3] In doing so, though, Irenaeus insists,
and in fashioning their account of the doctrine of creation in particular,
they repeatedly misappropriated and maltreated the imagery of Scripture,
showing no regard for "the order and the connection" between elements in
the patterns of the text (1.8.1), thereby jeopardizing a proper understanding both of God's character and of his relationship to "all things" and putting the gospel message itself significantly at risk. As we shall see, Irenaeus'
own appeal to the image of God as artist has two main theological objec-
tives—(i) to emphasize the immediate, personal, "hands-on" involvement
of God himself in the making of the cosmos and (ii) to assert that, despite
empirical considerations seeming to suggest otherwise, the world was in
the beginning and remains a work of supreme divine craftsmanship, an
artifact born of God's own wisdom and skill, worthy of our admiration
and enjoyment.

Irenaeus' most fundamental concern is to overturn the gnostic claim
that, since God himself is too exalted and too remote to have any direct
dealings with a world such as ours, the world's fashioning (and that of
its various sentient inhabitants) must therefore be ascribed instead to the
activities of a created demigod or angelic mediator, one delegated and sent
by God to do the relevant dirty work (1.4–5). The problem here, Irenaeus
realizes, is that the initial premise stands in stark contradiction to what
Christian faith actually knows to be true about God—namely, that, let
alone being fussy about the hygiene of creating, he was determined, in the
fullness of time, to get himself altogether more fully and messily involved
in the handling of "the flesh" even than this, entering the virgin's womb
in the power of his own Spirit and immersing himself to the hilt in the
contingencies and other conditions of human creatureliness (1.9.3; 2.32.5;

---

[2] Eric Osborn, *Irenaeus of Lyons* (Cambridge: Cambridge University Press, 2001),
22. Osborn's case builds on the observations of Hugo Koch, "Zur Lehre vom Urstand
und von der Erlösung bei Irenaeus," *Theologische Studien und Kritiken* 96–97 (1925):
183–214.

[3] Thus von Balthasar describes the heart of the gnostic vision of reality as an "aesthetic myth," noting that "Valentinus—to mention only him, though the same could be
said of the other great Gnostic myth-makers—is beyond doubt a powerful poet." Hans
Urs von Balthasar, *The Glory of the Lord: A Theological Aesthetics*, vol. 2, *Studies in Theological Style: Clerical Styles* (Edinburgh: T&T Clark, 1984), 33, 38. Cf. Osborn, *Irenaeus
of Lyons*, 22.

3.17.4, et passim). In order to see the divine ends already envisaged in creation duly brought to fulfillment, God (the Word/Son), Irenaeus maintains, became one with his own creation by entering it as a creature and thus united it through himself to God (3.4.2). A *deus antisepticus* who is either incapable or unwilling to get his hands soiled by any immediate involvement with the world's distinctive ontology is quite clearly not the God of this gospel, and nor, therefore, Irenaeus insists, can he be the God of creation, since creation and redemption are in effect two facets of a single overarching direct engagement of the triune God with the world.

What Irenaeus urges upon his readers is the importance of beginning in the right place and effectively reversing the flow of interpretation where biblical statements about creation are concerned. Rather than beginning (as the gnostics do) with first principles sourced outside the substance of biblical revelation itself or even with the Bible's own earliest statements about God's creative activity read in isolation, we should begin in the place where the most, rather than the least, light is shed upon the character of God's dealings with the world. For the Christian reader, in other words, Genesis 1 must be read in the light cast by the first chapter of John's Gospel, as well as vice versa. We must interpret things backward as well as forward, viewing the earlier dispensation from the perspective of this more full-blooded, unequivocally "hands-on" engagement with the world in the humanity of Christ.[4] And we must identify those very same "hands" as ones already decisively and directly involved in shaping earlier stages of the world's history under God, including its primordial fashioning into an inhabitable shape.

If we proceed in this fashion, then it is clear that the God of Christian Scripture has no need of angelic intermediaries to fashion, mold, and form the world for him (4.7.4; 5.1.3).[5] Echoing the poetry of the Genesis texts but fashioning his own highly distinctive Trinitarian image from the materials afforded by it, Irenaeus therefore insists that it is no created demiurge but the one true God and Father himself who molds Adam from the dust of earth (3.21; 5.14.2), apparently not even troubling to

---

[4] On the biblical hermeneutics of Irenaeus and his handling of the early chapters of Genesis as Christian Scripture, see Thomas Holsinger-Friesen, *Irenaeus and Genesis: A Study of Competition in Early Christian Hermeneutics*, Journal of Theological Interpretation Supplements (Winona Lake, Ind.: Eisenbrauns, 2009).

[5] The Hebrew texts themselves, as we have already seen, place a parallel weight on God's direct "manual" engagement in the formative processes of creation. As Osborn notes, though, for Irenaeus it is only in the light of a Trinitarian reading that the radical extent and implications of divine immediacy (in the respective economies of the fully divine Son and Spirit) can be fully and properly appreciated. Osborn, *Irenaeus of Lyons*, 53, 65.

wear protective gloves for the task but (here and more widely in the work of creation) laying hold of and shaping matter into a cosmos directly with his two "hands," the divine Word/Son and Spirit (4.pref.4; 4.20.1; 5.1.3). No artist's hands can meaningfully be thought or spoken of as external or subordinate to the artist herself or her artistic agency; they are distinguished both from the tools on her bench and from any other labor deployed in her workshop precisely as those aspects of the artist herself through which her most immediate engagements with the work in hand occur. Correspondingly, it is clear that, appealing to this image, Irenaeus intends and will tolerate no Trinitarian subordination: his point is that the Son and the Spirit, precisely because they are fully divine, are the natural extensions of God's own being through which the eternal Father handles the world in creation and redemption.[6] Thus the world in its entirety is, from first to last, God's own "peculiar handiwork" (*to idion autou plasma*, 3.19.3), that good workmanship that he himself fashioned and formed in the beginning and which, in the fullness of time, he sought out and laid hold of again in a radically new way in order to bring it to its due completion in Christ (3.19.3; 3.22.1–2; 4.41.4; 5.16.1; 5.36.3).

The parallelism and organic connection between these two distinct "hands-on" engagements and their theological significance is neatly captured by Irenaeus in the following allusion to the healing of the blind man's eyes by Jesus in John 9:

> Now the work of God is the fashioning [*plasmatio*] of man. For, as the Scripture says, He made [man] by a kind of process: "And the Lord took clay from the earth, and formed man." Wherefore also the Lord spat upon the ground and made clay, and smeared it upon the eyes, pointing out the original fashioning [of man], how it was effected, and manifesting the hand of God to those who can understand by what [hand] man was formed out of the dust. For that which the artificer, the Word [*artifex Verbum*] had omitted to form in the womb, [viz., the blind man's eyes], He then supplied in public, that the works of God might be manifested in him, in order that we might not be seeking out another hand by which man was fashioned, nor another Father; knowing that this hand of God which formed us at the beginning, and which does form us in the womb, has in the last times sought us out who were lost, winning back his own, and taking up the lost sheep upon His shoulders, and with joy restoring it to the fold of life. (5.15.2)

We can forgive Irenaeus the slight crunch of imaginative gears in the last few clauses, as one metaphor slides in unannounced and rudely displaces another, and the divine artist suddenly morphs into a shepherd. The fundamental theological point remains clear. The healing and salvaging hands of

---

[6] See Osborn, *Irenaeus of Lyons*, 89–93.

Jesus (i.e., of the incarnate Word empowered by the Spirit) are precisely the eternal Father's own, the same hands that formed Adam in the beginning and set him down securely and blessedly in a cosmos of their own design and making. This is a thoroughly Trinitarian and incarnational account of God's dealings with the world, and it is wedded to Irenaeus' vivid imaginative apprehension of God as a master craftsman/artist who in the beginning fashions an artifact with his own hands and then continues to work away at it over time, bringing it only at the last to its due completion and fulfillment.

Creation Not a Botched Job

This, though, might seem to ignore something else that, according to Irenaeus' own account, was central to the gnostics' doctrine of creation, shaping their particular treatment of the biblical image of the Creator as an artist or craftsman. In effect, they indulged in some art criticism, carefully considering the quality of the work in question and then disputing the traditional ascription of it to God's own hand. The world, they observed, when you stopped and looked at it, was not actually much of a masterpiece at all but contained blemishes and flaws of a fairly significant sort. Thus, even if it were possible in theory for God himself to have been directly involved in the world's fashioning (in fact, they believed, it was not, due to God's radical transcendence), the finished product was in any case hardly one that could be ascribed to him with any confidence, being quite unworthy of his supreme level of knowledge and power. Clearly, they maintained, a work of such quality was not that of a master craftsman at all but of some apprentice, one as yet relatively unskilled and lacking in creative vision, capable only of copying a model supplied by someone else and in the event making a botched job of it. Here, to be sure, we have the familiar imagery of the craftsman's workshop; but here the creation of the cosmos, far from being a project engaged in directly and underwritten by the master himself, has been entrusted instead to "an architect of no ability [*nullius momenti artifex*] or a boy receiving his first lesson" (2.7.5). That alone, according to the gnostic version of things, can account for the state we currently find it in.

This claim calls forth an emphatic response from Irenaeus, and for convenience we may trace three strands in that response. (1) While he certainly does not underestimate the problem posed by the presence of evil and suffering in God's world, he follows early Christian tradition in its refusal to lay the blame for this state of affairs at the door of the divine Creator, ascribing responsibility for its presence instead largely to a "fall" into sin by the ancient parents of the race (3.18.7; 3.21.10; 5.19.1).[7]

---

[7] Osborn notes that Irenaeus' lost tract to Florinus on divine monarchy (recorded in

(2) Thus, the world itself, Irenaeus indicates quite clearly, came to us originally from God's own hands as an unequivocally good work, one "fitted
and arranged [*aptauit et disposuit*] . . . by His wisdom" for our habitation
(2.30.9), and, despite sin's undeniable and terrible impact upon it, it continues to manifest goodness and order of a sort sufficient to bear witness
to that same divine wisdom. God's wisdom/skill (*sapientia*),[8] Irenaeus suggests, is in fact manifest simultaneously with his power and goodness, but
it is seen at work preeminently in the aesthetic unity of creation, rendering
the many varied elements of the cosmos "parts of one harmonious and
consistent whole" (4.38.3), establishing order and harmony where otherwise mutual opposition and disharmony would prevail (2.25.2). (3) It
is also true that while, in order to preserve certain theological capital, he
wishes to recognize the completeness of God's creative labors after the six
initial days of making recorded in Genesis 1–2, Irenaeus' development of
the image of God as artist tends in practice to soften this insistence, rendering the boundaries between creation, providence, and redemption less
than absolute,[9] and gesturing in the direction of some appropriate notion
of a *creatio continua*—that is, an aspect of God's "creative" engagement
with the cosmos that does not come to an end with the day of divine rest
but perdures beyond it. Thus, he acknowledges that the work of "shaping"
and "forming" attributable to the divine artist's hands continues throughout the whole of salvation history and, indeed, the various histories of our
individual lives within it that are, he urges, as much a matter of immediate
divine "workmanship" as the ancient formation of the cosmos itself and
continuous with it (4.36.6; 4.39.2; 4.64.2).[10] If, therefore, there is indeed
an element of divine creativity which is of necessity located uniquely and
unrepeatably in the beginning, there are nonetheless aspects of the same

---

Eusebius' *Ecclesiastical History*, 5.20) bears the subtitle "that God is not the cause of evils."
Osborn, *Irenaeus of Lyons*, 219.

[8] The term *sapientia* can denote practical wisdom as well as theoretical, and is rendered
variously as "wisdom" and "skill" in the English text. The wisdom of an artist/craftsman
is particularly closely allied to and manifest in embodied, "hands-on" practices as well as
"design," and thus "skill" is a fitting alternative rendering in the context. On the problems
of divorcing "head" from "hand" in craft through abstract and disembodied approaches to
design, see Richard Sennett, *The Craftsman* (London: Penguin, 2008), 37–45.

[9] These are boundaries that his explicit disavowal of all Marcionite tendencies
restrains Irenaeus in any case from pressing too hard or too far, always urging a fundamental continuity rather than discontinuity between them.

[10] Cf. Gustaf Wingren, *Man and the Incarnation: A Study in the Biblical Theology of
Irenaeus* (Edinburgh: Oliver & Boyd, 1959), 7. As we have seen above, this self-conscious
conjoining of aspects of primordial creation and a theology of providence also characterizes the use of the image of God as *yotser* in the Old Testament.

divine work of "making" which began there that have a vital extension through created time. God does not immediately let go of the cosmos as something finished, exhibiting it and handing it over for the public and the critics to make of it what they will. He holds onto it, carries on working away at it; in a vital sense, it never leaves his workshop. Viewed thus, it must be judged in some clear sense to be not yet complete and the locus of the final goodness and perfection of the divine "work" as a whole (the project that begins with "creation") situated in the eschatological future rather than the protological past, glimpsed for now by faith proleptically and under the forms of hope.

Thus, Irenaeus suggests, whether apprehended by the empirical or the eschatological gaze, it is not just the immediacy of God's personal engagement in making the cosmos but also the supreme judgment and skill evinced in his rendering of it as an aesthetically satisfying and ecologically viable whole, which compels religious imagination to picture God as a craftsman (*plasmator*) fashioning an artifact with his own hands (5.17.1) or an artist (*artifex*) combining disparate tones into a harmonious work (2.25.2). Those who hear the melody, he observes, should offer their praise to the composer for his demonstration of judgment, goodness, and skill (*iustitia, bonitas et sapientia*), a triumvirate of characteristics evocative, perhaps, of the "wisdom, understanding and knowledge" cited in Exodus 31, we recall, as the hallmark of all that issues from the divine workshop. By their attribution of the cosmos to the work of an incompetent and clumsy artisan, the gnostics, by contrast, despise the workmanship of God and thereby blaspheme against him (1.22.1).

As I have already noted, it may well have been the gnostic adoption and adaptation of the biblical image of God as artist/craftsman that led Irenaeus himself to make quite as much of it as he did, and it certainly shapes his particular way of handling the metaphor. The God pictured in Scripture, he insists, is a wise master craftsman bringing to bear all the authority of his profession, not an inept trainee learning "on the job" from his unfortunate mistakes as he attempts to follow the instructions and mimic the example of more experienced and skilled pairs of hands. Indeed, Irenaeus insists, there could be no question of this particular artist ever having to copy a design produced for him by someone else or emulating the technique of a greater practitioner; being God, he himself is and must be the sole source both of the blueprint in accordance with which the cosmos is duly fashioned and of the skill and power involved in actually fashioning it (2.16.3; 4.20.1). Of course, as we have already observed, even the greatest among human masters of art and craft must at some point in their illustrious careers submit to the authority of others, learning from and carefully imitating their techniques and their designs; but where God is concerned the social mechanisms of authoritative *traditio* cannot and do not apply, and to insist upon them as proper entailments of the image would be to make a fundamental theological mistake. The God to whom Scripture bears witness, Irenaeus insists, is *adeētos*, in need of nothing, and anything that he requires for his artistic engagement in creation must thus originate "from himself."[11]

This claim, then, is one that cannot be derived from the logic of the image of God as artist itself, existing, as it does, in apparent tension with some of the natural entailments of that image. Here, therefore, Irenaeus arrives at the threshold of a realization to which we have already alluded—namely, that any single poetic image can only be made to do so much work before it breaks down and threatens to generate misunderstanding rather than illumination. Images for God in particular (even biblically sanctioned ones) must thus be treated with enormous care and permitted to be broken open on the hard edges of reality as we apply them and allow them to inform and to guide our thinking and speaking about God's nature and activity. Thus there are points, Irenaeus sees, at which the analogy between God and human artists holds and is religiously and theologically enormously valuable, and others at which, even when used well and with orthodox intent, it does not hold at all and must not be pressed into service. The theologian's responsibility is precisely to discern the point at which the genuine poetic penetrations of a metaphor's insistence that "it is" needs finally to give way to the accompanying apophatic acknowledgment that, even so, "it is not," permitting other images, perhaps, to supplement and contradict and correct it.

The logic of images is always a matter of complex interplay between comparability and incomparability, and when one of the two terms is God himself this wider poetic consideration is reinforced and magnified, because in the final analysis and at the most basic of levels God is wholly unlike any creaturely entity, so that the instability of images (even inspired ones) is more pronounced and recognition of it more urgent. Furthermore, this fundamental difference, Irenaeus realizes, has to do precisely with the business of creation itself. The distinction between the uncreated (*infectus*) God on the one hand and all that is created on the other is, he holds, a defining distinction,[12] a boundary which must not under any circumstances be blurred (2.12.1; 2.25.3; 2.34.2; 3.8.3; 4.11.2). And if there are (as we have seen there are) aspects of God's creative relation to the world that permit of appropriate human analogies, there are other aspects that do not, in relation to which no image drawn from the sphere of human

---

[11] Cf. Osborn, *Irenaeus of Lyons*, 64.
[12] Osborn, *Irenaeus of Lyons*, 28.

agency will properly serve and where we are therefore driven regularly to resort to negations in order to establish the relevant point. Thus, unlike any human artist, God has no need to serve an apprenticeship in order to gain the skill and wisdom manifest in the ordering of the cosmos nor any need to refer to a long-standing tradition of design to inform his handling and ordering of the cosmos. These things are vital to any human artist if he or she is to get the best out of materials available and with which he or she must work. But here again, Irenaeus insists, our image runs aground if we try to press it too far; because, unlike any human artist (and unlike the gnostic demiurge), the divine artist is neither constrained by nor accountable to the forms and inherent qualities of various materials that already stand over against him. In this regard, too, he is radically "self-sufficient" (*ipse sibi sufficiens*), granting to everything else that exists (including the raw material with which he must work) its very existence (3.8.3), and thus from first to last "master" of the creative process in an altogether more radical sense than properly befits any human artist (2.10.4). So, whereas human artists must take what is given in the primordial plenitude of creation itself, working with it in order to fashion something new from its rich potential and bound by the teeming possibilities and impossibilities intrinsic within it, God's own "creative" action, Irenaeus insists, entails another aspect which has no legitimate parallel in human artistry, granting the privilege of existence itself not just to the form but to the very substance of the cosmos, calling into existence alongside himself that which (precisely as creature) is not himself but that can only meaningfully be pictured as *fecit ex eo quod non erat*—as something formed and fashioned "out of that which had no existence" (1.22.1).

No apprenticeship, no established tradition of design and construction, no raw materials to constrain the limits of his creative vision—these are just some of the vital negatives which Irenaeus recognizes must qualify our appropriation of the biblical image of God as an artist and of the world as the skilled and aesthetically supreme artifact issuing from his two divine hands. As Osborn notes, though, in making these vitally important theological points, Irenaeus does not depart from the logic of images but remains securely within it, making use of some of its self-correcting tendencies; in particular, he deliberately juxtaposes the image of God as craftsman to another—that of God as sovereign monarch who, by virtue of nothing other than his own word of command, speaks and sees his will immediately done.[13] The images collide at various levels (as discrete metaphors applied to the same reality often do), but in Irenaeus' hands the collision is a fruitful one, allowing the genuine insights of each image to

---

[13] See Osborn, *Irenaeus of Lyons*, 51–52.

complement those of the other and permitting each to correct some of the other's potential theological deficits. Thus, for instance, whereas the image of monarch for its part presupposes no preexistent "matter," emphasizes a fitting "distance" between God and the object of his sovereign utterance, and bespeaks an ease in the accomplishment of the divine creative will, the image of artist, as we have seen, connotes instead personal commitment to the hard graft of the processes of making, a personal vision seen through from the moment of its inception to successful fulfillment and underwritten by the immediate hands-on involvement of one whose skill cannot be surpassed. Each image has something important to tell us about the nature of God's "creative" engagement with the world, though neither tells us all that we need to know, and each, pressed to inappropriate lengths, risks serious theological misunderstandings. Each benefits from the imaginative collision of metaphorical entailments that Irenaeus' treatment facilitates, though as Osborn himself observes, Irenaeus cannot be given all the poetic credit here, since he finds the two images themselves already deeply embedded and coexisting in a suggestive tension within the final form of the biblical narrative of creation itself.[14]

Images and Things to Be Done with Words

In his commentary on Genesis, Claus Westermann reminds us that in the cosmogonic saga of chapter 1 it is not the author's intention "to describe creation in such a way that we can imagine how it took place."[15] To think of it thus would be to misunderstand both the purpose of ancient cosmogonies and the nature of poetry, where images typically suggest rather than describe and where, as we have already seen, several different images may happily coexist, collide, and modify one another in the process. A clearly defined picture of how things were at the moment of creation is in reality and by definition unavailable to us (being literally "unthinkable," since our thought is always cast in terms of structures and relationships proper to the creaturely world itself), and it is precisely the logic of the broken or chastened image, therefore, that preserves us from the fallacy of supposing that we possess any such thing. Accordingly, von Rad among others notes,[16] in

[14] Osborn, *Irenaeus of Lyons*, 51.
[15] Claus Westermann, *Genesis 1–11: A Commentary*, trans. John J. Scullion, S.J. (London: SPCK, 1984), 116.
[16] Gerhard von Rad, *Genesis: A Commentary*, trans. John H. Marks, 2nd ed. (London: SCM Press, 1963), 51–52. Cf. Walther Eichrodt, *Theology of the Old Testament*, vol. 2, trans. J. A. Baker (London: SCM Press, 1967), 99–100; Westermann, *Genesis 1–11*, 110–11; William P. Brown, *The Ethos of the Cosmos: The Genesis of Moral Imagination in*

the reports of creation in Genesis 1–2 what we find is precisely the poetic counterpoint of at least two quite distinct conceptions or images of God's activity in the beginning.

First, as we have already seen, there is the image of God's immediate "hands-on" making and fashioning (1:7, 16-17, 21, 25, 26; 2:7-8, 19), forming, and ordering into complex relational patterns the component parts of the cosmos and its sentient inhabitants, like a great artist or master craftsman, rendering a "work" that, when it is finished, passes muster and is pronounced to be "good work" by the one who has labored long and hard over it. Alongside and interlaced with this, though, there is the image of God as one whose brow remains unvisited by the sweat born of effort, creating not by skilled manual labor but by what is surely the supreme instance of a series of "performative utterances."[17] This is a God who has only to speak, and what he speaks is at once accomplished, as indicated by the reiterated antiphon: "And God said. . . . And it was so" (1:3, 6, 9, 11, 14, 20, 24, 26). The relevant image, Westermann observes, is that of the all-powerful Near Eastern potentate who issues a command from the throne and neither expects nor encounters any meaningful resistance to its immediate fulfillment.[18] Creation by the divine Word, it is generally claimed, suggests an element of unlimited freedom in what God does, his absolute sovereignty with respect to the entire creative process from beginning to end.[19]

In the final form of the text of Genesis 1, we might note, these two images do not simply stand in uncomfortable juxtaposition but are permitted to cross-fertilize. Thus, as William Brown notes, the "let there be" of divine commanding is in practice woven together in the text (e.g., in vv. 6-7, 14-18) with accounts of divine doing and making, the monarch getting off the throne, as it were, to get involved personally in tasks of fabrication and construction. "In the role of king," Brown suggests, "God is the consummate artisan, wielding a verbal stylus . . . and the cosmos is a thoroughly artistic product."[20] In verses 9, 11, and 24, God himself acts,

---

the Bible (Grand Rapids: Eerdmans, 1999), 39–40; Michael Welker, Creation and Reality (Minneapolis: Fortress, 1999), 9–13.

[17] The notion of "speech actions" in which certain uses of words accomplish rather than merely describe things was introduced by philosopher J. L. Austin more than half a century ago. See J. L. Austin, How to Do Things with Words, 2nd ed. (Cambridge, Mass: Harvard University Press, 1979).

[18] Westermann, Genesis 1–11, 111. Cf. Walter Brueggemann, Theology of the Old Testament: Testimony, Dispute, Advocacy (Minneapolis: Fortress, 1997), 146.

[19] See further Eichrodt, Theology of the Old Testament, 100; Wolfhart Pannenberg, Systematic Theology, vol. 2 (Edinburgh: T&T Clark, 1994), 13.

[20] William P. Brown, The Ethos of the Cosmos: The Genesis of Moral Imagination in the

it seems, only "remotely" by uttering his supreme authoritative word. In each case, though, Brown argues, the accompanying "and it was so" is envisaged as arising not *ex voce* alone, but *per collaborationi*,[21] from the responses of relevant creaturely elements and forces ("the waters," "the earth") addressed directly by the divine imperatives and therefore participant by their responsive obedience in the tasks and processes of world making itself.[22] Perhaps we should imagine ourselves here among the courtiers in the throne room, where an all-powerful sovereign issues irrevocable and irresistible commands and nervous minions scurry to see that they are put into effect quickly and with minimum fuss. But we might equally find ourselves transported once again to the divine workshop where a supremely authoritative and wise master craftsman oversees and instructs others who share in the realization of his personal artistic vision. Brown's account suggests that we need not choose between the two scenarios. As long as the distinctive contributions of each are kept securely in play, it seems, the images themselves need not be wholly disentangled but may be permitted to overlap and so modify one another all the more effectively. What we have to do with here, the text suggests, is precisely a king who is not merely a king but also an artist, one who treats his dominion as a thing of beauty and value, expending lavish care over it, while exercising an unmatched degree of skill and power in the processes of its making.

In fact, Brown's allusion to the "verbal stylus" wielded by God suggests the presence of a third image lurking largely unnoticed in the hinterland of this passage, one suggested to the biblical author naturally enough by the imaginative fusion of immediate artistic making and unimpeded authoritative utterance and, no doubt, by the fabled skill with verbal tools of Israel's own first and most auspicious human monarch, King David. Perhaps we are presented here, too, that is to say, with a fleeting glimpse of God as poet or wordsmith, one who "makes" with words rather than manually, whose acts of verbal utterance or inscription are themselves a form of rich *poesis* calling something into being and who exercises a certain unrivalled authority over it, determining what shall be the case in the "work" simply by speaking it "thus" rather than otherwise. This is a "speech-act" quite distinct in mode from the royal decree, and it compels us to hear the formulaic "Let there be . . ." that punctuates the text of Genesis 1 and rings the reader's mind's ear now in a rather different tone of voice—less

---

Bible (Grand Rapids: Eerdmans, 1999), 49. The same interplay is picked up helpfully by Irenaeus in his imaginative insistence that God's Word is nonetheless one of his "hands."

   [21] Brown, *Ethos of the Cosmos*, 41.

   [22] See Brown, *Ethos of the Cosmos*, 39–40. Cf. Welker, *Creation and Reality*, 9–13. *Pace* Westermann, *Genesis 1–11*, 111.

an injunction barked out than an excited ejaculation of imaginatively apprehended possibility, less authoritative utterance than the joyful play of artistic expression. For a poet is precisely an artist, one who fashions something in person and is involved at every stage of its production (rather than issuing injunctions and leaving others to figure out how they might realistically be implemented); but his work of fashioning—because it has words alone for its material—is by definition less "hands on," less immediately engaged with the world itself than that of the potter, the goldsmith, or the builder. For this very reason, it is often supposed, poets do indeed enjoy greater sovereignty over what they fashion than artists working with other more intractable materials. Again, creation by the word points us in the direction of a relative ease and freedom in the accomplishment of the creative will.

If, though, rather than moving swiftly on to the next available image, we linger over this one instead and explore its depths, the force of this initial suggestion fades, giving way to others. Quite apart from the vexed question of the relationship pertaining between a given "reality" or world external to language itself and to which even the most poetic of language users might be held in some sense to be accountable,[23] as a social and historical phenomenon characterized by shared and specifiable rules and conventions, the world of language as such has identifiable limits and potential as a medium of what may count as meaningful human discourse (or good poetry) in a given time and place and thus in its own way constitutes a definite "given" that the artist must work with and respect, rather than a material wholly pliable to the bidding of his or her artistic will. What makes a powerful metaphor powerful is certainly not the poet's decision that it shall be so but considerations largely outside his or her control. So, the freedom of the poet is far from "sovereign," if by that we intend the wholesale absence of external constraints and preconditions. What the poet utters into existence is only what the given potential of language will permit and nothing more. What such reflections draw rudely to our attention too, of course, is the fact that, despite surface appearances, in this respect not even the most powerful oriental potentate imaginable issuing uncontradictable edicts can be reckoned "wholly free" in the act of doing so but is compelled to express the royal will relying on linguistic "tools" the nature and availability of which lies beyond his own range of control. In this instance too, of course, the fulfillment of that will is hardly secured by the fact of its articulation alone but depends in turn upon the performance of those who hear, understand, and duly seek to obey it.

---

[23] See below, chap. 6.

If, therefore, as most commentators indicate, the image of God creating by word rather than by hand is indeed intended to suggest his incomparable unlimited sovereignty, it can nonetheless only suggest it, and in the moment that we trouble to pursue or extrapolate upon the logic of the image we find other things suggested instead or as well. From one perspective, this may appear simply as a natural and proper limitation of the poetic image as such which, we have already seen, always relies upon the play of comparability and incomparability between its two terms and urges us imaginatively to discern the difference. The genuinely incomparable element, of course, cannot be "imaged"; the image suggests it precisely by its own shortfall and brokenness, combining the vital apprehension that "it is" with the willing acknowledgment that "it is not." If we work any image too hard in this regard, trying to press it further than it should be pressed or make it bear more than it can reasonably bear, we threaten to kill it, robbing it of its illuminating force rather than benefiting from it.

David Brown has recently reminded us, though, that the semantic shortfall of the poetic image is not the only relevant manifestation of what we are calling its "brokenness." We must also reckon with the multivalence of many images, which grants our imagination the possibility of moving in more than one direction or operating on more than one level of meaning at once.[24] Far from commending the identification of a single imaginative "point" beyond the making of which no particular scriptural image ought to be troubled any further, Brown insists that images are mostly richer and more complex than this, that "part of the point may well be that there is no single point"[25] and that we ought therefore always to tarry with images, chewing on and digesting them to see what further epiphanic possibilities may yet be released.[26] This is a strategy more familiar in meditative and devotional uses of the biblical text, perhaps, than systematic ones; but theological bids to be faithful to Scripture must include faithfulness to the demands placed upon us as readers by the logic of its given literary forms, and Brown's claim is that, in the interests of systematic clarity, theologians too often rein the imagination in too soon, before the biblical author's chosen medium has done its full complement of work. Of course, we must still seek to discern the point at which the imaginative suggestion that "it is" should yield properly to the recognition that "it is not"; but the multivalence of images means we must always reckon seriously with the prospect of there being more than one such point

---

[24] David Brown, *God and Mystery in Words: Experience through Metaphor and Drama* (Oxford: Oxford University Press, 2008), 68.

[25] Brown, *God and Mystery*, 50.

[26] Brown, *God and Mystery*, 71–72.

available to us for consideration, as the image plays in more than one direction at once. Again, the relative instability of the image in these terms is a source of potential blessing rather than loss for theology: unburdened by expectations of the sorts of "truthfulness" attaching to more literal formulations, the image is liberated to suggest possibilities beyond and alongside those that, with our particular sets of theological prejudices, we might most naturally identify and proceed to isolate as its relevant "point."[27] It can suggest more than one thing at once and is naturally resistant to the sort of blinkered systematizing which, in a bid to tidy things up, too easily misses or dismisses whatever will not fit into its convenient schemas.

If we approach the image of divine creation *ex voce* in the light of this, it seems reasonable to insist at least that it affords more than one possible perspective on the sort of freedom possessed by one who "speaks" a world into existence. At first blush, the suggestion in the passage before us is certainly that of an incomparable sovereign authority which achieves precisely what it says more or less in the act of saying it. If we tarry with the image, though, the thought naturally arises that, in human terms, not even the most exalted use of words can disentangle itself entirely from some reliance on given conditions and constraints. What then are we to do? Must we choose between these two seemingly incommensurable suggestions where talk of God's creativity is concerned? Commentators have mostly supposed so, allowing the claims of the former suggestion wholly to displace the latter for theological purposes, guided a priori, no doubt, by wider systematic convictions about God's aseity and other allegedly incomparable attributes. But this would appear to be precisely the sort of imaginative "reining in" that Brown counsels us robustly against, robbing the image of some of its potential force, including, perhaps, its capacity as Scripture to urge reconsideration of some cherished theological assumptions. Is it possible, then, to keep both imaginative suggestions simultaneously in play, without fruitless contradiction arising? It seems to me that it is and that doing so may simply nudge us more clearly yet in the direction of a perception already latent in the wider imaginative texture of this passage, with its provocative juxtaposition of images of manufacture with those of oral accomplishment: namely, that God's "creative" role and action with respect to the cosmos should be understood to have more than one aspect or moment—one that, it seems, is wholly without creaturely analogy but another in which, far from being wholly unconstrained in what he does and how he does it, God himself is obliged (because he

---

[27] Brown, *God and Mystery*, 69; P. Agaësse and A. Solignac, eds., *La Genese au sens littéral en douze livres (VIII–XII)*, vol. 49 of *Oeuvres de Saint Augustin* (Paris: Desclée de Brouwer, 1972).

chooses and submits himself freely) to work with the given constraints and possibilities latent within the materials already to hand and at his disposal.[28] In the entailments of the image of God as poet, in other words, the tension between absolute sovereignty and kenotic accommodation which is shot through the whole imaginative logic of this passage is neatly encapsulated. Before exploring the implications of this suggestion further, though, we need to underwrite more securely the biblical perception that there is indeed something radically incomparable about God's status and activity as Creator, lest we seem simply to have called this into question.

Imaging the Unimaginable

The logic of images, I have argued, relies on a suggestive interplay between the comparable and the incomparable. When, therefore, the Old Testament wishes to point precisely and unequivocally to an aspect of God's creative activity which it holds to be wholly without comparison, it is compelled to leave images as such behind. Here, indeed, it finds itself up against the very limits of meaningful language use, obliged to forge a radically singular terminology to refer to the circumstance, setting it apart from any profane application. Thus, as commentators have long observed, the Hebrew verb *bārā'* is one that positively smoulders with holiness, used sparingly and (in the *qal* and the *niphal* forms) "only to describe divine activity and so dissociate it completely from any analogy with human doing or shaping."[29] Because it refers us to an action of which God alone is capable (one without appropriate analogy in the creaturely sphere), *bārā'* cannot function for us as an image. To ask (as we are naturally inclined to in our attempts to make sense of things) just what sort of action this is or is like is, of course, precisely to invite comparison and thus risk compromising the apophatic achievement of the deliberate neologism.[30] It is precisely to miss the point of

[28] Brown, *Tradition and Imagination*, 40–47.

[29] Wellhausen, cited in Westermann, *Genesis 1–11*, 99. Cf. Ludwig Koehler and Walter Baumgartner, eds., *The Hebrew and Aramaic Lexicon of the Old Testament*, trans. M. E. J. Richardson, rev. ed. (Leiden: Brill, 1994), 153–54; W. Bernhardt, "Bara," in *Theological Dictionary of the Old Testament*, vol. 2, ed. G. Johannes Botterweck and Helmer Ringgren (Grand Rapids: Eerdmans, 1990), 246.

[30] It is unlikely, of course, that the Hebrew term itself constitutes a linguistic *creatio ex nihilo,* fitting though that might be. Bernhardt notes that "[a]s yet, the root br' has not been found in the older Semitic languages outside the OT" but suggests possible links to an Old South Arabic root meaning "to build." Koehler and Baumgartner, meanwhile, indicate likely connections with terms for sculpting, or shaping by cutting. Whatever its prebiblical progenitors and extrabiblical relatives, though, the point that concerns us here is about its singular and distinctive use and meaning within the Old Testament canon itself, seemingly divorcing it from any earlier semantic entanglements.

its linguistic awkwardness. The word *bārā'* can be and often is used in close conjunction with other Hebrew verbs which can and do function for us as images (making, forming, building, and so on), and this helps to map out its proper domain of use; but, when it is used, the function of *bārā'* seems to be to provide a countermanding impulse, reminding us in no uncertain terms that, whatever legitimate comparisons may be permissible and needful, there is nonetheless an aspect to God's creative activity that sets it decisively apart, a distinctive semantic territory with respect to which all images necessarily fall woefully short and threaten to mislead rather than illuminate. Where LXX lost sight of this vital verbal discrimination (translating *bārā'* variously with *poiēn*, *ktizein*, and other terms with a widespread application),[31] English-language translations have generally preserved it by reserving the verb "create" to render occurrences of *bārā'* in the Hebrew text. This word, too, though, has both a prehistory and an afterlife beyond the biblical canon that entangle it in much more variegated associations,[32] dulling its impact on surface readers of the English text and raising questions, perhaps, about the usefulness of attempts to lop and chop its use to match the precise theological circumstance. To insist, within the wider context of a doctrine of "creation," that only God may be said to "create" (i.e., positing direct and unadulterated equivalence between the semantic ranges of "create" and *bārā'*) may, in other words, prove problematic, and for more than one reason alone.

As Westermann suggests, given the way in which *bārā'* is deliberately set apart from the profane lexicon by its use, in the case of this word in particular we can seek to grasp its range of connotations only by attending carefully to the precise contexts of that use.[33] When we do so, at least three things emerge. There is an association (sometimes explicit but otherwise tacit) with (1) the utter incomparability of Israel's God. So, for instance, Isaiah 40:18-31 contrasts the activity of God in fashioning and ordering a cosmos deliberately with anything that either human artists or human

---

[31] See Werner Foerster, "Ktizo, Ktisis, Ktisma, Ktistes," in *Theological Dictionary of the New Testament*, vol. 3, ed. Gerhard Kittel (Grand Rapids: Eerdmans, 1965), 1027. Significantly, though, in this particular connection LXX scrupulously avoids use of *dēmiourgein* with its explicit connotation of the craftsman's task of imposing form on given material. The NT, meanwhile, apparently reflects the Hebrew concern to identify linguistic holy ground, appropriating the verb *ktizō* and its derivatives to refer to something that God alone is understood to do (and by inference capable of doing). *Ktizō* may thus reasonably be taken as the NT equivalent of *bārā'*.

[32] The Lat. verb *crĕo* in classical and prebiblical/theological use could refer to a range of purely human actions including making, bringing forth, producing, and begetting. On its somewhat promiscuous afterlife, see below chap. 8.

[33] Westermann, *Genesis 1–11*, 98. For the wider point, cf. James Barr, *The Semantics of Biblical Language* (London: Oxford University Press, 1961).

rulers are capable of. "To whom then will you compare me, or who is my equal?" God inquires in verse 25. The answer—that there is none who could ever bear the comparison—is linked directly to the acknowledgment that the LORD alone is "the *Creator* of the ends of the earth" (v. 28).[34] So, too, in Psalm 89, it is because God alone created them that all those things catalogued in verses 5-12 (the heavens, the earth, and all that is in it) belong to him, owing him unrivalled fealty and praise; only this, the passage suggests, can account for his incomparable authority over them all (vv. 6, 8). "Who is like the LORD?" "Who is as mighty as you, O LORD?" In answering such inquiries unambiguously, appeal to what God does under the rubric of *bārā'* is, it seems, a rhetorical strategy second to none.

Part of what is incomparable about the divine action referred to by the verb *bārā'* is seemingly (2) the effortlessness with which it is effected.[35] The sort of sovereignty enjoyed by human agents is, no matter how exalted, always constrained to some extent by considerations of one sort or another. But, where God is concerned, the Old Testament invites us imaginatively to strip all constraints away, envisaging a global sovereign jurisdiction that nothing may resist unless God himself so chooses. This sovereign authority is understood to be both a consequence and a characteristic of God's trademark activity as the one who creates. Nothing in history can finally resist God's will (though for his own purposes he ordains or permits some things to do so for a while), because he has himself created all things (darkness as well as light, woe as well as weal) and is Lord of them all.[36] And while the Old Testament borrows materials from the dualistic cosmogonies of its neighbors, its use of these generally resists any suggestion that Israel's God was compelled to struggle with forces lying outside his own jurisdiction in the original creative act itself. So, for instance, the psalmist (89:9) imagines the "raging waters" of the primeval sea being stilled with a divine command, and "Rahab" (a symbolic personification of the forces of chaos)[37] swept aside contemptuously and left for dead. Having been created by the LORD himself in the first place (v. 12b), such purported challengers are, in Israel's version of the myth, incapable of genuine opposition. Instead, having been set firmly in their place by divine directive, the waters above the heavens and the sea monsters of the deeps are duly invited, together with the rest of God's creation, to praise their

[34] Cf. v. 26: "Who *created* these?"

[35] See Shalom M. Paul, "Creation and Cosmogony -in the Bible," in *Encyclopedia Judaica*, ed. Cecil Roth (Jerusalem: Keters, 1971), 1059; von Rad, *Genesis: A Commentary*, 47.

[36] Cf. Isa 45:7; 54:16.

[37] See Arthur Weiser, *The Psalms: A Commentary* (London: SCM Press, 1962), 592.

Maker.[38] In each case, use of the verb *bārā'* suggests a sovereign authority universal in scope and effortless in execution.[39]

At first blush the biblical account of creation opens with a fairly unequivocal statement of this sort. According to Genesis 1:1, God's creative action (the relevant verb is again *bārā'*) has "the heavens and the earth" for its object (ostensibly an all-inclusive phrase comparable in intent with the Nicene Creed's "all things, visible and invisible")[40] and constitutes "the beginning." Traditional exegesis tended to treat this verse as a free-standing caption, and much modern scholarship continues in this vein;[41] but a dominant strand of exegesis (followed by the translators of NRSV) understands this verse as a dependent clause, a move that places the "formless void" of verse 2 logically and chronologically, if not syntactically, before the act of creation itself.[42] It is increasingly common, therefore, for commentators on the passage to suggest that the biblical author imagined, and was untroubled by, the presence to hand of some already existing "chaotic" material alongside God that he then laid hold of and, in an act of "creation," shaped into an orderly cosmos.[43] This, it is mostly conceded, need entail no scriptural contradiction of the later idea of a *creatio ex nihilo*, because the questions and concerns informing that particular doctrinal development belonged to a different intellectual context and were not ones that the biblical mind was aware of;[44] by the same

[38] Ps 148:3-13, esp. vv. 4-7. Weiser, *Psalms*, 837–38; Eichrodt, *Theology of the Old Testament*, 103.

[39] That there is "an enduring force of chaos" at work in the world is of course something that the Old Testament also readily acknowledges, but that this is something "that has still not been brought under the rule of Yahweh" rather than a matter of divine sovereign permission seems to me not to be. For the contrary view, see Brueggemann, *Theology of the Old Testament*, 159, 534–43. Jon D. Levenson, *Creation and the Persistence of Evil: The Jewish Drama of Divine Omnipotence*, 2nd ed. (Princeton, N.J.: Princeton University Press, 1994).

[40] Cf. Karl Barth, *Church Dogmatics III/1* (Edinburgh: T&T Clark, 1958), 101.

[41] See, e.g., von Rad, *Genesis: A Commentary*, 46; Robert W. Jenson, "Aspects of a Doctrine of Creation," in *The Doctrine of Creation: Essays in Dogmatics, History and Philosophy*, ed. Colin E. Gunton (London: T&T Clark, 1997), 17.

[42] On the disputed interpretation of these verses, see, helpfully, Nic. H. Ridderbos, "Genesis i 1 und 2," *Oudtestamentische Studien* 12 (1958): 214–60.

[43] Brown, *Ethos of the Cosmos*, 40; Brueggemann, *Theology of the Old Testament*, 158, 529.

[44] See Westermann, *Genesis 1–11*, 108–9; Gerhard May, *Creatio ex nihilo: The Doctrine of "Creation Out of Nothing" in Early Christian Thought* (Edinburgh: T&T Clark, 1994); Frances Young, "'Creatio ex Nihilo': A Context for the Emergence of the Christian Doctrine of Creation," *Scottish Journal of Theology* 44 (1991): 139–51. May and Young both suggest that the questions that threw up the radical idea of a *creatio ex nihilo*

token, though, this interpretation insists, we certainly should not read the gist of that doctrine back into the passage, as though it were lurking there in another guise. Those minded to insist otherwise (i.e., that the intellectual root of the doctrine at least is properly identified here) are compelled to wrestle with the claim that God himself created something chaotic, at least in the first instance, a claim that some have found theologically problematic in its own right. Calvin was apparently quite untroubled by it, admitting frankly that "the world was not perfected at its very commencement, in the manner in which it is now seen, but . . . was created an empty chaos,"[45] while noting that God "did not create Adam until he had lavished upon the universe all manner of good things."[46] Irenaeus, though, could not tolerate any such two-stage process, deeming the prior production of an unformed chaos as such quite unworthy of God's artistic wisdom and insisting instead, therefore, upon the simultaneity of the origination of matter and its primal formation as a cosmos.[47] Barth, meanwhile, interprets the *tohu wabohu* of Genesis 1:2 to signify imaginatively a possible state of affairs that God deliberately excludes from the cosmos, a creative option that, because it is hostile to his sovereign purpose, he does not choose and thus does not permit to exist.[48] Barth takes his exegetical cue here from Isaiah 45:18. Again, in this passage the incomparability of the LORD is clearly in view (vv. 18d, 21-22), and again, therefore, we are in the natural domain of use of *bārā'* (vv. 18a, 18c). Strictly speaking, the verse itself need not conflict with Calvin's two-stage exegesis of Genesis 1:1ff., insisting merely that God's creative intent was not the origination of a mere *tohu* ("empty void") but the formation of an orderly cosmos fit for human habitation.[49] What Barth rightly discerns in it, though, is the suggestion that "creating" a "chaos" was something God might theoretically have chosen to do in the beginning (but graciously elected not to), and the existence or nonexistence of chaos itself is thus precisely a question

---

as a response were ones posed by the exposure of biblical thought to Greek categories only in the second century A.D. In defense of a much earlier Jewish origin for the idea, see Thomas F. Torrance, *The Trinitarian Faith: An Evangelical Theology of the Ancient Catholic Church* (Edinburgh: T&T Clark, 1988), 95–98.

[45] John Calvin, *Commentaries on the First Book of Moses Called Genesis*, vol. 1, trans. Rev. John King (Edinburgh: Calvin Translation Society, 1848), 70.

[46] John Calvin, *Institutes of the Christian Religion*, ed. John Baillie, John T. McNeill, and Henry P. van Dusen, The Library of Christian Classics 21 (Philadelphia: Westminster, 1960), 1.14.2 (p. 162).

[47] See Osborn, *Irenaeus of Lyons*, 52, 69.

[48] Barth, *Church Dogmatics III/1*, 102–10.

[49] See Joseph Blenkinsopp, *Isaiah 40–55*, ed. William Foxwell Albright and David Noel Freedman, The Anchor Bible (New York: Doubleday, 2002), 259.

for God's incomparable sovereign jurisdiction rather than falling within it. While falling short of the intentionality of *creatio ex nihilo*, this nonetheless indicates that questions about the provenance of the *tohu wabohu* vis-à-vis Israel's God were ones the biblical imagination might well ruminate on and suggests the sort of answer that came most naturally to it when it did.

We should not lose sight amidst all this of Westermann's reminder that we are not dealing here with an attempt to picture or describe the process of divine creation in any precise way but with the logic of imaginative formulations, albeit ones intended, we may suppose, to bear an appropriate theological charge. Perhaps, therefore, we should understand the "formless void" of Genesis 1:2 not as an allusion to any physical state of affairs at all (divinely created or otherwise) but simply, as Eichrodt suggests, as the poetic evocation of "a situation devoid of all creative potential" apart from the decision and act of God himself, precisely a way, in other words, of imagining absence rather than presence.[50] This, of course, brings the sentiment of Genesis 1:1-2 much closer to the root notion which, in a different theological and philosophical context, grew into the doctrine of *creatio ex nihilo*. It also resonates with a further peculiarity of the use of the Hebrew verb *bārā'* that has often been noted—namely, the fact that as well as being used exclusively of God, in the Hebrew Bible this word never takes a preposition or an accusative to indicate the presence of any indirect object.[51] Syntactically, at least, that is to say, God simply "creates"; he does not "create" with or from anything. To this, we may now add the testimony of a final association emerging from consideration of the contexts of use of this verb—namely, its connotation of (3) unprecedented and radical newness.

Creating the Otherwise Impossible

As Pannenberg observes, God's action concluded under the rubric of *bārā'* is not limited by biblical writers to what occurs in and as the world's "beginning" but crops up in history's midst too.[52] Where it does so, it generally occasions the occurrence of things radically new and utterly remarkable,

---

[50] Eichrodt, *Theology of the Old Testament*, 105.

[51] Eichrodt, *Theology of the Old Testament*, 103. Curiously, Westermann appeals to this fact to insist that for the biblical writers the question what God "created" the heavens and the earth "out of" was a wholly irrelevant one that could not arise, thus eschewing any link with the logic of *creatio ex nihilo*. Others have argued the opposite: the irrelevance of the question in this sense (testified to by the peculiarity of the verb use) *is* the root of the idea of *creatio ex nihilo*. See Westermann, *Genesis 1–11*, 98. Cf., e.g., von Rad, *Genesis: A Commentary*, 47.

[52] Pannenberg, *Systematic Theology*, 12.

unprecedented within the scheme of nature and history as common experience testifies to these, precisely because, it seems, they arise from the introduction into that scheme of conditions and possibilities hitherto unknown to it. Thus, the word *bārā'* is used in connection with the performance of certain miracles and wonders. In Numbers 16:30-31, for instance, it is because the LORD "creates something new" that the ground opens up precisely where and when Moses says it will, swallowing the unfortunate Korah and his associates directly down to Sheol, while in Exodus 34:10, at the renewal of the Sinai covenant, God promises to perform before Israel "marvels, such as have not been performed [*bārā'*] in all the earth or in any nation."[53] Echoing this,[54] Isaiah 48:6-7 contrasts the "former things" declared and done by God "long ago" with the imminent appearance of some remarkable "new things," things never seen or heard of before even by Israel, because they are only now to be created (v. 7). The same thought, that God has "created a new thing on the earth," arises in the preamble to Jeremiah's vision of God establishing a radically new sort of covenant with Israel, one wholly unconstrained by the conditions and possibilities evinced by Israel's checkered history of covenant keeping and covenant breaking to date (Jer 31:22, 31-34).[55] And unprecedented wonders of a spiritual and moral rather than a physical sort are apparently what the psalmist has in mind too when he urges God to "create in me clean heart . . . and put a new and right spirit within me" (Ps 51:10), capacities untrammeled by the dispositions of historical, fallen existence and equally unlikely ever to evolve out of them; if they are ever going to be had, the prayer suggests, God must simply put them there, overriding the generative incapacities of nature and history. The verse in which all this effectively culminates, though, is one which refers us not to a divine action within history but to one imagined as constituting its proper end: "I am about to create new heavens and a new earth" (Isa 65:17). This too, of course, bespeaks a radical new beginning for the world, one envisaged as an interruption and transfiguration of nature and history rather than constrained by or extending their given range of possibilities.

---

[53] "This act is of such an unprecedented nature that only creation language, combined with language of marvel and awe, can adequately describe it." Terence Fretheim, *Exodus*, Interpretation (Louisville: John Knox, 1991), 308.

[54] Brevard Childs, *Exodus: A Commentary*, Old Testament Library (London: SCM Press, 1974), 613.

[55] Isa 43:1-7 and 43:15-19 link *bārā'* to the miracle of Israel's own existence as a people, suggesting that her understanding of God's *creative* acts more widely might be patterned after the narrative of election, a people constituted only by the potentialities of divine promising. See Jenson, "Aspects of a Doctrine," in Gunton, *Doctrine of Creation*, 23; Pannenberg, *Systematic Theology*, 9.

In each of these circumstances, the newness of what God does and produces is radical and unprecedented precisely in the sense that it appears unconstrained by qualities and potentialities latent within the given context for action.[56] There are no limits placed on what is possible under the rubric of *bārā'*, because the relevant conditions of possibility are themselves, it seems, ones generated only in and with the creative act itself, transcendent to, rather than immanent within, history as such. This capacity to inaugurate wholly unprecedented and unconditioned new beginnings is, it might be argued, the most radical and unique aspect of the verb's pattern of use within the Old Testament. Given this wider understanding, if we revisit the opening declaration of the creation narrative itself, it seems reasonable to presuppose it there too and to interpret the poet's emphatic *bᵉrē'šīt* as envisaging an act of absolute origination, not just the beginning of a cosmos (i.e., as an ordered *habitus*) but equally of whatever conditions must be considered needful for a cosmos to exist at all. As Robert W. Jenson puts it, while the text is not concerned with arguing the point, the presumption tacit within its poetic vision is that "God and only God is the creature's antecedent."[57]

In due course, as Jenson notes, this is certainly how Jewish and Christian readers alike came to interpret the text, and when in the second and third centuries A.D. the doctrine of *creatio ex nihilo* was formulated in an unambiguous version, it was on the basis of such readings and, we should note, precisely as a careful way of qualifying the biblical image of God as craftsman/artist. One clear advantage of that image is its natural resistance to any suggestion that the world is itself divine, issuing from God's own being through a process of emanation or natural generation. Whatever we may wish to say about the sense in which an artist "puts something of himself" into whatever he makes, his relationship to the work is nonetheless to something identifiably external to himself, a product of his will and action, and not a natural extension or overspill of his "being." But picturing God as an artist throws up its own question naturally enough: If human artists fashion their works out of clay or words, what does the divine artist use, and where does he get it from? In his treatise *To Autolycus*,[58] Theophilus of Antioch (fl. c. 169–183) insisted that the answer to this question suggested in Plato's rather different use of the same image—that the "stuff" out of which the universe is fashioned existed

---

[56] Thus "Israel's testimony to Yahweh as creator concerns Yahweh's ultimate power to work an utter novum, one that on any other terms is impossible." Brueggemann, *Theology of the Old Testament*, 146.

[57] Jenson, "Aspects of a Doctrine," in Gunton, *Doctrine of Creation*, 22.

[58] Theophilus, *Ad Autolycum* 2.4. See Young, "Creatio ex Nihilo," 142.

eternally alongside God himself[59]—could never be accommodated within a Christian account, precisely because it compromised the incomparable sovereignty of God borne witness to in Scripture and tied decisively to his unique status as the only "uncreated" one (i.e., the one who himself created "all things"). Thus, Theophilus concludes, Christians must insist that God's artistry, whatever else we may wish to say about it, exceeds human artistry in this fundamental regard: that when God creates he is able to do so "out of things that are not" (*ex ouk ontōn*), since in his case (and his case alone) there is not and cannot be anything already lying conveniently to hand. We have already seen that Irenaeus of Lyons, for all his enthusiastic appeal to the image of God as artist, argues precisely the same sort of case in his response to the gnostics: unlike any human artist, the God of the Bible is wholly self-sufficient and provides himself with whatever materials he needs out of his own creative act alone, and in this sense "*ex eo quod non erat.*"[60] A thousand years later, Aquinas reiterates the argument in the *Summa Theologiae*: God is indeed properly pictured as an artist who lays hold of material and fashions it lovingly into a good work, thereby bringing something new and valuable into existence (1a.45.6);[61] but the sort of newness generated by the work of the human *artifex* is strictly limited, since it must presuppose the prior existence of the relevant material with its given potentialities (1a.45.2).[62] God's artistry, though, is set radically apart from any other in this very regard; God not only forms and orders the cosmos but simultaneously "causes" precisely that which all other artistry presupposes—that is, "existence tout court" (1a.45.4). It is to this uniquely divine artistic prerogative of absolute origination, Aquinas suggests, that the verb "create" in its fullest sense refers us. This, I have argued, is consonant in its outlook (if not the philosophical framework in terms of which it is articulated and developed) with the biblical use of the verb *bārā'*. "The God of the Old Testament is the Creator in this sense, and everything that is not God is opposed to him in this sense as creature."[63] Thus the distinction between the uncreated and created duly becomes another way for Christian theology to identify in the most precise manner God's own radical uniqueness, setting him apart from all else that exists.

---

[59] In the *Timaeus*, esp. §15–21. See Plato, *Timaeus and Critias*, trans. Desmond Lee (London: Penguin, 1971), 66–73.

[60] "Out of that which had no existence." See above p. 67.

[61] For the relevant portions of text, see St. Thomas Aquinas, *Summa Theologiae*, vol. 8, *Creation, Variety, and Evil (1a. 44–49)*, ed. Thomas Gilby, O.P. (London: Blackfriars in conjunction with Eyre and Spottiswoode, 1967).

[62] Aquinas observes that the "newness" of the radically particular events and objects produced by natural processes rather than works of human *ars* is similarly constrained.

[63] Barth, *Church Dogmatics III/1*, 17.

Recapitulation

We might sum up what we have seen in our first four chapters by saying that the imaginative field of God's role as Creator of all things visible and invisible suggests two discrete but related modes of divine activity with respect to the creation.[64] First, there is God's unique activity of bestowing existence and potential upon the creaturely and holding it in existence alongside himself as such, as something possessed of its own distinct integrity and proper ways of being. This mode of action, entirely lacking in antecedent condition or external constraint beyond God's own character as the one who wills it (and who in his sovereignty is free to realize that which he wills), is unique in kind, rather than merely in degree, and lacks any useful human analogy, being referred to typically by resort to neologism (*bārā'*) or negation (ex nihilo). This unique generative mode sets God apart decisively from all that is not God (the creaturely as distinct from the Uncreated One), and it must be allowed to inform and color the whole of our understanding of what it means for God to create. Nonetheless, it does not exhaust the range of activities or modes of action naturally and properly concluded under the rubric of divine "creating."

Second, therefore, other sorts of activity too are included within the orb of the biblical imagining of creation (planning, making, shaping, forming, developing, and so on), activities which not only bear fruitful creaturely analogy but, if we follow the suggestion of the biblical texts themselves, actually require, solicit, and conscript creaturely participation and initiatives in the course of their movement toward completion. There is, we might say, a distinct movement "from below" (from the side of the creature) as well as a logically prior movement "from above" within the dynamics of God's creative project to fashion a world in which he might dwell together with the creature and enjoy fellowship with it. Thus, the motif of divine sovereignty is set in apposition to a constantly renewed insistence upon divine accommodation, as God works (and thus we must suppose chooses to work) in and through the limitations, opportunities, and possibilities proper to the world that he has made, as well as transcending those same limitations and possibilities (which are, of course, ones that he himself has established in the first place). Put slightly differently, we could say that God puts himself willingly in a place where he needs the "creative" work of human hands to complement that of his own if the unfinished project of creation is finally to come to fruition.

---

[64] Fretheim helpfully identifies as many as twelve discrete "modes" of divine creation in the biblical text, but my point here is to distinguish between those bearing legitimate human analogy and those resisting it. See Terence Fretheim, *God and World in the Old Testament: A Relational Theology of Creation* (Nashville: Abingdon, 2005).

Such talk is likely to raise theological hackles quite quickly and in due course will need to be carefully qualified by being set within an adequate Trinitarian frame of reference; but for now it serves conveniently to make the point I wish to make indubitably clear before moving on: God's way of modeling what it means to be a "creator" is not one that jealously excludes or crushes the initiatives or contributions of others but instead inspires, solicits, and embraces them, drawing others actively into a wider dynamic in which the creative vision is enriched and effoliated beyond the scope of its initial venturing. Furthermore, since this same kenotic inclusion of the creature's free contribution brings with it the inevitable consequence of sin and idolatry, and the terrible costs borne by God in recapitulating the history of these and so bringing eventual good out of the chaotic interruptions of evil, we must also conclude that the most fundamental disposition of the sort of creator God is, is that of love— love that is willing to give its all to see its creative vision finally realized. According to Christians, it is precisely out of an overflow of love that God creates; it is a disposition of joy and love that characterizes God's creative action in calling a world into existence alongside himself; it is love for the creature that provides the subtext to the entire history of the world that God calls into being and continuously shapes through costly interaction, working always in accordance with the substance of his creative vision; and it is love that is the telos or goal of creation—as the site of God's promised cohabitation together with the creature, a love enjoyed eternally and without interruption. Again, all this demands fleshing out in terms of the particular shape taken by the interpenetrating economies of the incarnate Logos and the Spirit of holiness, returning us to where this chapter began, with reference to the two "hands" of God's creative engagement with the world; but such vital elaboration will have to await a later stage in our argument.

5

Cosmos
A World (Not) of Our Own Making

In the previous chapters, our primary concern was to reckon with the nature of God's creative action vis-à-vis the world as depicted in strands of Scripture and ecclesial tradition. What we saw was that while some of these depictions set God radically apart, emphasizing in no uncertain terms God's otherness from all that he has made and the incomparability of his actions in making it, others tend in a rather different direction, tracing analogies between aspects of what God does in his capacity as "Maker of the heavens and the earth" and certain familiar creaturely modes of making. Moreover, the image of God as an artist, central to the biblical portrayal of creation as such but extending too into Scripture's account of God's continuing "hands-on" shaping engagement with what he has made, unfolds to embrace within its poetic logic a demand for correlative creaturely acts of responsible "making." God's artistic project in creation, in other words, does not exclude or displace but actively calls forth and enlists appropriate acts of human *poesis*, mere analogy giving way now to creaturely *participation* in the pattern and the dynamics of God's own uncreated "creative" action. This is necessarily so, since the telos of that action (the "vision" or idea toward which this making is finally directed) is the establishment of a world in which God and the creature dwell together "at one" in peace and mutual enjoyment. Such a "world," by nature of the case, cannot be established "from above" by sheer primal fiat alone; it will entail a fitting "ethos" as well as an ordered physical "cosmos," manifestations of culture as well as nature, and thus its establishment is bound in the end to involve a corresponding movement from the side of the creature, a fully human component and contribution constructed in response to what is first received and acknowledged as something given.

Hints of this bilateral pattern in which uncreated and creaturely acts of *poesis* are clearly differentiated yet closely interwoven, God and God's creature making something of the world together, are, we saw, already identifiable in the saga of creation itself. They are to be found in the Priestly writer's accounts of primal processes in which "God's commanding performance . . . prompts also the positive performance of the elements" in a "friendly convergence of divine and earthly powers."[1] And they arise, too, in a different way in the Yahwist's story of Adam's creation with a view to the needful tilling of the earth (Gen 2:5, 2:15) and his subsequent appointment as creation's own poet laureate, called upon to name his fellow creatures in a primeval act of "symbolific"[2] response (2:19-23). These original human actions (as yet uncomplicated by the compromising presence of sin and evil) supplement "nature" with "culture," granting the newly born cosmos a distinctly human dimension and gesturing already toward the inseparability and interpenetration of the two spheres (Adam "cultivates" in both) in any world fit for human habitation and flourishing. There is, as it were, a symbolic counterpart to that set of finely tuned material conditions for sentient life referred to by advocates of the so-called anthropic principle, a basic level of accompanying ethos apart from which truly human existence cannot even be imagined, let alone supposed possible.

Scripture in general, we noted, has relatively little to say in explicit terms about human capacities for acts of artistic *poesis*. It is all the more telling, therefore, that its most concrete mention and endorsement of such capacities and practices is to be found not incidentally or in connection with matters peripheral to the writers' focal concern but rather at its very core, in connection with what must occur humanly to fashion and set apart a literal "place" where God himself will dwell identifiably in the midst of the world and its history. In this respect, we saw, the tabernacle traditions resonate with the patterns of action and reaction in the creation narratives, upon which they are in part modeled. In their turn, though, for Christian readers these same traditions look forward and find their eventual fulfillment in God's tabernacling in the "flesh" of Jesus, the unique "place" where the ancient creative Word finally abjures strategies of enlistment

[1] William P. Brown, *The Ethos of the Cosmos: The Genesis of Moral Imagination in the Bible* (Grand Rapids: Eerdmans, 1999), 41–42.

[2] See Susanne K. Langer, *Philosophy in a New Key: A Study in the Symbolism of Reason, Rite, and Art*, 3rd ed. (Cambridge, Mass.: Harvard University Press, 1956), 26–52, et passim.

and enabling in favor of one of hypostatic assuming and becoming.[3] By "taking flesh" (an action quite distinct in its mode from that ancient "taking clay" that it nonetheless echoes and evokes) and thus now *as a creature*, God himself supplies the requisite conditions for his own radical dwelling in our midst as one of us (there is, it seems, not merely an "anthropic" but a *theanthropic* principle to be reckoned with here), that very creaturely response that his own creative vision and purpose has cried out for from the beginning but has as yet always found wanting. Finding his chosen materials unremittingly intractable and resistant to his bidding, in other words, the divine artist at this point does what no human artist could ever do: in effect he himself "becomes" his materials and thereby renders them more fit for his purpose. Laying hold of our creaturely being with both hands, he fulfills here at last his own creative project, not "from above" alone but from both sides at once.

Thus, I shall argue duly, the most natural and adequate theological "home" for an account of human creativity is precisely the overlap between the doctrines of Trinity and incarnation, rather than any free-floating account of our creation in the image and likeness of God (the doctrinal locus where it has more typically been addressed). In Christ, God's primal creative vision finds its first and most decisive bodying forth in the world, as God takes up residence not just "in" but *as* part of his own creation, at last dwelling "at-one" with it. And, inasmuch as human actions of a constructive sort (of *ars* or *poesis* in a broader as well as the more precise sense) may properly be situated here, made sense of as a concrete participation in what God now continues to do through his Spirit to expand the scope of this ecology of divine-human at-one-ment in history's midst, they not only may but, I shall argue, *should* be identified with the lexical markers of "creation" and "creativity." To do so, far from either diluting or displacing the proper theological provenance and applicability of such terms (i.e., their original and originating reference to God's own unique actions and prerogatives), keeps securely in view the Trinitarian-incarnational context within which all human action actually occurs and apart from which it cannot properly be judged. Here, in other words, the interference set up between various fields of the words' actual use, far from presenting a scrambled message, may be made to serve a precise and positive theological purpose.

---

[3] The use of *skēnoō* in John 1:14 is widely acknowledged as an allusion to the tabernacle (LXX *skēnē*) in which God "dwelt among" his people. See, e.g., C. K. Barrett, *The Gospel according to St John: An Introduction with Commentary and Notes on the Greek Text* (Philadelphia: Westminster, 1978), 165–66.

But this is to rush too far ahead far too quickly. In the next several chapters, our focus will for the most part be concentrated quite deliberately on human actions as such, and on these as they are studied and accounted for by an assortment of "secular" intellectual disciplines. In particular, we shall attend carefully to what historians, philosophers, anthropologists, psychologists, and others have to tell us about what they variously identify as activities and practices of a "creative" sort, contributing in one way or another to the shape and the substance of what, following philosopher Anthony O'Hear, we shall refer to for convenience as "the human world"—that is, the world as experienced by human beings rather than as posited from some putative nonhuman perspective.[4] By comparison with earlier chapters, therefore, our strategy in what follows will be to draw self-consciously and repeatedly on perspectives "from below," keeping specifically theological perspectives, questions, and judgments deliberately in the wings, at least until we have heard what other voices are saying on their own terms and with their own distinct integrity. Of course, the question of how all this may finally be squared with a theological account of the world and our place as human in it will be ever in the wings and may, as occasion demands, trespass visibly onto the stage. Indeed, the classification "from below" itself is potentially misleading, since in practice few treatments of our theme can progress very far without necessarily venturing (deliberately or otherwise) into territory that theology rightly considers its own proper domain. Nonetheless, we shall seek to adopt a "conversational" model for the most part, permitting other voices to speak without constant interruption by specifically theological interlocutors.

The central organizing theme of this chapter is one that, like talk of "creation" itself, conveniently straddles theological and nontheological discourses—namely, the notion of the world's "givenness" as a premise and a context for human action and response. How much, and what different sorts of things, do we find to be a "given" starting point in our dealings with the world? What are the implications of such givenness for the shape, substance, and direction of our lives together as cohabitants of this same world? And what, if anything, are we called upon or compelled in our turn to give constructively to it?

Theologically, to speak of the world as something "given" entails reckoning with it at least as something that (1) comes to us from God's hand with its own proper "being" (it does not depend finally on us or our actions for its existence or to be what it is); (2) is already possessed of a given meaningfulness or order, both extant and in the form of myriad potentialities

---

[4] Anthony O'Hear, *The Element of Fire: Science, Art and the Human World* (London: Routledge, 1988), 23.

lying as yet far beyond realization (the majority of which, indeed, by nature of the prodigality of the case will never *be* realized), these having been both established and circumscribed (though they may be far reaching and infinitely rich and complex rather than easily traced by our attempts to encompass them) by its divine authorship; (3) is given to us precisely as a "gift," a blessing, or, in Barth's preferred phrase, a "benefit" (*Wohltat*)—something to be received, enjoyed, and celebrated, because "what takes shape in it is the goodness of God."[5] It is not, to be sure, the sort of gift that we may return or exchange upon production of the till receipt within fourteen days, and some, we shall see, have balked at this fact and the de facto constriction placed upon creaturely freedom which it undeniably entails. In many ways, it is a costly gift to receive, and its "goodness" will not be discerned as such if we expect it to be anything other than this. Yet this, I suggest, is precisely because the world's "givenness" is not of the absolute and fixed sort craved by positivists but a much more open-ended sort rooted in God's promise as surely as his love. The benefit or blessing of creation, it might be insisted, lies precisely here, in its being good "for" something and its being given to us not, in Iris Murdoch's phrase, "on a plate" for our easy consumption and immediate gratification but "as a creative task,"[6] something to "make something of," to work with (perhaps even to "play" with?) and explore and respond to, in each engagement "making the most of" it that we can and thereby allowing it to be what, in God's own creative design and desire, it is capable of being and becoming. Significantly, we shall see, this suggestion resonates audibly with the testimony of a host of nontheological versions of events. It is not only the more radical deconstructionists and nihilists who would have us take stock of the extent to which, in various ways at various levels and in quite different departments of the world as we encounter and are encountered by it (the "human world"), investigation quickly discovers us to be makers of and givers to that world just as surely as we are (grateful or ungrateful) recipients of it. However much and whatever we take to be given *to* us, it would seem, in its turn calls forth reciprocal and responsible acts of giving *from* us, some of which we are necessarily conscious of performing and others of which we perform so often and so naturally as to be unaware of doing so. Consideration of this claim as it arises authoritatively within various fields of intellectual concern will be our first port of call. Some readers, I recognize, may already be feeling uncomfortable by now, supposing that they discern nascent theological problems attaching necessarily to any qualified account of the world's "givenness," let alone the provocative suggestion that as human dwellers in God's world we are also in

[5] Karl Barth, *Church Dogmatics III/1* (Edinburgh: T&T Clark, 1958), 330.
[6] Iris Murdoch, *Metaphysics as a Guide to Morals* (London: Vintage, 2003), 215.

any meaningful sense involved in "constructing" it, making more of it than is in the first instance given, and thereby "helping it to be."[7] For the time being, I can only crave such readers' patience, inviting them to remain with the course I have elected to take and promising to address (and hopefully allay) such concerns in the light of what emerges along the way.

In those practices, institutions, and outputs which we habitually conclude under the rubric of "the arts," of course, we have to do precisely with a context characterized by acts of deliberate and self-conscious "making" of one sort or another. Generalizations about art (what art "does," what it is "for," etc.) are for the most part best avoided and should always come with a health warning marked clearly on the packaging,[8] but it seems safe nonetheless to suggest that artistry always involves somebody in some intentional acts of making and forming, whatever materials are used, however they are handled or deployed, whatever form the outputs may take, and whatever the purposes of such actions and outputs may be understood to be. The arts, we might say, are prominent among human ways of acting upon and engaging materially and symbolically with the given world, and—without wishing to get embroiled unhelpfully at this point in "the interminable and excruciatingly unedifying task of separating art from nonart"[9]—it therefore seems reasonable to suggest that, mutatis mutandis, artistry may usefully serve as a paradigm case for reckoning with that wider set of "poetic" actions and outputs in which, I shall argue, *Homo faber* is always and everywhere implicated and complicit.

It comes as no surprise to discover that one of the most fundamental issues underlying both theory and practice in the arts since ancient times (so fundamental, in fact, that it has dictated the way in which the history of the visual and plastic arts in particular has typically been narrated) has been precisely the question of art's own status vis-à-vis putative primordial acts and outputs of divine making. Finding herself situated in the midst of a world identifiably not of her own choosing or making but possessed of a given shape and structure and set of possibilities, that

---

[7] Cf. Murdoch, *Metaphysics*.

[8] Nicholas Wolterstorff insists that—while we may identify the arts as a human universal ("We know of no people which has done without music and fiction and poetry and role-playing and sculpture and visual depiction. Possibly some have done without one or the other of these; none to our knowledge has done without all.")—there is no single purpose underlying this universality. The question "what is art for?" is therefore misguided, resting on a flawed premise. In reality, "[a]rt plays and is meant to play an enormous diversity of roles in human life." Nicholas Wolterstorff, *Art in Action: Toward a Christian Aesthetic* (Carlisle, U.K.: Solway, 1997), 4.

[9] Kendall Walton, *Mimesis as Make-Believe: On the Foundations of the Representational Arts* (Cambridge, Mass.: Harvard University Press, 1990), 2.

is to say, the artist (painter, poet, playwright, sculptor, architect, composer, performer, or whoever) is bound at some point to ask just how what she does and what she makes in its midst is and ought to be related to the shape and substance of this same larger "given" reality. Artistry has been understood (by its practitioners, patrons, theorists, purveyors, and appreciators) to be and to do many different things, but all of them entail situating it in some relation to that given world of which it both is and yet, precisely as a work of *ars*, in some sense self-consciously is not (not yet, not necessarily, not merely) a part.

So, for instance, artistry has frequently been understood as an empirical and mimetic activity, concerned above all faithfully to capture and reproduce likenesses to elements in our experience of the given world (objects, people, events), sometimes aspiring to a degree and a sort of likeness that presses beyond the mere evocation of recognition to the generation of illusion, so that in our encounter with the work, the line between art and "reality" is momentarily a difficult one to draw. Others have understood the arts to be concerned primarily not with the external world of objects and events at all but with another world attendant upon it, a world of deeper—objective but nonmaterial—realities lurking present beneath or behind the empirical and mediated to us symbolically by the artist's careful handling of the "language" (whether natural or conventional) of some set of material forms. Closely related to this, though logically distinct from it, is the familiar suggestion that what art is really all about is the artist's expression of the rich inner world of his or her own "feeling," rendering the realities of the individual soul available in visual, verbal, tactile, or sonic media so as to enable us in our turn to "feel" the same way. For others still, art's chief task and achievement is precisely to modify or transform the given world, adding something new and unprecedented to the sum of things that there are in it, perhaps even deliberately breaking faith with its given forms in order to substitute for them others of the artist's own choosing and making. Such bids for something new (especially in the modern era) have undoubtedly arisen sometimes from a sense of disappointment or impatience with the given world, even outright hostility toward it;[10] but they need not do so. They can be born, too, from the intuition of a world richly endowed with promise, laden with a plenitude of as yet unanticipated form and meaning and inviting us to draw and to develop genuinely new realities from its stock of hidden and unrealized potential. Indeed, inasmuch as an artifact or work of art often entails

[10] Hence the sentiment of the quip variously ascribed to Virginia Woolf and Rebecca West: "A copy of the world is not what is required of art; one of the damned things is enough!"

the imaginative projection and indwelling of an accompanying "world" (a suggestion with which we shall reckon duly),[11] the generation of alternative realities would seem to be an occupational hazard for the artist, whether or not it lies at the heart of his or her personal manifesto. Then, lastly, we must add those approaches to art that—eschewing the pursuit of any stable meaning or order whatsoever in the given world and doubting art's capacity either to stabilize it for us or to furnish satisfying alternatives to it for our shared indwelling—treat the world as a repository of random flotsam and jetsam to be played with in a largely irresponsible manner, making whatever we will of it without any serious hope that doing so will achieve more than our temporary amusement (though in a world without meaning or purpose, that may be no mean consideration).

This, of course, is not a comprehensive list of ways in which art has been understood to be situated vis-à-vis the given world; there are other accounts of the circumstance to be had, and again we must reckon with the fact that in practice art is a great multitasker, so that more than one such answer to the question is likely to apply to any chosen instance;[12] but the underlying question itself haunts artistry as such. In the modern age in particular, this question and answers proffered to it have been more highly charged by the commonplace ascription to the artist of the status of one who "creates"—the "presumption of affinity" (in George Steiner's phrase) posited and felt, even as unacknowledged "background noise" to what the artist does, across the best part of five and a half centuries. As we have already observed, though, this first bold democratization of the language of creation and creativity at modernity's dawn has now long since been superseded. Today the verb "to create" includes within its range of accepted uses not just acts of God and certain exalted achievements of the human spirit identified in their turn as most "godlike" (as we shall see, the act of verbal trespass at the Renaissance was tied decisively to developments in theological anthropology) but all manner of human activities, practices, and outputs involving all sorts of people in more or less every sphere of life. "Creativity," we are wont to be told, is a basic human trait,

---

[11] See, e.g., Walton, *Mimesis as Make-Believe*, 57–67; Wolterstorff, *Art in Action*, 122–55. Wolterstorff notes that "pure" music and "abstract" art constitute exceptions to this (122).

[12] The portraits, still lifes, and genre paintings of the Dutch "Golden Age," for instance, are generally regarded in terms of the quality of their illusionistic naturalism in reproducing scenes and moments of an empirically available world; yet many of them also function at another level altogether, presenting some urgent moral, spiritual, or practical lesson carefully encrypted in a visual language for the benefit of those with eyes to see and ears to hear. See E. de Jongh, *Questions of Meaning: Theme and Motif in Dutch Seventeenth-Century Painting*, trans. Michael Hoyle (Leiden: Primavera Pers, 1995).

something we are all capable of at some level and in some portion of our lives, and realizing this is a matter of no small significance, since the exercise of creativity is vital for human well-being and flourishing, both in personal and in social terms.[13] If such claims seem to beg the question, the emergent discipline of "creativity studies,"[14] despite its typical insistence upon the inherent complexity of the phenomenon,[15] is nonetheless in broad agreement at least as regards a working definition of the term: in all manifestations of the creative impulse (the cognate nouns "creator" and "creation" are, on the whole, less widely claimed and distributed) possibilities lying latent within the given (our own inner selves, circumstances—problems, opportunities—confronting us in the external world) are intuited, grasped, explored, and developed to generate new ideas, new ways of seeing and doing things the outputs of which are of some identifiable benefit to self and society alike. In short, *creativity* (whatever the context for its manifestation) is the ability to produce something that is both innovative and appropriate (novelty itself will not suffice), original and useful, unexpected and fitting, unconventional and beneficial—not being

[13] So, e.g., the National Advisory Committee on Creative and Cultural Education (NACCCE) report *All Our Futures: Creativity, Culture and Education* (1999) advised the U.K. government's secretary of state for education: "Creativity is possible in all areas of human activity, including the arts, sciences, at work at play and in all other areas of daily life. All people have creative abilities and we all have them differently. When individuals find their creative strengths, it can have an enormous impact on self-esteem and on overall achievement" (6). See http://sirkenrobinson.com/pdf/allourfutures.pdf, accessed on April 13, 2014. According to the esteemed British psychoanalyst D. W. Winnicott, meanwhile, "creativity" is an essential feature of human mental hygiene, a "colouring of the whole attitude to external reality." See D. W. Winnicott, *Playing and Reality*, Routledge Classics ed. (London: Routledge, 2005), 87–114.

[14] See, e.g., Margaret A. Boden, ed., *Dimensions of Creativity* (Cambridge, Mass.: MIT Press, 1996); Margaret A. Boden, *The Creative Mind: Myths and Mechanisms*, 2nd ed. (London: Routledge, 2004); David Bohm, *On Creativity*, Routledge Classics ed. (London: Routledge, 2004); Rob Pope, *Creativity: Theory, History, Practice* (London: Routledge, 2005); Mark A. Runco and Steven R. Pritzker, eds., *Encyclopedia of Creativity*, 2 vols. (London: Academic, 1999); Mark A. Runco, *Creativity: Theories and Themes; Research, Development, and Practice* (London: Academic, 2007); R. Keith Sawyer, *Explaining Creativity: The Science of Human Innovation* (Oxford: Oxford University Press, 2006); Robert J. Sternberg, ed., *Handbook of Creativity* (Cambridge: Cambridge University Press, 1999). Two peer-review journals are also dedicated to the nascent field: *Journal of Creative Behaviour* (est. 1967) and *Creativity Research Journal* (est. 1988).

[15] See, e.g., Runco, *Creativity: Theories and Themes*, x. Sawyer acknowledges that part of the problem faced by the discipline is that "creativity—as we use the term in everyday language—is not a scientific concept; it's a culturally and historically specific idea that changes from one country to another, and from one century to another." Sawyer, *Explaining Creativity*, 36.

bound by the shape of the given but bringing forth from it something that is in the same moment new and worthwhile.[16]

Appeals to imagination (i.e., our capacity for acts of an imaginative sort) are commonplace in discussions of all this.[17] "Imagination," it should be noted, is a problematic and contested category in its own right, doubly so when laden with the qualifier "creative." Yet it is difficult to suppose other than that the two notions are naturally rather than unnaturally yoked, and if by no means all that is imaginative is "creative" in the sense we have now begun to associate with this term (nothing is more imaginative than a torture chamber), perhaps it is safe to suggest, nonetheless, that all that is creative is necessarily imaginative. The imaginative (those mental capacities and activities habitually clustered together under the rubric of "imagination") includes our capacity to "think outside the box," to conceive of states of affairs, and to act in ways that go beyond what is given to us by circumstance (what "stands over against" us materially or culturally or, in-so-far as each of us necessarily experiences *ourselves* as in some sense "other" too,[18] in the forms of prior personal experience and acquired habit), venturing or trespassing—we can select metaphors to suit the particular occasion—into identifiably new territory, whether that means "new" for the individual, the particular group, or (so far as anyone can meaningfully tell) human history as a whole.[19] Here there are inescapable echoes of those aesthetic discourses in which the power of "creative imagination" has not just been appealed to but on occasion effectively deified, the "work" of art being celebrated precisely as a unique *novum*, a phenomenon of unprecedented originality and (in this context more or

[16] See, e.g., Pope, *Creativity: Theory, History, Practice*, xvi; Runco, *Creativity: Theories and Themes*, 380; Sternberg, *Handbook of Creativity*, 3.

[17] See, e.g., NACCCE, *All Our Futures*, 30–31. Rob Pope suggests that the relationship between the two is of such a sort that "a radically recast notion of creativity entails some fundamental rethinking about what may be meant by imagination." Pope, *Creativity: Theory, History, Practice*, 14.

[18] A point drawn attention to by habits of speech in which, without any apparent sense of risk, we straddle ourselves awkwardly in syntax between the grammatical subject and object—in such phrases as "I look after myself," "She caught herself staring at him," and so on. French, as Ricoeur reminds us, suggests this internal opposition more consistently through its widespread use of pronominal verbs (conjugated by prefixing the reflexive pronoun *se* to the infinitive form of the verb—*Elle se promène, Tu te baigne, Nous nous habillons*, etc.). See Paul Ricoeur, *Oneself as Another* (Chicago: University of Chicago Press, 1992), 1.

[19] See NACCCE, *All Our Futures*, 32. Boden rests content with a twofold classification of "psychological" and "historical" creativity (*P*-creativity and *H*-creativity). Boden, *Creative Mind*, 2. Again, "creativity" in each case entails not just newness but acknowledged value or benefit.

less tautologously) unrivalled worth. Typically, texts in creativity studies begin by distancing themselves from the associations of such "romantic" or unashamedly elitist uses of the terms. Nonetheless, they remain within earshot of the echoes. And, since the reduction even for rhetorical effect of all instances to the level of some purported lowest common denominator ("I think the average person is almost indistinguishable from Mozart and Beethoven")[20] grates inelegantly against the grain not only of common sense but of most people's experiences of life, the field tends in practice to distinguish at least between "everyday creativity" and creativity of a publicly (i.e., socially or culturally) significant sort, or, as it is imaginatively indexed, c-creativity and C-creativity.[21] Indeed, while disentangling the point emphatically from any straightforward correlation with IQ (and thus from even the whiff of any notion of creative "genius"),[22] it is perfectly capable of differentiating a "creative type" of person from the hoi polloi.[23]

Despite the inevitable demurral of those wedded irretrievably to notions of the exceptional nature (and innate resistance to scientific accounting) of genuine human "creativity," it seems more likely that we should indeed reckon at least with the reality of a continuum on which various quite different instances of imaginative engagement with the world—some more and some altogether less notable and exalted, but all important—may helpfully be plotted and a corresponding sliding scale of applications of the term "creative." If the term is to be applied properly to human agency at all, that is to say, then there is no very good reason to restrict its application to the activities and outputs of a putative privileged class, even though we may still wish to argue for clear differences of degree between some of its manifestations and others. Of course, if *everything* is creative, then nothing is, the word in effect losing all distinctive and meaningful sense; but not even the most ardent among democratizers of the notion intend us to lose sight of the reality (indeed, the *prevalent* reality) of much that is *un*-creative in the ways we respond humanly to the given world. In due course, I shall suggest that this distinction remains essential to any theological account of the circumstance, not now in order

---

[20] M. Minsky, *Society of Mind*; cited in Runco, *Creativity: Theories and Themes*, 408.

[21] Sawyer notes, though, that to some extent this distinction serves equally as a fault line between differing camps within the field itself. See Sawyer, *Explaining Creativity*, 27–29.

[22] So, e.g., Sternberg, *Handbook of Creativity*, 251–69.

[23] See Runco, *Creativity: Theories and Themes*, 280–317; Sternberg, *Handbook of Creativity*, 137–52. This, though, is generally accompanied by the qualification either that creativity admits of degrees (there are "more" and "less" creative people) or that it rests on the deployment of "normative" rather than extraordinary human capacities and functions and is therefore latent even where it is not realized.

to maintain a respectful gap between divine and creaturely action (nor one between some "special" human actions/outputs and others) but to disentangle those human initiatives and achievements that are consonant with the patterns of possibility invested in the world by God at creation from those which are not.

Throughout the course of the previous century, and especially in its closing decades, voices in cultural theory began to urge upon us the claim that *nothing* is creative,[24] that even those achievements of the human spirit that we had typically deemed to be among the highest and best would prove, upon closer inspection, in reality to be little more than a hapless collage of bits and pieces harvested from old, tired, and broken projects— existential flotsam and jetsam endlessly recycled in a world that has, sensu stricto, run out of options and is going nowhere. This "eclipse of the messianic"[25] in human sensibility sees no genuinely new beginnings and expects none. It peddles the ultimate brand of "givenness," exalting pastiche as the highest form not of flattery but of all of which we are humanly capable.[26] Here again, the question of possible new beginnings within history resonates with religious and theological accounts of the beginning of history itself. Thus, the poststructuralist identification of categories such as "authorship" and "originality" as "myths" to be left behind gives us proper theological pause,[27] reminding us helpfully that the creaturely circumstance is indeed one marked by "the cruel fact of posteriority,"[28] thereby lancing unduly bloated accounts of human capacity and urging the careful disentangling of any remaining talk of creaturely "creativity" from liturgical and theological ascriptions of the category to God. But in theological terms, talk of creation (at any level of consideration) is precisely "messianic" both in its origins and in its orientation and will not leave us trapped—as its deconstructionist counterparts threaten to—in a labyrinth of exhausted and therefore literally "hopeless" possibilities.

As well as a primordial investment of the world with resources of potential and possibility that always transcend our grasp, faith in God as Creator also discerns God's dynamic presence in history's midst, "opening it up for the possible and the new in unexpected and unforeseeable

---

[24] Pope, *Creativity: Theory, History, Practice*, 6–7.

[25] George Steiner, *Grammars of Creation* (London: Faber & Faber, 2001), 7.

[26] See, e.g., Roland Barthes, *S/Z*, trans. Richard Miller (New York: Hill & Wang, 1974), 55.

[27] Rosalind E. Krauss, *The Originality of the Avant-Garde and Other Modernist Myths* (Cambridge, Mass.: MIT Press, 1986), passim.

[28] Steiner, *Grammars of Creation*, 19. "Has any painter invented a new colour?" he asks.

ways."[29] These openings, we may suppose, are the avenues of ever new possibility that we, in our most "creative" moments and modes of activity, intuit, grasp, explore, and develop.[30] If, therefore, as Steiner has suggested, our meaningful engagements with significant form (in language, in the arts, and elsewhere) are always contingent on a "wager on transcendence,"[31] theology reminds us that this wager has both a synchronic and a diachronic (eschatological) dimension. It is oriented, that is to say, not just toward the "real presence" of the meaningful other which (or who) transcends our own given reality and draws us into conversation but equally toward the presence (imminence) of a future filled with as yet unforeseen promise and worth pursuing. Whether or not we accept Steiner's further claim that this wager is finally always identifiable as one of a religious sort, so that "where God's presence is no longer a tenable supposition and where His absence is no longer a felt, indeed overwhelming weight, certain dimensions of thought and creativity are no longer attainable,"[32] it seems to be true at least—and prima facie paradoxically—that the postulate of human creativity is strengthened rather than weakened by the insistence (religious or otherwise) that we do not live in a world of our own making.

"We do not," philosopher O'Hear reminds us, "live in a world of our making. Our existence and survival depends on our recognizing this fact, and in coming to terms with the world as it actually is, not as we would like it to be."[33] As O'Hear suggests, the observation that as human beings we inhabit a world not of our own making has all the compelling force not just of common sense but of practical adaptation to life's circumstance. If we pretend otherwise, we shall quickly become ill fitted to the realities of our environment and swallowed up by the relentless machinery of natural selection. From a very different angle, of course, the claim is also basic to a theology of creation, for which the world is to be received from God's hand as a gift, an initiative of God's grace, and thus in some clear sense "given." And yet, as several millennia of philosophical skepticism have suggested—and a handful of centuries of scientific discovery served merely to confirm—the matter is much more complex than this. Sheer

---

[29] Ingolf U. Dalferth, *Becoming Present: An Inquiry into the Christian Sense of the Presence of God* (Leuven: Peeters, 2006), 30.

[30] "Scientific" descriptions of creativity typically posit some staged account of the process such as the four-stage model of "preparation," "incubation," "illumination," and "verification." See Runco, *Creativity: Theories and Themes*, 19.

[31] George Steiner, *Real Presences: Is There Anything in What We Say?* (London: Faber & Faber, 1989), 4 and passim.

[32] Steiner, *Real Presences*, 229. For a critical response to Steiner that finds his argument lacking at this point, see Dalferth, *Becoming Present*, 43–48.

[33] O'Hear, *Element of Fire*, 161.

positivism (of a commonsense, idealist, empiricist, or any other variety) is unsustainable, and we must reckon with the countervailing claim that as grateful recipients of a given world we are—at the same time, in the same action (in ways of which we are sometimes more and sometimes less conscious), and to some extent—complicit in the construction and the giving of it. This claim and the dialectic that it sets up are what will concern us in this section.

Reality, it has been insisted, is in some sense precisely that which we do not choose or make for ourselves but that which we "bump into," which resists our will and frustrates or damages our personal desires, purposes, and interests as often as it cooperates with or blesses them.[34] If this is true, if the world manifests a givenness that will not be gainsaid, we must nonetheless reckon again with Murdoch's insistence that "the world is not given to us on a plate" like some fast-food dish served up for immediate human consumption. Our human activities of receiving and indwelling it are neither wholly posterior to nor wholly distinct from the relevant action of "giving," but make a fundamental difference to the shape and substance of the gift itself. "[I]t is given to us as a creative task," and, working "at the meeting point where we deal with a world which is other than ourselves," "we of necessity shape it and 'make something of it.' We help it to be."[35] From a distinctly theological perspective, H. H. Farmer echoes Murdoch's point, referring us to God's determination "to create creators," setting them "in a world which in a sense was as yet uncreated, a world in which the full working out of His (creative) will would depend on the responses and decisions of" the creatures themselves.[36]

It is a commonplace of modern philosophy that all our experience and knowledge of the world is, in some sense, *mediated* knowledge. It is indirect, rather than direct, knowledge. Think for a moment of some of the different sorts of things that we come to know or to be conscious of as human beings: physical objects, of course, but also feelings, memories, ideas, hopes, beauty, goodness, evil, fantasies, fears, and so on and so forth.

---

[34] "Reality is what I 'come up against,' what takes me by surprise, the other-than-myself which pulls me up and obliges me to reckon with it and adjust myself to it because it will not consent simply to adjust itself to me." John Baillie, *The Sense of the Presence of God* (London: Oxford University Press, 1962), 33.

[35] Murdoch, *Metaphysics*, 215.

[36] Herbert H. Farmer, *The World and God: A Study of Prayer, Providence and Miracle in Christian Experience* (London: Nisbet, 1936), 69. Ingolf Dalferth reflects the same dialectic: "We are all born into a world not of our inventing. But we differ from other creatures in that we cannot live in it without inventing it. . . . We are born into a world not of our own making. But we cannot live in it without making it. We are—in a phrase dear to Austin Farrer—'made to make ourselves.'" Dalferth, *Becoming Present*, 34–35.

By the time we become conscious of any of these things, a lot has usually already happened to them in one way or another, depending on just what sort of thing they are. They present themselves to us already clothed in sensory, conceptual, and verbal form, laden with intellectual, practical, emotional, aesthetic, and moral significance of one sort or another. They are, for that matter, already presented to and apprehended by us as discrete objects or ideas, possessed of form and pattern which disentangles and differentiates them clearly from other things that we know or are conscious of or are experiencing at the same time. In other words, we never have to do consciously with "raw" experience that thrusts itself at us in an unedited version. The objects of our experience and knowledge seem already to have been worked on, tidied up, edited, packaged for our easy reception. And we make sense of individual objects not in isolation but, as I have already suggested, by locating them within some wider pattern or framework of meaning. We *interpret* them. Sometimes we do so consciously (as when we look at a photograph of an apparently unfamiliar object and try to decide what it is), but often we do so virtually simultaneously and subconsciously. We simply "see an approaching car" or "hear a bird singing." But the activities referred to in this way are in reality far from simple; they involve highly complex and involved formative and interpretative processes.

The distinction between the way in which we as human beings experience the world and an occult reality "as it is in itself" has a certain vulgar self-evidence about it, but it entered the intellectual mainstream with devastating and epoch-defining force in the writings of Immanuel Kant (1724–1804).[37] Kant's fundamental point was to observe that the experiences of which we are humanly capable are limited in range and determined in nature by the particular apparatus with which, as human beings as distinct from beings of any other sort, we have been supplied (our organs of sense, our brains, our central nervous systems, etc.).[38] It follows from this that there may well be (almost certainly are) all sorts of things in reality of which, because we do not have apparatus capable of registering their existence, we remain wholly unaware. Of those things that we can and do apprehend, however, it also follows that they cannot themselves exist (privately, "in themselves") in the same apparatus-dependent forms

---

[37] As Strawson notes, "The vulgar *distinguish*, naturally and unreflectively, between their seeings and hearings (perceivings) of objects and the objects they see and hear." P. F. Strawson, "Imagination and Perception," in *Experience and Theory*, ed. Lawrence Foster and J. W. Swanson (London: Duckworth, 1970), 36 (emphasis in original). With Kant, though, the nature and extent of the presumed gap assumed new proportions.

[38] The following account is indebted to the helpful treatment in Brian Magee, *The Tristan Chord: Wagner and Philosophy* (New York: Metropolitan Books, 2000), 152–62.

under which we necessarily perceive and subsequently think about them.[39] Reality, Kant is insisting, exists independently of human beings and their experiences and possesses its own integrity. The way it appears to us (the way we experience it) is precisely the way (and the only way) in which it is bound to appear to human beings, beings with the particular epistemic equipment and capacities that we possess. To seek to know it apart from this would be to seek to escape altogether from the range of perspectives available *in principle* to our humanity itself—in other words, to know it apart from any genuinely *human* knowing of it.[40]

When it comes to our knowledge of realities external to ourselves, Kant supposes that we are wholly dependent initially upon our senses and the barrage of stimuli (sensations of vision, taste, sound, smell, and touch) with which they supply us. It is indeed a barrage, though, and a potentially confusing and overwhelming one were we to notice everything going on around us at once. Indeed, whereas some of his philosophical predecessors had supposed that sensations presented themselves to us already conveniently packaged into identifiable clusters (the "objects" we experience) for us to reckon with and make sense of, Kant insists that the various strands of basic sensation are in principle wholly separable, part of a swirling chaotic manifold of stimuli threatening to engulf us. And yet, of course, we do not experience things in this way.[41] Even in our most immediate and unreflective engagements with the world, what we apprehend is a reasonably stable environment of discrete and bounded material "objects" existing in orderly and meaningful relationships which, when we stop and take notice, we can chart and predict, "make sense" of. How, then, are we to account for this? Kant's own answer is to insist that "percepts," the objects of sensory experience, have already been worked upon and edited into a stable and coherent form before we become conscious of them, an arcane activity which he ascribes to two distinct functions, or modes, of

---

[39] As Magee notes, the point here is a straightforward logical one: "People who say, 'But why *shouldn't* things actually be as they appear to us?' are radically failing to understand this. It cannot possibly be the case that things exist in experience-dependent forms independently of experience. To say so is self-contradictory: the nature of their independent being *must* fall outside any categories of thought or apprehension that are available to us." Magee, *Tristan Chord*, 155 (emphasis in original).

[40] We should note that even the enhancement of our bodily apparatus by sophisticated scientific apparatus remains firmly within the sphere of what it is in principle possible for human beings to experience. It extends the *range* of human experience but remains human experience for all that.

[41] For helpful treatment of this aspect of Kant's thought, see Mary Warnock, *Imagination* (London: Faber, 1977), 41–66; Strawson, "Imagination and Perception," in Foster and Swanson, *Experience and Theory,* 31–44.

the imagination:[42] the "transcendental" or "productive" imagination com-
bines separate sensory stimuli into composite objects possessed of particular shape, color, mass, smell, taste, and so forth; and the "reproductive" or
"empirical" imagination subsequently links these objects to concepts provided by the mind, situating them within wider patterns that "make sense
of" them for us. In all this, the imagination works strictly in accordance
with certain fundamental structures or rules laid down by the constitution
of the mind itself (a priori categories of space, time, and causality), so that
in a real sense the orderly world that we all experience is one first legislated
for and then called into being by the very physical and mental processes
through which reality is mediated to us.[43] None of this, of course, is at the
discretion or the disposal of our individual will; it is a function of our species being and occurs prior to the point at which we become conscious of
anything. As such, the world is in a real and important sense one "given"
to us. Yet it is also, in an equally clear sense, a world of our own making,
or at least one in the active construction of which our personal bodily and
intellectual equipment is involved to the hilt. We are not, according to
Kant, that is to say, passive registers of an already ordered world but active
participants in the construction of the world we experience, and it is to
imagination—the very feature or function of our humanity which, at a
conscious level, permits us to "range beyond the sensory,"[44] deconstructing
and reconstructing the world's given patterns in our mind's eye for one
reason or another—that Kant ascribes the chief responsibility in forming
the world disclosed by sensory perception itself.

We are not, of course, obliged to accept Kant's precise account of how
things stand with human beings in the world, though his so-called Coper-
nican shift has certainly had a profound impact—philosophers, theologians, and others alike tending ever since to situate themselves relative to
its claims and implications. Some theologians in particular have resisted
or rejected the basic moves Kant makes as an example of overweening
hubris, necessarily antagonistic to the proper concerns of a doctrine of
creation, though this seems to me to be quite mistaken. In any case, Kant
was neither the first nor the last (though he may remain the most significant) of those who have suggested in one way or another that the world as
we take it to be in our daily dealings with it (the world of "commonsense"

[42] See Immanuel Kant, *Critique of Pure Reason*, trans. Norman Kemp Smith (London: Macmillan, 1929), A115–30.
[43] The human understanding is, in a famous though sometimes harshly judged
phrase, "itself the lawgiver of nature." Kant, *Critique*, A126.
[44] Daniel Nettle, *Strong Imagination: Madness, Creativity and Human Nature*
(Oxford: Oxford University Press, 2001), 2.

empirical encounter) does not exist in any such guise apart from our peculiarly human interactions with it but is in some way precisely the result of what occurs when our humanity interacts with whatever reality is external to itself, just as light refracts into the colors of the rainbow when it interacts with a prism. Philosophers, physicists, physiologists, psychologists, and others all have their versions of this claim, and they can hardly be swept conveniently aside even if, as I shall suggest, the status of these claims vis-à-vis talk about what "reality" is finally like (or what counts as "real") must be more carefully weighed and considered than they sometimes are.

Philosophy and science prior to Kant had already suggested long since that material objects in the world external to us were possessed only of qualities measurable by mathematics (shape, size, number, position, etc.), all the other qualities we typically perceive in them (color, taste, smell, sound, texture) being the result of the way in which these objects impact upon our sense organs and brains.[45] The rich, sensuous world of daily experience, in other words, must be located not outside us but "in" us or at least at the notional interface between ourselves and that which is not ourselves. This sounds very odd at first blush (and perhaps even beyond that), but something like it has been held as a firm conviction by modern science ever since.

Physics today continues to posit a world that, at its most fundamental level, consists of infinitesimally small particles in constant motion, invisible, tasteless, soundless, odorless—in short, unobservable entities which become observable only when certain finely tuned apparatus (that of our human bodies and brains and whatever further technology we may have invented or developed) is brought into play. Physiology, for its part, tells us that when we "see" or "hear" or "smell" things, the relevant sensation is generated by complex processes involving photons, sound waves, or particles of gas stimulating our physical organs of sight, hearing, and smell, which in their turn transmit signals along our central nervous system to the brain for eventual unscrambling. The process takes time (albeit generally very little time indeed), and the stimulus may have passed or even ceased to exist (the night light emitted by perhaps long-dead stars makes the point) before we "have," as we say, the relevant experience itself. In the case of the sensation of touch, again, electrical repulsions between atoms in our finger and atoms external to our bodies send signals to the brain in an analogous manner, no material contact (at least as we think of it) ever actually having taken place. Again, therefore, all that we see, hear, touch,

---

[45] The following is indebted to the more detailed account in O'Hear, *Element of Fire*, 29–43.

taste, and smell around us is not some set of qualities belonging to a world existing independently of our acts of perceiving but precisely the product of a transaction between external reality and the efficient functioning of our complex machinery of perception itself. For its part, psychology observes that even when this rich sensory field has been generated for our indwelling, it remains in itself a bewildering, unstable, and indeterminate environment, dizzying in its constant Heraclitean variations of shape, color, and brightness—like the terrible wedding video shot at the reception by the drunken uncle. That we do not often notice this is due to the functioning of psychic stabilizing mechanisms known to psychologists as "constancies," adjustments made to the incoming signals in order to render a more stable and orderly world. As Ernst Gombrich notes,[46] it was precisely painters who, in their attempts to render likenesses of the three-dimensional world on a flat surface, learned to break down the effects of these stabilizers, uncovering and putting on canvas not what we actually "see" (for what we see is precisely the already carefully edited version of things) but the unsettling peculiarities of the unexpurgated version. By successfully doing this, they elicited from their viewers the arcane "beholder's share" in constructing a sensory environment, their painted image—being carefully suggestive rather than overdetermined—stimulating the same sort of perceptual responses as the world itself constantly demands from us as we bring it to order, with the result that their pictures "look" and feel much more, rather than less, like elements of that world itself—more "natural," as we would say. Thus artistic illusion is achieved precisely by *not* replicating accurately on canvas exactly what we see (it is hard to know in any case exactly what that could mean) but by the artist securing our imaginative participation in a constructive editing process whereby something "like" it is nonetheless generated in our visual field.

Gombrich also points to other editorial tricks and tools essential to our apparently simple and straightforward perceiving of things. From an astronomical background plethora of sensory input, he reminds us, we can and do grant our attention at any moment and across time to a mere selection of that which we deem most significant for the various practical purposes of living. Much of the "world" presented to us, in other words, ends up in practice on the cutting room floor or forming a hazy backdrop to the main action.[47] And, even among the elements isolated, selected, and

---

[46] Ernst H. Gombrich, *Art and Illusion: A Study in the Psychology of Pictorial Representation*, 5th ed. (London: Phaidon, 1977), 236–38, 253–54, et passim; Ernst H. Gombrich, *The Image and the Eye: Further Studies in the Psychology of Pictorial Representation* (London: Phaidon, 1982), 18–20.

[47] Gombrich, *Image and the Eye*, 15.

attended to, much more than we notice remains indeterminate; our perceiving involves repeated imaginative acts of projection (we "see" what we
expect to see and correspondingly often fail to see what we do not expect),
guessing, testing our guesses, and adjusting our expectations accordingly.[48]
The whole business is very far indeed from being one of passive registra-
tion and much more a matter of continuous small-scale acts of imaginative
construction, deconstruction, and reconstruction as we seek to identify
things by fitting them into given and familiar patterns of meaningfulness
and significance. There is no "innocent eye" (or ear or nose or whatever) in
all this; perceiving and interpreting (*making* sense of) are all of a piece and
contingent on the "creative" capacities and functioning of our complex
perceptual apparatus, just as Kant said they were (if not necessarily in the
precise way he supposed to be the case).

The question about creation, Steiner avers, is not just "Why is there
not nothing?" but "Why is there not chaos?"[49] As we saw in the previous
chapter, this latter line of inquiry is perhaps even more fundamental to
the concern of the biblical writers than the former (the answer to which
they nonetheless take for granted). The beneficent ordering of a cosmos to
be inhabited rather than the summoning forth of a chaos is of the essence
of the LORD's primordial activity (Isa 45:18). What, then, are we to make
of the suggestion—difficult to gainsay other than in terms of incidental
detail or variations among schemes of presentation of the case—that in
significant measure the orderliness and other qualities of the world we
inhabit (namely, the world as it presents itself to us in everyday conscious
experience) is contingent on the factoring in of the particular "apparatus" (bodily and mental) with which we are all equipped, apart from the
efficient functioning of which the world would be for us a very different
place indeed (something, in fact, much more fittingly described in terms
of "chaos" than "cosmos")? If it is indeed our equipment of sensation and
imagination which, as Mary Warnock puts it, "creates for us the world we
like to have, . . . without which we could not bear to inhabit the world,"[50]
and if, when this same equipment is taken out of play, what remains is a
reality made up largely of "colourless, tasteless, silent, odourless corpus-
cles,"[51] a dull, aesthetically barren and humanly uninhabitable place, how
then are we to hear the prophet's enjoinment to praise and obedience? We
might be tempted to conclude that the very sorts of things that we value

[48] Gombrich, *Art and Illusion*, 170–201.
[49] Steiner, *Grammars of Creation*, 46.
[50] Warnock, *Imagination*, 25. Warnock's words at this point in her text refer to
Hume alone, but they are equally applicable to the wider point at issue here.
[51] O'Hear, *Element of Fire*, 33.

and celebrate most—the harvest moon that hangs heavily on the horizon, the intoxicating perfume of the rose, the sudden cooling breeze on a sultry afternoon, the morning song of the blackbird, the burst of fresh raspberries on the palette—are all products not of a prior divine ordering but of our own capacities of physical and supraphysical response and representation. Is the poet's ecstatic celebration of "dappled things,"[52] then, anything more than a peculiar form of narcissism, and art's wider "mimetic" engagements with Nature an example of ostentatious self-referencing (like the sort of academic who loves endlessly to footnote and comment on his or her own previous publications)? Ought we, perhaps, to consider redirecting the shuddering climactic "Praise him" of Hopkins' heavenward verse, allowing it to shower back down instead upon our own heads?

Such questions cannot be shirked, even though they may flirt dangerously with blasphemy. It is important to ask them precisely because so much rests on the answers we are finally minded to give. Any suggestion that the reality summoned into existence by God in the beginning and held in being by him from moment to waking moment is "in reality" a swirling chaos—and that in our daily intercourse with an ordered world rich in color, texture, sound, taste, and smell, therefore, we are effectively "victims of a systematic illusion"[53] perpetrated and sustained by our sensory organs in collusion with the imaginative powers of preconscious intelligence—is likely to be as disturbing to simple religious faith in creation as it is unacceptable to formal religious doctrine. We may value the artistry of a Jackson Pollock painting enormously, but the claim that it might turn out finally to be more deserving of the tag "realist" than a Botticelli *Virgin and Child*, an early Rembrandt, or a landscape by Constable is likely to upset more than the neat canons of art history alone, and rightly so.[54] But it does not take religious belief to balk at the suggestion, challenge the presumption of the terms in which it is cast, and so view the relevant considerations from a different perspective altogether.

As O'Hear argues,[55] the absolute "de-centred" conception of things (i.e., one from which, as far as is possible for us, every trace of a distinctly human standpoint or concern has been purged), whether in its scientific

[52] Gerard Manley Hopkins, "Pied Beauty," in *Poems and Prose of Gerard Manley Hopkins*, ed. W. H. Gardner (London: Penguin, 1953), 30.

[53] O'Hear, *Element of Fire*, 33.

[54] The sense in which any painting may properly be considered "realist" (i.e., approximate to a visual transcription of reality onto canvas or some other surface) is, of course, a complex one, and will concern us later in this chapter.

[55] O'Hear, *Element of Fire*, e.g., 65–73.

or its metaphysical versions,[56] needs to be treated with caution, not least in its aspiration to provide a reliable account of "reality." The problem is, of course, that human beings can never finally prescind from some possible human perspective or other,[57] and as embodied and conscious beings any attempt to do so is bound itself to depend on acts of a highly imaginative sort. Thus, science purports to offer a description of "reality" in terms of clouds of miniscule particles and their erratic dance, a vision which discloses itself only in part to the multimillion-dollar equipment on which massive research grants are spent, needing the further assistance of acts of inference, interpretation, and inspired hypothesizing to construct an account of how things really are "out there" beyond the level of observation to which alone our technology will as yet carry us. Kant's radical distinction between "phenomena" and "noumena," meanwhile, projects an apophatic "reality" that is in principle and *by definition* beyond our reach (limiting the advances of science to ever more refined descriptions of "phenomena"— namely, those things which are in principle knowable by embodied and conscious beings like us).[58] While the two conceptions are thus subtly but vitally distinct, each insists on disentangling and divorcing "reality" from the world as it appears to us in our everyday dealings with it. Each affords the status of "reality," that is to say, to some state of affairs knowable only independently of those constraints by which human experience is in fact characterized—that is, by taking all that is distinctly human (the way things are bound to be perceived by beings situated at particular points in time and space and with the sensory and intellectual equipment we in fact possess) out of the equation altogether. "Reality" then becomes a technical term used to refer to a circumstance which human beings are incapable in practice (and perhaps in principle) of experiencing or, arguably, even imagining. But is that not rather an odd way of choosing to distribute the available terms? Surely, O'Hear suggests, "something which belongs, and necessarily belongs, to the way in which certain sentient beings perceive some physical reality . . . has for that very

[56] Kant's account of what lies beyond human apprehension also posits something resembling a chaos at this point, since "noumenal" reality cannot possibly be structured in terms of the categories of space, time, and causality that order our experience of the "phenomenal" or empirical world (space, time, and causality themselves being precisely a priori categories of human understanding, and hence "internal" to or a function of our experience as such). See Magee, *Tristan Chord,* 157–58.

[57] O'Hear, *Element of Fire,* 14.

[58] This too, of course, is a highly imaginative act; but for Kant (unlike the scientist) we can never gain any imaginative purchase on reality, since the noumenal, by definition, excludes the categories in terms of which our thinking and speaking, and hence our imagining, are all structured. Cf. Magee, *Tristan Chord,* 158.

reason a perfectly good title to be thought of as part of what the world is really like"?[59]

We have acknowledged already that the reality we experience humanly is always a mediated product, and one the particular contours and qualities of which are bound up with peculiarly human capacities and perspectives. To admit this is to admit that there are almost certainly other ways of experiencing it, other nonhuman perspectives (that of God, say, or the electron microscope or the earthworm) from which the world appears very different indeed. But we are those, we might suppose, who are programmed by our particular natures to perceive the world in certain given ways and, by the same token, discouraged or even prohibited for the most part from experiencing it otherwise. For practical purposes, therefore, without in any way denigrating the various alternative perspectives afforded by scientific instruments or posited by philosophical imagining, we may nonetheless reasonably elect to ascribe the status of "reality" to that set of experiences most typically available to most of us most of the time.

Putting the same point now in distinctly religious and theological terms, we might say simply that, since the physical and psychical processes and powers of perception with which we are equipped as human beings are part of the particular nature God has bestowed upon us, those same perceptual responses which undeniably mediate and "construct" reality for us are themselves part of the fundamental "givenness" of the world that issues from God's own creative activity. That God creates not "chaos" but an ordered cosmos fit for creaturely indwelling and enjoyment, therefore, is not a fact that excludes consideration of creaturely responses to reality but one that includes the range of such responses within itself and is contingent upon them. On this account, it is precisely God's gift and calling to human beings to experience the world in those ways in which, for the most part, we do in fact experience it—namely, as an orderly presentation of material objects richly endowed with color, taste, smell, and the rest. We do not (and probably cannot) know how God's other creatures experience the world, though we have good reason to suppose that their perceptions are calibrated rather differently than our own. We certainly cannot know how God experiences it (the one perspective deserving, perhaps, of the description "Reality" with a capital R). The utility, for certain purposes, of extending the range of sensory perspectives available to us (by magnification or amplification or whatever) or of imagining how things might look if we did not possess the bodies we do in fact possess has long since been demonstrated by the progress of science in its dealings with

---

[59] O'Hear, *Element of Fire*, 9.

the world. But for the most part, surely, we can be thankful that we were *not* created with the perceptual capacities of the electron microscope, able to see only "atoms and the void" rather than the world of light, color, form, and line which our own eyes and brains disclose to us. This is the world to which, from our technologically enhanced encounters and our flights of intelligent imagination alike, we must always return at the end of the day.[60] It is the world that God created us, as human beings rather than beings of some other sort, to inhabit. It is the world into which, let us not forget, in the fullness of time God himself entered, having taken to himself a "flesh" endowed with the selfsame sense organs, central nervous system, and brain as facilitate our own distinctly human vantage point on reality—thus giving himself a quite new and different "taste" of things than that which, as God, he enjoys eternally—and living out his divine life from within it. And it is the world that God calls us to take and "make more of" than that which (through a sovereign divine giving/gifting that incorporates the dynamics of human bodily response) empirically it already is.

---

[60] As O'Hear notes, while scientific theory often ranges way beyond the level of the humanly observable, the testing and verification of such theories (i.e., the ascription to them of some truth value) always returns of necessity to questions of empirically available fact. Indeed, the point of such theories is not to escape from the observable world but to enable us to make practically advantageous (as well as intellectually satisfying) predictions about that world. See *Element of Fire*, 49–58.

6

Ethos

Give and Take in the Order of Signs

In the previous chapter, we concentrated on ways in which aspects of our embodied nature function to construct a world fit for human habitation. Physiological and psychological mechanisms hardwired into our system involve us in imposing an order on the world of a sort that simply would not obtain in our absence. As dwellers in the world, it seems, we are active shapers and builders of it rather than mere passengers; even at this most fundamental of levels, there is both give and take to be reckoned with. Of course, since much of this has as yet to do with animal processes rather than actions, it is something of which we remain largely unaware (except when the mechanisms malfunction) and for which we can neither take the credit nor shoulder the blame. In the current chapter, we turn our attention to a further dimension of this creaturely construction of the world, one that is (so far as we can tell) unique to the human species, and in which considerations of responsibility make a sudden, unavoidable and uncomfortable, appearance. I refer, of course, to the ways in which human beings habitually supplement the sphere of "nature" with another, equally deep and complex, tier of reality—the sphere of the symbolic, of "language" and of "culture" in the broadest sense of both of those terms, the sphere in which meanings and values and feelings are identified, articulated and explored, shaped and reshaped, and within which human lives find their distinctive direction and their realization.

The Complex Grammar of Immediate Experience

The given reality of everyday living is not limited to encounters with material objects, of course. Even if we concentrate on the "here and now," that segment of reality which presents itself to us in particular times and places, falling more or less immediately within our individual purview and demanding our attention,[1] the things confronting us and making their presence felt are not just things that can be weighed and measured but things of wholly other sorts too—celebrations, cities, concerts, constellations, and conversations; wars, wealth, and work; criminality, education, government, and the market; religions, reconciliations, and responsibilities; images, thoughts, arguments, memories, hopes, fears, disappointments, desires, purposes; descriptions and lists. And persons. Our world is irreducibly intersubjective,[2] populated by and shared with others who are certainly not reasonably reducible to the net material substance of their bodies (and likely to meet with indignation any attempt to treat them as though they were).[3] The "grammar of experience," Nicholas Lash suggests,[4] thus proves upon inspection to be varied and complex, determined both by the many different sorts of things there are and by the equipment and competencies for registering them supplied now not just by our bodies but by the social institutions of human culture too. Even our encounters with physical objects amount to much more than can be described in terms of the mechanics of sensory perception alone, and, as Ingolf Dalferth observes, any account ignoring this is bound to miss what in reality matters most—namely, "that which our experiences *mean to us*" and that makes us live our lives in one way rather than another.[5]

John Macmurray draws our attention to the fact that, of the vast amount of information presented to us by the world at any given moment

---

[1] See Peter Berger and Thomas Luckmann, *The Social Construction of Reality: A Treatise in the Sociology of Knowledge* (London: Penguin, 1967), 35–36.

[2] Berger and Luckmann, *Social Construction of Reality*, 37.

[3] "The other's will stands as a limit to ours. Physical objects also limit our purposes, but the limitation is of an entirely different kind, as our response to it clearly shows. The resistance of physical objects can only be overcome, if it is overcome at all, by direct manipulative control. The resistance of a will can never be overcome save by what we call agreement or reconciliation. For in the degree that it is otherwise overcome it ceases to be a personal will any longer, and so cannot, *qua* will, be said to be overcome at all." Herbert H. Farmer, *The World and God: A Study of Prayer, Providence and Miracle in Christian Experience* (London: Nisbet, 1936), 21.

[4] See the essay "On What Kinds of Things There Are," in Nicholas Lash, *The Beginning and End of "Religion"* (Cambridge: Cambridge University Press, 1996), 93–111.

[5] Ingolf U. Dalferth, *Becoming Present: An Inquiry into the Christian Sense of the Presence of God* (Leuven: Peeters, 2006), 114 (emphasis in original).

in time, most necessarily goes unnoticed by us. Impressive though our capacity for engaging with the world is, we can attend consciously to (concentrate upon, think about, reflect upon) only one thing at once. The rest of our environment we remain aware of and able perfectly well to navigate and respond to in meaningful ways, but it is not, as we say, "on our mind," for the moment at least. We are immersed in it, "living it" rather than stepping back and attending to it as something singled out, abstracted temporarily from the mix and set over against us for observation and analysis.[6] "Immediate experience" of this sort is thus precisely the form that most of our "knowing" of the world takes most of the time, "the effortless result of living in it and working with it and struggling against it."[7] It is "unreflective" experience—experience, that is to say, which has not been thought about or expressed in the effort to understand.[8] But it is certainly not "raw" or chaotic; on the contrary, we apprehend it as a world already shot through with pattern and significance, structured in significant part, indeed, by the products of chronologically prior acts of human reflection and expression (our own and those we inherit from and share with others), and constantly growing and developing through its enrichment by further such acts.[9] And, whereas in our attempts to understand things we typically tear them from their particular context in the fabric of existence to consider them in splendid isolation, the fabric of given reality itself (i.e., the world as it actually presents itself to us for indwelling) is one in which different sorts of things and different aspects and dimensions of experience (sensation, cognition, conation, imagination, feeling) are all woven together into a seamless and meaningful whole.[10] Thus, in our day-to-day dealings with things, we typically encounter individual physical phenomena not in

---

[6] John Macmurray, *Interpreting the Universe* (London: Faber, 1935), 21.

[7] Macmurray, *Interpreting the Universe*, 16.

[8] As such, of course, it is also the logical presupposition and condition of all our understanding. "*All thought presupposes knowledge*," Macmurray reminds us, and while "[i]t may be true that some things that we know cannot be understood or even described . . . it is certain that nothing that is unknown can be described or understood." Macmurray, *Interpreting the Universe*, 15 (emphasis in original). Macmurray's account shares much in common with Michael Polanyi's description of the "tacit components of articulate knowledge," a mix of sensory, symbolic, theoretical, and learned-active (skilled) elements that together form a coherent framework of which we are aware only in a subsidiary manner while attending in a focused way to other things, but upon our active indwelling of which all attempts to make sense of those same things rely. See Michael Polanyi, *Personal Knowledge: Towards a Post-critical Philosophy* (London: Routledge & Kegan Paul, 1958), 98. See further Michael Polanyi, *The Tacit Dimension* (London: Routledge & Kegan Paul, 1967).

[9] Macmurray, *Interpreting the Universe*, 19.

[10] Macmurray, *Interpreting the Universe*, 22.

rarefied (and by definition artificial) "scientific" abstraction but as components of "synthetic intuitions"[11] which discover them already irretrievably implicated in webs of significance. Objects present themselves to us (and we grasp them involuntarily) already laden with meaning for some existential circumstance—Proust's madeleine, the eucharistic wafer, the black squiggles and lines on the white page of a letter or a musical score, the dog that does not bark in the night, the granular blemish that appears suddenly on a sun-weathered back. The significances of such things are untraceable by physical, chemical, or biological analysis alone, and they are nowhere found inscribed on the hard material surfaces of things; yet they provide the mesh around which the "human world," as O'Hear calls it,[12] is constructed and without which it would be quite unrecognizable and wholly uninhabitable by creatures such as ourselves.

Culture and the Predicament of Being Human

To be human, it seems, is to be obliged to dwell in two spheres of reality at the same time, spheres at once identifiably distinct yet equally clearly demanding to be held together and interpenetrating in every genuinely human encounter with things. Thus the Welsh poet and painter David Jones notes that, according to the teaching of his own Catholic tradition, it is part of "the predicament of being human"—part, that is to say, of the kind of creature we are and were made by God to be—that we should straddle and hold together in our own distinctive species being the spheres of material and nonmaterial reality and thus be both capable of and bound in practice to commit those acts of sense making, signification, and re-presentation which transgress and refuse to be bound by the putative border between the two spheres.[13]

From a nonreligious perspective, O'Hear makes a parallel observation. We are, he suggests, embodied consciousnesses embedded by our particular constitution both in the animal processes of material nature and in the world of linguistic, cultural, and artistic traditions that transcend nature and articulate self-consciously human perspectives on and responses to it.[14] We seem, he says, to need to inhabit a world that is structured by objects and at the same time suffused with distinctly human meanings

[11] See Farmer, *World and God*, 34–38.

[12] Anthony O'Hear, *The Element of Fire: Science, Art and the Human World* (London: Routledge, 1988), 14.

[13] See the essay "Art and Sacrament," in David Jones, *Epoch and Artist* (London: Faber & Faber, 1959), 143–79; for the cited phrase, see p. 166.

[14] See, e.g., O'Hear, *Element of Fire*, 18–28.

and feelings (rather than indifferent to our existence, as the physical cosmos considered on its own terms alone otherwise appears to be); and it is language and culture that manage this interface for us, furnishing an objective symbolic habitat to accompany its material counterpart, a finely constructed web in which such meanings, values, and feelings are carefully encoded and via the mediations of which we apprehend them shot through the texture of every human encounter with our environment.[15]

"Nature is not itself a home for human beings," writes Jürgen Moltmann. "It is only when nature has been moulded into an environment that it can become the home in which men and women can live and dwell."[16] Moltmann is thinking here chiefly of those acts of physical "cultivation" by means of which the world's human inhabitants respect and work together with its physical forces and processes, harnessing and ordering them toward specifically human goods and goals. Identifying and articulating those goods and goals, though, already trespasses beyond the level of a merely physical engagement with things, and Moltmann's observation holds good for acts of human cultivation more widely defined. Nature alone will not suffice to engender or sustain truly human existence. Human beings being what human beings are, something more is needed, something that human beings themselves can and must provide through appropriate acts of cultivation. Endowing the world with human meanings, we might say, the symbolic *habitus* provided by culture both arises from the needs and demands of a distinctly human existence in the world and in turn renders such an existence possible. A classic study of our theme by Lotman and Uspensky reaches similar conclusions: as a system of signs designed to structure and explore the world from a distinctly human perspective, culture, they suggest, provides the conditions necessary for genuinely human existence in a manner directly parallel to the biosphere itself.[17]

[15] O'Hear, *Element of Fire*, 141–42. Language itself, of course, in most of its forms entails the dialectical counterpoint of material and nonmaterial elements, on the one hand demanding "the play of muscle and vocal cords," yet on the other remaining something impalpable and elusive to sense alone. Thus, Steiner argues, it "confirms the dual mode of human existence, the interactions of physical with spiritual agencies." George Steiner, *After Babel: Aspects of Language and Translation*, 2nd ed. (Oxford: Oxford University Press, 1992), 60.

[16] Jürgen Moltmann, *God in Creation: An Ecological Doctrine of Creation*, trans. Margaret Kohl (London: SCM Press, 1985), 46.

[17] Yu. M. Lotman and B. A. Uspensky, "On the Semiotic Mechanism of Culture," *New Literary History* 9, no. 2 (1978): 213.

Symbolization: Representing and Transforming the World

We ought not, in speaking of "culture," to narrow our focus of consideration too far or too quickly. Even understood in its broadest sense, the term "culture" refers us to the public and social manifestations of a more basic and widespread human phenomenon—namely, the capacity to transform our experiences into symbolic form for storage and subsequent revisiting and use.[18] Data received empirically (not via the testimony of our senses alone but from the whole pattern of "immediate experience" resulting from our immersion in the world) is instantaneously converted by the brain into symbols (images, ideas, words) by means of which we are able to represent it to ourselves and to others after the fact and in absentia.[19] Symbols are signs we use not to *indicate* things but to *represent* them. The symbolic order thus frees us from the tyranny of the physically and temporally proximate in merely animal experience, allowing us to remember, to reflect upon, to talk about things. A symbol in this particular sense, Macmurray notes, can be anything which, in the currency of thought or interpersonal exchange, "stands for" something other than itself, taking its place either by virtue of some degree of likeness to the thing represented or through the more indirect ministry of socially accepted conventions.[20] Language (i.e., our capacity for words—thought, spoken, written) is the most familiar and pervasive manifestation of this symbolic supplement to the world, though both inwardly and outwardly symbolization amounts to more than words alone. Thus there is always that which we "know" but find that we cannot "put into words."[21] And there is that which is more naturally articulated instead in the alternative "languages" of gesture or of material objects to which meaning is imputed over and above whatever, in and of themselves, they may already possess.[22] In the order of signs, Rowan Williams notes, "the flesh is

---

[18] See Susanne K. Langer, *Philosophy in a New Key: A Study in the Symbolism of Reason, Rite, and Art*, 3rd ed. (Cambridge, Mass.: Harvard University Press, 1956), 26–52.

[19] Langer, *Philosophy in a New Key*, 31.

[20] Macmurray, *Interpreting the Universe*, 44–45. Thus, in this sense nothing is a "symbol" by virtue of some intrinsic property but only by virtue of its deliberate use or function in the relation of representing something else. See Macmurray, *Interpreting the Universe*, 50.

[21] Macmurray, *Interpreting the Universe*, 47. Cf. Langer, *Philosophy in a New Key*, 41.

[22] Symbols properly belong to "languages" in this broader sense—i.e., to systems of articulate expression—and the process of symbolization terminates naturally in the peculiarly human activity of expressing ideas, attitudes, and feelings. See Langer, *Philosophy in a New Key*, 43.

more than it is, gives more than it (as flesh) has."[23] In our technologically advanced age, of course, the encryption, storage, and rapid transmission of data in symbolic forms has reached new and dizzying heights, generating an entire "worldwide" symbolic "web" within which most citizens of Western societies consciously and constantly situate themselves courtesy of their laptops, smartphones, and other electronic extensions of bodily apparatus.

In reality, "[s]ymbol and meaning," Susanne Langer suggests, "make man's world, far more than sensation."[24] Consider just a handful of examples: the busy homemaker, consulting a long shopping list and taking a basket filled with groceries at last to the checkout for payment; the meteorologist plotting the likely course of an approaching weather system; the couple engrossed in conversation on a park bench, making plans for the weekend, perhaps, or sharing in office gossip; the girl flicking idly through the pages of a fashion magazine; the child whose daydreams transform a bunk bed into a pirate ship braving the high seas; the psychoanalyst scribbling on her notepad as a client rehearses fragments of childhood memory or last night's dreams; the wedding guest apparently more intent on capturing the moment on camera for subsequent retrieval than on actually living it; the undergraduate multitasker, composing an essay for the next day's tutorial while simultaneously surfing for news online and "chatting" with friends via "text," or providing a constant commentary on events by "tweeting." In each case (and the list could be extended indefinitely), the reality in which we are all immersed—in which we live and move and have our being—is one identifiably teeming with symbol as well as sensation, and one in which even the flesh itself, therefore, is always "more than it is, gives more than it (as flesh) has."

Again, as its inhabitants we are not just passive recipients but active makers and constructers of this symbolic world. Much of our time, Macmurray notes, is spent in various activities (in thought and speech but elsewhere, too) directed toward the deliberate modification and reconfiguration of the symbolic order as distinct from engaging directly with "the real world."[25] Thought itself and as such involves either the symbolic reduction of experience or its rendering by means of some arbitrary semiotic convention, rather than its duplication. So, *representation*, we should note,

[23] Rowan Williams, *Grace and Necessity: Reflections on Art and Love* (Harrisburg, Pa.: Morehouse, 2005), 61.

[24] Langer, *Philosophy in a New Key*, 28. In a related vein, in a discussion of the ubiquity of language, Steiner alludes to it as providing the "skin of consciousness, a vital cover more intimately enfolding, more close-woven to human identity than is the skin of our body." Steiner, *After Babel*, 115.

[25] Macmurray, *Interpreting the Universe*, 39.

even at this very basic level of symbolic engagement necessarily entails some element of *transformation*. There is and can be no sheer replication, faithful in every detail to the original experience. Even were such acts of reduplication possible in some imaginary state of affairs,[26] they would hardly be useful, since it is precisely a function of our symbolic engagement with things to render them manageable (able to be thought and spoken of) in ways that their full-blown reality is not and could never be, being at once too voluminous, too complex and protean. "What is left out, and how much is left out," Macmurray notes, "depends on the particular purpose for which the image is required."[27] Symbolic reduction also enables us to think about things in a manner that trespasses immediately and inevitably even further beyond the given experiences from which it begins. In reflecting on things, we seek to "make sense" of them, manipulating their symbolic substitutes, editing and reconfiguring them, trying out different patterns in pursuit of the best imaginative "fit." Supposal (inference, judgment), Macmurray observes, is fundamental to the grammar of thought; and supposal involves a willingness deliberately to free ourselves from the given facts of the case. "Thought," he concludes, "is always an advance in imagination beyond 'what is given.'"[28]

Whistler's Fog

In this regard, we might note, every act of symbolic engagement with reality shares the basic structure and circumstance of those acts of representation habitually concluded under the rubric of the "fictional" or "artistic." In each case, representation (no matter how thorough or faithful) involves transformation too, and in each case (in the arts no less than in our more "scientific" engagements with things) the texture of what we take reality itself to be is at stake. For the relationship between reality and its symbolic representations turns out to be a complex rather than a straightforward affair, with give and take evident on both sides. Nature and culture, too, prove on inspection to be interpenetrating layers caught up in a constructive and mutually modifying play, rather than permitting any convenient disentanglement of the one from the other for classification.

That our experiences of material nature should have a direct shaping impact on our symbolic representations is hardly surprising; indeed

---

[26] Baudrillard refers us to the Borges fable in which "the cartographers of the Empire draw up a map so detailed that it ends up covering the territory exactly." Jean Baudrillard, *Simulacra and Simulation*, trans. Sheila Faria Glaser (Ann Arbor: University of Michigan Press, 1994), 1.

[27] Macmurray, *Interpreting the Universe*, 44.

[28] Macmurray, *Interpreting the Universe*, 55.

it seems to belong to what it means to say that they are "representations" at all. But it appears that the impact of our embodied state on the construction of a symbolic habitus goes much deeper than this. So, for example, Mark Johnson has argued that recurrent and familiar patterns of our embodied existence in the world (bodily motion, manipulation of objects, perceptual interactions) "work their way up into the mind" to be developed figuratively as abstract structures ("image schemata") around which meaning is subsequently organized, thereby both constituting and constraining the ways in which we experience, reflect upon, and represent the world itself as a meaningful environment.[29] That the traffic moves in the other direction too is clear enough. According to urban legend, unlike most readers of this book, Eskimo peoples are able to differentiate among (and hence "experience") many different varieties of snow, having a suitably developed lexicon that permits the relevant subtle distinctions to be articulated and "invented."[30] It is language, too, George Steiner notes, which, courtesy of its possession of past and future tenses and conditional and subjunctive moods, constructs our experience of time and of possibility, enabling us to speak of what has been and what may yet be and thus to live in a present whose texture is saturated with memory and anticipation, rather than locked in an endless cycle of sameness. Again, without the benefit of adjectival qualification, there could be no conceptualization (and no meaningful experience) of things as good or evil, hot or cold, black or white. In this sense and in all these ways and many more besides, Steiner urges, language *generates ways of experiencing the world* by virtue of

[29] Mark Johnson, *The Body in the Mind: The Bodily Basis of Meaning, Imagination and Reason* (Chicago: University of Chicago Press, 1987), 18–40, et passim. So, e.g., one of the most pervasive features of embodied existence in time and space is "our encounter with containment and boundedness," the recurrent organizational patterns "entailments" of which furnish an experiential basis for a range of *in-out* schemata that duly structure the world and orient us within it on lots of different levels of experience, cropping up eventually in the habitual patterns of our speech—I wake *out* of a deep sleep, I climb *out* of bed, I am *in* a hurry, I enter *into* a conversation with a colleague, I speak *out* at a meeting, I find myself *out* of a job (all *in* the space of a single morning!), and so on. See Johnson, *Body in the Mind*, 21–22, 30–31.

[30] The particular claim was made initially by adherents of the Sapir-Whorf school of linguistic relativity, but its accuracy has since been repeatedly disputed. The wider point, though, i.e., that there is an evident extent to which "language forces us into its patterns" (Berger and Luckmann, *Social Construction of Reality*, 53) by permitting the objectification of some experiences while leaving others necessarily mute or inarticulate (and to that extent not fully "experienced" at all) relies neither on the veracity of the particular (convenient) example nor on acceptance of the strong Whorfian theory of discordant and incommensurable linguistic mappings of reality. On the latter, see, helpfully, Steiner, *After Babel*, 92–98.

its capacity (or its incapacity) to name it.[31] On the visual front, meanwhile, Ernst Gombrich observes that, once the initial shock and rash of resistance to impressionist paintings had worn off, people soon discovered that, upon revisiting the Paris boulevards or the fields and woods of the surrounding countryside, they could hardly help noticing gradations of color and light that seemed not to have been there before. Having seen a Monet or a Renoir, they now "saw" the world quite differently, having had their "mental set" (their expectations and capacity to configure or "read" visual signals) appropriately adjusted. If, in some sense, therefore, art sometimes imitates nature, then so too, it seems, nature in its turn often "imitates" or follows the symbolic representations of art and culture—hence Oscar Wilde's quip that there was no fog in nineteenth-century London before Whistler painted it.[32]

As O'Hear observes, therefore, we certainly should not make the mistake of supposing that "experience" is something which exists fully formed, requiring symbolic transformation only as a logically posterior instrument of storage and transmission.[33] On the contrary, the states of mind, attitudes, and responses to reality we are capable of having (our "experiences" of it) are themselves frequently contingent upon (rather than logically prior to) our active participation in the languages and institutions of human culture in its broadest sense—that is, "that public realm in which human beings express their feelings, attitudes and concerns objectively."[34] In short, language does not simply map the reality we experience but constructs it for us, too.

Let us remind ourselves briefly again of Kant's insistence that, whatever may exist "out there" beyond us, the experiences of which we are humanly capable are contingent on the particular apparatus we have at our disposal. Kant was thinking chiefly of the apparatus supplied by our bodies for dealing with a world of material objects, but what we must now reckon with is the claim that something essentially similar pertains in the case of the symbolic "apparatus" supplied by culture and in our dealings with a world the reality of which refuses to be constrained to the level of its materiality alone. Our immediate experience is, we have seen, of a world already saturated with meanings and values, and our personal apprehension and articulation of these on a day-to-day basis is linked decisively to

[31] See George Steiner, *Real Presences: Is There Anything in What We Say?* (London: Faber & Faber, 1989), 56.

[32] Ernst H. Gombrich, *Art and Illusion: A Study in the Psychology of Pictorial Representation*, 5th ed. (London: Phaidon, 1977), 275.

[33] See O'Hear, *Element of Fire*, 23–24.

[34] O'Hear, *Element of Fire*, 19.

the symbolic tools made available to us by the language we share together with others and to prior articulations of such meanings and values by our fellow users of that same language. We can only "say" what our language will permit us to say, and this has a decided (if not wholly decisive) impact on the shape of the reality we experience. Rather than being a neutral tool at our disposal to express a wholly prelinguistic experience, therefore, to a considerable extent, Berger and Luckmann observe, our language forces us (and our experience) into its own given patterns;[35] language "speaks us" rather than vice versa. "Significance," that is to say (the ways in which things undeniably "matter" to us in one way or another), is bound up necessarily with webs and systems of "signification." It is this point, perhaps, that lies behind the postmodern rhetorical overstatement which insists that language (or "text") is all there is[36] and compels R. G. Collingwood to insist that we cannot properly be said to have had an "experience" of something at all until we have "expressed" the occurrence at least to ourselves—namely, placed it within some public scheme of meaningfulness and thereby "made sense" of it.[37] But in this case, if the shape "reality" takes for us is constructed in part by the socially mediated products of human representation (culture, language), then questions of accountability and moral responsibility attaching to our deliberate manipulation and modification of such symbols (in thought, in speech, in art) seem to arise naturally and quickly; for symbols, it would seem, have a habit of returning to reality with interest added.

Shared Subjectivity and the "Third Realm"

This is perhaps a convenient juncture at which to raise the question of the locus and status of these nonmaterial elements in the *empeiria*. The ghost of a by now largely discredited philosophical materialism still haunts modern culture, and it is not uncommon even today for claims about humanly perceived patterns of meaning and value to be diagnosed or treated without further question as mere "subjective" human constructs, duly projected onto a physical cosmos that is "in reality" morally, aesthetically, and spiritually neutral. Perhaps our own earlier talk of a "need" duly met by the provision of humanly constructed cultural forms might be supposed to tend naturally

---

[35] Berger and Luckmann, *Social Construction of Reality*, 53.

[36] Thus: "The doctrine that there is nothing outside the text is neither esoteric or difficult: it is merely that there is no knowledge, of which we can speak, which is unmediated." Kevin Hart, *The Trespass of the Sign: Deconstruction, Theology and Philosophy* (Cambridge: Cambridge University Press, 1989), 26.

[37] See, e.g., R. G. Collingwood, *The Principles of Art* (Oxford: Clarendon, 1938; repr. London: Oxford University Press, 1958), 244. Citations are from the 1958 edition.

in this direction, human beings "making up for themselves" whatever they need as they go along, as it were, and projecting it onto the surface of the cosmos in order to provide it with a friendlier face (a habitation more fit for human dwelling).[38] When it comes to the order of signs, it may well be suggested, we are at last up against that which is unequivocally and unashamedly a product of human devising and making, and thus, viewed from a larger cosmic perspective, *technikos*—"artificial" rather than "natural." Such claims (and responses to them) need to be handled carefully. After all, we have already seen that, where the qualities of the physical cosmos itself as we experience it are concerned, crude distinctions between what pertains "out there" and what only arises "in here" in, with, and under the shape and substance of our particular creaturely responses to the world are not easy to draw in any helpful manner and, if drawn at all, must probably finally be drawn very low down indeed.[39] If, therefore, as I have argued above, notwithstanding this there is no very good reason to relegate our perception of a world rich in color, sound, and smell to the category of "illusion" or the merely "subjective," then by the same token now we may reasonably challenge the attempt without further ado to relegate our apprehensions of meaning and value (as qualities undeniably shot through our immediate experience of the world) to the same qualified and provisional status, simply on the grounds that, in apprehending them, we are also involved in activities of construction and projection.

There is one very clear sense in which the world of meanings, values, and feelings is not subjective, of course, and that is in its status precisely as a "world," a public habitation structured by language. No human being ever views the world from the vantage point imaginatively aspired to by scientific description, entirely denuded of its human significances. Nor, as dwellers in the world, do we remain wholly immersed in the radically personal perspective afforded by our own "subjective" responses to it. The world as we experience it, chock full of significances, is at the very least a "shared subjectivity,"[40] a reality we indwell together with others (subject not to our own individual perceptions, judgments, desires, and goals alone but to those of a "great cloud of witnesses"[41]) and thus something very different indeed from a merely "subjective" project. Our reports concerning

---

[38] A classic instance of such "naturalism" is found in Bertrand Russell's insistence, "We are ourselves the ultimate and irrefutable arbiters of value. . . . It is we who create value." Bertrand Russell, *What I Believe* (London: Kegan Paul, Trench Trubner, 1925), 24–25.

[39] Cf. John Baillie, *The Sense of the Presence of God* (London: Oxford University Press, 1962), 49.

[40] O'Hear, *Element of Fire*, 25.

[41] Baillie, *Sense of the Presence*, 57,

such aspects of experience are, as John Baillie notes, certainly typically intended as reports of our perceptions of a shared "real world" and not of some discrete private experience or purely personal judgment.[42] Human culture, O'Hear suggests, thus constitutes a "third realm," mediating between the world of objective fact and the purely private "inner world" of the individual self and its responses. At one level it is something "collaboratively created,"[43] the identifiable product of our shared responses to the world, and thus precisely something given to or "made of" the world humanly; yet the human world itself comes to us individually and moment by moment already transformed by such responses, laden with value and meaning, "mattering" to us in ways that go far beyond the level of its mere "matter" alone.[44] Culture, as well as nature, that is to say, is in the first instance precisely an inheritance, something "given" to us by the accidents of our particular situation in time and space. Paradoxically, Berger and Luckmann suggest, it seems that man is "capable of producing a world that he then experiences as something other than a human product."[45] But is there anything more to it yet than this? Or are we bound to concede that those teeming moral, aesthetic, social, and other nonmaterial "realities" we suppose ourselves to apprehend shot through the world's fabric, which confront us in our every engagement with things and function constantly to shape and reshape our dispositions and actions, are in reality nothing more than an elaborate projection, an artificial canopy supervening wholly on humanly constructed and sustained webs of signifiers?

Culture, Construction, and Creation

These are important questions, for all the things that matter most to us in the living of life, and that we suppose to dignify and ennoble our humanity, fall by definition and without exception within this bracket. As Baillie observes, human history is littered with accounts of those who have gladly sacrificed their own lives for the sake of love, loyalty, liberty, justice, beauty, and the like, whereas few have felt it incumbent upon themselves to do so in the name of any empirically verified scientific doctrine.[46] That the apprehension and articulation of such values involves us in acts of symbolic construction and reconstruction is undeniable. "Man," Iris Murdoch notes, "is a creature who makes pictures of himself, and then comes to resemble

---

[42] Baillie, *Sense of the Presence*, 52–58.
[43] Leavis, cited in O'Hear, *Element of Fire*, 23.
[44] O'Hear, *Element of Fire*, 96.
[45] Berger and Luckmann, *Social Construction of Reality*, 78.
[46] Baillie, *Sense of the Presence*, 29.

the picture."[47] The role of various imaginative forms in guiding and inspir-
ing the best—and indeed the worst—of human behavior is well attested
and documented. And, of course, for much of what is to be found in such
imaginative visions (from Homer's *Iliad* to Homer Simpson), human beings
must themselves be willing to take both the credit and the blame as appropriate. Yet when it comes to the fundamental values embedded and elabo-
rated within them, it is quite another matter to claim that these too are the
sheer products of human imagining (albeit, no doubt, ones buried deep in
the evolutionary past and now lost to memory). In the case of the very best
and most cherished of such values (such as those mentioned above), quite
apart from the overweening hubris attaching to such a claim, it seems to be
untrue to the shape of much of our moral experience, where our intuitions
are of such values breaking in and confronting us, as it were,[48] from beyond
the sphere of any merely human capacity and incapacity and placing us
under an obligation of an unconditional and absolute sort.[49] Again—and of
course—the particular ways in which we apprehend, make sense of, articulate, and respond to such intuitions will be mediated symbolically, in terms
of the particular language at our disposal and prior uses of that language in
analogous contexts. But to acknowledge the inevitable symbolic and social
mediation of our intuitions and expressions of value and meaning is one
thing; to insist that such things originate without remainder in the order
of signs—as nothing more than the projection of human aspirations and
desires out into an empty cosmos or constructions born of the play of particular sign systems themselves, "elevated by social ideologies to a privileged
position," and ripe for the liberating act of "deconstruction"[50]—is a quite
different sort of claim, as regards both its assumptions and its implications.

Theology, of course, has its own particular reasons and grounds for
insisting that moral, aesthetic, and other noncorporeal qualities transcend
the human order of signs, belonging to the world's "primordial plenitude"
and thus having their proper origin in God's creative action rather than
our own. Might we now, nonetheless, pursue a line of thought similar to
that which occupied us at the end of the last chapter and suggest again
that while reality itself has its own proper existence apart from us and
our modes of apprehending it, the precise ways in which we apprehend
and experience it are always contingent not just upon what is there but
upon the apparatus we happen to possess for registering and perceiving it?

[47] Iris Murdoch, *Existentialists and Mystics: Writings on Philosophy and Literature* (London: Penguin, 1999), 75.
[48] On "intuition" as the relevant mode of apprehension in such circumstances, see Baillie, *Sense of the Presence*, 52–53.
[49] See, e.g., the discussion in Farmer, *World and God*, 24–25.
[50] See Terry Eagleton, *Literary Theory: An Introduction* (Oxford: Blackwell, 1983), 131.

Our concern now, of course, is not just with our bodies and their mediation of material objects but with the mediation of nonmaterial realities
by creaturely responses of language and culture. Might these responses,
too, though, now be safely factored into a story about the dynamics of
God's particular way of blessing us, of "giving" an ordered and meaningful world for our indwelling? It seems to me that some such story may and
must indeed be told if we are to be true both to the logic of a theology of
creation and to the apparent realities of our epistemic circumstance (i.e.,
the extent to which our world is indeed structured and enriched from top
to bottom by the mediations of language and other forms of signification);
but we must reckon at once with the realization that the considerations
involved here are in some ways rather different from those pertaining at
the level of our physiological and psychological responses to things.

Response-ability and Responsibility

The first thing to be noticed, of course, is that language and culture involve
us in responses to the world of a much more fully conscious and responsible
sort than attend to the neurophysiology of sensation. In some clear sense,
language itself, as well as its particular uses, arises within the world not just
as a peculiarly human phenomenon but as the direct outcome of human
acts of making. Older theology, to be sure, speculated about a prelapsarian Edenic *Ursprache*, a symbolics possessed of "direct divine etymology,"
given to Adam so that he might reenact the divine mechanism of creation.[51]
In the tradition preserved by Dante, for instance, having spoken the world
into existence, God then helpfully supplies humankind with the lexicon
and grammar in terms of which sense must subsequently be made of it,
a linguistic circumstance obtaining globally down to the building of the
Tower of Babel and surviving in some manner in the tongue of the ancient
Hebrews.[52] In its own rather different way—obviously without appeal to
any such divine inception of language and with a very different set of implications—contemporary social and linguistic theory, too, draws our attention to a fundamental "givenness" of language for any particular participant
in it, emphasizing its function as an all-embracing symbolic habitus into
which we are born (we do not choose it or make it for ourselves), and which
serves in significant measure to construct and shape not just our sense of the
world as a reality external to ourselves but (since even self-consciousness is

---

[51] See Steiner, *After Babel*, 60–61. See further James H. Stam, *Inquiries into the
Origin of Language: The Fate of a Question* (New York: Harper & Row, 1976); Graham
Ward, *Barth, Derrida and the Language of Theology* (Cambridge: Cambridge University
Press, 1995), 35–52.

[52] See Ward, *Barth, Derrida*, 35.

shot through with language) our sense of "self" too.[53] Rather than consisting in a tool box from which tools may freely be selected by a prelinguistic
self to express prelinguistic meanings, there is thus, as we have already had
occasion to notice, an important sense in which we are always already in the
hands of language rather than vice versa.

Nonetheless, there is more and other to be said than this. I have
already gestured toward a reading of Genesis 2 in which the responsibility invested in Adam by God is not as the first user of a divinely donated
dictionary (matching each signifier appropriately to its preordained signified) but as one invited to *give* a name to each creaturely form and presence, an act of *onomatothesia* in which human language itself is forged and
extended—and with it culture as a distinctly human dimension—and the
process of creation extended rather than merely reenacted.[54] Be that as it
may and notwithstanding the insights of theory concerning culture's role
as a given heritage and matrix with and within which we must each live
and work, viewed from another angle it is in any event clearly the case
that, as they arise and develop in history's midst, languages and cultures
are indeed themselves the products of human action, and our participation in them is of a deliberate (and thus responsible) as well as a tacit sort.
We do things within and with and to the order of signs, even if the things
we can choose to do are themselves constrained by that order and may in
turn escape the limits of whatever intentions we may have in acting as we
do. Our linguistic responses to the world, in other words, are subject to the
dictates of human will in a way that our bodily responses are generally not.
This is not, of course, incompatible with the suggestion that language (i.e.,
language as such, not just some putative long-lost primal tongue) is part of
God's own "giving" of a world to his human creatures. As the eighteenth-
century philosopher Hamann observes in a classic treatment of the question, within the context of a theology of creation everything is *ultimately*
of divine origin, and divine and creaturely agency ought not in any case to
be treated as alternative explanations but understood frequently as coin-
herent and concurrent.[55] Thus, language may be acknowledged as a fully
human product without compromising the claim that, precisely as such,

[53] See Eagleton, *Literary Theory*, 130.

[54] This is the reading offered in the eighteenth century, for instance, by Vico, according to whom Adam was granted both the capacity and the responsibility of naming things
poetically in accordance with their natures. See Giambattista Vico, *New Science*, trans.
David Marsh (London: Penguin, 2001), 158.

[55] See "The Last Will and Testament of the Knight of the Rose-Cross" (1772), in
Johann Georg Hamann, *Writings on Philosophy and Language*, trans. Kenneth Haynes
(Cambridge: Cambridge University Press, 2007), 96–110.

both its ultimate provenance and its continuing development and unfolding fall within the dynamics of God's creative action. Nonetheless, such acknowledgment introduces a distinctive new theme—namely, that this particular gift (the human capacity for acts of signification and culture) cannot possibly be received passively but implicates us in conditions of responsible use apart from which it may be experienced not as blessing but as something else altogether.

The picture is complicated further by the fact that, whatever may be imagined to have pertained in the instance of the Edenic vernacular, we find ourselves situated now in any case in a very different economy—one lying both east of Eden and after Babel. The order of signs as we indwell and participate in it in history's midst, we discover upon reflection, is a remarkably fragile structure, being at once indirect, unstable, and plural. Semiotic theory has often cast these features of language in an essentially negative light, identifying them as a function of human fallenness rather than human creatureliness as such and thus something (from a theological perspective) to be struggled with, overcome, and finally redeemed from, rather than something to be celebrated, enjoyed, and redeemed in promised new creation of God.[56] That there are direct and illuminating parallels to be drawn here with attitudes toward the body is no accident, since it is precisely the *materiality* of the sign (the necessary embeddedness of language itself in our embodied existence) around which much of the perceived fragility clusters. An account of the mediation (and construction) of reality as proper to the human condition rather than accidental to it, though, points us in a rather different direction. In the next chapter, we shall continue our consideration by attending to each characteristic mentioned above briefly in turn.

[56] Thus, Derrida observes, for the tradition of "metaphysics," "[t]he sign is always a sign of the Fall." Jacques Derrida, *Of grammatology*, trans. Gayatri Chakravorty Spivak (Baltimore: Johns Hopkins University Press, 1976), 283. See further Hart, *Trespass of the Sign*, 3–21.

7

Response-able

Reality and Its (Mis)representations

Indirectness—Imprisonment or Extension?

George Steiner observes that it follows logically from the appeal to a primal divine donation of language that originally all linguistic signs applied "naturally," directly, and easily to their referents, rather than arbitrarily as semiotics after Saussure typically insists.[1] Thus, "[t]he tongue of Eden was like a flawless glass; a light of total understanding streamed through it."[2] Whatever we make of this suggestion, it is apparent that our own linguistic circumstance is rather different, language, as it were, interposing itself across the board "between apprehension and truth"[3] and denying us the opportunity to step momentarily altogether outside its framework in order to judge the authenticity of its mediations, any more than we can step outside our bodies to validate theirs. At this point, of course, the parallelism between sense and sensibility holds good, each mediating reality to us in a version shaped and edited decisively by its own capacities and categories. Perpetuating the parallelism momentarily, the only total leap out of language, Steiner insists, is death (though those who hope for the resurrection of the flesh may

---

[1] George Steiner, *After Babel: Aspects of Language and Translation*, 2nd ed. (Oxford: Oxford University Press, 1992), 61. For a helpful summary of Saussure's central positions, see Terry Eagleton, *Literary Theory: An Introduction* (Oxford: Blackwell, 1983), 96–97.

[2] Steiner, *After Babel*, 61.

[3] Steiner, *After Babel*, 61.

complain that even this is to presume too much!).[4] Of course such indirectness of access may be construed in different ways. It may be judged negatively and as a problem (and thus a distinguishing feature of any symbolics
situated "after Babel"),[5] breaking our relation and preventing our immediate access to "reality," or distorting and warping such access as we have,
"trapping" or "imprisoning" us in its own systems. (Compare the familiar
post-Cartesian suggestion that we are in some sense "trapped" in our own
bodies and cannot be sure that anything exists beyond the testimony furnished by them.) But again, we have to inquire about the meaningfulness
of such talk (and again the parallelism of our sensory responses to the world
is instructive). Exactly what sort of reality would it be, we might ask, that
was not "significant" for us in one way or another in our encounter with
it? But if significance is bound up by definition with signification—that is,
with systems of meaning making—then a world bereft of the mediations of
language is just as impossible for us to imagine as one from which the constructive contributions of our bodies and brains had been entirely erased. In
either case, what would remain would not be a humanly recognizable world
at all. Viewed in this light, language is what makes human experience of the
world possible at all, enabling us to inhabit reality as a meaningful environment, to extend ourselves out into reality and "make sense" of it.

That language is itself also a product of responsible human activity certainly has serious implications for reckoning with this "covenant"
between word and world, but it does not of itself undercut or fatally compromise it. On the contrary, Colin Gunton suggests, the indirectness
of the linguistic relation (as distinct from the odd notion that language
somehow "mirrors" reality or provides a 1:1 mapping of its coordinates)
tends in itself to engender an appropriate humility in the face of reality,
respecting its mystery and otherness rather than squeezing it into the particular set of containers we happen to have available to us. Here again we
notice the flip side of the important recognition that language shapes reality; reality, for its part, returns the compliment, reshaping and "making
new" our language as we find ourselves compelled to modify it so as better

---

[4] Steiner, *After Babel*, 116. So, again, "[o]nly death is outside discourse." George
Steiner, *Real Presences: Is There Anything in What We Say?* (London: Faber & Faber,
1989), 88.

[5] So Steiner: "Babel was a second Fall, in some regards as desolate as the first."
Steiner, *After Babel*, 61. The punishment of Babel, though, was that of the fragmentation
and subsequent plurality of human language. There is no biblical suggestion that I am
aware of that an immediate relation to the world through a wholly transparent language
was ever part of "unfallen" human existence. The suggestion rather presupposes that indirectness is a problem (a function of sin) rather than a necessary part of the human condition as such.

to fit new insights, new intuitions, new thoughts. Metaphor, Gunton suggests—the most indirect of all linguistic devices—far from distancing us from reality, is thus in actual fact the most natural and fitting tool for a realist epistemology to wield, "cutting the world at its joints" to gain epistemic access, while at the same time maintaining a disposition (habitus) of openness, receptivity, and humility in the face of it, eschewing the idolatrous identification of statements with states of affairs.[6] The point is a wider epistemological one, but we can hardly fail to notice in passing that such a disposition is exactly what we might suppose fitting for creatures in a world received consciously as a gift from God's hand.

Instability, Excess, and Gratuity

As well as being indirect in their relation to reality, signs are also an inherently unstable medium of engagement with it. Far from being fixed and secure, their meanings are slippery, difficult to pin down precisely, and prone to constant change. Language, Steiner avers, is in reality "the most salient model of Heraclitean flux."[7] If, as linguistic theory after Saussure insists, meaning is not mysteriously immanent within signs (the particular material markers inscribed on paper or uttered aloud have no necessary connection with what they are taken to signify) but largely a matter of cultural and historical convention (quite different signifiers may and do evoke the selfsame "signified"— "horse," *cheval*, *Pferd*, *equus*, ἵππος, and so forth), then the meanings of signs are in significant measure a function of their distinction from and particular relation to all other signs within the synchronic system. (Saussure appeals to the analogy of the "meaning" a piece on the chessboard has at a particular point in a game, something determined wholly by its relation to other pieces on the board as identified within the given rules of the game.) Thus the meaning of "horse" is bound up with the fact that it is not "house" or "morse." But the concentric circles of differentiation involved here spread out in principle to the thresholds of the system itself, each sign in turn defining itself in terms of its difference from those aurally or graphically proximate to it, the buck of meaning never quite stopping or settling anywhere, being "the spin-off of a potentially endless play of signifiers."[8] And, if we turn to a dictionary

---

[6] See Colin Gunton, *The Actuality of Atonement: A Study of Metaphor, Rationality and the Christian Tradition* (Edinburgh: T&T Clark, 1988), 27–52. The image of "cutting the world at its joints" (among other things in Gunton's account) is borrowed helpfully from Richard Boyd, "Metaphor and Theory Change: What Is 'Metaphor' a Metaphor For?" in *Metaphor and Thought*, ed. Andrew Ortony (Cambridge: Cambridge University Press, 1993).

[7] Steiner, *After Babel*, 18.

[8] Eagleton, *Literary Theory*, 127.

in order to help us define the meaning of a particular word within a given language, what we are confronted with are more words of the same sort, words, that is to say, that themselves come laden with questions about their own (potentially diverse) meanings. We can look these up in the dictionary too, of course, but, absent our capacity to step outside language as a medium, the process is a potentially endless one.[9] At this point we might naturally suppose speech to have the advantage over writing, appealing to the speakers to clarify precisely what they mean by their words; but this is to overlook the fact that thought itself is already mediated to consciousness by language, and all the complicating elements of the materiality and ambiguity of the sign (its difference from that which it ostensibly represents) are thus already present in the speaker's "inner" formulation of utterance. Meaning, it seems, is never fully present, never "pure" or "immediate," but always incarnate in the flesh of language and hence necessarily "deferred," unarrestable in principle, flickering ever further down the corridors of signification whenever we seek to put our finger on it, no matter how far we choose to pursue it.

Diachronically, too, meaning refuses to stand still for observation and classification. Here, too, meaning is a function of "difference," of the permeation of "presence" by that which is absent from or other than the sign itself and as such.[10] Language is a temporal process (the meaning of words is always "in a state of being constituted,"[11] constantly unfolding rather than something fixed in amber), the sense of every word in a sentence, and each sentence in a paragraph or a conversation, being held in suspense, deferred, to be modified by what is yet to come.[12] "For the words to compose some relatively coherent meaning at all," Terry Eagleton suggests, "each one of them must, so to speak, contain the trace of the ones which have gone before, and hold itself open to the trace of those which are coming after."[13] Furthermore, it belongs to the nature of signs as such that they must be capable of repetition. In order to function as signs at all, they cannot be the linguistic equivalent of the "single-pad" codes employed by military cryptographers (the point of which is precisely to resist decipherment in absolute terms).[14] Yet this very capacity for "iterability" and empirical resituation, combined with the sign's material difference from that of

[9] See Jonathan Culler, *On Deconstruction: Theory and Criticism after Structuralism* (London: Routledge & Kegan Paul, 1983), 95.

[10] Culler, *On Deconstruction*, 94–95.

[11] Kevin Hart, *The Trespass of the Sign: Deconstruction, Theology and Philosophy* (Cambridge: Cambridge University Press, 1989), 26.

[12] Eagleton, *Literary Theory*, 128.

[13] Eagleton, *Literary Theory*, 128.

[14] Cf. Steiner, *After Babel*, 54.

which it is a sign, renders it intrinsically vulnerable to an uncontrollable shifting and slippage in its meaning.[15] Each fresh use of a word or a phrase in language is haunted by the history of its previous uses, so that in the strict sense the same words can never mean exactly the same thing twice.[16] But the precise context of inscription or utterance modifies the sense of signs in other ways too, Steiner observes, each contingent circumstance invoking a distinctive set of associations, both public and private in nature (we speak "at the surface" of ourselves, he observes, beneath which lies a wealth of subconscious associations "so extensive and intricate that they probably equal the sum and uniqueness of our status as an individual person").[17] In this sense, no particular context of utterance or writing, hearing or reading, can completely circumscribe or "totalize" the meaning of signs; by virtue of their nature as signs, they are always open to change (susceptible to what "befalls" them, as Derrida puts it),[18] and a surplus or "remainder" of potential meaning thus haunts their every use.

For all these reasons, language is a medium shot through with levels of "undecidability" or "alterity," making it an unstable and in some ways a risky rather than a secure environment in which to dwell. And the "hermeneutic motion"[19] of interpretation, therefore, is as vital to our indwelling of the world as the systole and diastole of cardiac function or the rhythm of inhalation and exhalation in respiration. The latter, of course, are themselves signs of organic health rather than pathological, and, although the instability of signs may bring its obvious problems and challenges (we may wish it were otherwise), it, too, might be viewed as a natural feature of what it means to be human in the world and cast in a positive rather than a negative light. In other words, the absence of any pure congruence between the material sign and that which it signifies (and the consequent need for us constantly to interpret and explore possibilities of alternative meaning), rather than being construed as a distinctly postlapsarian circumstance, might instead be understood as part of what it means to be embodied beings in a world which refuses reduction to materiality alone—part of the "predicament of being human" as David Jones has it. As Kevin Hart notes, this is really Derrida's fundamental point: "full presence" (a meaning unmediated by signs and hence determinable in an absolute manner) is neither a prelapsarian ideal nor an eschatological hope but an illusory

---

[15] See Hart, *Trespass of the Sign*, 12.
[16] Steiner, *After Babel*, 18, 24.
[17] Steiner, *After Babel*, 181.
[18] See Hart, *Trespass of the Sign*, 19.
[19] See Steiner, *After Babel*, chap. 5.

goal.[20] Presence is always elusive, but this is not a matter of the failure of signs to do their work (of signs in a "fallen" economy) but rather a structural feature built into language as such by virtue of its materiality. On this view, we should no more bewail the constraints attendant upon our indwelling of systems of signs (and hope for their eventual removal) than we should bewail those arising from our circumstance as embodied beings situated at particular points in time and space. The parallels are precise and more than accidental, and those who espouse a theology centered on the incarnation have good reason at least to applaud the challenge Derrida presents to the residual Platonism of some accounts of our relationship to language (many of which would apparently prefer to strip it of its "flesh" altogether in pursuit of an immediate engagement with a preexistent *logos asarkos*, a move challengeable on christological grounds alone).

In any case, we must not overstate the negative aspects of the circumstance. The simple fact of our ability to communicate meaning more or less effectively across and within languages in a plethora of everyday life contexts bears witness to the fact that, for the most part, we have more than sufficient determinacy to work with.[21] Again, though, the fact that meaning is ultimately (but only ultimately) unfathomable and frequently less determinate than we should like demands of us not just the hard work involved in acts of interpretation but a sense of respect, mystery, and humility in the face of reality, rather than the arrogant assumption that, with a set of state-of-the-art precision linguistic tools at our disposal, we can capture it and pin it down definitively for inspection and analysis. And, what from one angle appears as instability, of course, may, from another be construed instead as potential richness, flexibility, and adaptability, the protean capacity of language to accommodate itself to a reality that is itself constantly on the move, permitting words, texts, and utterances to speak to ever new contexts, rather than remaining shackled to one precise circumstance of use, again holding out the promise of an as yet unborn surplus of meaning to be had in a world still brimming with unrealized possibility.[22] Again, such richness, depth, and mystery attendant upon things is precisely what we might expect, perhaps, in a world received as a

[20] Hart, *Trespass of the Sign*, 14.

[21] As Eagleton notes, it is *absolute* grounds for our habitual uses of words that Derrida and his followers are concerned to deconstruct, not determinate meaning of any sort and at any level. Eagleton, *Literary Theory*, 144, 148. Clearly, in practice the levels and sorts of certainty necessitated by and available in different existential circumstances are in any case very varied.

[22] Cf. Steiner, *Real Presences*, 42. See further Trevor A. Hart, *Faith Thinking: The Dynamics of Christian Theology* (London: SPCK, 1995), 141–422.

gift from God's hand, and not "givenness" of a precise, literal, and wooden sort, a world patient in the final analysis of only one "reading."

Plurality and Pentecostal Flame

Here we can and must be ruthlessly brief. We live on an ever more over-crowded planet and in an increasingly "globalized" world, yet as a race we speak a remarkable number of different languages, many of them mutually incomprehensible apart from acts of skilled and careful translation. Compared to what is to all intents and purposes a universally shared anatomy and neurophysiology across the species, the development of our "language-skin"[23] across the millennia has resulted in a prodigal plurality of tongues which, Steiner observes, can hardly be supposed an obvious evolutionary advantage.[24] Even within common languages, mutations and adaptations arise, resulting in subcultures and tribal "lingo" often every bit as remote from the vernacular as the technically "foreign" tongue, and thus further dividing us from one another. For different languages, while not wholly incommensurable (translation between language groups happens), nonetheless map the contours of the world to some extent differently, each affording a distinctive outlook, a unique edition, or "tasting," of its reality. According to the Babel myth, such linguistic fragmentation arose from a gracious act of divine judgment, placing limits on human hubris and its destructive potential. The challenges and difficulties consequent upon this second fall are clear enough. Quite apart from the practical difficulties of ordinary communication, the inability to understand one another at a level much deeper than that tackled by the provision of linguistic equivalents alone so easily breeds suspicion, fear, and contempt. Yet the vision of Pentecost, we should recall, is not one of linguistic otherness finally erased but of the redemption of otherness, a baptism of fire in which mutual understanding and enrichment are to be had in and through, and not despite, linguistic difference. The idealistic project of Esperanto may have failed because it overlooked this fact. And, experience testifies, different ways of "speaking" reality can indeed modify, qualify, and complement one another, and our everyday acts of translation (in which, as Humboldt reminds us, "[a]ll understanding is at the same time a misunderstanding, all agreement in thought and feeling is also a parting of the ways")[25] often result in the enlargement and enhancement of our being. "Each language," Steiner reminds us, "speaks the world in its own ways. Each edifies worlds and counter-worlds in its own

---

[23] Steiner, *After Babel,* 52.
[24] Steiner, *After Babel,* 58.
[25] Quoted in Steiner, *After Babel,* 181.

mode. The polyglot is a freer man."[26] Nevertheless, such symbolic give and take means that the tribes of humankind indwell what are in many respects rather different "given" worlds and must learn responsibly to navigate and negotiate the practical and political adjustments entailed in inhabiting and exploring together a shared reality.

Archimedes or Bust?

Such admitted plurality of perspectives thus drives us back again to the question we posed earlier. The fact that the sphere of human meanings, values, and feelings—embedded and entangled as these inevitably are in deliberate acts and outputs of human signification—is a sphere in which the human "construction" of reality is prominently to the fore might itself suffice to explain the diversity of symbolic "takes" on the world arising in different human communities and groups. If language is the symbolic "skin of consciousness" which, analogously to our actual skin, puts us in touch with, mediates, and grants order to whatever reality stands over against us, then the evolution of incommensurate cultural mechanisms of response (whatever explanation be proffered for this ostensibly odd fact) is bound to result in very different experiences of reality itself. But is there any reason to suppose that, rather than being differing responses to a shared reality that transcends them (and thus, in principle at least, accountable in the face of it for their various representations), different linguistic systems are not themselves the ultimate source of value and meaning, and the human world just irredeemably fragmented into a series of different projections, a cacophony of signals in which none therefore has any greater claim (no matter how humbly and generously advocated) to perspectives on the "truth" than any other?

As I have already indicated, it seems to me that much in our experience suggests otherwise than this and, as Steiner observes, "everything in our speech habits protests against" it.[27] Of course, there is no Archimedean point from which to refute the claim, and positivist models of meaning certainly will not serve us well by way of a response. If, that is to say, "meaning" or "presence" be supposed to mean something certain, indisputable, grounded either in immediacy of access to or in the direct mirroring of reality, then there is indeed no such thing to be had. But why should anyone ever have supposed that there was? Absolute certainty and absolute despair of finding any sort of certainty at all are, of course, a natural pair, the one typically spawning the other; but they are not the only alternatives, and neither matches the apparent realities of our circumstance in the world very well.

[26] Steiner, *After Babel*, 56–57.
[27] Steiner, *Real Presences*, 97.

Steiner speaks of our epistemic disposition as involving instead a necessary "wager on transcendence"—that is, a leap of faith which, in the absence of any demonstrable proof that it is so, nonetheless trusts that there is meaning and value out there beyond our various humanly constructed versions to be engaged with and finds itself rewarded by the gracious yielding of reality to our advances, giving itself to be known in ever new and unexpected ways, transforming and enlarging our experience and reordering the very same linguistic, visual, and other codes through whose mediations alone, paradoxically, we are able to apprehend it in the first place. Language, Macmurray observes, serves naturally as a conservative force, stabilizing and fossilizing "the analysis of the world which has already been produced by thought," and thus furnishing an orderly world for our habitation.[28] Yet there are occasions, and thankfully plenty of them, when imagination runs ahead of experience and anticipates hitherto unforeseen possibilities of meaning[29] or when apprehension outruns comprehension so far that the poverty of established patterns of language becomes painfully apparent,[30] and we discover that we know more than we can say. In such circumstances, wherever they arise, we find ourselves compelled deliberately to adjust and recalibrate our symbols better to fit the shape of a world that, as it were, intrudes into, interrupts, and imposes itself upon the accounts we currently have to give of it.

Without collapsing into overblown nonsense about language mirroring reality, our sense in such situations is nonetheless of a better "fit" between the two having been accomplished, rather than the indulgence of a merely playful reorganization of the symbolic furniture (what Coleridge, as we shall see, refers to as "fancy"). Human cultures, Lotman and Uspensky remind us, have a history, and they do so precisely because they are bound constantly to absorb and encode new information about a world that, to be sure, remains tantalizingly forever beyond the limits and configurations of our language but nonetheless unfolds and unveils itself in our presence and in and through our continually renewed efforts to speak it more fully into presence.[31] Thus, notwithstanding the needful critical cautioning about meaning never being fully present in the sign and being unavailable to us at all, indeed, apart from the intrinsically unstable constructions of language, it seems appropriate nonetheless, as Steiner

---

[28] John Macmurray, *Interpreting the Universe* (London: Faber, 1935), 47.

[29] See Macmurray, *Interpreting the Universe*, 43.

[30] See Susanne K. Langer, *Philosophy in a New Key: A Study in the Symbolism of Reason, Rite, and Art*, 3rd ed. (Cambridge, Mass.: Harvard University Press, 1956), 149.

[31] Yu. M. Lotman and B. A. Uspensky, "On the Semiotic Mechanism of Culture," *New Literary History* 9, no. 2 (1978): 226.

suggests, to predicate (or postulate?) the "presence" of "a realness, of a 'substantiation' . . . within language and form."[32] Artists—among those whose reconfigurations of the symbolic order are most constant, deliberate, and striking—frequently testify to a sense of something coming from beyond the threshold of their own supple imaginings on the one hand and social conventions of representation on the other, to place them under obligation. What makes a good metaphor a good metaphor (as distinct from the arbitrary redistribution of signifiers from their familiar contexts), we tend to suppose, is precisely its capacity to "cut reality at the joints" for us, opening up new perspectives on and new ways of experiencing the world. Here, again, we are bound to notice that there is both give and take involved on both sides of the putative relationship. We adapt our language in order better to fit the world we apprehend, yet it is precisely via playful and exploratory reconfigurations of our language that new apprehensions of reality most typically arise—good metaphors, whether they arise in the sphere of poetry or cutting-edge science, "are new mappings of the world, they reorganize our habitation in reality."[33]

In this territory of imaginative venturing beyond the given, therefore, Mark Johnson observes, recognition and construction, apprehension and projection, are clearly not the logical opposites of popular report but in fact are found frequently to stand and fall together, heuristic and creative ventures alike being contingent on our ability to configure and constantly reconfigure the world into novel symbolic orderings that yet "make sense"[34] to us precisely because we take them to be related not arbitrarily but in some positive manner to the world we already know—that is, constrained rather than wholly unconstrained by "external circumstances."[35] We ought not to miss the marvel here, Macmurray observes, namely, "that we can ever manipulate images, combining them and recombining them in novel ways, and find that the pattern we have constructed does result, in spite of the play of imagination which has produced it, in a complex symbol which can sometimes be directly referred to reality."[36] And it is precisely in this return from the level of symbol alone ("thought") to the practical demands of living and acting amidst a symbol-enriched

[32] Steiner, *Real Presences*, 4.

[33] Steiner, *After Babel*, 23.

[34] Mark Johnson, *The Body in the Mind: The Bodily Basis of Meaning, Imagination and Reason* (Chicago: University of Chicago Press, 1987), 158. Johnson is here expounding Kant's account of the role of imagination in reflective judgment, but the claim is one he endorses and develops further in his own work.

[35] Cf. George Lakoff and Mark Johnson, *Metaphors We Live By*, 2nd ed. (Chicago: University of Chicago Press, 2003), 228.

[36] Macmurray, *Interpreting the Universe*, 67.

immediate experience, he suggests, that the verification of our symbolic adjustments takes place; new thoughts, new ways of speaking, new possibilities charted, either enable us better to act and more successfully to navigate the territory of experienced reality or not. Of those that do, of course, we cannot say that their purchase on reality is absolute, certain, or guaranteed. But, Macmurray insists, "[a] rational belief is not a belief which is known to be certainly true. It is simply a conclusion which it is reasonable to believe. And it is reasonable to believe a conclusion when the evidence in its favour is greater than the evidence in favour of any other suggested alternative. It is this that verification through action achieves."[37] Eagleton makes a related point: language, he observes, may well be ultimately undecidable if we consider it contemplatively, in abstraction from its actual uses in life; but it becomes altogether more decidable (not absolutely but sufficiently so) when the contexts of its use are restored.[38] Again, in the interplay of sign and world, the traffic is not all in one direction; each has a shaping impact on the other.

The world of meanings as a whole, Lakoff and Johnson suggest, is never cut and dried but always necessarily the product of our human interactions with and successful functioning within given physical and cultural/personal environments.[39] We "construct coherences" using the tools and skills proper to our physically embodied and culturally embedded natures,[40] but—to reiterate our conclusion—it certainly does not follow immediately from this that they are mere constructs of human imagining or mere projections of human subjectivity. As Charles Taylor observes, some such things might well in theory—exactly like their sensory counterparts—be viewed as "projections" belonging precisely to certain involuntary ways in which, as human beings, we cannot help responding to and experiencing the world[41] and thus, as I have suggested, part of the world "given" to us by God together with (and not apart from) our creaturely being itself. Others may arise identifiably from more complex, prolonged, and responsible engagements with things the particular cultural genesis of

[37] Macmurray, *Interpreting the Universe*, 78.

[38] Eagleton, *Literary Theory*, 147. To this extent, Steiner's talk of a "wager" might also mislead, since in the moment of day-to-day action and decision, we are hardly ever conscious of having to wager anything. We "trust," but even this is for the most part something we need to have pointed out to us. The wager, like the radical indeterminacy to which it responds, belongs in large measure to the rarefied atmosphere of the contemplative and "academic" mode of reckoning with such matters, important though these may be.

[39] Lakoff and Johnson, *Metaphors We Live By*, 194, 229–31.

[40] Johnson, *Body in the Mind*, 137.

[41] Charles Taylor, *Sources of the Self: The Making of Modern Identity* (Cambridge: Cambridge University Press, 1989), 53–54.

which can be traced but nonetheless be held to have roots securely sunk
in the soil of "reality," rather than—as the ephemeral products of a purely
human fabrication—only loosely attached to its surface. Others again
(think, for example, of the complex semantic structures of the Inland Rev-
enue or the internationally acknowledged rules governing games such as
soccer, cricket, and rugby) may no doubt safely be acknowledged as being
of purely human provenance, a means by which we choose to order our
world and to live in it. That all meaning and value is of this latter sort,
though, is, all things considered, a very unlikely scenario indeed, albeit
one we cannot entirely dismiss by means of some convenient demonstration. To do that, we should have to step outside the "skin" of language
itself, a feat accomplishable only by death (and, arguably, not even then)
or by otherwise ceasing to be the symbolically endowed and symbolically
dependent human beings that we in fact are.

Misrepresentation—Ethos, Error, and Evil

It is via our participation in the order of signs far more fully and directly
than in our navigation of the material world (though the two cannot, of
course, finally be disentangled) that our hearts and minds are engaged and
our fundamental dispositions in the world thereby shaped and reshaped.
The socially generated and socially generative matrix of language furnishes
an ethos, a habitation or environment that "makes possible and sustains
moral living, establishing the direction and parameters of human conduct,"
providing the cement that binds society itself together.[42] Taylor refers us to
the importance in this connection of various "frameworks" or "imaginaries," as he calls them (metaphysical, cosmic, social), imaginative visions of
how things stand finally with human beings in the world, stories that we are
told and in turn tell ourselves about ourselves and about what it is good to
be and become and what really matters in life which (though we may well
remain largely unaware of them much of the time and may never actually
articulate them) function to situate and orient ourselves within the world
and within society, making sense of our lives, as it were, on the grand and
the medium scale, yet filtering down in ways that have a precise, profound,
and identifiable impact upon our moment-to-moment ways of living.[43]

As we have already had reason to notice, though, such structures
are not empirically given, as the material structures and qualities of the

[42] William P. Brown, *The Ethos of the Cosmos: The Genesis of Moral Imagination in the
Bible* (Grand Rapids: Eerdmans, 1999), 11.

[43] See, e.g., Taylor, *Sources of the Self*, 3–49; Charles Taylor, *Modern Social Imaginaries* (Durham, N.C.: Duke University Press, 2004), 23–30; Charles Taylor, *A Secular Age*
(Cambridge, Mass.: Harvard University Press, 2007), 164–76, 322–51, 361–69.

cosmos mediated by our bodies in some sense clearly are. Here, much more fully and obviously, we are called upon to build, to construct, to "make something of" the world, interpreting, evaluating, and responding to what confronts us in experience. Here, as Iris Murdoch puts it, we have to work, and work hard, "at the meeting point where we deal with a world which is other than ourselves."[44] If, nonetheless, as I have argued above, our struggles to "bring the world to language," as it were, are indeed constrained by and accountable to "a reality which is beyond us"[45] (and finally beyond language), rather than a sheer projection outward and upward of a playful plurality of humanly generated expectations, aspirations, and desires, then we are at once in territory where we must face questions not just about the sort of "truthfulness" that may reasonably be said to belong to whatever together we make of the world but about the impact of our misrepresentations and misconstructions of it too, whether accidental or deliberate. The order or network of signs, Murdoch suggests, is "the border wherein the interests and passions which unite us to the world are progressively woven into illusion or reality."[46] An ethos or cosmic or social imaginary woven in substantial measure or constructed at key (weight-bearing) points from the materials of illusion, we may reasonably suppose, is bound to be one judged sooner or later (and hopefully sooner rather than later) unfit for human habitation, though in the meanwhile it may cause significant difficulties and damage, disposing and fitting us ill rather than well for the realities of our circumstance in the world.

Oddly, it is our very capacity for symbolic transformation and expression that sets human beings up for a fall. By comparison with other animals, Susanne Langer notices, we suffer from language and have no sooner acquired its rudiments than we begin to misinterpret the world by reason of it.[47] Hallucinations, superstitions, misconceptions, and irrational beliefs are all possible only because we have the capacity to represent (and so to misrepresent) the world as it presents itself to us. As we have already observed, language also has a subversive capacity. We can manipulate its signs, deliberately reconfiguring the patterns apprehended in experience and so liberating ourselves in thought from the constraints of a given actuality. This may sometimes modify our understanding and experience of present actuality itself (if the new configuration commends itself as "making better sense" of things than the dominant paradigm). Or

---

[44] Iris Murdoch, *Metaphysics as a Guide to Morals* (London: Vintage, 2003), 215.

[45] Murdoch, *Metaphysics*, 214.

[46] Murdoch, *Metaphysics*, 214–15.

[47] Langer, *Philosophy in a New Key*, 35. Langer draws here on Stuart Chase, *The Tyranny of Words* (London: Methuen, 1938), 46–56.

our concern may be instead to explore how things might be quite different than they currently are, thought running ahead of actuality in pursuit
of solutions to today's seemingly insurmountable problems or glimpsing
exciting new possibilities the conditions for which themselves lie as yet
hidden from empirical view. Again, though, the possibility of error dogs
the heels of every such act, and the "heuristic fictions"[48] we successfully
construct will inevitably be accompanied by many misapprehensions and
illusory expectations.

Much more disconcerting than our capacity for error in navigating
the interfaces between symbol and reality, perhaps, is our capacity to
construct or engineer falsehoods, deliberate misrepresentations of reality
designed to serve the interests of those who generate and sustain them. Let
us differentiate at once between "falsehoods" in this sense and "fictions."
Both are counterfactual modes, but fictions (whether in the arts or those
continual ventures into the subjunctive and conditional moods that bind
artistic imagining so closely to every human act of discovery and invention) typically announce themselves as such, posing the question "What
if . . . ?" and asking us, for the time being or the sake of argument, to
suppose that it is thus.[49] Falsehoods, meanwhile, are deliberately dupli-
citous, soliciting not the temporary suspension of disbelief but wholehearted
commitment to the artificial account of things they lay before us. The
simple lie may be the smallest unit of such symbolic dissimulation known
to us, and its destructive capacity is familiar enough. The ideologies and
"mind-washing" propaganda associated with various tyrannical regimes
in modern times afford an obvious example on the larger scale. Today,
we must reckon too with falsehoods perpetrated on a scale even more
widespread than this, embedded subtly but securely in our own social and
cultural institutions and enjoying unrivaled (precisely because unnoticed)
ease of access to our lives through the very media by which we typically
seek to extend ourselves out into the world and take stock of it.

Already half a century ago, Daniel Boorstin was testifying to the
flooding of North American experience with illusions and "pseudo-events"
courtesy of the regnant print and electronic media, especially those concerned with news and the new growth industry of advertising.[50] A "thicket

[48] Paul Ricoeur, *The Rule of Metaphor: Multidisciplinary Studies of the Creation of
Meaning in Language*, trans. R. Czerny and others (Toronto: Toronto University Press,
1977), 239.

[49] See George Steiner, *Grammars of Creation* (London: Faber & Faber, 2001), 5. Cf.
Macmurray, *Interpreting the Universe*, 56.

[50] Daniel Boorstin, *The Image: A Guide to Pseudo-events in America* (New York: Vintage, 1992). The work was originally published in 1961.

of unreality," Boorstin suggested, now interposed itself between viewers and readers and the actual realities of life, a host of vivid, carefully manufactured, and airbrushed "images"—by comparison with which reality itself seemed a pale and uninteresting substitute—telling people what sort of reality to expect and persuading them what sort it was they wanted, shaping their attitudes, their desires, and thereby their actions (especially those involving their wallet). More recently the colorful and often hyperbolic writing of Jean Baudrillard has traced the further evolution of this same phenomenon. In truth, we no longer exist in an age of representation at all, Baudrillard argues, but in one of "simulation" in which the sign or image either masks absence or "is its own pure simulacrum."[51] So complete and so successful has been the saturation of daily experience by deliberately manufactured and "artificial" images of this sort, he suggests, that they (and the technologies by which they are produced and mediated) have long since soaked into the fabric of reality itself, ruthlessly colonizing both our "inner and outer spaces"[52] and thus becoming a familiar and indispensable part of the ways in which habitually we construct and experience the world. Rather than such images obscuring or "denaturing" reality (or "misrepresenting" it), therefore, our subliminal exposure to them is so complete that they are now in effect simply part of the texture of the "reality" that we all indwell, unable to see things any differently. Sociological analysis of this phenomenon may, as Walter Wink has suggested, furnish the theologian with useful categories in terms of which to make sense of biblical imagery concerning "principalities and powers," an objective legion of destructive, dehumanizing, and evil forces abroad in the postlapsarian world that hold us securely in their thrall and cause us to dance to their tune, unable in large measure any longer even to turn and glimpse the good, let alone to do it.[53] In the age of the simulacrum, Baudrillard writes, "[i]llusion is no longer possible, because the real is no longer possible."[54]

Discernment—Language, Sin, and Responsible Action

This, of course, is a counsel of despair if we take it too seriously, since it leaves us, as Baudrillard himself appears willing (if not altogether happy)

---

[51] Jean Baudrillard, *Simulacra and Simulation*, trans. Sheila Faria Glaser (Ann Arbor: University of Michigan Press, 1994), 6.

[52] Richard Kearney, *The Wake of Imagination: Toward a Postmodern Culture* (London: Routledge, 1988), 380.

[53] Cf., e.g., Walter Wink, *Engaging the Powers: Discernment and Resistance in a World of Domination* (Minneapolis: Augsburg Fortress, 1992).

[54] Baudrillard, *Simulacra and Simulation*, 19.

to admit, unable to discern at all when we are being duped and thus wholly unable to resist the mechanisms of pernicious social control lying behind the regime of the simulacrum. Like the biblical imagery of our enslavement to objective powers, pressed too far and unqualified by other considerations,[55] the account threatens to rob us wholly of any meaningful sense of responsibility for our dispositions in the world and, together with that, our dignity as human beings. Again, it is one thing to insist that since reality, insofar as it is humanly significant, is by definition always mediated and structured by language, the sort of hard and fast distinction between reality and representation (or misrepresentation) to which Boorstin occasionally appeals will not hold. But, again, hard and fast distinctions are not the only sort worth drawing here, and it is another matter altogether to suggest that the slide into an undiscriminating and ethically paralyzed and irresponsible relativism is the inevitable outcome of all this.

For reasons already rehearsed above, I see no reason to suppose the "undecidability" of significance to be absolute, let alone deadly. As Richard Kearney suggests, postmodern deconstruction may actually perform a valuable ground-clearing exercise, robbing us of the illusion of absolute certainties in our dealings with the world (whether grounded in premodern or modern models of knowing) and thus encouraging a more respectful disposition to the mystery and otherness of things.[56] But if, in the name of its insistence that nothing can be known for sure, it effectively abdicates in the face of any responsibility to choose between different accounts of things and the courses of action most naturally associated with them, then it becomes a dangerous enervating influence, turning its adherents into hapless (albeit not wholly unwitting) victims, incapable of mounting any strategies of resistance to the system whatever. But "epistemological undecidability," Kearney argues, "does not necessitate ethical undecidability" and must not be permitted either to encourage or to excuse it.[57] Otherwise, respect for the other collapses in practice into sentimentality or indifference, and the very basis of human culture and human life itself is put at stake. Specifically, it is human "others" in particular—those persons whose being as such we cannot "prove" beyond doubt but who nonetheless confront and address us in, with, and under the various mediations of sense and sensibility—who place us under an ethical demand, and

[55] The Bible typically juxtaposes such language to other accounts of our status, for instance, as those held accountable by law or within the dynamics of personal relationships. Recognition that in some sense we are "bound" to sin in no way lessens the force of these other images that bespeak responsibility and accountability for our actions.

[56] Kearney, *Wake of Imagination*, 387.

[57] Kearney, *Wake of Imagination*, 388.

concern for whose well-being compels us not to prevaricate endlessly but, even when "rock solid" epistemological grounds cannot be provided for doing so, to respond, to choose, and then to act in one way rather than another.[58] Again, in the moment of action we have sufficient to work with and must work with whatever we have, taking a stand and resisting what we discern (rightly or wrongly) to be false and dehumanizing visions and versions of things. The fact that we do not always do the good that we would do, therefore, but find ourselves inexorably drawn by compulsions identifiable in both "inner" and "outer" space in the direction of the evil that we would not do (see Rom 7:15-19) thus leaves us in some clear sense without legitimate excuse, and we ought not to turn to semiotic theories of linguistic indeterminacy in search of one! Without invoking a now untenable model of truth and its representation, it seems to be incumbent upon us nonetheless to continue to speak of "truth" and forms of faithful and unfaithful witness to it, precisely in order to articulate the reasons for the particular morally significant judgments we make and the actions we undertake (or fail to).

In this same connection, we can usefully revisit Taylor's account of the imaginative frameworks that grant us our standpoints within "moral space," perspectives generated, acquired, sustained, extended, and modified, he reminds us, within particular "webs of interlocution"[59]—culturally constituted, plural, and providing us at best with "contestable answers to inescapable questions."[60] Such frameworks are not, of course, mostly the product of deliberate attempts to dissemble or deceive (though the ideologies of some totalitarian regimes might be judged to fall into this category); nor are they "fictions," at least in the sense outlined above; but they are nonetheless imaginative visions, indirect in their purchase on reality and, as noted, de facto if not de jure, plural in their representations of it. Questions about the relevance and possibility of acts of discernment therefore properly arise. Taylor strongly resists any suggestion that pluralism here collapses naturally into relativism. On the contrary, such frameworks, he argues, provide the means by which we extend ourselves out into the world as other, seeking the "Best Account" of the meaningfulness of human existence available, exercising discernment, and being willing to adjust or modify our position as we proceed.[61] Here again, therefore, the heuristic and the creative belong together; we construct (and reconstruct) as we discover and discover as we construct, finding "the sense of life through

[58] Kearney, *Wake of Imagination*, 362, 388.
[59] Taylor, *Sources of the Self*, 36.
[60] Taylor, *Sources of the Self*, 41.
[61] Taylor, *Sources of the Self*, 71–75.

articulating it."[62] The postmodern model of imaginative "play," therefore, Kearney reminds us, is not wholly pernicious; for a form of "play" is precisely what any attempt to see beyond and to subvert given patterns of permission and possibility entails—reconfiguring things at the level of the symbolic, trying out different patterns for size, and in the process perhaps grasping one that holds out genuine new resources of meaning and spurs us into new forms of sociopolitical action. In the immediate moment of personal ethical response, too, Kearney notes, it is precisely a playful and creative imagination that sees beyond the limits of the self and its desire, apprehending (precisely through an act that is at once one of construction) the other in his or her otherness than the self and making possible our ventures (never absolutely assured) in the direction of appropriate, as distinct from an inappropriate, response.[63]

We are inhabitants of language and cannot long survive as human beings outside its environments. But we are not the sheer passive products or servants of language. We take from it (and a good deal in our encounter with reality is given to us by our language) to be sure; but precisely from within language we also give back to it, use it, and modify it in our turn, not arbitrarily or for the sake of mere "playfulness" alone but responsibly and in accordance with the contours of reality itself as we apprehend these opening up and unfolding before us. Thus, Paul Ricoeur notes, some ways of symbolizing the world, of "representing" it in language and image, seem undeniably to be more "fortunate" than others, to exude an "air of rightness" which drives us to what is as much an aesthetic as it is a moral or an intellectual judgment in their favor. "Does not the fittingness, the appropriateness of certain verbal and non-verbal predicates" in this sense, he asks, "indicate that language not only has organized reality in a different way, but also made manifest a way of being of things . . . ? It would seem that the enigma of metaphorical discourse"—and other modes of our linguistic redescription of the world—"is that it 'invents' in both senses of the word: what it creates, it discovers; and what it finds, it invents."[64] We cannot be absolutely certain, of course. Yet it is upon this same dialectic motion of imaginative response to the world, the systole and diastole of symbolic give and take "along an 'interface' of which we have no adequate formal model,"[65] that our most fully human engagements with things (and

[62] Taylor, *Sources of the Self*, 18.

[63] Kearney, *Wake of Imagination*, 370. See also Trevor Hart, *Between the Image and the Word: Theological Engagements with Imagination, Language and Literature* (Farnham, U.K.: Ashgate, 2013), 97–117.

[64] Ricoeur, *Rule of Metaphor*, 239.

[65] Steiner, *After Babel*, 19.

our strategies of resistance to the inhuman and dehumanizing) are compelled at the last to rely. The world is not handed to us on a plate. We are called to make something of it, to help it to be and, we might now add, to become what it is capable of becoming.

God and the Order of Signs

In this chapter I have sought for the most part to keep explicitly theological considerations in the wings, though, as we have seen, they crop up in one way or another quite directly even in "secular" discourses relevant to the subject. In closing, it seems appropriate now to reckon further with just a couple of those more germane to what we have been discussing. Both have to do with the relationship God might be supposed to have with language.

First, by now it is likely that some readers will be responding to all this talk of linguistic indeterminacy and its peculiar challenges by asking whether religious claims concerning a subsequent authoritative revelation do not effectively short-circuit some of those same challenges, pointing us to a place where God, as it were, serves as the transcendent giver and guarantor of some copper-bottomed, crystal clear meanings, on and around which others may duly be based and built. The suggestion is an important one, but by inviting reflection on the ways in which, according to Christian theology at least, God has actually given himself to be known, it points us finally, I would suggest, in a rather different direction.

According to the testimony of Christian faith, God has placed himself variously not just within the world and its history but thereby also within the order of signs,[66] tabernacling, as it were, within the "flesh" of the semiotic economy itself—in inspired Scripture, in the symbolics of sacraments and preaching, and supremely and definitively by clothing himself with our nature and dwelling among us as the man Jesus Christ. Such appropriation of our "language," we may suppose, endorses sign making as part of what it means to be fully human, commandeers it as a normative means of our meaningful communion with God himself, and perhaps in some sense "redeems" language in the process (a suggestion demanding some careful dissection, to which we shall return in our final chapter). This divine assumption and appropriation of language, though, is precisely a kenotic accommodation to the human condition (including its linguistic condition), and not a "transcendental" abrogation or overriding of it. By nature of the case, therefore, it cannot and does not involve any sheer "givenness" or donation of absolute and unchallengeable meaning. The humanity of Christ is and remains always "other" than God, or

---

[66] Cf. David Jones, *Epoch and Artist* (London: Faber & Faber, 1959), 179.

"not-God" as Karl Barth puts it;[67] in and of itself, it has no necessary or proper reference to that which, here, it signifies. Precisely here, therefore, at the point where faith certainly apprehends the glory of God himself, Godhead is and remains nonetheless paradoxically "veiled in flesh," as Charles Wesley's lyric reminds us. There is no direct, unmediated encounter with the naked "presence" of God facilitated by this sign. Instead, we are called to attend unceasingly to the "flesh" of the sign itself, to the presentation of Jesus' humanity, borne witness to and made sense of within that wider dynamic web or matrix of signs that is Christian Scripture and tradition. Indeed, it would be supremely ironic if, here of all places, the flesh of the sign ceased either to mean more than, as flesh alone, it means or else to fade into insignificance, becoming the wholly transparent conduit to a pure (fleshless) "transcendental signified."[68] In christological terms the former would amount to semiotic psilanthropism, the latter to semiotic docetism. That this is not how things stand in God's dealings with us—that the divine Word himself, in taking flesh and entering the order of signs, subjects himself to "the vicissitudes of all signs"—seems to me to be part and parcel of the church's historic insistence upon the abiding integrity of Christ's humanity (in all its fleshy particularity and contingency) within the revelatory dynamics of the hypostatic union itself.

Precisely because God takes this way of dealing with his human creatures (accommodating himself to the order of signs, the way of mediated communion rather than some putative immediate union), our access to him is always indirect and solicits from us meaningful response rather than urging passive receptivity in the face of an irresistible download directly "from above." Here, too, in other words, we are compelled to "make sense" of what presents itself to us. Thus, while we ought not to underplay the extent to which faith does indeed begin with a divine initiative of communication originating beyond the web of human language

[67] See Karl Barth, *The Göttingen Dogmatics: Instruction in Christian Religion* (Edinburgh: T&T Clark, 1991), 1:136.

[68] "Transcendental signified" is Derrida's term for a putative point outside the system of language and hence existing (and known) in a manner free from the constraints and vicissitudes of language as a medium. Kevin Hart suggests that, for Derrida, "since Christ is God, what He signifies is signified in and of itself," and thus Christ (as God) is a transcendental signified in this sense. See Hart, *Trespass of the Sign*, 8. My suggestion is that, on the contrary, the logic of incarnation as understood in the classic doctrine of hypostatic union can be taken to prohibit any such conclusion, the relationship between Christ's "deity" and his humanity being paradigmatic of the wider semiotic economy rather than rupturing or abrogating it. For related (and more substantial) discussions, see further Graham Ward, *Barth, Derrida and the Language of Theology* (Cambridge: Cambridge University Press, 1995), 31–41, 235–51.

itself and involves sorts and levels of "certainty" and clarity wholly comparable with those pertaining in other day-to-day practical epistemic circumstances, we must nonetheless reckon with the fact that it is equally a response to signs that prove upon closer inspection to be rich and multivalent rather than shallow and "literal," which subsist within wider webs of signs upon which their meaning depends, and which demand constant revisiting and rereading. We revisit and reread precisely in the expectation that new possibilities of meaning await to be discovered in (or sense to be "made" of) them as yet and that new and surprising (and sometimes uncomfortable) "words" will indeed be heard issuing from their time- and culture-conditioned forms, addressing the contingencies of each new human circumstance. In the dynamics of a revelation of this sort, the give and take of the order of signs is upheld rather than abrogated, and any easy appeal to the availability of an absolute (because divinely revealed) meaning is displaced by acknowledgment of a Word who transforms the world finally always from within, and only by first submitting to its conditions.

My second point takes us back to our discussion of creation and to God's fashioning of the world as an orderly and meaning-full cosmos rather than a swirling chaos upon which order has yet to be imposed. Significance, we have seen, is bound up inextricably with the forms and processes of signification—that is to say, with some "language." In this sense, therefore, the meanings that we apprehend in the world are certainly always ones constructed and mediated in terms of human language itself. We have also spoken, though, of the interpenetration of acts of linguistic construction and ones of discovery or discernment, about the importance of holding on to talk of truth and falsehood, and of continuing to make judgments about more and less adequate linguistic standpoints on the world. Meaning, therefore, I have argued, need not (and theologically cannot) be supposed to be a pure epiphenomenon supervening upon the structures of human language alone. In some sense it "comes to" our languages as something other from beyond, interrupting it and compelling us to modify our speech, "fitting" its meaning better to the world's own. But what meaning can the world itself possess if meaning as such is necessarily a linguistic construct, a product of some response to things mediated by the forms of some language? Who, apart from human beings themselves, has "language" to generate and sustain such significances?

Here, it seems to me, theology has an answer to proffer that is unlikely, perhaps, to commend itself more widely (or even across all theological versions of things) but at least affords one way of resolving the seeming conundrum attendant upon our experience. Language, theology holds, is not limited to human beings but has its uncreated counterpart in God's own life as the one who has and is his own Word and who, according to the biblical narration of creation, speaks the cosmos itself into existence. This powerful metaphor already entails the suggestion that the world as it comes to us as gift from God's hand is neither mute nor inarticulate but shot through with a plenitude of meaning and pregnant with possibilities of further meaning to come. God's world, that is to say, has significance for God—is brimming, as it were, with divine Logos. This, though, is a tongue none of us speak, and the creaturely forms constructed by it are ones that, as dwellers in this world, we must therefore learn, as it were, to make sense of in terms of the constructions permitted by parlance more familiar to us.

Hamann pictures the Edenic circumstance as follows: "All that [Adam] heard at the beginning, saw with his eyes, looked upon, and his hands handled was a living word; for God was the word. With this word in his mouth and in his heart the origin of human language was as natural, as close and easy, as a child's game."[69] Notice that Hamann does not suggest that God's own language is the language Adam himself actually speaks. If God's uncreated otherness means anything, this would be impossible. Instead, Adam forges his own, distinctly human language, placing new poetic constructions upon the world that respond to and resonate with rather than contradict the significances God himself has invested in it and finds in it. Thus in some sense the phenomena of nature already have meaning (for God), but from Adam's creaturely standpoint they also require to be given meaning, to be named and made sense of. In the prelapsarian world, Hamann suggests, this task of constructive response was both a joyful and playful one, and also a responsible one, for "human nature is from the beginning until the end of days as like unto the kingdom of heaven as leaven, with whose smallness every woman can make ferment three measures of meal."[70] The human creature, therefore, is no passive recipient or passenger in this newly created cosmos but one whose presence and action alone suffices to "leaven" its human significance, to "make sense" and thus "make more" of it than, humanly speaking, it will otherwise be and become, discovering and unfolding (for meaning does not happen all at once, and not all potential meaning will be realized) the primordial plenitude of potential meaning that God himself has granted it in his creative utterance. Without such activity of responsible meaning making, apart from the introduction of human language as such, the world would remain "unleavened" from the human standpoint, relatively mute and inarticulate, despite the fact that (like complex utterance in a

[69] Johann Georg Hamann, *Writings on Philosophy and Language*, trans. Kenneth Haynes (Cambridge: Cambridge University Press, 2007), 108–9.

[70] Hamann, *Writings on Philosophy*, 109.

tongue we cannot speak and thus fail to comprehend) it has an abundance of meaning for God himself.

Strictly speaking, therefore, the world we indwell is never actually the world exactly as God himself constructs and experiences it, but then, of course, theology has never supposed that it was. That is just one of the things setting God decisively apart as the world's uncreated creator from any of his creatures, whose experience is always shaped and limited by the contingencies and potentialities of their own given forms, both bodily and cultural. In any case, as we have already noted, even among human tongues themselves, different linguistic standpoints often render available quite different constructions, qualities, and possibilities of experience in this world. As in the case of exchange between human tongues, too, something is invariably lost in translation in our intuitions and attempted renderings of the divine speaking of the world, and some versions prove to be altogether more apt, more illuminating and "fitting," than others. Some renderings, meanwhile, are wholly and perhaps wantonly misleading, deliberately contradicting or misrepresenting rather than following the lead or elaborating upon the intuited trajectories of divinely inscribed significance and substituting for them others of purely human provenance. To rely on such, or to be disposed toward the world in terms of them, is inevitably to be ill disposed, ill fitted, and ill equipped for flourishing in the world's midst, being at odds, as it were, with its stock of God-given possible significances. To seek to be faithful in the dialectic of give and take, construction and discovery, which translation and interpretation everywhere involves, and thus to forge an ethos (or culture) that resonates with rather than contradicts or frustrates those infinite possibilities of fruitful significance God himself has spoken into the world at its birth is, we may suppose, the responsibility and privilege that God lays on his human creatures. Like Adam in the garden, we are called—playfully but responsibly—to share in the discernment and bestowal of significance in God's world and so, in fellowship with God himself, to enjoy its potential fruits.

We ended chapter 5 with the claim that the constructive role played by our human physical and psychic processes of perception might legitimately be factored into any account we wish to give in theological terms of the world as an orderly cosmos coming to us as a blessing from God's hand. At this point we may and must now go further and suggest that something essentially similar holds true as regards the contributions of human language and culture to the "construction" of reality. The shape and meaning that the world has for us is undoubtedly contingent in large measure upon the particular ways in which we "speak" it. Since, as we have seen, nature and culture cannot be entirely disentangled in our reckoning with them, this is true to a certain extent even of our ways of experiencing the material world, though it seems that there is much here that is shared to a high level across the species by virtue of the bodily processes we share in common. (There is probably little culturally specific about the experience of a raging toothache.) Where the "third realm" of human meanings, values, and "ethos" is concerned, though, we are faced with much higher levels of creaturely responsibility for the constructions we place on things and consequently much greater diversity and plurality apparent in the "realities" we variously indwell. Such diversity can be enriching, of course, and understood as part of the teeming prodigality of meaning and ever-fresh perspectives available to us as creatures in God's world. Yet not every perspective need or can be held to be equally valuable or equally valid, and in the preceding I have suggested grounds for supposing that, notwithstanding our embeddedness within language (from the webs of which we can no more be successfully extricated than we can from our bodies), damaging misrepresentations of the world are things we are quite capable of identifying and rectifying as well as capable of perpetrating. To suppose that the origin and development of human languages is not only a fully human phenomenon but also "divine" (in the sense that God intends and enables us to be creatures of precisely this sort, for whom the world holds more, the more—through acts of continual redescription and reinterpretation—we make of it together) is thus certainly to suppose that God's "giving" of a world is for us an act of costly rather than "cheap" grace. Again, though, the circumstance is one that we cannot fully appreciate without reckoning with the fact (and the implications of the fact) that, in the fullness of time, God himself becomes a speaker not only of his own eternal Logos but of human language too, with all its capacities for semantic shortfall and excess, truthful witness and duplicity, creativity and destructiveness. The claim that the gift to human creatures of language (i.e., the capacity for forging and speaking it as distinct from the donation of a divinely fixed *Ursprache*) might reasonably be considered a mixed blessing needs thus to be weighed finally in the light of what happens with the second form of divine utterance (that issuing from the side of the creature and not the first alone). For now, this is a suggestion we must leave hanging, to be returned to at a later point. But it permits us, perhaps, to close this part of our discussion by suggesting again that to be a creature embedded in language—with all its possibilities, its constraints, and its dangers—is part and parcel of what it means to be fully human and the linguistic "construction" of reality part, therefore, of God's own "giving" of the world to us, to see what we may make of it.

8

Art, Mimesis, and Transformation

In the previous three chapters, we have been concerned in particular to consider the dialectic of give and take involved in our circumstance as inhabitants of an orderly and meaningful world. What we have seen is that at every level of our existence as human creatures (from the preconscious material processes of body and brain to the most fully conscious and voluntary engagements with meaning and value that we are capable of) there is indeed both give and take to be reckoned with, and the line between a world existing "out there" apart from us and ourselves as dwellers in a world that we take to be shot through from first to last with human significance is a very difficult one to draw precisely. O'Hear sums up the circumstance helpfully: "We do live in a world that is not of our own making," he writes, "but in our lives and in our theorizing we are constrained by our human perspective. We have also built up worlds of culture and of meaning, through which the implications of human perspectives on the world are explored and developed in various directions and within which we live out our lives as creatures of passion, flesh and blood."[1] We are, it seems, securely embedded in the world, complicit in the various structures and processes both of nature and of culture, and whatever "givenness" presents itself to us for consideration, therefore, is one into which our own embodied and imaginative responses of one sort or another must already be factored. The "human world" (the world as we experience it humanly), in other words, is precisely

[1] Anthony O'Hear, *The Element of Fire: Science, Art and the Human World* (London: Routledge, 1988), 162.

one that has and could have no meaningful existence apart from our own distinctly human perspectives on and responses to it. If this is in some identifiable sense indeed a "constraint" (the desire to transcend all possible human vantage points and see things "as they really are" is perhaps ineradicable from creatures to whom curiosity comes so naturally and plays such an important part in their development and achievement), from a theological vantage point we must nonetheless insist that it is more fundamentally still a blessing, a function of our being situated in creation as the particular sorts of creatures we are, capable of experiencing the world in a given range of ways including those in which we do in fact find ourselves experiencing it. Furthermore, these same constraints furnish the given context and limits within which we are in our turn called to free, responsible, and reciprocal acts of "cultivation," making more of the world through our various constructive engagements with it than we initially receive, fathoming just some of its primordial plenitude of possibility, and so further enriching its significance as a human habitation.

In this chapter I want to direct our attention specifically to the place that human artistry might be supposed to have amidst all this. Acts of intentional "making" and "cultivation" of one sort or another can readily be traced across the entire spectrum of human action in the world, of course, and my warrant for concentrating on art in particular lies in a conviction that it constitutes a paradigmatic case rather than just one more instance of the phenomenon. In art, as in language, agriculture, trade, technology, politics, religion—all the varied manifestations of human "culture" in the widest sense—we have to do both with the symbolic transformation of experience and with the transformation of elements in the material environment attendant or consequent upon that. Art is one way, but more than just one way, in which human beings negotiate the fragile interface between matter and meaning, the interface along which significance is variously traced, grasped, and fashioned. Artistry, as Nicholas Wolterstorff helpfully reminds us, has in any case traditionally been understood and practiced as part of the warp and weft of the fabric of human life as a whole, despite modernity's myopic tendency to treat it as something to be set apart in splendid isolation. The products of the arts—paintings, poems, plays, carvings, musical compositions, dance, and all the rest—have historically found their proper place and purpose not in the hushed silence of galleries, museums, and auditoriums but as instruments and objects of a wide variety of human actions in the busy flow of life itself—praising, remembering, communicating, celebrating, interpreting, accompanying, entertaining, lamenting, invoking—the means, in fact, whereby we carry out a whole range of our intentions "with respect to the world, our fellows, ourselves, and our gods."[2] So, artistry has been (and, of course, in large measure remains) a pervasive rather than a rarefied and specialized feature of human culture. This point is clearer and sharper still if we permit ourselves to forget for a moment the immediate associations that talk about "the arts" typically has in modern Western societies and remind ourselves of the more expansive classical and medieval understanding of *ars* as a term referring to forms of human productivity in general, whether in what we would nowadays identify as works of "art" or in wider manifestations of craftsmanship, technique, and cultivation.[3] Lamenting the loss of this expansive and integrative vision of human "art" (and its implications for understanding our distinctive place as human beings in the world), David Jones traces the essence of *ars* in certain qualities of action (intransitivity, gratuity, and signification) contingent upon human freedom and capable of manifestation across "the whole field of human making."[4] In a related vein, but more expansively still, Wendell Berry prefers to define art as "all the ways by which humans make the things they need," which means, he adds pointedly, that "everybody is an artist—either good or bad, responsible or irresponsible."[5] Everything that we do in, to, and with the world that is our home, Berry maintains, *has significance* for ourselves, for others, for the world itself; we *make something* of it, even if what we make turns out to be a mess. All action, then, is a form of *poesis*.

Turning back from this wider canvas to consider "the arts" through the more familiar lenses furnished by what Wolterstorff calls modernity's Institution of High Art,[6] O'Hear suggests that one thing that artists have always done and continue to do in their work is to explore the human world (the avenues of actual and possible human experience and response to the world) self-consciously from within.[7] In an important sense, he notes, all human culture consists in just such an imaginative exploration, charting the appearances of things from our perspectives as embodied consciousnesses and then expressing our findings for others to examine. Art, though, does so in a more deliberate and obvious manner. Rather than eschewing or seeking to eliminate the "distortions" of the way the world

[2] Nicholas Wolterstorff, *Art in Action: Toward a Christian Aesthetic* (Carlisle, U.K.: Solway, 1997), 3.

[3] See E. N. Tigerstedt, "The Poet as Creator: Origins of a Metaphor," *Comparative Literature Studies*, no. 5 (1968): 474.

[4] David Jones, *Epoch and Artist* (London: Faber & Faber, 1959), 153.

[5] Wendell Berry, *The Art of the Commonplace: The Agrarian Essays of Wendell Berry* (Berkeley, Calif.: Counterpoint, 2002), 315, 316.

[6] Wolterstorff, *Art in Action*, 21–23.

[7] See O'Hear, *Element of Fire*, esp. 74–93.

looks and tastes and feels to us as its human inhabitants, as science does in its own imaginative bid for a "decentered" account of things, therefore, the artist adopts an unashamedly anthropocentric standpoint, concerned precisely to explore, capture, give expression to, and thus develop our ways of experiencing and evaluating the world as it presents itself to us for consideration.[8] What the artist offers, therefore, is always a vision of some way of experiencing things as already endowed with human value and significance, presenting us "with ways in which those aspects of the world might be experienced."[9] In this sense, art is always informed by the perspectives of human "subjectivity," and human responses to the world constitute both its proper point of departure and its intended point of return. But we must not mistakenly suppose that this renders it inevitably "subjective," as though art were simply a pouring out of the artist's own inner world onto canvas or paper or whatever sensory medium. On the contrary, art is central to and paradigmatic of that "third realm" to which we alluded in chapter 6; what it offers is offered publicly and in terms of some recognized "language" (visual, tactile, kinetic, aural, or whatever sort) and it is mostly subjective only in the sense that, like every other meaningful human encounter with things, it offers or evokes or suggests an account of things already transformed by the conditions and possibilities of some recognizable human perspective or other (not necessarily the artist's own). Thus, while in one sense every work of art is necessarily a projection of "egocentric attitude,"[10] in reality it is so only in a manner more self-conscious and sustained than our manifold daily engagements with things, through which we experience reality by placing some "construction" or other upon it. Reality, as we have already seen, can be disclosed to us only in and through some possible human concern or viewpoint (empirical or imaginative), and in its deliberate depictions, enactments, or evocations of the quality of our relatedness and responses to the world, therefore, art either brings us face to face with the ways in which things affect us or matter to us humanly or fails to do so;[11] its "truthfulness" (its "objectivity" in a perfectly proper sense),[12] therefore, can and should be evaluated by its capacity to render faithfully the familiar qualities of the world as experienced humanly or to open up for us new possibilities of experience that yet "make sense." It does so in its own distinctive modes, but its basic form, manipulating matter in order to

---

[8] O'Hear, *Element of Fire*, 89.

[9] O'Hear, *Element of Fire*, 108.

[10] O'Hear, *Element of Fire*, 22.

[11] O'Hear, *Element of Fire*, 89.

[12] See Trevor Hart, *Faith Thinking: The Dynamics of Christian Theology* (London: SPCK, 1995), chap. 3.

express and articulate a vision of the world rooted in human custom and sentiment,[13] is one that it shares with human culture across the board. It is, arguably, the basic form of all truly human action, straddling the boundary between the material and the nonmaterial, holding them together, and navigating the territories of each in terms that bear the trace of our citizenship and movement in the other.

Whether we think in terms of *ars* as a wider category, inclusive of a whole range of human activities of production and cultivation or concentrate our attention on those practices and products that we more typically identify among "the arts" nowadays, my suggestion, therefore, is that no absolute hard and fast distinction should be drawn between the two (we might visualize the relationship between them as the occupancy of different points on an inclined plane on which all distinctly human engagements with things may be situated) and that each serves properly as a (more or less explicit) paradigm of the give and take that is everywhere and always characteristic of our human engagements with things. In chapter 5 I suggested that the question of how the artist's "work" is situated relative to the "givenness" of the world we indwell is a question never far from that artist's mind and often prominently situated in the foreground of artistic consideration. For the sake of convenience, I want to turn next to consider the idea that the artist's primary goal and responsibility is most helpfully understood in terms of some form of faithful reproduction or representation of the given "text" of the world and what exactly might be involved in the processes of "mimesis" where it is attempted.

Complicating Mimesis

All artistry must begin in some sense with whatever is placed at its disposal by the world in which it finds itself. The question is, what should art do with what is given to it in this manner (by way of materials, models, and so forth)? How should it situate its products vis-à-vis the given world? In his 1953 monograph *The Mirror and the Lamp*, M. H. Abrams traced the influence of two underlying metaphors on a seismic shift in thinking about this question.[14] The tremors of the shift could already be felt in the Renaissance, Abrams claimed, but it erupted most impressively with the romantic movement and its heirs in modernism. More recently, Richard Kearney has suggested that the advent of postmodern aesthetics demands a supplement to Abrams' scheme, both the mirror and the lamp now having in effect been

[13] O'Hear, *Element of Fire*, 146.
[14] M. H. Abrams, *The Mirror and the Lamp: Romantic Theory and the Critical Tradition* (Oxford: Oxford University Press, 1953).

displaced by a "labyrinth of mirrors" in which the distinction between art
and world itself is understood as problematic, making the question of the
relation between them difficult to ask, let alone to answer in any meaningful way.[15] Like most schemes, this one has its usefulness in drawing our
attention to some broad shifts; but like all schemes, if pressed too hard or
too far, it is capable of obscuring rather than illuminating the realities of
a circumstance. In what follows we shall see good reason for shifting our
angle of approach slightly and so tracing some closer connections between
the putative stages of development.

In this chapter we shall concentrate in particular on the first of the
three images, that which encourages us to think of the artist holding up
a mirror to the world and capturing the likeness of some feature of it,
presenting it in a recognizable form that duly generates pleasure or grants
satisfaction on the part of the beholder. What we shall find, though, is that
for the most part, where it has arisen or dominated across the centuries of
reflection on our topic, the ideal of mimesis or faithful representation of
reality has only rarely involved the pursuit of some notional duplication
or precise "mirroring" of the empirical world. Of course, there have been
repeated attempts to trompe l'oeil ever since the days of Zeuxis of Heraclea
(fl. c. 465–397 B.C.), who reputedly painted grapes so realistic, so firm
and juicy looking, that the birds flew up and tried to pilfer them from
the painted surface.[16] And, in broader terms, the quest to depict the likeness of objects extended in three spatial dimensions in the terms afforded
by just two was without doubt central to the development of painting in
the Western tradition, a development which, as is well known, under-
went a quantum leap with the rediscovery of the laws governing visual
perspective in the early Renaissance. But this observation serves to make
an important point. Where visual art is concerned, as Ernst Gombrich
demonstrates, there can be no simple or straightforward transcription of
empirical reality onto its flat surfaces, and even where optimum verisimilitude and illusionism has been entertained as the ideal, therefore, the
process of securing it actually involves complex processes of translation
and encoding, designed precisely to fool the eye into supposing that it
sees things that, in actual fact, are not being presented to it at all.[17] Even
here, then, mimesis entails something much more complicated than the

---

[15] Richard Kearney, *The Wake of Imagination: Toward a Postmodern Culture* (London:
Routledge, 1988), 253.

[16] The account is found in Pliny, *Natural History: Books 33–35*, trans. H. Rackham
(Cambridge, Mass.: Harvard University Press, 1952), 308–11.

[17] See Ernst H. Gombrich, *Art and Illusion: A Study in the Psychology of Pictorial
Representation*, 5th ed. (London: Phaidon, 1977), passim.

image of "holding up a mirror" to the world suggests, and it results in a visual encounter to which the beholder must bring his or her own share if it is to succeed at all. Ironically, artists who fail to recognize the principle at work here—supplying too much detail or seeking to be too "faithful" in visual terms by leaving too little work for the imagination to do— end up rendering relatively lifeless facsimiles which neither look nor feel very much like the reality in question. Since, as we have seen, our experience of reality itself always solicits from us some active contribution to the shape and substance reality takes for us, the artistic overdetermination of things is bound finally to fail in its efforts to ring true, giving too much (rather than, as we might naturally suppose, too little) ever to be convincing. In practice, though, few versions of artistic mimesis across the centuries in any case have understood the representation of reality as concerned primarily with conjuring up an accurate duplication of its empirical manifestations. Most have realized that, in art as in actuality, a faithful engagement with things demands not a largely passive secretarial reportage but a transformation that "makes something of" the world even in the process of bearing witness to it.

Classical Accounts

Theorists from Aristotle to Girard have insisted that the mimetic impulse is one that comes naturally to human beings and lies at the root of all human learning and culture in one way or another.[18] As Girard notes, though, mimesis is not one consistent relation or function but manifests itself in various different modalities in human life. Thus, not all mimesis has to do with *representation*,[19] and, even within the category of representation itself, different strands, layers, or modes may properly be discerned and disentangled. The mimetic impulse, Aristotle suggests, is linked to the epistemic drive to understand, and the pleasure or delight we take from a picture or a dramatic performance has in large measure to do with the arousal of our power of *recognition*, thus being contingent on our familiarity with the thing being represented or "imitated."[20] While Aristotle refers to the need for "the most accurate possible images" in order to secure such pleasure, though, David Ross reminds us that it is of "objects which in themselves cause distress when we see them"[21] in everyday life that Aristotle speaks, so that mimesis,

[18] See René Girard, *Things Hidden since the Foundation of the World* (Standford, Calif.: Stanford University Press, 1987), 7–8; Aristotle, *Poetics*, trans. Malcolm Heath (London: Penguin, 1996), 6.

[19] Girard, *Things Hidden*, 8.

[20] Aristotle, *Poetics*, 7.

[21] Aristotle, *Poetics*, 6.

for Aristotle, cannot possibly mean the simple duplication of objects or episodes arising in the midst of life but rather always involves their deliberate transformation and *re-presentation* in terms of the forms proper to some "poetic" art.[22] Thus, for instance, what the poetic arts imitate is not sensible objects but "characters, emotions and actions,"[23] the poet's concern being to lay bare the necessary connections among these in the fabric of human existence, connections all too often obscured in real life by the indeterminacy of "a thousand casual interventions."[24] In Aristotle's own more familiar terms, "the function of the poet is not to say what *has* happened but to say the kind of thing that *would* happen"[25] in the event of a certain kind of person finding herself facing a particular set of circumstances. Clearly, there is a sense in which this is an attempt to depict the reality of human life in the world; but equally clearly it is something quite different from the sheer replication of empirical experience, which is altogether more fragmented, fluid, and formless than we often care to notice. The poet does in a more sustained, deliberate, and complete manner what each of us is called constantly to do in the hurly-burly of living itself—namely, to edit, interpret, and thus make some sense of what we do and suffer in the world. What the poet offers to us for consideration, therefore, is a vision earthed solidly in the stuff of "real life" but one the mimetic pretensions of which go far beyond the mere replication of particular phenomena. Life here is transformed into something more orderly and meaningful than "raw realism" could ever permit.

Aristotle's account of mimesis is thus rather different from that seemingly supposed by his teacher and mentor Plato. Plato has several reasons for being cautious about the place of the arts in society, and each of them is linked to the notion of artistic mimesis and its implications. As Murdoch reminds us, there is a wider theological context for this, and we ought not to lose sight of it.[26] Thus, in the *Timaeus*, Plato pictures the creation of the world itself as a venture of artistic mimesis, something that sets his theological vision apart decisively from the sort of organic cosmogonies that mostly preceded it in Greece[27] and might at some level be thought to sanctify artistry as a practice. Plato's creator Demiurge is precisely a craftsman who, working with the limited materials at his disposal,

[22] David Ross, *Aristotle* (London: Methuen, 1964), 280.

[23] Ross, *Aristotle*, 278.

[24] Ross, *Aristotle*, 279.

[25] Aristotle, *Poetics*, 16 (emphasis in original).

[26] See "The Fire and the Sun: Why Plato Banished the Artists," in Iris Murdoch, *Existentialists and Mystics: Writings on Philosophy and Literature* (London: Penguin, 1999), 429–30.

[27] So Desmond Lee, in Plato, *Timaeus and Critias*, trans. Desmond Lee (London: Penguin, 1971), 8.

fashions the material cosmos in accordance with a blueprint provided by the eternal Forms or Ideas. Unlike the world summoned into being by the biblical Creator, in this instance the resultant *kosmos aisthetos* is necessarily imperfect, "a changing sensible copy of an unchanging intelligible original."[28] Inasmuch as human artistry duly participates in this very same bind (the original refuses to be reproduced fully and precisely in another medium, and the material in any case resists the artist's conceptions and powers), it too, we may suppose, must be judged a failure. But what the artist "copies," Plato insists in his classic discussion of the matter in book 10 of *The Republic*,[29] are precisely objects and states of affairs arising in the *kosmos aisthetos* itself, phenomena that are themselves, we recall, already pale shadows of their eternal exemplars, so that even the most skilled and accomplished acts of human mimesis are, as it were, necessarily at least two stages removed from reality.[30] As R. G. Collingwood points out, on Plato's account this need not yet condemn the artist's product as such as something obnoxious or worthless, so long as we are not confused about its standing.[31] It is deficient only if we judge it in accordance with standards pertaining to the pursuit of truth, but properly speaking we should not. It is artifice and, strictly speaking, pretends to nothing more. Thus Collingwood comments, "The object of art neither is real nor appears to be real: . . . the aesthetic experience neither is nor believes itself to be knowledge."[32] The standards by which we judge art, therefore, should, in theory, be purely aesthetic ones. For as long as we keep all this clearly in mind, art's representations are harmless enough. Our minds, Plato suggests, must be inoculated against the commission of such category errors, and it is to this task that he attends, though he is ambiguous about the likelihood of successful immunization. In practice, he supposes, by

---

[28] Murdoch, *Existentialists and Mystics*, 429.

[29] See Plato, *The Republic*, trans. Desmond Lee (London: Penguin, 1974), 421–39.

[30] We should note that Plato distinguishes in this context, for instance, between the artisan who (like the Demiurge of the *Timaeus*) fashions a bed or a chair by attending to ("having his eye on") the relevant Form (so that what the artisan produces is only a copy of "what a bed really is") and the painter who aspires only to produce a representation of the empirical bed under the mode of painting. It is the latter that is "at third remove" from reality. See Plato, *Republic*, 423. Cf. R G. Collingwood, "Plato's Philosophy of Art," *Mind: A Quarterly Review of Philosophy and Psychology* 34 (1925): 157. Plato could not yet imagine the further complication attaching the work of art in an age of mechanical reproduction.

[31] To this extent, he suggests, what Plato offers might properly be understood as a positive theory of art and not a mere attack on it. See Collingwood, "Plato's Philosophy of Art," 154.

[32] Collingwood, "Plato's Philosophy of Art," 161.

directing us continually toward and immersing us more fully in the world of material particulars, art's counterfeits make the soul's ascent to a vision of the truth more difficult to achieve rather than more straightforward. Since, as Murdoch observes, Plato's epistemology is finally also a form of soteriology, concerned with the adjustment of the human soul to the reality of things, unimpeded vision of the real is bound up with moral and spiritual as well as intellectual rectitude, and Plato's concerns about the dangers of mimetic art are themselves appropriately described as "fundamentally religious" ones.[33]

While Plato's account of the nature of artistic mimesis is thus rather more measured and nuanced than is sometimes supposed, his objections to it do nonetheless presume a basic concern on the artist's part to do little more than "hold up a mirror to" aspects of our empirical experience.[34] This empirical ideal was, as Abrams notes, supplemented with and challenged by others from very early on in the Greek tradition itself, so that what art was held properly to "imitate" was not the raw substance of our sensory encounters with things, but rather selected aspects, qualities, or forms, "veridical elements in the constitution of the universe which are of higher worth than gross and unselected reality itself."[35] We have seen something of how this plays out in the poetics of Aristotle where, through the careful re-presentation of patterns discerned in and through the world of concrete particulars, "universals" proper to the drama of human existence are disclosed for consideration. In all this, though, Aristotle is still concerned with faithfulness to "nature" and the external world of objects and events that we indwell. A rather different, "transcendental" impulse is to be found in the thought of another of Plato's heirs, one that was to leave its stamp identifiably on the rebirth of classical ideals in the early modern era and which rendered the artist's role as the faithful "copyist" of a given reality intrinsically ambiguous. In the *Enneads*, Plotinus disagrees directly with his intellectual forebear and insists that the arts "give no bare reproduction of the thing seen, but go back to the Ideas from which Nature itself derives and . . . add where nature is lacking."[36] This, Plotinus suggests, is why art so often departs identifiably from actuality and why its depictions are frequently to be preferred to their empirical counterparts. Having the same immediate access to the Forms possessed by Plato's Demiurge and having the same materials to work with, the artist on occasion at least renders the original more fully and perfectly than

---

[33] Murdoch, *Existentialists and Mystics*, 443.

[34] The image of mirroring is quite explicit in 596d–e. See Plato, *Republic*, 423.

[35] Abrams, *Mirror and the Lamp*, 35.

[36] Plotinus, *Enneads* 5.8.1; cited in Abrams, *Mirror and the Lamp*, 42.

nature herself. Here, then, the category of mimesis effectively encompasses the act of artistic fashioning itself, which directly replicates (and in some sense even outstrips) the dynamics of God's own shaping of the cosmos, and works from the selfsame blueprint. Furthermore, since in terms of the mythological constructs of Platonism, the Ideas may properly be said to exist "in" the human mind just as meaningfully as they are pictured subsisting in their own ideal space (or the Mind of God, or wherever), the artist must turn inward to find what he seeks just as surely as he is called to look to something "external" to himself (his biological eyes at this point can show him nothing and are best kept closed lest they detract from the ideal vision).[37] At a single stroke, this Neoplatonist version of things shifts the center of gravity decisively—art is still to be measured by its correspondence to something other than itself rather than attended to in its own right, but it is no longer the external world of nature as it actually exists and is experienced to which we should turn in search of a yardstick; instead, art's faithfulness is to an ideal world, untarnished by the messy contingencies of actual existence and existing in a notoriously difficult to identify "space" that straddles and apparently softens both the distinction between objective and subjective and, it seems, that between God and the human soul. Here, the image of art as a faithful mimesis "inventing" the forms of a given world and that of the artist as a figure possessing genuinely "godlike" creative qualities and capacities are held together and, within the relevant paradoxes and ambiguities proper to Greek idealism, permitted to cross-fertilize rather than simply contradicting one another. The deity in question, of course, was not yet the God of Israel whose utter incomparability and otherness from the world and its human inhabitants in many ways provides the cantus firmus around which the biblical doctrine of creation is composed. The rediscovery or "rebirth" of such ideas in a distinctly Christian religious context would in due course place a rather different construction on the issues, raising the relevant theological stakes and giving the questions of the proper relationship between "imitation" and "invention" and the artist's place as a "creator" rather than a mere copyist a new sense of urgency.

The Rebirth of Mimesis

In her magisterial treatment of the subject, Agnes Heller observes that it is a favorite commonplace of studies of the Renaissance to point to humanity as its overriding intellectual concern, whereas, she suggests, one might just

---

[37] Cf. Abrams, *Mirror and the Lamp*, 43.

as readily argue the case for a concentration on nature.[38] In practice we are not dealing here with an either/or, Heller maintains, since it is the question of *our relationship to nature* that presents itself in one guise or another at the dawn of modernity, inviting answers that both reach back self-consciously to classical visions and forge radical new departures. Prominent in the texture of those answers, there was, to be sure, a new emphasis on human conquest and mastery of the natural world and a corresponding rediscovery of the ancient classical conviction that, mutatis mutandis, "the attributes of God were in fact the attributes of man."[39] As we shall see duly, this insistence on human dominion and capacity was enmeshed too with versions of the Christian doctrine of creation—in particular the biblical insistence that Adam was created in the image and likeness of God—and it fed directly into new currents in the understanding of artistry that trespassed boldly into the regions of hitherto sacrosanct vocabulary, speaking of the artist himself now as a "creator," a claim the breathtaking audacity of which in its day is difficult for us to sense but which served to make its passage into habitual use a slow and uncomfortable one. Even so, the intellectual fabric of the Renaissance was more complex than concentration on such impulses alone might suggest, and my purpose here is to reckon with the fact that, for much of the period and many of its key representatives, it is an emphasis on art as a respectful imitation of nature that dominates the scene but one which acknowledges to the full that, in one way or another, faithful mimesis also involves some sort of transformation, some element of *invenzione*, on the part of the artist.[40]

Frederick Antal credits Cennini's short manual for painters, *Libro dell' arte*, with the reintroduction of the mimetic ideal to Western art.[41] It is clear from the content of Cennini's work that his concern is with techniques by means of which the novice artist may quickly be able to render visual likenesses of natural phenomena, and he therefore urges his readers for the most part to take their models directly from nature itself, rather

[38] Agnes Heller, *Renaissance Man*, trans. Richard E. Allen (London: Routledge & Kegan Paul, 1978), 11.

[39] Heller, *Renaissance Man*, 79–80.

[40] This is one of the key theses of Martin Kemp, "From 'Mimesis' to 'Fantasia': The Quattrocento Vocabulary of Creation, Inspiration and Genius in the Visual Arts," *Viator: Medieval and Renaissance Studies* 8 (1977): 347–98.

[41] See Cennino d'Andrea Cennini, *The Craftsman's Handbook ("Il libro dell' arte")*, trans. Daniel V. Thompson (New York: Dover, 1954). Cennini is thought to have been born c. 1370 (a pupil of Agnolo Gaddi), and Antal dates the composition of this work to "about the 1390s," a dating supported in the more recent work of Ames-Lewis. See Francis Ames-Lewis, *The Intellectual Life of the Early Renaissance Artist* (New Haven, Conn.: Yale University Press, 2000), 5; Frederick Antal, *Florentine Painting and Its Social Background* (London: Kegan Paul, 1947), 277.

than prioritizing the imitation of what other artists have produced.[42] Thus, "[i]f you want to acquire a good style for mountains, and to have them look natural," he writes, "get some large stones, rugged, and not cleaned up; and copy them from nature."[43] Such technique already admits of a degree of artifice and composition, of course (stones are *not* mountains and can at best provide the painter with a starting point), and it is clear elsewhere that Cennini certainly does not think of the artist as a mere copyist or technician. So, for instance, in the introductory chapter of his book, he suggests that, as well as possessing the relevant "skill of hand," the painter must also be permitted to follow the dictates of his or her "fantasia," a term that Martin Kemp suggests is best translated "inspired insight."[44] Cennini's understanding of mimesis, therefore, expounded in a manner that deliberately situates human artistry as a practice within the Christian narrative of creation, fall, and redemption,[45] while concerned at one level with the "copying" of divinely created reality as it presents itself to us, also acknowledges the artist's power, by choosing to represent things in one way rather than another, "to discover things not seen, hiding themselves under the shadow of natural objects, and to fix them with the hand, presenting to plain sight what does not actually exist."[46]

Another painter's manual written some forty years later follows Cennini's naturalistic lead but presses the newly revived mimetic impulse now in a much more scientific direction. In the dedicatory letter to the 1436 Italian translation of *Della pittura* (*On Painting*),[47] Leon Battista Alberti (1404–1472) refers to the first of its three books, which, he suggests, "is entirely mathematical, [and] shows how this noble and beautiful art arises from roots within Nature herself." As Anthony Blunt observes, this sort of mimesis went well beyond the surface level of appearances, relying on

[42] See Cennini, *Craftsman's Handbook*, 14–15.

[43] Cennini, *Craftsman's Handbook*, 57.

[44] See Cennini, *Craftsman's Handbook*, 1–2; Kemp, "From 'Mimesis' to 'Fantasia,'" 367.

[45] Cf. Cennini, *Craftsman's Handbook*, 1–2.

[46] Cennini, *Craftsman's Handbook*, 1. On these grounds Cennini argues already, here in the earliest throes of the Renaissance, that the painter should be afforded the same accolades more typically reserved in his day for the poet. This shift in the social position of the artist is another key element in the transition from art's identifiable situation within the wider body of human "craftsmanship" to the more specialized and rarefied position it has typically enjoyed and assumed in modernity. See Anthony Blunt, *Artistic Theory in Italy 1450–1600* (Oxford: Clarendon, 1962), 48ff.

[47] The dedication was to the architect Filippo Brunelleschi. See Leon Battista Alberti, *On Painting*, trans. Cecil Grayson (London: Penguin, 1991), 34. Grayson's translation is nonetheless of the original Latin text of *De pictura* (1435).

newly acquired knowledge in intellectual fields such as anatomy and the laws of visual perspective to achieve its likenesses.[48] Here painting becomes a vehicle for the accurate indexing of nature's manifold forms, and it requires of the artist no superficial copying but a deep understanding of how things in nature hold together, a grasp of the fundamental principles by which nature herself works, so that correspondingly "natural" effects may be "remade" in the artist's own works.[49] Despite this, Alberti is not interested in a documentary approach as such, urging the novice always to "choose those things that are most beautiful and worthy" as a subject for depiction.[50] Accuracy of depiction is here held in tension with a clear editorial policy, though Blunt points out that the standard Alberti seeks is sought in nature herself by a sort of "mathematical averaging" of empirical examples, and not in some abstract ideal world. "From what he says about choosing the best and the typical from nature," Blunt writes, "it follows that the artist can create a work which is more beautiful than anything in nature. But with Alberti this can only be done by a series of processes all of which keep the artist in the closest touch with nature."[51] If Alberti owes a debt to the Greeks, therefore, it is to Aristotle rather than Plotinus, and his determination to remain true to the nature of things fluctuates between two senses of the term "nature"—as the sum of things existing and not made by human hands and as the end or telos toward which such things are properly and naturally directed.[52] Mimesis thus reveals "what nature is always aiming at but is always frustrated from producing."[53]

In his own writings on the art of painting,[54] Leonardo (1452–1519) is more insistent than Alberti on the importance of exact imitation without editing or aspiration to improvement which, he suggests, will result only in an unnatural and mannered style.[55] Again, though, Leonardo recognizes that even the most scientific faithfulness to nature's forms is bound to involve the artist in something altogether more complex than the simple transcription of whatever presents itself to the eye. Painting, he insists,

[48] Blunt, *Artistic Theory in Italy*, 1.
[49] Cf. Kemp, "From 'Mimesis' to 'Fantasia,'" 381.
[50] Alberti, *On Painting*, 91.
[51] Blunt, *Artistic Theory in Italy*, 18.
[52] Blunt, *Artistic Theory in Italy*, 19.
[53] Blunt, *Artistic Theory in Italy*, 18.
[54] See Martin Kemp, ed., *Leonardo on Painting: An Anthology of Writings by Leonardo da Vinci with a Selection of Documents Relating to His Career as an Artist* (New Haven, Conn.: Yale University Press, 1989).
[55] Cf. Blunt, *Artistic Theory in Italy*, 30.

precisely as the highest form of mimesis,[56] is rather an art of "subtle invention," demanding "philosophical and subtle speculation," rather than any crude or superficial reflection of material forms.[57] The mind of the artist must "transmute itself into the very mind of nature,"[58] for only thus will he be able to interpret and mediate its reality in a convincing manner for the viewer, grasping and thus working with the grain of its deep principles and laws (see, e.g., fig. 1 in the appendix). Kemp has documented the way in which Leonardo's own "hypernaturalism" is constructed precisely on the basis of such profound awareness, attending not only to the optical laws attaching to "what is out there" but equally to the "subjective effects . . . resulting from the perceptual apparatus with which we have been equipped."[59] Leonardo, in other words, is already aware of the need to solicit what Gombrich calls "the beholder's share" if a convincing imitation of reality is to result. Discovery and mimesis on the one hand, and invention or construction on the other, therefore, far from being logical opposites, here coincide and serve the very same ends, since the task of *representing* reality accurately necessarily involves the artist in an activity of interpreting or mediating, *making sense* of it for the viewer. Imaginative *invenzione* is understood to be an extension of the processes of excogitation rather than a deliberate departure from or negation of them,[60] and even where Leonardo grants somewhat freer rein to *fantasia* (in the depiction of demons and dragons for instance), he insists that "natural plausibility" will only be maintained if the same deep understanding of nature's workings forms the basis of what is imagined.[61] In each case (in "mimesis" and "fantasia"), the artist is involved in the "remaking" of natural effects, a remaking made possible by a deep insight into the underlying dynamics of their "making" in the first place.

Sir Philip Sidney (1554–1586) plied his particular artistic trade with words rather than paint, but, with the relevant adjustments duly made, the argument of his *Defence of Poesy* reflects the selfsame fluctuation between the give and take of artistry that we have identified among his Renaissance forebears in the field of the visual arts. Thus, Sidney confirms, poetry is certainly an "art of imitation," as Aristotle held—an act of representing,

[56] It is "the sole imitator of all the manifest works of nature." Kemp, *Leonardo on Painting*, 13.

[57] Kemp, *Leonardo on Painting*, 13.

[58] Cited in Kemp, "From 'Mimesis' to 'Fantasia,'" 376.

[59] Martin Kemp, "Leonardo and the Idea of Naturalism: Leonardo's Hypernaturalism," in *Painters of Reality: The Legacy of Leonardo and Caravaggio in Lombardy*, ed. Andrea Bayer (New Haven, Conn.: Yale University Press, 2004), 68.

[60] Cf. Kemp, "From 'Mimesis' to 'Fantasia,'" 365.

[61] Kemp, "From 'Mimesis' to 'Fantasia,'" 381.

counterfeiting, or figuring forth through "speaking pictures," with the compound end to both "teach and delight."[62] But the poet is no mere secretary of nature's forms, borrowing from and clinging tenaciously to the substance of what is, what has been, or even what shall be.[63] No, poetic mimesis, Sidney holds, is of a quite distinct sort, ranging, "only reined with learned discretion, into the divine consideration of what may be and should be."[64] The poet, indeed, is properly termed a "maker" as well as a "prophet," since he alone among those termed "artists"[65] "bringeth his own stuff, and doth not learn a conceit out of a matter, but maketh matter for a conceit."[66] In other words, rather than simply granting verbal expression to some already experienced reality, the poet's vision penetrates beyond the horizons of the actual to present for our imaginative consideration a "conceit" (a conceivable state of affairs) that duly *shapes* experience or opens up for us new ways of experiencing the world, moving the world forward in the direction of what it *ought* to be. Thus, the goal of this poetic re-presentation of things, Sidney reminds us, is "to lead and draw us to as high a perfection as our degenerate souls, made worse by their clayey lodgings, are capable of."[67] Sidney had apparently read Scaliger's *Poetices*,[68] and his allusion to Aristotle's work also clearly indicates classical influences on his thought at this point. He takes great care, though, to situate what he says within an identifiably Christian narrative, daring to compare what the poet is capable of favorably with nature's own capacities ("[h]er world is brazen, the poets only deliver a golden"[69]), yet countering the suggestion that this is too "saucy" a claim by insisting that, on the contrary, such recognition alone gives due honor to "the heavenly Maker of that maker," who has created human beings in his own image and set them over all the works of nature in such wise that, "with the force of a divine breath," they may bring forth from its given plenitude of possibility things far surpassing the empirically familiar.[70] Given his allusion to the "perfection" of natural forms and his appeal to the divine "breath" as that which inspires

[62] Sir Philip Sidney, *An Apology for Poetry; or, The Defence of Poesy*, ed. Geoffrey Shepherd (London: Thomas Nelson & Sons, 1965), 101.

[63] Sidney, *Defence of Poesy*, 102.

[64] Sidney, *Defence of Poesy*, 102.

[65] Sidney has the old, broader notion of *ars* in his sights here and mentions astronomers, geometricians, arithmeticians, natural philosophers, grammarians, and others among those who merely "follow" nature.

[66] Sidney, *Defence of Poesy*, 120.

[67] Sidney, *Defence of Poesy*, 104.

[68] See Sidney, *Defence of Poesy*, 131, line 19.

[69] Sidney, *Defence of Poesy*, 100.

[70] Sidney, *Defence of Poesy*, 101.

and drives the poet's imaginative insight, Sidney's, it might be reasonably be maintained, is an *eschatological* poetics, concerned with a form of mimesis that is faithful to nature precisely by transforming it, bathing it in the light of what as yet it is not, and—by granting us new imaginative "conceits"—transforming our ways of experiencing actuality and, thereby, our ways of living in the world.

Both Leonardo and Sidney remain committed to a mimetic model for artistry and thus to the accountability of the artist and his or her work in the face of a given reality that stands over against them. Yet both, we have seen, construe artistic mimesis as an imaginative engagement with reality in which there is both give and take to be reckoned with, the artist taking what the world offers as his or her starting point but handing it back transformed and enriched, some new meaning having been disclosed or invested in it through artistic labors. Both men, furthermore, are willing on occasion to flirt deliberately with a vocabulary that exalts the artist to a unique and somewhat ambiguous place vis-à-vis the natural order of things and the one who is understood to have called it into being. We have already noted Sidney's carefully measured reference to the "gold standard" of poetry compared to what nature has to offer. So, too, Leonardo reminds his reader that whereas nature produces only elementary things (*semplici*), the painter is capable of taking these and multiplying them infinitely by acts of imaginative construction that, in effect, repeat all the works of God the most high, the artist himself thus being "*signore e dio* of all the things he wishes to generate."[71] Such sentiments and analogies are carefully cast and remain within the bounds of a religiously orthodox respect for the world as it comes to us from God's hand; yet in them we draw close to the brink of a related but quite different territory of Renaissance sensibility, one in which reserve and respect for the givenness of the world and its forms are rendered more problematic, not least (albeit not uniquely) in relation to the arts. Already, in Leonardo's own later writings, the verb *creare* makes an occasional, unapologetic appearance to refer to what the painter does with brush in hand. Prior to this, Kemp notes, "[t]he verb invariably used to denote the production of a work of art was *fare*, which could be applied as readily to pasta as painting."[72] Whatever the precise historical origins of this new, highly charged metaphor,[73] its entailments for human self-understanding more widely were considerable and, as we

[71] Cited in Kemp, "From 'Mimesis' to 'Fantasia,'" 377–78, 382–83.

[72] Kemp, "From 'Mimesis' to 'Fantasia,'" 397.

[73] The earliest known use is its application to the poet by Cristoforo Landino (1424–1498) in a 1481 edition of Dante's *Divine Comedy*. See Tigerstedt, "Poet as Creator," 457, et passim.

shall see in the next chapter, once released into discourses about the arts in particular, it tended naturally to foster accounts and impulses rather different in their basic orientation to the various modalities of mimesis.

Mimesis amidst Modernity

Walter Benjamin reminds us that the real question about photography confronting those who bore witness to its birth in the nineteenth century was not whether photography itself might be considered an art form but whether its invention "had not transformed the entire nature of art" itself and as such.[74] It was not yet apparent that it had, but the availability of technologically produced (and reproducible) images documenting objects and events in the real world from the advent of the daguerreotype in Paris in 1840 onward certainly had a marked impact on contemporary theory and practice in the visual arts. Nowhere was this more evident than in France itself, where the accuracy and level of attention to detail now associated with photography set new standards for those inclined in the direction of artistic verisimilitude and lifelike illusionism in painting to measure up to. So, for instance, the "academic" painter and sculptor Jean-Léon Gérôme (1824–1904) pursued a form of visual "realism" that placed a huge premium on precise and polished draftsmanship and wealth of detail in order to give the viewer the painted equivalent of an "eye-witness" vantage point on his subjects. Of course, many of Gérôme's chosen subjects were, in the best traditions of academicism, taken from the stock of great historical, mythic, and biblical events, and the drive in the direction of an illusionistic "faithfulness to reality" was therefore of necessity compromised by a high level of imaginary recomposition.[75] As it happens, the compromise involved duly took its toll on Gérôme's reputation, many critics judging that the academic style of *grande peinture* was here sacrificed on the altar of populism and in the interests of an obsession with a false visual ideal (i.e., precisely that of accomplishing a "photographic" likeness).[76] Of Gérôme's *The Death of Caesar* (1859–1867),[77] the critic Théophile Gautier observed wittily, "If photography had been known in the days of Caesar, we might think that the

---

[74] "The Work of Art in the Age of Mechanical Reproduction," in Walter Benjamin, *Illuminations* (London: Pimlico, 1999), 220.

[75] Laurence des Cars, "Gérôme: Painter of Histories," in *The Spectacular Art of Jean-Léon Gérôme*, ed. Laurence des Cars, Dominique de Font-Réaulx, and Édouard Papet (Paris: Skira, 2010), 29.

[76] Scott C. Allen, "Gérôme before the Tribunal: The Painter's Early Reception," in Cars, Font-Réaulx, and Papet, *Spectacular Art of Jean-Léon Gérôme*, 95.

[77] See Cat. 67 in Cars, Font-Réaulx, and Papet, *Spectacular Art of Jean-Léon Gérôme*, 122–23.

painting had been done from a print made on the spot at the very moment of the catastrophe."[78] But the "feel" of reality generated by visual verisimilitude alone might be had at the cost of imaginative grasp on the "reality" of the event at another, bigger and deeper, level. The observation was barbed.

In fact, Gérôme himself did indeed eventually toy with the practice of using photographic records as models for elements in some of his paintings, especially in his works ostensibly documenting contemporary scenes from the Ottoman Empire and the Arabian Orient.[79] On a visit to Egypt undertaken in 1855–1856, he was accompanied by the sculptor Auguste Bartholdi (1834–1904), who took a camera with him, supplying Gérôme in due course with a series of prints to serve in lieu of the time-honored artist's sketchbook. But although Gérôme made no secret of his intention to exploit this efficient new data-gathering strategy, what duly emerged from his studio was very far from being an authentic ethnographic record. In a revealing study of these paintings, Sophie Makariou and Charlotte Maury demonstrate that the apparent photographic precision of the work "only rarely proceeds from a totally faithful imitation of reality"; more often than not, the overall composition is identifiably cobbled together, apparently drawing as much from fragments of half-remembered visual material and images culled from literary sources as from the photographs placed at the artist's disposal.[80] In any case, candid journalistic "snapshots" of daily life were not, of course, what Gérôme was working with; Bartholdi's photographic images themselves were necessarily carefully "staged" and composed (rather as a painting might be) in order to meet the demands of the new visual technology for adequate lighting and long shutter exposures. Some (of individuals wearing "authentic" oriental costume) were actually taken in Paris once the trip was over.[81] The painted result, far from constituting any meaningful form of "realism," is in fact often a scene utterly incongruous to anyone actually familiar with the details and realities of oriental life at the time. That it convinced Gérôme's intended audience of its integrity and "likeness to life" was hardly surprising, since it offered them a romanticized vision of the Orient that they were already expecting to see, an "invented, literary Orient" shaped decisively, Dominique

[78] Cited in Dominique de Font-Réaulx, "Gérôme and Photography: Accurate Depictions of an Imagined World," in Cars, Font-Réaulx, and Papet, *Spectacular Art of Jean-Léon Gérôme*, 215.

[79] See Font-Réaulx, "Gérôme and Photography," in Cars, Font-Réaulx, and Papet, *Spectacular Art of Jean-Léon Gérôme*, esp. 215–18.

[80] See Sophie Makariou and Charlotte Maury, "The Paradox of Realism: Gérôme in the Orient," in Cars, Font-Réaulx, and Papet, *Spectacular Art of Jean-Léon Gérôme*, 262.

[81] Font-Réaulx, "Gérôme and Photography," in Cars, Font-Réaulx, and Papet, *Spectacular Art of Jean-Léon Gérôme*, 218.

de Font-Réaulx suggests, by Antoine Galland's early eighteenth-century translation into French of *The Arabian Nights*.[82] Despite the reputation for accuracy upon which he traded, therefore, and the "photographic" quality held to attach to his paintings, far from simply "rendering what he saw" on his exotic travels, Gérôme deliberately constructed an imaginative vision of the Orient for his viewers' consumption[83] (see, e.g., fig. 2 in the appendix). As with his "history" paintings (though for rather different reasons), the aspiration to a "photographic" quality of visual representation in the medium of paint eludes him, the element of imaginative construction stubbornly refusing to be dispensed with and distancing the result significantly from any straightforward "mirroring" of the world as it really is or was. His works were from first to last "skilful subterfuges,"[84] rather than the slices of visual reality they were readily mistaken for.

Once again, therefore, even the most forthright and sustained efforts to achieve an illusionistic mimesis prove, on closer inspection, to have a far more complex relation to reality than first meets the eye. For those committed to a notion of artistic realism as the faithful transcription of nature's realities onto canvas (or its equivalents in other media), the new visual technologies of the nineteenth century furnished the ideal of a mechanical process from which the editorial and hermeneutic role of the artist's eye was, prima facie, conspicuous by its absence. Others were far less convinced of photography's capacity to render the visual truth in this way, let alone the whole truth and nothing but the truth, and their own artistic commitment to "reality" thus led them in a quite different direction. So, for example, writing in 1859, Eugène Delacroix (1798–1863) observes that photography, precisely because of its often arbitrary way of framing objects (isolating the part shown from the larger whole not able to be shown), its relentless reproduction of every minute detail (most of which experience filters out in our actual visual encounters with things), and its unforgiving faithfulness to the uninterpreted "facts" of visual perspective, often "falsifies our seeing of objects by reason of its very correctness."[85] In our empirical encounters with nature, Delacroix notes, imagination is hard at

---

[82] Font-Réaulx, "Gérôme and Photography," in Cars, Font-Réaulx, and Papet, *Spectacular Art of Jean-Léon Gérôme*, 215-6.

[83] Ironically, Gérôme's popularity as a painter was boosted considerably by the widespread availability of his own paintings in the form of cheap photographic reproductions. See Pierre-Lin Renié, "Gérôme: Working in the Era of Industrial Reproduction," in Cars, Font-Réaulx, and Papet, *Spectacular Art of Jean-Léon Gérôme*.

[84] Font-Réaulx, "Gérôme and Photography," in Cars, Font-Réaulx, and Papet, *Spectacular Art of Jean-Léon Gérôme*, 218.

[85] In Charles Harrison, Paul Wood, and Jason Gaiger, eds., *Art in Theory 1815–1900: An Anthology of Changing Ideas* (Oxford: Blackwell, 1998), 362.

work editing and interpreting, filtering and framing, things in a meaning-ful manner. If what photography reproduces is indeed in some sense to be identified as "reality," therefore, it is nonetheless not reality as anyone actually experiences or "sees" it (its "decentered" perspective remains by definition one unpopulated by any human agent), and it is for this reason that, as we look at it, a photograph frequently feels false rather than ringing true.[86] Where painting is concerned, Delacroix suggests, the artist under-takes a role analogous to that of imagination in experience, presenting the visual subject concretely in terms of a language (conventions of composi-tion and execution) that edits and interprets as it shows, placing a definite construction on things, and so encouraging the spectator to perceive them in a particular way. In the process, the artist also typically leaves much more for the imagination itself to do (ironically, Delacroix avers, the most striking photographs are those that, due to some defect in equipment or process, fail to reproduce everything lying within the visual field of the image), suggesting much rather than showing all and thus involving the viewer in a collaborative give and take consistent with the dynamics and texture of our wider sensory engagement with the world. So art (even that art that aspires to visual transcription) cannot avoid passing through the mind's eye of both the painter and the beholder, being transformed at each stage of the process,[87] and gaining whatever semblance to "reality" it has for us courtesy of this same ineradicably imaginative human stand-point, rather than from some putative faithfulness to an unedited nature accessible only by stripping the human factor out and approximating to a mechanical form of "seeing." We can never achieve the latter in any case, Delacroix insists (even a photograph is finally viewed from some human perspective or other), but more importantly, he suggests, we ought not to try if it is the reality of the human world (rather than the world as per-ceived by a machine) that we are genuinely concerned to capture.

In his discussion of visual style in *Modern Painters*, volume 3 (1856), John Ruskin (1819–1900) maintains that "he who is closest to Nature is best" and eschews all forms of artistic idealism in favor of a faithful

---

[86] Delacroix underestimates the extent to which photography itself can also be a medium susceptible to careful editorial and hermeneutic strategies. Cf., e.g., Susan Son-tag, *On Photography* (London: Penguin, 1979), 51–82. As we have seen, this was already an issue in Delacroix's own day (with scenes allegedly from the Orient being composed and shot in Paris studios), though the development of photographic technology in subse-quent decades no doubt encouraged more deliberately creative uses of it than he could be familiar with. Notwithstanding this, Delacroix's basic point (which concerns what pho-tography renders when the photographer aspires simply to document reality, and so *erases* herself and her perspectives as fully as is humanly possible from the process) holds good.

[87] Harrison, Wood, and Gaiger, *Art in Theory*, 363.

attention granted to the "facts" of actuality as it confronts us.[88] Yet, Ruskin argues, closeness to nature is not at all the same thing as the production of shallow visual resemblances to its external forms. What must be sought instead is that inner and deeper resemblance to which the "penetrative imagination"[89] alone reaches and the successful showing of which is necessarily quite incompatible with techniques of superficial verisimilitude. The artist must therefore choose between these, and the best artists are those whose work draws the viewer's own imagination directly into play as an active force. Thus, he argues, "[b]etween the painter and the beholder, each doing his proper part, the reality should be sustained; and after the beholding imagination has come forward and done its best, then, with its help and in the full action of it, the beholder should be able to say, I feel as if I were at the real place, or seeing the real incident. But not without that help."[90] The painter, as it were, keys us more fully into reality through his representations when he solicits our active imaginative participation in a *poetic* project—that is, one that, precisely in its bid to represent "as much truth as possible" involves both artist and beholder identifiably in a project of *making*, transforming what is given to the senses in order more fully to fathom its intrinsic depths of meaning and possibility. It goes without saying that no artistic image can possibly show reality in all its fullness; but this, Ruskin suggests, is precisely a gain rather than a deficit. The artist suggests, selects, and filters by what he presents for our consideration, guiding us in the direction of what really matters. "Reality" itself in its full-blown version, Ruskin argues, is too much for us to cope with, quickly taxing and overwhelming us with its plethora of undifferentiated detail, and the sort of "dangerous realism" that concentrates on a superficial "life-likeness" tends to fail for the same reason, leaving the imagination languid and enervated rather than summoning it into a focused and directed activity. (It is on these grounds that Ruskin favors the impressionistic style of Turner's landscapes and seascapes over the more visually "accurate" depictions by Constable or De Wint.)[91] We *need* an editorial perspective on nature, Ruskin indicates, and if in ordinary empirical experience our own imagination gladly bears the responsibility for providing one, what a painting can do is to stimulate us to imagine things *differently*, to experience the world through someone else's eyes rather than our own. Great painting, then, Ruskin insists, is not the successful mimicry of nature

[88] John Ruskin, *Modern Painters* (London: George Allen, 1904), 3:136.

[89] A notion Ruskin had introduced to his readers ten years earlier in the second volume of his work (1846).

[90] Ruskin, *Modern Painters*, 3:147.

[91] See, e.g., Ruskin, *Modern Painters*, 3:135–36.

offering its surface appearances to us "as in a mirror" but rather the provision of a profound and fertile imaginative standpoint and starting point, granting others access to new ways of seeing and experiencing its truth for themselves.[92] Far from erasing all traces of the artist as far as humanly possible in the pursuit of a "photographic" likeness, therefore, here again we find precisely the opposite impulse—namely, the deliberate interposing and exploration of concrete human perspectives in the pursuit of more rather than less truth. In effect, Ruskin suggests, to the great painter, we say, "Come between this nature and me—this nature which is too great and too wonderful for me; temper it for me, interpret it to me; let me see with your eyes, and hear with your ears, and have help and strength from your great spirit."[93] This is clearly "mimesis" of a sort,[94] an art concerned first and foremost, that is to say, faithfully to reflect the truthfulness of a given world rather than substituting for it some other reality of its own making. Yet, like most of the other examples we have considered, it is a form of mimesis which appreciates that the successful representation of reality necessarily involves its imaginative transformation and redescription and thus, paradoxically, *augments* reality for us even as it offers faithful testimony to its contours. In Paul Ricoeur's words, by representing one thing imaginatively in the terms and media proper to another, such art " 'invents' in both senses of the word."[95]

Despite the broad shift in aesthetic concern since the Renaissance that Abrams traces from a dispensation of "representing" to one of "making," modes of mimesis continue to flourish today in the arts as elsewhere in human life. Paintings, theater, novels, films, and other art forms all provide plenty of examples of works that take their starting point, their basic component parts, and their bearings from some reality wholly familiar to us from the substance of "real life." Again, though, according to philosopher Kendall Walton, such works are not best thought of as mere facsimiles or clones of everyday objects and events but as "props" which function (like

---

[92] Ruskin, *Modern Painters*, 3:148–49.

[93] Ruskin, *Modern Painters*, 3:149.

[94] Ruskin embarks upon his treatment of visual style by alluding to the observation of Sir Joshua Reynolds that the maxim according to which art should "imitate nature" is more often inculcated than explained and ought not to be understood in a merely mechanical sense. See Ruskin, *Modern Painters*, 3:4.

[95] Paul Ricoeur, *The Rule of Metaphor: Multidisciplinary Studies of the Creation of Meaning in Language*, trans. R. Czerny and others (Toronto: Toronto University Press, 1977), 239. Ricoeur's observation pertains specifically to metaphorical discourse, but the logic of visual representation (and other sorts) shares a basic pattern with the phenomenon of verbal metaphor, as one thing is shown or suggested in terms proper to another quite different thing.

the toys that children play with) in games of make-believe, stimulating far-reaching imaginative activities in which fictional truths and "worlds" are duly generated, providing an imagined supplement to reality.[96] Such fictional worlds, Walton argues, go far beyond the particular content of the works themselves and as such, but remain identifiably earthed in and constrained or authorized by that content. Thus, for instance, the purpose of Georges Seurat's *Sunday on the Island of La Grande Jatte* is "to serve as a prop in certain sorts of games—games involving a principle of generation which results in the functionality (in those games) of the proposition that a couple is strolling in a park," and not ones "in which fictionally hippos are wallowing in a mud hole."[97] Of course, all sorts of things *may* be imagined in connection with this particular painting, but not all of them will be "authorized" by its content and by the conventions of "reading" within which, by virtue of their time and place, they are situated.[98] If Walton's account of artistic mimesis as bound up in this way with activities of make-believe is correct, then the purpose of such works is clearly not to replicate or "mirror" segments of empirical reality (in fact, a prop need not bear any close resemblance to that which it represents but needs only to suggest it effectively) but precisely to stimulate acts of imaginative construction on our part that transform the work itself and thereby generate fictional supplements to the "real world," inducing us to imagine what we might not otherwise ever imagine.[99] Of course, Walton suggests, the deeper purpose of such playful departures from actuality (and the reason mimetic activities of one sort or another are so residual a feature of human cultures) may be precisely to enable our imaginative exploration of the possible or to serve as a form of role playing fitting us better to meet unfamiliar circumstances that may sooner or later confront us.[100] In this sense, the "fictional truths" generated by them may nonetheless also often prove to be what Ricoeur dubs "heuristic fictions,"[101] imaginative redescriptions of the world which, precisely in the act of showing it otherwise, grant us epiphanies of its more profound and far-reaching realities.

Ricoeur himself provides our final example of an understanding of mimesis as something more and other than the image of "mirroring,"

---

[96] See Kendall Walton, *Mimesis as Make-Believe: On the Foundations of the Representational Arts* (Cambridge, Mass.: Harvard University Press, 1990), esp. 11–69.

[97] Walton, *Mimesis as Make-Believe*, 60.

[98] "What is fictional in a painting depends not only on splotches of paint on canvas but also on relevant traditions about how to interpret them." Walton, *Mimesis as Make-Believe*, 49.

[99] Walton, *Mimesis as Make-Believe*, 22.

[100] Walton, *Mimesis as Make-Believe*, 12.

[101] Ricoeur, *Rule of Metaphor*, 239.

taken at face value, seems to suggest. In narrative discourse, he suggests, artistic mimesis in fact stands in a complex, threefold relation to what it represents.[102] Following Aristotle, Ricoeur understands mimesis as an act of *poesis* in the full sense, rather than a matter of mere copying or replication;[103] it is thus always a "creative imitation"—not the attempted "redoubling of presence" but "the break that opens the space for fiction" and the invention of the "as-if."[104] Narrative is concerned in particular with the temporal configuration of human action and events in the field of practical experience. In the substance of lived experience itself, though, Ricoeur notes (drawing on Augustine's account in the *Confessions*), time as such is confusing, characterized by aporias that render the moment of existence discordant—expectation, memory, and attention being perichoretically interlaced and stretching the soul or mind in three ways at once. In Aristotle's account of narrative emplotment as "the imitation or representation of action,"[105] Ricoeur identifies a tension between "a lived experience where discordance rends concordance and an eminently verbal experience where concordance mends discordance."[106] Through an act of imaginative *composition*, he suggests, narrative discourse "resignifies the world in its temporal dimension"[107] and in doing so constructs and proposes a meaningful whole for our indwelling. Thus, according to Ricoeur, mimesis has three distinct but interwoven moments or modes. Mimesis$_1$ draws materials from the familiar world of action and experience—experience already informed and mediated tacitly ("prefigured") by prior acts of symbolization but fragmented and inchoate, possessing a "prenarrative quality" that thus cries out for acts of imaginative reconfiguration.[108] Mimesis$_2$ is the moment in which artistic imagination configures rather than merely reproduces what it borrows from experience, imposing order upon (or perhaps tracing order latent within) the flux of a world encountered from the standpoint of action and suffering. Mimesis$_3$, meanwhile, is the moment or mode in which all this feeds back directly into the field of action, as it gains imaginative purchase in the reader or (in the case of a drama) spectator and serves to *refigure* his or her experience of temporal

[102] Paul Ricoeur, *Time and Narrative*, vol. 1, trans. Kathleen McLaughlin and David Pellauer (Chicago: University of Chicago Press, 1984), esp. 52–87.

[103] Ricoeur, *Time and Narrative*, 1:34.

[104] Ricoeur, *Time and Narrative*, 1:45.

[105] Ricoeur, *Time and Narrative*, 1:33.

[106] Ricoeur, *Time and Narrative*, 1:31.

[107] Ricoeur, *Time and Narrative*, 1:81.

[108] Ricoeur, *Time and Narrative*, 1:74. Ricoeur's account here has structural similarities to Macmurray's account of the dialectical relationship between the qualities of "immediate" and "reflective" experience discussed in chap. 6.

existence itself (through moments of recognition and disclosure). Here the worlds of the text and the reader intersect, and an imaginative "as-if" proposes new possibilities of meaning and experience for our indwelling. What the artist does, of course, is merely to continue, intensify, and offer back the products of an imaginative activity in which we are all constantly and necessarily engaged at another level in our bids to "make sense" of things as they happen to us. Time, Ricoeur notes, only becomes "human" to the extent that it is articulated through a narrative mode, and we are all storytellers.[109] But it is the achievement of the artistic imagination in particular to offer us "fictions" which, by the fittingness of their conventions of representation (constantly modified under the pressure of engagement with particular realities by a process of "rule-governed deformation"),[110] mediate the world to us as a meaningful environment and in doing so constantly *augment* the "reality" it holds for us, bringing new experience to language through the unfolding of meanings "that themselves depend on the virtues of abbreviation, saturation, and culmination, so strikingly illustrated by emplotment."[111] The point of such mimesis, we might say, is not to make the text "look like" the world but to make the world itself look and feel different when viewed from the imaginative perspectives afforded by the text. Again, faithful mimesis and imaginative transformation prove to be overlapping rather than distinct (let alone opposing) impulses and activities.

[109] Ricoeur, *Time and Narrative*, 1:52.
[110] Ricoeur, *Time and Narrative*, 1:69.
[111] Ricoeur, *Time and Narrative*, 1:80.

9

Origination, Image, and Autonomy

Modifying the Grammar of "Creation"

In chapter 8, we saw that the great painters and sculptors of the Renaissance found their inspiration in the glories and intricacies of Nature and in a conception of artistry as a faithful exploration and representation of these. If this rebirth of the mimetic ideal amounted in principle (and necessarily in practice) to something much more subtle and complex than the simple transcription of empirical data, it was nonetheless driven and sustained by a deeper mode of fidelity to the shape and substance of a reality given to it for consideration and inviting truthful response and report. Art and due deference went hand in hand, and a disposition of wonder in the face of a world brimming with meaning and possibility as yet undisclosed typically lay at the heart of artistic endeavor. In the wider intellectual ethos of the Renaissance, though, a new and shrill note was already sounding out about the place of humankind in the cosmos, one that shifted the center of gravity in the vision of human *ars* in general and that duly found its way in some form or other into the self-understanding and aspiration of poets, painters, sculptors, and architects—effectively giving birth to the distinctly modern notion of the "artist" in the process. This new vision (which in reality was a very old vision resuscitated and given a new lease on life) was one the implications of which were much less accommodating of deference and accountability, gesturing instead toward a quite different set of dispositions (conveniently summed up under the rubric of "dominion") as befitting the world's human inhabitants. The rhetoric in which this vision was gradually articulated in the discourses of philosophy, science, technology, agriculture, and other manifestations of *ars* in its more expansive classical and medieval sense was already shot through with religious and theological allusion and warrant. Arguably, though, it is in discourse concerning some of those practices and outputs which we today typically include among "the arts," those conveniently paradigmatic instances of human *poesis* lying at the heart of every human culture, that the most revealing symptom of this cultural moment manifested itself. It did so in a singular act of linguistic trespass, in its day at once breathtaking, brazen, and blasphemous, but bound eventually to pass permanently into the lexicon of nonliturgical speech, reshaping the public perception of artistry and much else besides as it did so.

As we saw in the early chapters of this book, the presumption of affinity between acts of divine and human making has firm scriptural warrant in the biblical depiction of God as an artisan, working with his hands to fashion something good and worthwhile. We saw too, though, that these same traditions consistently picture human artistry as subordinate to divinely furnished guidelines, supervision, and standards—a matter of apprenticeship and labor in the workshop of a master craftsman whose authority exceeds all other and must be respected. And while all this may properly be said to lie within the legitimate semantic range and implications of the doctrine of creation, we also saw that the Bible contains other traditions in which certain aspects of God's identity, relationship, and activity with respect to the cosmos are clearly marked out and set apart as something wholly unique and radically incomparable. In their specifically theological uses, the English noun "creation" and its cognate adjectival and verbal forms themselves often serve to flag vital difference rather than putative likeness or analogy between God and the world; but in wider patterns of language use this is not so at all, and even theological uses (as reflected, for instance, in what is typically treated under the rubric of the doctrine of "creation") embrace that which, in biblical terms, is comparable as well as the divinely incomparable within their proper scope.

This complex and—for the theologian at least—arguably unsatisfactory linguistic circumstance is in significant measure a direct outcome of the cultural shift alluded to above. The theologians of the medieval era may well have done much to elaborate an account of God's relationship to the world in which the notion of analogy figured large, but they were equally clear about the fundamental importance of that unspeakable otherness referred to obliquely in the paradoxically nontransferable adjective "uncreated." The second constitution of the Fourth Lateran Council (1215) drives the relevant point home: "between the Creator and creature there cannot be a likeness so great that the unlikeness is not greater."[1] And, as the wording here suggests, it is precisely what God is and does as Creator that, for the medieval mind, most self-evidently transcends all analogy and sets him apart. Or, putting the same point the other way around, in medieval use the Latin verb *creare* and its cognates are rigorously preserved for religious and theological use, permitted to refer to God and God alone and more precisely to aspects of God's being and *actiones ad extra* that transcend all analogy and set him apart from everything else that is. Like its Hebrew equivalent *bārā'*, in other words, in the medieval lexicon *creo* smolders with holiness, other perfectly serviceable verbs (*fingo, facio*, and others) being both available and religiously adhered to in order to characterize the actions of the human artist or artisan, even—no, especially—those activities of forming and making deemed most fitting of divine analogy.[2]

This same scrupulous linguistic discrimination, designed to flag and respect the "unbridgeable chasm" between God and the creature, was preserved, Tigerstedt observes, by all the early Renaissance humanists, and it is not until the closing decades of the fifteenth century that the habit of centuries was eventually broken and the verb *creo* applied transgressively for the first time, as a metaphor now to describe human endeavors and achievements.[3] First poets—and then those hitherto contentedly classified as craftsmen (painters, sculptors, and others)—found themselves drawn gradually but irresistibly into the fold of those now held capable of an activity daringly but fittingly described in terms of this at first faltering but increasingly bold and presumptuous predicate.[4] Early examples of this linguistic innovation—in some of the later writings of Leonardo for instance, or further north from the pen of Albrecht Dürer—were

---

[1] The full text may be found at http://www.fordham.edu/halsall/basis/lateran4.asp (accessed April 14, 2014).

[2] See E. N. Tigerstedt, "The Poet as Creator: Origins of a Metaphor," *Comparative Literature Studies*, no. 5 (1968): 468.

[3] Tigerstedt, "Poet as Creator," 468. Drawing on Edgar Zilsel (*Die Entstehung des Geniebegriffes* [Tubingen: 1926], 280–81), Tigerstedt's essay identifies this first transgressive use in the writings of the minor Latin poet Cristoforo Landino (1424–1498), noting Landino's appeal by way of justification to the ambiguity of the Greek *poieō*, used in LXX and Greek Christianity indiscriminately to refer to divine and human modalities of making alike.

[4] On the history of the application of *creo* and *creare* to artists as distinct from poets, see Martin Kemp, "From 'Mimesis' to 'Fantasia': The Quattrocento Vocabulary of Creation, Inspiration and Genius in the Visual Arts," *Viator: Medieval and Renaissance Studies* 8 (1977): 347–98.

generally circumspect in their willing acknowledgment of analogy, preserving a due sense of the difference between divine and artistic creativity.[5] Furthermore, as Kemp suggests, the verb *creare* in its metaphorical use was at first only occasional, and its passage into the standard vocabulary of artistic production was not a rapid one. Nonetheless, he admits, the shift itself was momentous enough and reflects a growing sense on the part of the artist of "man's unique place in the natural order of things."[6] And the circumspection was certainly not evenly distributed. Cristoforo Landino, the poet to whom the first extant use of the metaphor is generally traced, seems almost grudging in his admission of divine otherness. God, he readily admits, "produces out of nothing whatsoever He will, which we call 'create.'" Yet the poet, too, he insists, by skilled composition, generates the deepest meanings "nearly out of nothing (ex nihilo)."[7] This presses up hard and unashamedly against the sanctum of that capacity which God alone and God as such was traditionally understood as possessing and exploits the suggestive potential of the metaphor to the full, the scrupulousness of qualifiers such as "nearly" and "almost" being all but overwhelmed by the positive force of the image, and, if not wholly eliding the distinction between them, at least "elevating the poet to a middle station between God and man."[8]

In this regard, though, the poetic trespass was symptomatic rather than causal, and the relevant shift in perception whereby the sorts of capacities and prerogatives associated hitherto with God's own role as Creator of the cosmos began now to filter into the aspirations and ideals of human artists—effecting a radical and irreversible transformation in the notion of the artist as they did so—was simply the particular crystallization of wider intellectual currents already well established, especially in the Italian culture of the mid- to late fifteenth century. Thus, if Landino was indeed the first to cross the line and boldly conscript the language of "creation" into wider poetic service, ironically it is nonetheless clear that this was itself far from being a case of semantic origination ex nihilo; Landino simply dared clumsily to utter the gist of what others, such as his close friend and associate Marsilio Ficino (1433–1499), had been thinking and implying for some time.[9] And—equally ironically—the underlying

[5] See Kemp, "From 'Mimesis' to 'Fantasia,'" 382–83. On Dürer, see Erwin Panofsky, *Idea: A Concept in Art Theory*, trans. Joseph J. S. Peake (Columbia: University of South Carolina Press, 1968), 121–24.

[6] Kemp, "From 'Mimesis' to 'Fantasia,'" 383.

[7] Cited in Tigerstedt, "Poet as Creator," 459.

[8] Tigerstedt, "Poet as Creator," 459.

[9] See Tigerstedt, "Poet as Creator," 470–71.

vision of human *ars* that found concrete and radical expression in this potentially blasphemous bit of *poesis*, although itself at best theologically imprudent and at worst sacrilegious in its inferences, found its external warrant if not its deeper inspiration in the words of the same biblical poet the authority of whose imaginative vision had thus far kept the blasphemy securely at bay.

The Image of God and the Apotheosis of Humanity

In Genesis 1:26-30, the first of the two biblical creation narratives begins to build toward its climax in the announcement of God's restful enjoyment of all that he has made and his blessing of the seventh day for perpetuity. It is a passage positively crackling with theological energy, and several major themes are fused together in the heat generated by just a few verses. First, there is the theme of the wider creation as a good gift from God's hand to the newly created and blessed humankind ("see, I have given you . . ."); then there is the indication that enjoyment of this gift will involve not passive consumerism but a "fruitful" mode of occupation and possession of this rich habitation, one unpacked further in terms of the image of mastery ("sudue it, and have dominion over . . ."); and finally, all this is cast in the wider context of the remarkable indication that among all creatures great and small it is upon human beings that God bestows the peculiar privilege and responsibility of being fashioned in his own image. The exegetical and theological problems associated with the latter theme are sufficient to fuel several monographs in their own right, and we will have more to say on the subject later. For now, though, it suffices to observe that, unsurprisingly, the nature of this "imaging" relation has more often than not been understood as yoked inexorably to the concomitant indication that humans are called to exercise dominion in the wider creation.

Of course the notion of "dominion" itself demands interpretation, and its biblical connotations are easily misunderstood. With the rise of nuclear and ecological consciousness in the closing decades of the twentieth century—and a growing awareness in the twenty-first that human behavior can have, has had, and is even now having a damaging impact not just on the surface of our planetary habitat but on its deeper systemic processes and prospects too—blame has often been laid at the door of modernity's Christian heritage for providing, in effect, a scriptural warrant for the willful despoiling and destruction of nature.[10] The charge is not wholly

---

[10] The locus classicus for this charge (echoed many times since) is Lynn White, "The Historical Roots of Our Ecological Crisis," *Science* 155 (1967): 1203–7. For a measured response, see the argument in Richard Bauckham, *God and the Crisis of Freedom* (Louisville: Westminster John Knox, 2002), 128–177.

groundless, but it is extremely misleading. For, in biblical and premodern Christian understanding, human "mastery" with respect to the wider creation was generally understood to be of a circumscribed and relatively modest sort, having to do chiefly with the harvesting of nature's resources (animal, vegetable, mineral) and a limited ability to control natural forces and processes (of wind, water, animal reproduction) for the ends of human flourishing.[11] Furthermore, while patristic and medieval interpretations of the "cultural mandate" in Genesis 1:28 were indeed typically anthropocentric in orientation (i.e., viewing the wider creation as put there for the singular benefit and utility of human beings distinguished from it and exalted above it by their possession of a rational soul), as Richard Bauckham suggests, the connotations of the relevant biblical texts themselves (Gen 1:26-28; Ps 8:6-8; etc.) when read in their wider canonical context are altogether different.[12] Here what we find instead is a clear acknowledgment of the fundamental horizontal relationship of humans with their fellow creatures and an understanding of "dominion" or authority cast precisely in terms of the wider characterization of God's own distinctive way of exercising "Lordship" as, indeed, "a sacred trust in which God delegates some aspect of God's own rule over creation," a rule that is "undoubtedly for the good of all God's creatures" and manifest in "God's compassionate and salvific care" for them all.[13] Nothing could be further from this than the endorsement of anthropocentric instrumentalism, let alone the domineering exploitation and rape of God's good gift to satisfy artificially stimulated human appetites for power, wealth, and glory.

In the early modern period, though, a seismic shift occurred in the rhetoric pertaining to the place of humankind within the cosmic scheme of things, albeit one not wholly without precedent in the history of scriptural interpretation. The new vision was thus one securely wedded to biblical language but fundamentally at odds with biblical ways of thinking and a radical departure even from the moderate human-centered utilitarianism of much premodern exegesis. Now, the advent of new scientific and technological advances mixed its DNA in a most regrettable manner with

---

[11] See Cameron Wybrow, *The Bible, Baconianism, and Mastery over Nature: The Old Testament and Its Modern Misreading* (New York: Peter Lang, 1991), 163.

[12] Bauckham argues that the loss of a sense of "fellow-creatureliness" and consequential anthropocentricism were due largely to the influence that Stoic and Aristotelian currents of thought exercised over the interpretation of the biblical text. In this sense, he points out, while the Renaissance certainly represents a sea change in its estimation both of human capacity and of divine permission, the way was in some measure already prepared for it. See Bauckham, *God and the Crisis*, 133–42.

[13] Bauckham, *God and the Crisis*, 128, 173–74.

the recent rekindling of interest in elements borrowed ultimately from an ancient pagan religious heritage, giving birth eventually to an anthropology less modest than anything seen in the best part of a millennium, and situated uncomfortably alongside the bulk of the church's traditional teaching about creatureliness, fallenness, and the human creature's need of redemption not just from the neck downward but in every part. We saw in the previous chapter how Leonardo's drawing and painting was linked to a notion of artistic mimesis as the penetration beneath physical surfaces to the deeper principles and hitherto secret processes of things,[14] and this same newfound confidence in and celebration of the capacity of the human mind to fathom nature's depths and understand her from the inside out, as it were, generated some unfortunate theological and practical inferences in the thought of those already so inclined. That nature now lent itself to such unlimited penetration, some supposed, could only mean on the one hand that the human mind-soul should be understood as a microcosm (rather than a delegated extension) of God's own sovereign rule over creation and on the other that such unlimited mastery placed in human hands could and should now express itself in the wholesale subjection of nature as a means to the end of realizing human designs and gratifying human needs and desires—a supposition that reveals just how little their notion of sovereignty was actually shaped by the biblical texts to which this sort of theology typically appealed.[15] In this central strand of Renaissance thought, Cameron Wybrow notes, the scriptural theologoumenon of the creation of human beings in God's image is interpreted in a manner that goes far beyond even this presumptuous claim to rule over nature and to do so in accordance with the dictates of human reason and will alone; in the final analysis, among its more vociferous and daring advocates, the theology of the image involved the claim "that man shared in the most fundamental activity of God—the activity of creation," of bringing something radically new and self-originated into the world.[16]

In his definitive two-volume treatment of the topic, Charles Trinkhaus identifies such themes as gestured toward already in the work of Giannozzo Manetti (1396–1459), who applied his skills as a linguist to translate editions of both scriptural and classical texts and whose treatise *On the Dignity and Excellence of Man* (1452) sounds a distinctive new anthropological note.[17] Whereas medieval theology tended to understand the dignity of

[14] See above, 166–67.

[15] So, Wybrow, *Bible, Baconianism*, 163–93.

[16] Wybrow, *Bible, Baconianism*, 167.

[17] Charles Trinkhaus, *In Our Image and Likeness: Humanity and Divinity in Italian Humanist Thought*, 2 vols. (Notre Dame, Ind.: University of Notre Dame Press, 1995), 1:230.

humanity in terms of its capacity for salvation and remained relatively pessimistic about human achievements in a fallen cosmos,[18] Manetti presents a quite different picture, insisting that the creation of the human soul in the divine image and similitude is manifest in a natural ingenuity, inventiveness, and excellence which exalts humankind above nature and establishes its dominance over all other creatures.[19] For Manetti the shadow of this essentially optimistic account of human worth remains a vestigial doctrine of sin and fallenness, albeit one with relatively slender practical purchase. Within a generation, though, a resurgence of Neoplatonism among Florentine intellectuals gave birth to an even more brazen articulation of man's place in the cosmos.

In his unashamedly titled *Platonic Theology* (composed between c. 1469 and 1474), Ficino is sufficient of a Neoplatonist to take seriously the radical transcendence of God and sufficiently Christian to maintain the orthodox line that, strictly speaking, "no creature . . . *creates* anything."[20] For Neoplatonism, though, the human soul, if never to be confused with God in himself (*autotheos*), is nonetheless of a wholly different order than the material creation, belonging naturally to the mediating metaphysical stratum of "divine" (*theios*) ideas and essences from which it issues and to which it is destined eventually to return. Ficino's anthropology fuses the biblical allusion to the creation of human beings in the image of God with this same parabolic narrative, then injects both with the potent ideological steroid derived from the rapid advance of early modern science and technology. The stupendous achievements of human *ars* in every sphere of life, he insists, rest squarely on the soul's natural similitude to God—in intellectual prowess, natural skill, and spiritual disposition—by virtue of which humanity "imitates all the works of divine nature," "performs the office of God," and in effect "is a kind of god" (*quidam deus*) with respect to all other living and nonliving things.[21] But what kind of "god"? Ficino appeals to the care with which the planet's human occupants foster and

---

[18] Cf. Paul Oskar Kristeller, *Renaissance Concepts of Man and Other Essays* (New York: Harper & Row, 1972), 5. Kristeller notes that the early humanism of Manetti, Bartolomeo Facio (c. 1400–1457), and others was in large measure a response to the pessimism apparent in such texts as Pope Innocent III's *De miseria humane conditionis* (c. 1195).

[19] Trinkhaus, *In Our Image*, 1:239.

[20] "nulla creatura creat aliquid. Nec inuria." Marsilio Ficino, "Platonic Theology Books V–VIII," in *Marsilio Ficino: Platonic Theology*, ed. Michael J. B. Allen and James Hankins (Cambridge, Mass.: Harvard University Press, 2002), 86 (emphasis added).

[21] Marsilio Ficino, "Platonic Theology Books XII–XIV," in Allen and Hankins, *Marsilio Ficino*, 171, 175.

train other living creatures,[22] but it is clear throughout that this is for the good of humankind rather than any other, and more typically his construal of human "lordship" over nature is characterized by aggressive and self-interested metaphors—using, conquering, trampling, and the like.[23] This wholesale subordination of the elements and "brutes" of the earth, Ficino argues, demonstrates that man is capable of thinking God's thoughts after him, being blessed with "almost the same genius . . . as the author of the heavens" himself and thus capable, indeed, of making the heavens were he ever to possess the tools and material required for the task![24] Again, the peculiar prerogatives proper to the Creator of all things visible and invisible are acknowledged—but grudgingly so, and in an attenuated form.

Ficino's pupil and intellectual heir Pico della Mirandola (1463–1494) was next to step up to the plate, and his *Oration on the Dignity of Man* (c. 1486) reiterates many of Ficino's favorite themes; but Pico adds to the narrative an existentialist twist: Unlike every other creaturely being in the heaven and on the earth, he suggests, human being and becoming is not fixed within the cosmic scheme of things or circumscribed by spheres of action prescribed in advance. Man, it seems, is never merely what he is but (like the God of the burning bush) will be what he will be, and that depends on what he chooses to make of himself—capable in theory of descending to the level of animality but equally (and more naturally) ascending toward deity.[25] Thus, in an imaginative recasting of the biblical saga of creation, Pico's God informs the newly created Adam: "[Y]ou may have as your own whatever place, whatever form, whatever gifts you may choose, according to your wish and your judgment. All other beings have received a rigidly determined nature. . . . You alone are bound by no limit, unless it be one prescribed by your will, which I have given you."[26] Here, all trace of human weakness or incapacity has effectively been banished from consideration. In its place, an emphasis on sovereign will associated

[22] Ficino, "Platonic Theology Books XII–XIV," in Allen and Hankins, *Marsilio Ficino*, 175.

[23] See, e.g., Ficino, "Platonic Theology Books XII–XIV," in Allen and Hankins, *Marsilio Ficino*, 173.

[24] "[W]ho will deny both that he has almost the same genius [*eum esse ingenio*], so to speak, as the author of the heavens, and that he is capable in a way of making the heavens, should he ever obtain the instruments and the celestial material, since in fact he is making them now, albeit from a different material, yet in the same order?" Ficino, "Platonic Theology Books XII–XIV," in Allen and Hankins, *Marsilio Ficino*, 177.

[25] See Ernst Cassirer, *The Individual and the Cosmos in Renaissance Philosophy* (Mineola, N.Y.: Dover, 2000), 83–85.

[26] Cited in Cassirer, *Individual and the Cosmos*, 85.

hitherto with God alone is now vested in God's creature, *Homo spiritua-lis*—the original "self-made man" in fact.[27]

Against charges that such notions were at best irreverent and at worst blasphemous, Ficino, Pico, and others could claim that all this was simply an acknowledgment and due celebration of the "godlike" quali-ties invested in humanity by its Creator (whose radical transcendence of the entire circumstance remained technically unscathed), taught clearly enough in Genesis 1:26 and witnessed to independently in the Hermetic literature.[28] In reality, the appeal to serious scriptural warrant was specious, the biblical figure of Adam having here been more or less conflated with that of Prometheus, the unfortunate offspring of an act of divine-human miscegenation who in Greek myth raided heaven to steal its fire and bear it down to earth.[29] As Agnes Heller notes, in their rush to redescribe the human condition, one early Renaissance writer after another followed the Promethean trajectory and "discovered that the attributes of God were in fact the attributes of man."[30]

Creation, *Communicatio Idiomatum,* and the Birth of the Artist

Such was the wider climate of ideas, then, within which the first daring and halting uses of the verb *creare* itself to refer to the highest among human endeavors and achievements arose and gradually found purchase in popular discourse. With it, the last verbal bulwark against a theologically and reli-giously imprudent "presumption of affinity" between divine and human ways of engaging with the world was effectively breached. Of course, the strict insistence that God and God alone could call something into existence ex nihilo remained—though even this, we have seen, was only grudgingly conceded by some. But the term "creation" had served much more widely than this to mark God's uniqueness vis-à-vis the "creaturely" cosmos, its preservation as lexical holy ground reminding whoever uttered or inscribed it in liturgical and theological contexts that, even in those modes of divine activity *ad extra* lending themselves to human analogy, the quotient of uncreated otherness was set unimaginably high, demanding the continuous breaking and radical reordering of every linguistic sign in its "strange-mak-ing" appropriation by God within the dynamics of revelation and stretching

[27] See Agnes Heller, *Renaissance Man*, trans. Richard E. Allen (London: Routledge & Kegan Paul, 1978), 9.

[28] See Wybrow, *Bible, Baconianism*, 169. Ficino produced a Latin edition of Her-metic texts (the *Corpus hermeticum*) from fourteenth-century manuscripts.

[29] So Cassirer, *Individual and the Cosmos*, 93.

[30] Heller, *Renaissance Man*, 80.

to breaking point the suggestion of any easy contiguity between modes of divine and human action. The steadfast resistance of *creo* and its cognates to metaphorical transference, in other words, had hitherto functioned as an invaluable reminder of the fact that, where God was concerned, the whisper "it is not" was more of a roar threatening to drown out metaphorical transference more widely and as such.

The breaching of this terminological boundary may have been symptomatic rather than causal so far as the wider cultural shift at the Renaissance toward religious immanentalism and the concomitant glorification of humanity was concerned,[31] but it gave a particular shot in the arm to the bids increasingly being made by some of those formerly content to be considered artisans and craftsmen now to be acknowledged, together with poets and philosophers of one sort or another, as a breed apart—practitioners in the *artes liberales* rather than mere ignoble manual laborers.[32] This new breed of *artifex* would have to be not just a thinker as well as a supreme technician but ideally a polymath, a full member of the humanist intelligentsia, schooled in the new learning of the sciences as well as the classics and other intellectual pursuits. We saw in the previous chapter, for example, how far Leonardo's approach to visual and plastic mimesis was from that of a mere copyist, being grounded in a profound grasp of the principles and processes of natural phenomena themselves and a capacity, as it were, to supplement nature with new additions to its extant inventory precisely by working "inventively" with the same blueprints employed by its original Maker. All this is a far cry from Plato's insistence in the *Ion* that, since it is of the essence of what artists do that they depict things they do not themselves properly understand, art can lay no serious claim to purchase on truth,[33] and his effective relegation in the *Timaeus* of the divine architect of the cosmos himself to the role of a skilled copyist of eternal exemplars.[34] So, too, whereas painters, sculptors, and others had typically been furnished by their patron or his advisers with a "cut-and-dried invenzione" for technical execution, it now became more common for the dichotomy between inventor and executant to be broken down and for artists to use their own powers of imaginative composition to modify familiar literary subjects.[35]

---

[31] See Heller, *Renaissance Man*, 377.

[32] See Anthony Blunt, *Artistic Theory in Italy 1450–1600* (Oxford: Clarendon, 1962), 51–55.

[33] Blunt, *Artistic Theory in Italy*, 51.

[34] See, e.g., Plato, *Timaeus and Critias*, trans. Desmond Lee (London: Penguin, 1971), 43, 51.

[35] Kemp, "From 'Mimesis' to 'Fantasia,'" 355–59.

The slow but sure introduction of the vocabulary of "creation" to poetics and artistic theory from the 1490s onward encouraged—and no doubt
seemed to provide convenient lexical warrant for—a set of novel variations
on this wider motif of upwardly mobile "refined mechanicals," pressing
the analogy between God and the human artist now in new directions and
to new (and potentially problematic) lengths. In biblical and theological
tradition, the main traits of God's own distinctive role as "Creator" might
be summed up conveniently under three main heads:[36] First, God grants
things their very existence as such, summoning them into being ex nihilo
(without prior external condition or constraint upon his deciding and acting) and holding them in being by a continuous donation of his Spirit
apart from which they would be swallowed up once more by that absolute
absence of being and potential (Tò οὐκ ὄν) that, apart from God himself
and that which God wills and in due course enables to exist in distinction
from and communion with himself, is all there is, has ever been, or ever
can be.[37] Second, as their Creator, God exercises a complete sovereign freedom over his materials and what he duly fashions from them, even though
he grants all that he creates its own distinct and contingent existence over
against himself and, in the case of some of the creatures, their own distinct
mode of freedom too. In all this, God remains fully and finally free to
bring what he has made to the point where it realizes his own design and
vision for it, as something "good" in which he finds personal satisfaction,
something that, in its own distinctive mode, reflects to the full who he
himself is. Third, therefore, what God summons forth in unimpeded creative freedom is precisely and necessarily (since prior to this summoning
there is "nothing" other than God himself) the expression of God's own
self and inner vision—radically "new" and unprecedented realities given
concrete existence alongside God by the application of his sovereign will
to some (needless to say not all) of the objects of divine imagining and
foreknowing.

It takes relatively little reflection to see how these selfsame traits have
fed directly into and then shaped the conceptions of the artist and of artistic "creativity" that have dominated the larger part of Western culture for
the last five hundred years. In a more dilute (and less toxic) suspension, as
we shall see, they also continue to inform the wider democratization of the
term in popular discourse about the "creative" potential of individuals and
how that might variously be overlooked or repressed, or recognized and

[36] Cf. Nicholas Wolterstorff, *Art in Action: Toward a Christian Aesthetic* (Carlisle,
U.K.: Solway, 1997), 50–52.

[37] On the doctrine of *creatio ex nihilo* and its relationship to biblical accounts of God
as Creator, see above, chap. 4.

permitted to flourish.[38] For now, though, we will remain within the sphere of discourse about the arts and the modification which marked it in the wake of early modern humanism.

No doubt there had always been individual craftsmen whose personal skill, achievements, and self-belief pressed their aspiration for their work in the direction of a desire and determination to master their materials as none had ever done before and to leave their distinctive mark on the world by doing things in a way that none had ever done them before.[39] But such Promethean spirits had found themselves bounded securely around and held in check by the demands, expectations, and other constraints of their social circumstance, embodied concretely in the late Middle Ages and early Renaissance, for example, by the standards and structures of the guilds to which craftsmen by definition belonged.[40] If the wider intellectual climate represented by Ficino, Pico, and others furnished a context that fanned the flame of artistic ambition, then the bold addition of *creare* and its cognates to the lexicon of art-theoretical description added the equivalent of aviation fuel to the relevant fire, encouraging the confident identification of analogical entailments that the traditional image of God as *artifex* had never before been intended or supposed to bear. Like the artist, it had always been understood, God (albeit in his own "divine" way) fashioned a world with great skill and wisdom, producing something good and pleasing and for the identifiable benefit of all concerned. Like God, it now came increasingly to be held, the artist (albeit in his own "creaturely" way) was concerned to call something radically novel and unprecedented into existence rather than merely replicating or imitating an object to order from a given design or template—something that was the product of his own personal and inner vision rather than

---

[38] As we have seen, aspirations to a relationship with the world marked by such traits actually arose first in wider intellectual discourse about human potential, feeding into artistic theory only subsequently and in connection with the suggestion that the artist, like God, is one who "creates."

[39] Dorothy L. Sayers' characterization of the twelfth-century architect William of Sens in her play *The Zeal of Thy House* (written for the 1937 Canterbury Festival in celebration of craftsmen) is, of course, bound to be colored to some extent by postromantic notions of the hubris attendant upon creative "genius"; but we need not dismiss it as entirely anachronistic. Sayers' poetic eye for human traits likely to span the particularities of time and place lend her drama a compelling verisimilitude, and it is precisely in bumping uncomfortably up against the limits to his freedom presented respectively by church, guild, gravity, and God that William's pride results in the literal fall that, we are led to suppose, ultimately redeems him. See Dorothy L. Sayers, *The Zeal of Thy House* (London: Harcourt, Brace, 1937).

[40] See above, pp. 23–28.

the dictates of any external circumstance, something in the fashioning of which he might properly expect by the exercise of his will and power to transcend the limits ordinarily supposed to belong to his chosen materials, and something the result of which was intended first for his own personal delight and satisfaction before that of others.

Out of this intellectual and poetic fomentation, the distinctly modern notion of the artist was duly born. Of course it took not just decades but several centuries for these new entailments of the presumed analogy between God the Artist/Creator and man the "creative artist" to take shape and develop in their most pronounced forms. But already, as early as the late sixteenth century in Italy, the power of the craft guilds had been challenged and effectively broken, and significantly earlier than that the artist had begun to be perceived no longer as "a purveyor of goods which everyone needed and which could be ordered like any other material goods"[41] but as an individual facing an educated and sophisticated public, competing with others (through individual skill and accomplishments) for patronage within a widening economic market, and producing a "work of art" that critics increasingly treated not as an object of practical utility (even though in the cinquecento it was usually still also precisely that) but as something "justified simply by its beauty and . . . [as] a luxury product."[42] In northern Europe, meanwhile, the iconoclasm associated with some strands of the Reformation displaced many craftsmen in Protestant states from their former happy alliance to the mission of the church and its channeling of their energies and abilities in the singular service of its architectural and liturgical needs. Those finding themselves suddenly redundant in this new climate of formal hostility to the arts' abiding presence in sacred space were liberated to seek new markets as well as new subjects,[43] and the most gifted among them were often swept thereby into the arms of a newly emergent individualism, secularism, and capitalism.[44]

---

[41] Blunt, *Artistic Theory in Italy*, 56.

[42] Blunt, *Artistic Theory in Italy*, 55.

[43] The religious and theological issues underlying such hostility were both various and complex, and different strands of the newly born Protestant movement granted them more or less prominence in their particular versions of ecclesial reform. See Trevor Hart, "Protestantism and the Arts," in *The Blackwell Companion to Protestantism*, ed. Alister McGrath and Darren Marks, 268–86 (Oxford: Blackwell, 2004).

[44] As Simon Schama observes, it was the burgeoning cloth trade as well as the religious austerity of high Calvinism that decisively shaped the social and economic context of Rembrandt van Rijn's birth and upbringing in Leiden, and the skill of Dutch merchants in controlling markets in spices, silks, copper, saltpeter, and all manner of other goods furnished by Amsterdam's place as a hub of international trade routes at the turn of the seventeenth century was one of the earliest omens of just where Europe's economic

The age of the exhibition, the creative manifesto, the turbulent and tortured spirit of individual genius, and "art for art's sake" may still have been a long way off, but the ideas from which such institutions, conventions, and aspirations developed were already safely lodged in an embryonic, although for the time being nameless, modern "aesthetics."[45]

Freedom without Grace and the Grammar of Co-creation

Of course, the various constituent elements of this newly born understanding of what it meant to be an "artist" were not—and are not—inherently problematic as such. In this sphere, as in so many others, the spirit of the Renaissance bestowed a new confidence in human abilities and possibilities that was at once liberating and invigorating and that generated a rate of progress and a level of cultural achievement quite unprecedented in human history, for which the heirs of modernity have good reason to be grateful. Yet this apparent flowering of human freedom in so many areas of life was unfortunately wedded to a cosmic imaginary which could not hope finally to sustain it, placing a far heavier burden of expectation and responsibility upon human shoulders than they were ever intended to bear and under the weight of which the rapid march of progress and achievement was bound eventually either to go awry or to run out of steam. As Jacques Maritain notes, the problem with Renaissance humanism and its progeny was not its aspiration to see humanity rise above many of the conditions that hitherto had hampered it but the essential anthropocentricity of its vision, setting an apotheosized humanity at the center of its cosmos and—in practical terms if not always in theory—banishing God to the margins of consideration.[46] Even in the catholic Christianity of the day, Maritain observes, a distinctly

---

future lay, as well as providing the adult Rembrandt with many of the more esoteric props that populate his paintings of oriental scenes. And, Schama notes, despite the Reformed prohibition on images in liturgical and devotional space, "[i]mpeccable Calvinists were not averse to sitting for their portraits," and, even at the height of iconoclast polemic against idolatry, the art-buying nouveau riche of Dutch society continued to snap up paintings of biblical and religious themes on a large scale for domestic use. For a gifted and enterprising artist, it seems, there was a decent living to be made. See Simon Schama, *Rembrandt's Eyes* (London: Penguin, 1999), 200–212. Cf. James Fulcher, *Capitalism: A Very Short Introduction* (Oxford: Oxford University Press, 2004), 4.

[45] On the history of the term "aesthetics" in its distinctly modern senses, see Paul Guyer, "History of Modern Aesthetics," in *The Oxford Handbook of Aesthetics*, ed. Jerrold Levinson, 25–60 (Oxford: Oxford University Press, 2003).

[46] Jacques Maritain, *True Humanism*, 3rd ed. (London: Geoffrey Bles, 1941), 19. Maritain suggests that an external symptom of this self-aggrandizement can be seen in the shift from Romanesque and Gothic architecture to the Baroque style. In a related

new note is sounded with the suggestion that, in the orders of goodness and salvation, human agents should be acknowledged as the sole primary cause (rather than the free secondary cause) of their own good acts.[47] On this territory as on all other, it seems, Renaissance man was ready to dispute the ground with God and lay claim to the right (and the ability) to determine his own destiny on his own terms. If culture was indeed being born anew, this was nonetheless clearly not a birth from above, and the effective denial or loss of any sense of divine transcendence and grace from its matrix meant that it was orientated from the first in a direction that would turn it finally and naturally back in upon itself and its own resources, where its logical center of concern and gravity lay and its hopes were—somewhat insecurely—invested.[48] If, therefore, there was nothing wrong with the self-image of the new artist as such—within this deliberately disenchanted cosmos and with the immodest aspirations attaching naturally (if not necessarily) to the new rhetoric of artistic "creation"—the stage was certainly set for the development of a warped and misdirected notion of human artistry and its situation, capacities, accountability, and accomplishments.

The suggestion that in the deliberate refashioning of matter by the human arts there is to be found a direct parallel with God's role as the artificer of the world was well established by the end of the fifteenth century[49] and is echoed in Leonardo's heroizing of the master painter whose mind is transformed into "the likeness of the divine mind" as his hand summons into being a myriad of forms, "not only the works of nature, but infinitely more than those which nature produces."[50] Leonardo's account is measured, containing no suggestion as yet that the artist might let his or her imagination run riot and conjure up realities wholly divorced from or contradictory of the world of actual experience. Even the most imaginative forms he has in mind are ones securely moored in and modest

---

vein, Panofsky observes that whereas medieval architecture is designed without reference to the proportions of the human body (so that a Gothic cathedral even of a relatively small size compels awareness of our own diminutive stature by comparison), the columns of Renaissance structures deliberately reflect these proportions, inviting the visitor "to expand his own ideal stature in accordance with the actual size of the building" so that, no matter how gigantic it may be, its dimensions generally fail to impress. Where the one style engenders a sense of transcendence and humility, Panofsky avers, the other "proclaims the dignity of man." Erwin Panofsky, *Renaissance and Renascences in Western Art* (New York: Harper & Row, 1972), 29.

[47] Maritain, *True Humanism*, 11.

[48] Maritain, *True Humanism*, 17. Cf. Nicholas Berdyaev, *The Meaning of History* (London: Geoffrey Bles, 1936), 129–30.

[49] See, e.g., Ficino, "Platonic Theology Books XII–XIV," in Allen and Hankins, *Marsilio Ficino*, 175.

[50] Cited in Blunt, *Artistic Theory in Italy*, 36–37.

extrapolations from the givenness of the empirical realm.[51] Nonetheless, the implicit thought that the role of the work of art is not simply to act as nature's secretary (intended first and foremost to point beyond itself in a motion of perpetual mimetic deference to the world) but might be understood as furnishing a cultural supplement to nature that has some value and importance in its own right and, as such, marks another important development. God has called the world as we know it into being, and in a similar vein, mutatis mutandis, the artist now calls something new into being that adds to and perhaps even improves upon the world. In short, as Julius Caesar Scaliger puts the matter just a few decades later in his *Poetics* (1561), the poet or artist "makes another nature (naturam alteram) and . . . makes himself another God (Deum alterum), as it were."[52] The seeming impiety of such a claim needs to be offset by the acknowledgment that this productive paradigm for artistry—the artist, Scaliger points out, does not simply rehearse the given shape of the world as made by God but himself makes things that are not borrowed from but add to that world—is understood as falling within the scope of divine providence and as such in effect as a sort of vocation. The same notion is captured by the admittedly eccentric but nonetheless influential Paracelsus (1493–1541), according to whom the human artist is entrusted with the task of transforming the given world of nature into something vastly superior.[53]

The context for such ideas about artistry in particular is once again to be traced to the wider anthropocentric vision of the Renaissance, not least, paradoxically, to its deliberate attempt in the first instance to erase humanity entirely from its account of things. To be sure, as Heller notes,

[51] Blunt, *Artistic Theory in Italy*, 37–38. This was typical of the age, though there were occasional contrary voices. Kemp cites the dreamscapes of Francesco Colonna's *Hypnerotomachia poliphili* (1499) as affording an exceptional instance of an appeal to *inventione inexcogitabile*—i.e., imaginative invention deliberately at odds with the general processes of excogitation. See Kemp, "From 'Mimesis' to 'Fantasia,'" 365. Among the artists of the Northern Renaissance in the same era, one might also cite Hieronymus Bosch's (c. 1450–1516) works, such as the *Garden of Earthly Delights*.

[52] Cited in Tigerstedt, "Poet as Creator," 456, 477. Scaliger (1484–1558) was a pupil of Dürer. His *Poetices libri septem* was written toward the end of his life and published posthumously.

[53] Famous for his advocacy of alchemy, Paracelsus was committed more broadly to the notion that God created the world in such a state that much remained hidden within it, requiring human *ars* (in the characteristically broader premodern sense, but including the arts of music, sculpture, carving, etc.) to transform it and so bring it to its full potential. The highest that nature produces, he insists, is taken by human *ars* and transformed into "something greater" for the ends of human flourishing. See, e.g., Jolande Jacobi, ed., *Paracelsus: Selected Writings*, trans. Norman Guterman (Princeton, N.J.: Princeton University Press, 1951), 108, 112, 120, 131, 145.

the "self-made man" of the period was one who measured his success not in terms of the accumulation of money or power but in terms of "*how far he had placed his own stamp on the world*"[54] and thus left it in a different (and better) state than he had found it. But the flip side of this same humanizing impulse was a new "scientific" approach to the world that consciously divorced subject and object, objectifying nature by seeking a rigorously decentered and value-neutral epistemic perspective, and codifying the results in terms of logically consistent and empirically verifiable laws of cause and effect. We have already seen in chapter 5 the benefits for certain practical purposes (chiefly scientific and technological ones) of this imaginative venture; but we noted there, too, both the oddity and the potential dangers of privileging this particular standpoint (though in truth it is a point where no one ever actually stands) with the unchallenged status of "reality." Unsurprisingly, once carefully stripped of its sheath of distinctly human perspectives and responses in this way, the "world" that remains takes on a new and somewhat forbidding aspect. From a grace-filled habitat received as gift from the hand of God and fitted naturally to secure human flourishing in covenant with God, the cosmos that presented itself to the gaze of the knowing Renaissance intellectual was one transformed now into a "Nature" at best indifferent and at worst hostile to human affairs and interests and needing to be conquered and tamed, therefore, if humanity was to flourish and realize its full potential.[55] If the world could no longer be supposed to exist for the sake of humankind, it might nonetheless be made to serve human ends, a "second nature" being superimposed upon the first by human fiat. That human beings were uniquely equipped to achieve this act of *creatio ex natura*, and to do so without any resort to assistance proffered from the heavens, was another basic dogma of the age. It is as if, Ficino muses, human beings were not nature's slaves but her rivals in the scheme of things, correcting and emending nature's works and so perfecting them.[56]

This, then, is a vision of a world that—if it is to provide a dwelling fitted to the shape of human needs, capacities, and aspirations—needs first to be transformed by human input of one sort or another. More than this, though, the input envisaged is of a very particular sort. First, it is, in Maritain's phrase, the instantiation of "freedom without grace,"[57] an action in which humanity (albeit a humanity vested with "divine" capacities by

---

[54] Heller, *Renaissance Man*, 8 (emphasis in original).

[55] See Heller, *Renaissance Man*, 375–85.

[56] Ficino, "Platonic Theology Books XII–XIV," in Allen and Hankins, *Marsilio Ficino*, 169, 171.

[57] Maritain, *True Humanism*, 12.

virtue of its creation in the image of God) holds the primary initiative and bears fruit for which humankind alone, therefore, must take all the credit. There is little thought here of a grace-endowed or Spirit-filled human participation in the dynamics of God's own continuing activity in the world and its history. There is, to be sure, a presumption that in all this human beings are cooperating with the divinely initiated scheme of creation as such and in doing so fulfilling their own creaturely potential or telos. But it is nonetheless as those who add their own independent contribution to the project, supplementing and perfecting the rudimentary forms of nature with designs and schemes of their own devising and accomplishment that they take up their role as, in effect, co-creators. Second, in their dealings with nature these human co-creators are envisaged in the sort of terms we have already noticed, not as those who work "with the grain" of the cosmos, cooperating with natural capacities and tendencies to draw the best out of them, but rather as those who will have their way with nature, wrestling it into submission and forcing it to do what, otherwise, it is understood as having no inclination whatsoever to do—namely, to serve distinctly human interests and ends. The figure of the creative *divina artista* stood as a convenient type and symbol of this broader concern to harness the capacities of human *ars* to place an indelible stamp on the world, transforming the commonplace materials and processes of nature into something altogether more splendid and satisfying. Indeed if, as Heller suggests, it was through such deliberate transformation of an incomplete and otherwise indifferent nature that, reciprocally, "human nature" itself was understood as moving toward its creaturely end,[58] the new artist was, above all others, an index of the advent (or perhaps the renascence) of *Homo spiritualis* or *Homo intellegire* after a long period of what in retrospect was perceived as cultural "darkness."[59]

[58] "Mankind itself is no more 'completed' than nature is. By gaining knowledge of nature, and making use of her, man can make everything which hitherto contained him, as a goal, only objectively, into 'being-for-himself.'" Heller, *Renaissance Man*, 382.

[59] On Renaissance attitudes to the cultural heritage of the Middle Ages, see Panofsky, *Renaissance and Renascences in Western Art*, 1–41.

10

Imagination, Alterity, and Contradiction

The previous chapter traced the advent of a new, distinctly modern understanding of human artistry as a "creative" venture, calling something new and unprecedented into existence, something issuing forth from the artist's individual creative vision, appropriating elements of the external world, and imposing form upon them in accordance with the dictates of artistic will. In its early modern versions, we saw, this notion contained within it a tension between the recognition of a given context for responsible human action (understood in effect as "co-creation," the enhancement or elaboration of a work divinely begun and directed) and an emphasis upon the "divine" capacities and autonomy of the human subject as one "sovereign" within his own allocated sphere of jurisdiction. This tension sometimes resolved itself in the direction of more agonistic accounts of human creativity in terms of struggle against and triumph over a nature otherwise lacking in what it takes to provide for human well-being and enjoyment, needing not so much to be completed or enhanced as subjugated and reconstructed, and demanding what human vision and energy alone can supply to underwrite this bold "redemptive" task. Increasingly, the idea of the artist "making something new" shifted its connotation from "renewal" by working with the grain of a divinely ordered and oriented cosmos to the effective "replacement" by human innovation and agency of a world marked otherwise by absence, formlessness, and chaos. In this chapter we will attend briefly to just some strands in the further development of such ideas, more Oedipal than filial in their disposition toward the given world and its presumed source and more Promethean than Adamic, we might say, in their understanding of that to which human "creativity" amounts and may properly aspire.

Creativity, Co-creation, and Counterstatement

The constructs of the artist, George Steiner observes, are in one sense always a counterstatement to the world, setting up a dialectical interplay "between the constraints of the observed and the boundless possibilities of the imagined."[1] Even mimetic representations, I have argued above, are transformative, and thus they too in their own way bear witness to the fact "that things might be (have been, shall be) otherwise"[2] than they actually are. In the case of art less concerned to reflect the world's forms than deliberately to modify them or add to their number, the potential critical force of such apposition is at once more pronounced and more apparent. Counterstatement, of course, may be of more than one sort. It may take the form of a rich counterpoint which—precisely in and through rather than despite its alterity—enhances the original given theme, resonating with and developing possibilities of meaning inherent within it. Viewed thus, as a deliberate form of human response to the world, art is (in continuity with all our other human responses, whether tacit or conscious) "dynamically implicated in the realization of" the world, just as reception theory's readers and viewers are essential to the possible significations of art itself.[3] Without them, nothing "means" anything to anyone, and the works in question are thus structured precisely with a view to the responsive capacities and possibilities available to us. Not all responses are equally constructive, though, either in our engagements with works of art or in art's own engagements with the world. Counterstatement can also be critical, corrective, and even contradictory in its force.

The Renaissance notion of a "second nature" that must be fashioned by human hands is, as we have seen, not necessarily indicative of a negative disposition toward nature itself, often being couched in terms redolent of autonomous cooperation rather than competition with the given world. Nonetheless it is but a small sideways step from the logic of enhancement (especially when wedded to models of human dominion such as those we have already considered) to that of correction, and if suggestions of such a shift were already apparent in Ficino's fifteenth-century account,[4] by the latter decades of the sixteenth century more discordant notes still

---

[1] George Steiner, *Real Presences: Is There Anything in What We Say?* (London: Faber & Faber, 1989), 11.

[2] Steiner, *Real Presences*, 11.

[3] George Steiner, *Grammars of Creation* (London: Faber & Faber, 2001), 53.

[4] So, e.g., "In sum, man . . . perfects all the works of lower nature, correcting and emending them." Marsilio Ficino, "Platonic Theology Books XII–XIV," in *Marsilio Ficino: Platonic Theology*, ed. Michael J. B. Allen and James Hankins (Cambridge, Mass.: Harvard University Press, 2004), 171.

were being sounded, pointing the percipient toward an unavoidable conclusion—the world as it comes to us from God's hand is in some sense
unacceptable or unbearable and must be gainsaid, broken, and "unna-
tured" (rather than "cultivated") for the sake of its being rendered fit for
human habitation. With Giovanni Lomazzo's allusion in 1584 to "errors
in nature" that must duly be "corrected" by the artist,[5] for instance, to the
familiar Neoplatonist longing for a higher and better world than this one
is added a perceptible note of impatient dissatisfaction bordering on "con-
temptuous disdain"[6] for empirical reality. Now we begin to find the idea
of the artist as one who sits in judgment rather than serving as a skilled
apprentice in the workshop of a divine master. Now what he expresses
is not a desire for more of what God has purposed but something that
improves upon and competes with it. Now what he proposes is not so
much a divinely sanctioned and initiated enhancement of nature but a
veritable *creatio nuova*, a making of all things new—and by the artist
rather than God.

Imagination and "the Infinite I AM"

Two centuries later, rather different philosophical currents were to give
added impetus and mileage to notions of this sort. As we have already seen
in chapter 5, the epistemology associated with Kant encouraged the supposition that human processes of sensation and cognition must be factored
into the substance and structures of the world as we experience it, giving
the human subject, in effect, some sort of partnership (with whatever reality
may be taken to exist objectively) in the construction of this same "world."[7]
In Kant's thoughts in particular, key roles are granted in this constructive
engagement to the imagination, situating the processes of our everyday perception of objects firmly within the same domain as those poetic and artistic ventures in which we trespass deliberately beyond and reconfigure the
given world in one way or another in "our mind's eye." This insight (if we
take it to be such) inevitably bears with it an ambiguity and a gray area. In
what sense and to what extent is the world "given" to us and/or constructed
by us? And in what sense and to what extent, therefore, is our partnership
(executed through the ministry of our imaginative capacity) an arcane and
unconscious (and thus "given") one or an active, deliberate, and *responsible*
one? The answers to such questions do not come easily, though it is possible

---

[5] Giovanni Paolo Lomazzo (1538–1600), *Trattoro dell'arte della pittura* 6.50; cited
in Erwin Panofsky, *Idea: A Concept in Art Theory*, trans. Joseph J. S. Peake (Columbia:
University of South Carolina Press, 1968), 81, 222–23.

[6] Panofsky, *Idea*, 81.

[7] See above, pp. 99–102.

to identify a shift in some eighteenth- and early nineteenth-century poetics, exploiting the relevant ambiguity in a manner that appears to grant the
conscious human subject a far greater role in and responsibility for the initial shaping and subsequent poetic *reshaping* of the world than had hitherto
been reckoned with.

Abrams notes this bold appropriation of new epistemologies already
in the middle of the eighteenth century and the *Night Thoughts* of English poet Edward Young, according to whom our senses "[g]ive taste to
fruits; and harmony to groves; / Their radiant beams to gold . . . ," and
"half create the wondrous world they see. / But for the magic organ's powerful charm," the poet concludes, "Earth were a rude, uncolour'd chaos
still."[8] Young's consistent deployment of active verbs—giving, creating,
making—to describe the mode of the human mind's participation in the
processes of perception, Abrams notes, effects a metaphoric substitution
in which Locke's sensationalism is to be found "converting itself into what
is often considered its epistemological opposite."[9] Once again, the precise relationship between the dynamics of give and take in the texture of
human experience proves difficult to pin down and the threads impossible
to disentangle without the whole unraveling.

A kindred estimate of the human contribution to the given world is
found at the turn of the nineteenth century in the poetry and musings of
the young Samuel Taylor Coleridge, where threads from sources as diverse
as the Bible, the Cambridge Platonists, and Schelling's peculiar variations
on Kant are woven into a suggestive but often elusive and indeterminable
pattern. In particular, his oft-cited account of imagination in chapter 13
of the *Biographia Literaria* (1815), with its twin distinctions between primary and secondary imagination and between imagination and fancy[10]
suggests at least two things: First, the texture of the world as it is given to
us in daily experience, on the one hand, and the deliberate reconfigurations and redescriptions of this world issuing from the eye of the poet and
the hand of the artist alike, on the other hand, each fall within the sphere

[8] Edward Young (1681–1765), *The Complaint; or, Night Thoughts on Life, Death and Immortality* (1743); cited in M. H. Abrams, *The Mirror and the Lamp: Romantic Theory and the Critical Tradition* (Oxford: Oxford University Press, 1953), 62.

[9] Abrams, *Mirror and the Lamp*, 63.

[10] See, Samuel Taylor Coleridge, *Biographia Literaria; or, Biographical Sketches of My Literary Life and Opinions*, ed. James Engell and W. Jackson Bate, *The Collected Works of Samuel Taylor Coleridge* (Princeton, N.J.: Princeton University Press, 1983), 7:304–5. Coleridge's account deliberately echoes Kant's distinction between the transcendental and the empirical imagination (see above p. 101), but should not be confused with it. See fur-ther the discussion in Trevor Hart, "Who Am I? Imagination and the God of *Biographia Literaria*," *Coleridge Bulletin* 38 (2011): 53–66.

of jurisdiction (albeit under distinct modes of operation) of a common agency—that of human imagination.[11] Second, this agency is itself at least continuous (and perhaps more than just continuous) with the impulses of that creative Spirit or force to whom (or to which) responsibility for the constantly unfolding manifold of nature and history must finally be ascribed—"the infinite I AM."[12] The exalted status ascribed here to imagination was quite deliberate and reflects Coleridge's conscious departure from the empiricism and "associationist" psychology of his early philosophical education.[13] The self, he now believed, was not a pliant and passive wax tablet upon which the world simply impressed itself as something "given" and nonnegotiable. Rather, the self (as it were) receives a world in the construction of which it has itself already had a significant hand, and it has now both the power and the responsibility to make something more of it. The poet, as one in whose hands the task of continuous symbolic reordering occurs most obviously and profoundly, is thus, in effect, a high priest ministering on our behalf in the sanctuary where, through the zenith of a divine-human imaginative *poesis*, the world is ever made anew for human indwelling.

---

[11] The "primary" imagination functions below the level of consciousness to construct "the fixities and definites" of our empirical experience. As such it reiterates the eternal creative act of God, furnishing a world for our shared indwelling. The "secondary" imagination differs from it not in kind but only in the degree and mode of its operation when, fused now with the conscious operations of will, it "dissolves, diffuses, dissipates, in order to re-create" such structures and so modifies the shape of the reality we inhabit. See Coleridge, *Biographia Literaria*, 304; Hart, "Who Am I?" 59–64.

[12] The consistent idealism of Schelling, with which Coleridge flirted but would eventually part company, pressed beyond Kant to elide two key distinctions: that between external reality (the "*Ding an Sich*") and the products of thought, and that between God and the world (Mind and mind) that were understood as perichoretic aspects of a single cosmic process. Thus, for the Coleridge who wrote *Biographia Literaria*, the imagination held an ambiguous status as part of an organic nature designed to vibrate and resonate as over it swept "one intellectual breeze, / At once the Soul of each, and God of all . . ." (line 48 of "The Eolian Harp" [1795], in Richard Holmes, ed., *Samuel Taylor Coleridge: Selected Poems* [London: Penguin, 1996], 37.)

[13] Coleridge's early intellectual debt to the "great Master of Christian Philosophy," David Hartley (1705–1757), was acknowledged in the naming of his firstborn (David Hartley Coleridge) in September 1796, but his enthusiastic discovery of Kant that same year eventually compelled him to part company with any account of human experience cast in fundamentally passive rather than "poetic" terms. See Richard Holmes, *Coleridge: Early Visions* (London: Hodder & Stoughton, 1989), 124, 368. Cf. Hart, "Who Am I?" 55–56.

Unbridled Romanticism and Countercreation

As yet, this account of the human circumstance is one remaining within striking distance of theological orthodoxy, though flirting dangerously with the pantheistic currents latent within post-Kantian idealism. Indeed, Coleridge's longing for a world shot through with divine significance, pregnant with the very presence and energy of God himself, and for an account of every human engagement with this world as being of a potentially creative and responsible sort (crystallized most fully in the work of the poet and the artist) would eventually be translated by the poet himself onto the soil of a more biblical and creedal understanding of God as Trinity.[14] Other currents in romanticism, though, took idealism's key dogma (that nothing is absolutely given to the self) and wove around it a very different sort of story about artistic creativity and its relation to the world. Whereas for Coleridge the imagination's natural transport was in a shared realm of "spirit"[15] in which creativity and discovery (and hence accountability) were at points wholly coterminous, for others the ambiguity of the Neoplatonic and idealist insistence that reality was to be sought by a process of introspection provided a natural stepping-stone to a radical emphasis on the individual creative will as something to which even the products of the "primary" or "productive" imagination were in principle susceptible.[16] Alongside this solipsistic impulse, two further factors deserve mention. First, the notion of nature as a benevolent, ordered system in harmony with whose range of available possibilities human beings were meant to exist and to act was once again displaced after Kant by a vision of nature as amoral,[17] at best neutral and at worst hostile to human flourishing, and of humanity as most fully realized, therefore, in actions that imposed the demands and values of human personality upon it. Second, while Kant himself maintained a view of moral values as in some sense a shared subjectivity (to the question "what is the right thing to do in this sort of circumstance?" reason would supply the same answer to all regardless of accidents of particular time and place), some of his heirs pressed the emphasis on the primacy of

---

[14] See further Daniel W. Hardy, "Coleridge on the Trinity," *Anglican Theological Review* 69 (1988): 145–55.

[15] See, e.g., Coleridge, *Biographia Literaria*, 80.

[16] Copleston identifies this key shift in Novalis and Schlegel. See Frederick Copleston, *A History of Philosophy* (New York: Image Books, 1965), 31. On the shift to individualism, cf. Abrams, *Mirror and the Lamp*, 7:43–44.

[17] Because nature is determined by causal necessity of one sort or another, whereas humanity is at its highest and best in its transcendence of necessity and "heteronomy" and its manifestation of "autonomy." See Isaiah Berlin, *The Roots of Romanticism* (London: Pimlico, 2000), 75–77. I say "once again," because as we have already seen, something similar is already apparent in strands of Renaissance humanism. See above pp. 200–201.

the will in another direction altogether, insisting upon the freedom of the individual to construct for him- or herself a set of personal values in accordance with which to act.[18]

If, as Isaiah Berlin suggests, the leitmotif of unbridled romanticism is to be found precisely here, in a conviction that reality presents no pattern that the indomitable will of the individual may not modify or reject; that the universe is thus, to some extent at least, as the individual *chooses to make it*; and that the world is humanized precisely and only by the individual's struggle to create something new and worthwhile out of an otherwise chaotic, intractable, and inhumane "nature,"[19] then again we find notions of the artist as "creator" cherished as a convenient symbol—because understood to be the highest instantiation—of all this. Or, one might view the matter from the other end and suggest instead that romanticism of this sort amounted in effect to the transposition of a certain sort of aesthetic (a particular understanding of the artist's "creative" relation to the world) into numerous other registers of human concern and practice.

Of course, there were more and less moderate versions of this romantic vision available, and not all of them were "unbridled." Thus, while for Coleridge art is indeed never merely "mimetic" but always "creative," the engine of secondary imagination pressing ever further on to bring something genuinely new and unprecedented into existence, opening reality up further thereby for our shared indwelling and participation, he nonetheless envisages the poet penetrating and realizing new possibilities that are in some sense already "there" to be created (or discovered and unfolded) and thus possessed of a natural "authenticity" that others may duly recognize and confirm in acts of aesthetic judgment.[20] More radically individualistic currents of thought, though, duly gave rise to notions of artistic *poesis* as the expression of a unique imaginative vision surging up from within an individual center of consciousness, concerned now not to break reality open so much as to break it up into its inextinguishable particles, deliberately flouting any apparent givens or latent trajectories in the flow of existence and struggling to impose new visions, new values, new ways

[18] Thus, Berlin notes that, for Schiller, "[i]f man is truly to be free . . . [h]e must stand above both duty and nature and be free to choose either." Berlin, *Roots of Romanticism*, 81. Cf. Copleston, *History of Philosophy*, 30.

[19] Berlin, *Roots of Romanticism*, 119–20.

[20] I have argued elsewhere that it is precisely this poetic purchase on something that straddles the distinction between subjective vision and objective value that sets imagination apart from mere "fancy" in Coleridge's account of the matter. See Hart, "Who Am I?" 60–64. As we shall see in chapter 12, the testimony of artists to something being "given" or coming unbidden as gift and seemingly "out of nowhere" rather than summoned into being ex nihilo by the deliberate exercise of artistic will is quite common.

of arranging the manifold of the human world in accordance with particular preference. This was art—and not just art but life—as an attempt to return the world to its primeval chaos in order to begin over again and order it anew.[21] This was art understood not as "co-creation"—intended to enhance the given habitus of nature or even to rectify its perceived shortcomings and amend its faults—but as a quite different form of "counterstatement" to the given world, one that celebrated the capacity of language not just to modify the world but finally to contradict and eliminate it.[22] This was art as protest, as an attempt to *displace* the given world; it was, in the convenient phrase of the Austrian satirist and playwright Karl Kraus, a *gegenschöpferisch* art—art intended and attempted as an initiative in imaginative "countercreation."[23]

Art, Creativity, and Oedipal Revolt

The artists of premodernity, it has been suggested, found themselves already at one with a cosmos that manifested itself fundamentally as home, and they were thus content to generate mimetic inventories in celebration of the extant, or symbolic, presentations of its perceived deeper meanings.[24] By contrast, the typical spirit of modernity, from its origins in the Renaissance onward, tends to reflect a profound dis-ease with the world in both its natural and its social manifestations—an unsettling sense, as it were, of cosmic homelessness or homesickness—and finds expression in a disposition to reality that is frequently "rebellious individualistic, unconventional, sensitive, irritable."[25] It should come as no surprise, therefore, that the art of modernity is on the whole far less concerned with exploring, celebrating, or interpreting the given forms of the human world and replete with instances of carefully imagined abstractions or alterities, some (though by no means all) of which take their leave from the given world by way of an Oedipal revolt against it,[26] whether by way of tragic protest in the face of its perceived meaninglessness or a bid to escape from the same or by annexing some small segment of it and—by imposing new form upon it—infusing it with

[21] Cf. Peter Conrad, *Creation: Artists, Gods and Origins* (London: Thames & Hudson, 2007), e.g., 54, 61, 92.

[22] "Language" is used here, as throughout this book, in the wider sense of humanly devised and developed schemes of signification, including visual, nonverbal aural, and other schemes besides those of words as such—i.e., the bedrock of human "culture." See further the discussion in chap. 6 above.

[23] See Conrad, *Creation*, 211.

[24] See, e.g., Robert Motherwell, in Herschel B. Chipp, *Theories of Modern Art* (Berkeley: University of California Press, 1968), 563.

[25] Chipp, *Theories of Modern Art*, 563.

[26] Steiner, *Grammars of Creation*, 19.

a meaning and feeling springing from the individual artistic vision alone, thereby rendering it a habitable dominion, a fiefdom to call home, and with which the artistic imagination may therefore, by virtue of a relation at once tautological and narcissistic, at last find itself dwelling at peace and at one.

The problem posed by such art, it should be noted at once, lies not in its formal abstraction as such, since, as I have argued above, some level of abstraction and transformation is necessarily involved in any case even in the making of the most painstaking of realistic representations,[27] and works of more marked abstraction may also pose a helpful challenge to the finality of the surface appearances of reality or draw our attention helpfully to the provisional and partial status of any and every perspective we occupy in approaching it.[28] So, for instance, while the cubist style in painting pioneered by Pablo Picasso and Georges Braque at the dawn of the twentieth century[29] has been interpreted as a "seismic assault" on the staid forms of given reality, a conflagration in which the artist—godlike in this—rearranges the form of the universe to suit his or her own personal preferences,[30] one may read it differently, as (among other things) a refusal to allow any single spatial perspective to be privileged over others and thus identified naively with the reality of the thing itself. Even the more extreme journeys into visual abstraction taken by artists such as Wassily Kandinsky and Mark Rothko, while they prescind wholly from the sphere of familiar empirical forms, nonetheless do so in the firm conviction that a deeper, shared reality (for Kandinsky one of spiritual energies or, in Rothko's case, of mood or emotion) is rendered accessible thereby to the viewer, abstract form and color serving here, as it were, as a language in terms of which a larger, more complex, and mysterious reality is brought to expression than that which otherwise meets the eye.[31]

[27] See above, pp. 157–59. Cf. H. W. Jansen and Anthony F. Jansen, *History of Art: The Western Tradition*, rev. 6th ed. (Upper Saddle River, N.J.: Pearson Prentice Hall, 2004), 810.

[28] Thus: "Art challenges the finality of appearance here and now, the actual 'conditions of existence,' not in order to destroy but to ground, amplify, fulfill." Rowan Williams, *Grace and Necessity: Reflections on Art and Love* (Harrisburg, Pa.: Morehouse, 2005), 21.

[29] See, e.g., Picasso's *Les demoiselles d'Avignon* (1907), illustrated in Carsten-Peter Warnke, *Pablo Picasso* (London: Taschen, 2006), 67. Cf. Georges Braque's *Bottle and Fishes* (1910–1912), which can be viewed at https://www.tate.org.uk/art/artworks/braque-bottle-and-fishes-t00445 (accessed January 12, 2014).

[30] See Conrad, *Creation*, 481.

[31] See, e.g., Wassily Kandinsky, *Concerning the Spiritual in Art*, trans. M. T. H. Sadler (Mineola, N.Y.: Dover, 1977), 24–25; Mark Rothko, *Writings on Art* (New Haven, Conn.: Yale University Press, 2005), 126–28; Mark Rothko, *The Artist's Reality: Philosophies of Art* (New Haven, Conn.: Yale University Press, 2004), 34–37. For illustration,

And yet, as Rowan Williams observes in a penetrating discussion of Maritain's aesthetics, for embodied creatures such as ourselves the apprehension of nonmaterial ("spiritual" or "emotional") realities is never immediate or "pure" but bound up with a more complex environment in which such realities are always grasped together with the perception of concrete objects.[32] Forms of abstraction that seek to bypass the forms of the material world altogether, therefore, by straying too far from "a clear sense of *any* externally given reality, intellectual or material," run the constant risk of losing touch with that reality and its intrinsic semiosis in which "things visible and invisible" belong and are held together. They collapse all too easily instead into an egoistic autism that merely transubstantiates the contents of the artist's own secret self into pigment, stone, or word.[33] The proper task of artistic abstraction (indeed of artistry as such), Williams suggests, is not to change the world till it accords with the artist's inner vision in this way but rather, paradoxically, through a dynamic of imaginative give and take that penetrates deeper and further into reality than its surface appearances, "to change it into itself."[34] Only in the case of God himself, we might presume, might these two tasks naturally and readily coincide. For the rest of us, such happy coincidence is bound to be partial at best. It arises, perhaps, only through an insight (one suffused with and engaged by the Spirit of God, knowingly or otherwise) into the given actualities and positive potentialities of the world, calling forth from us a respectful and joyful response in which the boundaries between the creative and the heuristic break down, and we find, perhaps to our surprise, that at their highest and best the dynamics of giving and receiving no longer contradict but coinhere.

The fleeting trespass into specifically religious and theological territory at this juncture is warranted by the terms in which artists and theorists themselves have often articulated their personal mandates and manifestoes in the modern era, especially those who have understood the

---

see, e.g., Kandinsky's *Tension in Red* (1926), in Ulrike Becks-Malorny, *Wassily Kandinsky* (London: Taschen, 2007), 154; Rothko's *Untitled* (Seagram Mural; 1959), in Jeffrey Weiss, ed., *Mark Rothko* (New Haven, Conn.: Yale University Press, 1998), 171.

[32] See Williams, *Grace and Necessity*, 18.

[33] Williams, *Grace and Necessity*, 20 (emphasis in original). The parallel with the concerns of Christology here is instructive, where the allure of an idealism that quickly loses touch with the particulars of Jesus' actual historical existence has frequently blunted the cutting edge of the doctrine of the incarnation. See Trevor Hart, "Through the Arts: Hearing, Seeing and Touching the Truth," in *Beholding the Glory*, ed. Jeremy S. Begbie (London: Darton, Longman & Todd, 2000), 19–25. Cf. Richard Bauckham, "Christology Today," *Scriptura* 27 (1988): 20–28.

[34] Williams, *Grace and Necessity*, 18.

artistic impulse as already complicit in a sort of practical atheism, adding infidel forms to the sum of things. "God, having created everything, left little room for human creativity."[35] This reading of the circumstance, especially when fused with a typically modern disdain for or protest against the given nature of things as such, has generated among some the aspiration to a defiant artistic creativity of a "godlike" sort, able to displace the world and substitute for it a freshly imagined, more congenial reality—one better suited to human flourishing than that we currently find ourselves saddled with. The romantic poet John Keats places the relevant sentiment provocatively on the lips of Saturn:

> cannot I create?
> Cannot I form? Cannot I fashion forth
> Another world, another universe
> To overbear and crumble this to naught?
> Where is another chaos? Where?[36]

Here, then, a gauntlet is thrown down, a challenge issued both to the given cosmos with its order divinely wrought and sustained in the face of an otherwise all-consuming dissolution into chaos and nothingness and to God's own prerogatives as Creator. Writing more than a century later, the painter and sculptor Barnett Newman revisited his own scriptural heritage to offer a reading of the Jewish story of creation and fall cast in related terms. Adam's fall, he suggested, was not one from grace into sin as generally understood but, was due to his aspiration to creativity, to be "like God, 'a creator of worlds,'" an aspiration cruelly thwarted and punished in a fit of divine jealousy. Yet the artistic act, Newman maintained, is our personal birthright, and the "seemingly insane drive of man to be painter and poet" is best understood as an act of defiance that would reclaim and realize it.[37] The "Creative Credo" (1920) of painter and poet Paul Klee toys with the same religiously incendiary presumption of "collegial affinity"[38] between the primeval achievement of God and the labors of the artist who, burning with a creative fire more naturally associated with Prometheus than Adam, struggles to leave behind things visible on earth, to dissolve them once again into a chaos out of which wholly new realities may emerge.[39] In the heat of such creative energy, Klee observes, the artist is given to fancy just for a moment that he is God, a fancy to which Klee himself duly gave voice and

[35] Conrad, *Creation*, 103.

[36] From "Hyperion" (1818–1819), in John Keats, *The Poetical Works of John Keats* (London: Frederick Warne, 1892), 241.

[37] Extract from Barnett Newman, "The First Man Was an Artist" in *Tiger's Eye* (New York), no. 1 (1947): 59–60; reproduced in Chipp, *Theories of Modern Art*, 551–52.

[38] Conrad, *Creation*, 473.

[39] See Chipp, *Theories of Modern Art*, 182–86.

perpetuated in one of his own poems.[40] Some thirty years earlier, the French postimpressionist painter Paul Gauguin (1848–1903) had dispatched some friendly advice to his fellow artist Émile Schuffenecker that, whether ostentatiously or more innocently, laid the essential presumption bare: "Do not paint too closely after nature," he wrote. "Art is an abstraction to be extricated from nature as you dream in the face of it, thinking less about nature than about the creation that will result. The only way of ascending to God is to create as God, our Divine Master, himself creates."[41]

Art as Disengagement and Revolt

Others, less prone to explicitly religious allusion, have been even more forthright in their construal of artistic creativity as a deliberate departure and self-isolation from the given state of play in the human world. In his own bleak account of the human circumstance, for example, the nihilistic philosopher Arthur Schopenhauer (1788–1860) presents the world as a dreadful place bereft of underlying meaning or value and sentient existence within it as unavoidably tragic, a constant and unending drive toward imagined goods we can either never possess or never find satisfaction in, blighted with incredible cruelty and suffering while it lasts, and destined to end without exception in the maw of death and decay.[42] Unsurprisingly, therefore, Schopenhauer's prescription is one in which withdrawal from all this (and the sooner the better) figures largely. Dismissing suicide as an option, Schopenhauer looks instead to other forms of human action that afford a means of deliberate disengagement from the world and its processes. Chief among these he lists the "aesthetic" practices of artistic creativity and contemplation in which, he supposes, a state of "peace," "blessedness," or "pure knowledge" is attained that, because it is by definition divorced from the maelstrom of intellectual and practical categories and concerns by which empirical experience is otherwise structured and driven, transcends the relentless dialectic of suffering and satisfaction attendant upon them.[43] Music, in particular, he suggests, due to its largely nonrepresentational relation to the world, liberates us from its grip and affords another, more direct, way of engaging with the underlying reality

---

[40] Conrad, *Creation*, 473.

[41] "Un conseil, ne peignez pas trop d'apres nature en rêvant devant et pensez plus à la création qui résultera, c'est le seul moyen de monter vers Dieu en faisant comme notre Divin Maitre, créer." Maurice Malingue, ed., *Lettres de Gauguin a sa femme et a ses amis* (Paris: Bernard Grasset, 1946).

[42] For a helpful overview setting all this in context, see Brian Magee, *The Tristan Chord: Wagner and Philosophy* (New York: Metropolitan Books, 2000), 152–73.

[43] See, e.g., Arthur Schopenhauer, *The World as Will and Representation*, vol. 1, trans. E. F. J. Payne (New York: Dover, 1969), 195–200.

of things, the perpetual interplay between tension and resolution in melody and harmony, for instance, furnishing an aural window onto "will," the noumenal force that Schopenhauer identifies as the "inner being" of the visible world and of the human soul alike.[44]

Schopenhauer's notion of deep reality as a meaningless chaos, forever surging and abating and giving the lie to our attempts either to discover or to fashion lasting order and value for ourselves, captured the imagination of the composer Richard Wagner (1813–1883), who duly sought to bring music (as the art-form uniquely fitted to lay all this bare) to the appointed peak of its achievement. His opera *Tristan and Isolde* (1854–1860), for instance, turns the deferred gratification of harmonic suspension into an art form all by itself, toying constantly with audience expectations from the spine-tingling double dissonance of the opening chord of the *Vorspiel* onward, forever eschewing the longed-for resolution via a skillful incessant modulation from one seeming tonal center to another until at last—the unsatisfied passion of hero and heroine having built to an almost unbearable tension—in the aural world of the work as in Schopenhauer's cosmos, the final glorious chord arrives and with it death both for the eponymous protagonists and (by way of anticipation) for us as hearers of the work too, since only in death are the perpetual dissonances of life resolved.[45] By lifting us out of the world, art thus points and propels us toward death as its natural tragic fulfillment.

Being-toward-death in a quite distinct but not wholly unrelated sense is one of the characteristics of an "authentic" and free humanity in Martin Heidegger's version of existentialism,[46] though it is perhaps more helpful for our immediate purposes here to consider briefly instead the thought of one of Heidegger's near contemporaries, Jean-Paul Sartre (1905–1980), on the themes of creative imagination and the arts.[47] Like Schopenhauer,

[44] See Schopenhauer, *World as Will*, 1:255–67. Cf. Arthur Schopenhauer, *The World as Will and Representation*, vol. 2, trans. E. F. J. Payne (New York: Dover, 1966), 447–57.

[45] On the *Vorspiel*, see, e.g., Donald Tovey, *Essays in Musical Analysis* (London: Oxford University Press, 1936), 4:124–26. On *Tristan and Isolde* and Schopenhauer more widely, cf. Magee, *Tristan Chord*, 207–24.

[46] See, e.g., Martin Heidegger, *Being and Time*, trans. John Macquarrie and Edward Robinson (Oxford: Blackwell, 1962), 299–311. For brief but helpful commentary, see John Macquarrie, *Existentialism* (London: Penguin, 1973), 193–98, 218. Perhaps the most obvious disparity between Schopenhauer and Heidegger at this point is the latter's insistence that death, far from being that which permits final retreat from the world, is that which, once owned as the horizon of creaturely finitude, charges every moment of Dasein's existence with authentic meaning and thus both permits and demands a deeper immersion in the world.

[47] The following account is indebted to that in Richard Kearney, *The Wake of Imagination: Toward a Postmodern Culture* (London: Routledge, 1988), 224–48.

Sartre holds that the basic state of given reality is contingent and absurd, a world bereft of significance and value into which humankind finds itself cruelly thrown and within which it is constantly haunted by the desire for a meaningful existence. Whereas Schopenhauer counsels disengagement from the world, though, Sartre calls for a very different sort of response— one in which imagination conceives of, constructs, and projects its own set of meanings, thereby granting some overall sense of direction and purpose in the light of which life may be lived in the midst of the world in a worthwhile manner.

Drawing a sharp distinction between the psychological processes of perception and imagination,[48] Sartre notes that the latter (the positing of an "image") in an important sense always involves the displacement or denial of given reality, directing us instead to something apprehended precisely and only in its literal *absence*. To imagine what a friend might presently be doing is precisely to posit a circumstance not present within the immediate perceptual field and one that may well not exist at all outside the generative matrix of the imaginary world itself.[49] Other imaginative acts posit their objects precisely as *nonexistent*—as when we imagine, for instance, how things might have turned out very differently if only we had worked harder or a world in which disease, poverty, crime, and injustice have been eradicated without trace or the tantalizing set of variations on a slow and painful demise inflicted on the person currently most deserving of our ire. Whatever its object, imagination always presents us with something other than what the perceptual world presently yields, unhindered by the objective constraints of the given. Thus, the basic mode of operation of imagination, Sartre suggests, is one in which creativity always proceeds in some sense ex nihilo, the world of the image first *negating* reality by refusing to be bound by its limits and, second, itself being posited precisely as a "nothing," an *absence* or *nonexistence* rather than an actual presence, albeit one in dogged attachment to which human life may and must be lived as an act of resistance to the actual nature of things. This same generative movement from reality to the "imaginary" via the process of *néantisation*, Sartre holds, is proper both to the heroic production of "humanizing" meaning and values (in the face of the actual meaninglessness of one's existence otherwise) and to the creation of works of art. Whatever its precise relation to the

---

[48] Like David Hume, Sartre acknowledges that memory/anticipation constitutes a third, hybrid category sharing certain features in common with both the relative passivity of perception and the constructive alterities of imagination. See, e.g., Jean-Paul Sartre, *The Imaginary: A Phenomenological Psychology of the Imagination*, trans. Jonathan Webber (London: Routledge, 2004), 181–82. Cf. David Hume, *A Treatise of Human Nature*, 2nd ed. (Oxford: Clarendon, 1978), 8–10.

[49] See Sartre, *Imaginary*, 12–13.

flesh and blood realities of the sensual or to particular configurations of material objects, the "aesthetic object" is not and cannot be had at the level of the empirical alone, he insists, but "is constituted and apprehended by an imaging consciousness that posits it as irreal."[50] This is not to rob art of its "reality" in another sense, of course, since, as we have just seen, strictly speaking for Sartre all that truly matters to us as human beings falls into this same category of "irreality"[51]—that is to say, that which imagination generates from its own resources and superimposes on an absurd world to furnish a place fit for human dwelling.

The analogy between the artistic vision realized in the particular work and the process of imaginative self-projection and self-creation in which the individual wills himself to be what he first imagines himself to be lies readily to hand here, and Sartre grasps it gladly in one of his later writings: "[i]n life man commits himself, draws his own portrait and there is nothing but this portrait."[52] Just as the painter composes a picture, aesthetic values arising only in and through the dialectic that unfolds between the artist's will and her materials to produce the finished work, so the individual human subject too must compose his or her own authentic self in and through the choices and actions of a life lived, generating and sustaining meaning and values along the way rather than finding these ready to hand in some predefined template or authorized version. For all its heroism—and despite its avowed humanism—this picture of the self as a work of art created ex nihilo in the teeth of an absurd and inhospitable reality is nonetheless finally crushing and inhumane in the weight of responsibility it places upon human shoulders. Eschewing all sense of givenness in the supposed interests of human "freedom," it has no sense whatever of the world as gift or of a grace beyond the self that conscripts responsible (and genuinely free) human action and initiative without leaving these isolated and defenseless against the evils of failure, defeat, and loss. Creativity and authenticity are to be had here only at a considerable price.

A humanist vision of artistry close to that of Sartre in many respects is found in the writing of the French novelist, explorer, and art historian André Malraux (1901–1976), whose critical magnum opus, *The Voices of Silence*, offers an essentially Hegelian narration of the history of human art as the struggle for artistic self-awareness, a struggle reaching a decisive breakthrough, Malraux suggests, in the art of modernity.[53] In the

---

[50] Sartre, *Imaginary*, 191.

[51] Sartre, *Imaginary*, 125–48.

[52] Jean-Paul Sartre, *Existentialism and Humanism* (London: Methuen, 1948); cited in Kearney, *Wake of Imagination*, 241.

[53] André Malraux, *The Voices of Silence* (Princeton, N.J.: Princeton University Press,

peculiarly modern notion of the artist as a uniquely gifted individual who
"creates" a work that is its own end and generates its own standards of
evaluation, who imposes his or her will on the world to give expression
to a radically individual vision, struggling to break free from the given
constraints both of nature's forms and of the conventions of representation
embodied in artistic traditions, and who does all this first and foremost
in order to satisfy his or her own need to create—in all this, Malraux
believed, art had attained, if not quite its appointed eschatological telos,
nonetheless an epiphanic new consciousness of its own proper place in the
larger scheme of things, a messianic disclosure, as it were, of things hidden
from the foundation of the world. Thus, he suggests, the great works of
antiquity could now be resuscitated and granted a new and unprecedented
power to speak by liberating them from their original social and practical
contexts in life and submitting them instead to the canons of modern aesthetic interpretation.[54] Whatever the artists concerned may have supposed
about their work and its semantic charge, a decorated terra-cotta vase from
China's Xia dynasty (c. 2070–c. 1600 B.C.), an Assyrian winged bull with
human head carved in the eighth century B.C., a late medieval altar screen
and a painting by Titian, once translated to the hushed sanctuary of that
peculiarly modern institution, the art museum, may all be baptized retrospectively into the now audible conversation of human art, discovering
for the first time (and perhaps to their surprise) that—approached in the
right way—they possess the relevant grammar and vocabulary and can
hold their own alongside a Van Gogh, a Picasso, or a Francis Bacon. The
underlying language, Malraux believed, was global if not exactly demo-
cratic (being the privileged tongue of artistic genius alone). But what was
it saying to those with ears to hear?

In effect, for Malraux as for Sartre, human artistry wherever and
whenever it is to be found amounts to an articulate cry of indignation
and protest in the face of a fate worse than death—namely, the otherwise
meaningless and brutish nature of our animal existence and a material cosmos indifferent to our achievements.[55] Art is a challenge (albeit ultimately
a fleeting one) to the ephemerality and transience of human existence
itself and a defiant projection of meaning into the void of nothingness,
furnishing sufficient cultural moorings in the bestial terrain of "nature"
for human life to be lived with a self-generated dignity and purpose. Art
(and most obviously modern art with its impulse toward abstraction and

---

1978). For a sympathetic but critical reading of Malraux, see Nicholas Wolterstorff, *Art in
Action: Toward a Christian Aesthetic* (Carlisle, U.K.: Solway, 1997), 203–13.

[54] See, e.g., Malraux, *Voices of Silence*, 607–16.

[55] Malraux, *Voices of Silence*, 639–42.

formalism) is the deliberate negation of a tainted world, devalorizing reality and annexing it in order to "build up a world apart and self-contained, existing in its own right," a fragile enclave of original human meaning making in which the artist alone is sovereign.[56] Artistic creativity come of age thus inevitably involves a struggle for autonomy from demands and constraints on several fronts—from nature and its forms, from tradition and social expectations, from any supposed "givens" in fact beyond those the individual artist chooses to appropriate or generate afresh in structuring the world of his or her work. Despite a closing gesture in the direction of a "religious" interpretation of all this,[57] there is here, as Nicholas Wolterstorff observes,[58] little sense at all of the artist as one sharing in a divinely ordained calling to humankind to "master" the world through nonaggressive engagements, making more of it than its given empirical form already presents and offering it back in grateful thanksgiving. There is no notion of human glory (including that of the artist) as springing naturally from a freedom exercised and realized most fully in obedient response. For Malraux (and we may take him as typical of a sort), the artist's glory lies rather in the note of defiant revolt against the given world—noble, pointed, and tragic—protesting eloquently in the face of perceived oblivion rather than "voicing creation's praise."

In the Image and Likeness of Whom?

The story that this chapter and the last have been concerned to tell is a complex one, and constraints of space necessarily compel a more limited selection and exploration of its characters and plot lines than the telling might otherwise seem to demand. Furthermore, as we shall see in the next chapter, while it is a story the influence and institutions of which are still all too apparent in one way or another in the culture of early twenty-first-century Western societies, in other respects (not least in the ways in which artistry is currently theorized) it is a story that has long since passed its sell-by date, the modern image of the artist (or anyone else) as "creator" having been interrogated exhaustively and found wanting by theorists, critics, and practitioners of more postmodern sympathies. Nonetheless, since the appellation "postmodern" itself (with characteristic irony) betrays its considerable debt to the milieu of modernity even as it announces its determination to leave it behind, the story remains important, being formative in ways that will continue to exercise all the more power over us if we presume already to have escaped their grip (should that indeed be our aspiration).

---

[56] Malraux, *Voices of Silence*, 320, 461, 616.

[57] Malraux, *Voices of Silence*, 642.

[58] See Wolterstorff, *Art in Action*, 213.

What we have seen is that a peculiar synchronicity of intellectual, practical, and religious elements furnished the conditions for an alchemic reaction out of which (among other things) a decisively new understanding of human artistry would duly emerge. The advent of a new scientific approach to the world, by its deliberate erasure of all available human perspectives or responses, eventually engendered a sense of alienation from nature itself as a human-friendly environment. Developing technologies, meanwhile, made rapid strides forward in their capacity to control and exploit natural forces and processes, bending them as necessary (or desirable) to human advantage. And, outside the "hands-on" contexts of the laboratory and the workshop, the educated gentlemen of early modernity were also to be found resuscitating ancient religio-philosophical aspirations and ideals concerning the place of humankind in the cosmos. When, in the midst of all this cultural fomentation (as most of the early Renaissance humanists still did), they sat down and opened their Bibles and began to read, many of them found themselves drawing strikingly different conclusions from those of their Christian forebears concerning the semantic force of the description of the first human creatures in the divine image and likeness, and the image of the Creator himself as an artist, reversing the direction of the metaphor in a manner that rode roughshod over some of the vital qualifications and acknowledgments of "otherness" between the two terms that make it a metaphor at all. The result, as we have seen, was not just a flawed hermeneutics and poetics but a potentially disturbing new way of thinking about the place of the human artist—and with the artist (whose significance in this regard is paradigmatic) humankind as a whole in its presumed new "creative" disposition and birthright—in the larger cosmic scheme of things.

The typically modern mood of disenchantment and lack of at-one-ment with the material cosmos has, to be sure, been felt more and less acutely. It has also provoked a wide range of artistic responses: from the desire to probe more deeply into a presumed reality lying as yet hidden beneath or beyond the world's mere surface appearances; through the felt need to humanize nature by swamping or supplementing it with a world of subjective meaning and value (humanly generated, and thus only loosely attached to the surface of "reality," to be blown away eventually like so much spume by the winds of history and mortality); to the angry and embittered rejection of the given world as a whole, gesturing the severity of its protest by deliberately violating nature's forms and renouncing its citizenship of prevailing cultures, seeking instead the establishment of aesthetic silos within which retreat and sanctuary (if not ultimate redemption) may—at least for the while—be found. These are not the only responses to be found, of course, but they are prominent among the sorts of responses most characteristic of the modern cultural moment, and each of them departs from an imaginative disposition which finds itself fundamentally ill at ease with the given world and seeking an exodus from it.

Of course, as we have had reason to observe several times, some form or level of dissatisfaction with the given state of things or desire for more or other than the world currently affords to experience is a vital existential condition of the imaginative life in general and thus of artistry in particular. And the moods of the subjunctive and the conditional, counterfactuality and counterstatement, supply the oxygen that artistic imagination needs to breathe if it is to survive, just as surely as they render the atmosphere within which alone human freedom is able to subsist and heuristic ventures (whether of scientific or other sorts) into as yet uncharted territories of reality are possible. Even the deliberate flouting and contradiction of nature's laws by the poetic eye has an ancient pedigree stretching from Ovid's *Metamorphoses* to the playful visual alchemy of Flemish Renaissance painter Hieronymus Bosch's triptych the *Garden of Earthly Delights* (c. 1475).[59] And yet, the aesthetic counterstatements of modernity to the given world, especially those born of a response more Oedipal than filial in nature, are wedded to an ideal and aspiration idiosyncratic in its temerity, calling into being objects as wholly unlike anything in nature as possible and drawing close to the vertiginous brink of an absolute incipience of meaning, a distinctly human repetition of the primordial "Let there be" that sounded out authoritatively across the waters. That the ideal was flawed and the aspiration doomed to failure was something artists knew well enough from the outset and something which postmodern critics have tirelessly reminded those who have remained wedded to it, a fact that has served, it seems, merely to raise the stakes of the game and, for those so minded, to heighten the sense of ill will toward the given world and furnish further warrant for abetting its eventual disintegration and displacement. Had more attention been paid to those same biblical texts from which the term "creation" was originally lifted and press-ganged into wider service, though, it might have been noticed that the entailments of really modeling human "creativity" (artistic or otherwise) on the example of the divine Creator are altogether more radical and costly than the gesture of any attempted coup d'etat or doomed storming of the gates of heaven, and in reality they point us in a quite different direction.

[59] For illustration, exposition, and probable dating, see Laurinda Dixon, *Bosch* (London: Phaidon, 2003), 226–78.

11

Creativity, Art, and Originality

Creativeness, Capacity, and Incapacity

Despite the grandiose aspirations and mystique attaching to the figure and the practices of the artist in the modern Western world, artistry remains at root an earthbound and earthy business. It is just one way in which human beings manipulate matter in order to explore, express, and articulate distinctly human perspectives on the world—how the world appears or feels to some at least of its human inhabitants—presenting these objectively for the consideration and response of others. In the arts, in other words, we are very far from the sort of imaginative leap attempted by the sciences into a cosmos shorn of all human sensations, values, and significance. Indeed, it is precisely some identifiably human perspective or other (whether actual or merely possible) that art is generally concerned imaginatively to explore and exploit and express, infusing the world of objects and events again with the sorts of meaning and feeling characteristic of the quality of our immediate experience, but which processes of reflection and intellection bracket early out of consideration. To be sure, art itself is a product of careful articulation, making use of and developing "languages" of one sort or another; but its languages are ones that arise naturally out of and appeal to the whole of our embodied existence, articulating and provoking responses in which sensation, imagination, emotion, and conation are inextricably and properly tangled up with the cognitive. The arts, that is to say, are a central instance of that wider "third realm" (between the purely "objective" deliberations of science and the private or "subjective" inner worlds of our particular

personal responses to things) that Anthony O'Hear identifies as the realm
of human "cultures."[1] Indeed, if the phenomenon of language itself might
properly be supposed fundamental to this realm,[2] then artistry might reasonably be identified as one of its most significant manifestations, at least in
the sense that the artist does deliberately and carefully something that all
of us are involved in doing all the time in the give and take of our dealings
with the world—taking and transforming matter in humanly significant
ways. Whether or not the achievements of the artist (let alone those of any
particular artist) are to be judged better or more exalted than any one of a
number of other ways of taking the world and transforming it is a question
likely to arouse vigorous contest and perhaps generate more heat than light
unless granted more space than that available to us here. But the suggestion
that artistry, inasmuch as it constitutes an articulate human response to
and transformation of the world as we find it to hand, affords a convenient
paradigm of our wider condition as embodied beings indwelling a world
mediated not by our bodies alone but equally by the conventions and institutions of human culture, is hopefully beyond reasonable dispute. We are
creatures who, in one way or another, make matter matter, and in doing so
make ourselves at home in the world.

   If artistry is indeed paradigmatic of this necessarily and unashamedly
anthropocentric venture, then shifting assumptions about the nature of
artistry itself may perhaps tell us something about what we presume to
be true more widely as regards our human dispositions, permissions, and
possibilities as recipients, inhabitants, and modifiers of a world. In the
previous two chapters, we have seen how the theologically charged language of "creation" entered art-theoretical discourse, serving to reinforce
and undergird (if not actually to generate ex nihilo) an emergent humanist account of artistic prowess, potential, and achievement quite distinct
in shape and substance from anything that had preceded it. We also saw
that this new understanding of the artist was enmeshed within and supported by a wider, religiously and theologically informed, and sustained
account of human capacity and prospects within the cosmic scheme of
things, one courtesy of which in due course, by (in Karl Barth's phrase)
"thinking of ourselves what can be thought only of God," human beings
found themselves increasingly "unable to think of Him more highly than
we think of ourselves"[3] and party to a form of anthropocentrism that, far

   [1] See the discussion above, pp. 109–23.
   [2] Cf. Anthony O'Hear, *The Element of Fire: Science, Art and the Human World* (London: Routledge, 1988), 19.
   [3] Karl Barth, *The Epistle to the Romans*, trans. Edwyn C. Hoskyns (London: Oxford
University Press, 1933), 45.

from finding itself at home in the cosmos as an environment divinely fitted for our indwelling, found itself instead increasingly alienated from a godless Nature perceived as indifferent and hostile to human interests and incapable finally of exercising the sort of dominion required to tame and domesticate it to satisfy its inflated aspirations and demands. In theological terms, one might construe this as a shift from an economy of gift and response to one centered and reliant instead on autonomous human merits and achievements and discovering the hard way that such a path leads finally only to exile, disappointment, and death.

In many respects, as the cultural and intellectual heirs to modernity, the sense of exile or homesickness still pervades Western cultures today in the era of postmodernity. By its very nature, though, the postmodern tends to be more tolerant of strategies for the world's "re-enchantment," and the disillusionment resultant upon its playful deconstruction of modernist humanism's more Promethean postulates is perhaps in many ways a more hopeful and advantageous place from which to propose a theologically informed response (including a theologically informed account of the nature and place of human artistry and creativity) than those afforded by various versions of modernity itself. Typically, it is only when we have reached the point of despairing in our own autonomous resources that we are open to consider other possibilities. And while there are no doubt those wedded to an (ironic and oxymoronic) absolute determination to reject a priori the possible truthfulness or worth of any and every local announcement of good news or hopeful initiative, the self-referential incoherence of such a stance liberates those with stories worth sharing to venture them forth without fear of being swept aside or drowned out by the strident demand for empirical verification, logical certitude, or some other shibboleth arbitrarily appointed and enjoying unrivalled authority in the name of supposed common sense. In an intellectually, culturally, and religiously plural context, and one which has long since ceased to be patient with various forms of arid materialism, particular stories about the way things stand between God and the world can again be told, even if the telling of them may need to adopt a rather different tone of voice than that which has characterized its more imperialistic forms across human history from the age of Constantine onward.

In such a context, a vision of human creatureliness understood as gift rather than unbearable constraint and of human creativity as a matter of costly and responsible accountability rather than sovereign caprice and individual self-projection may offer one way (one that Christians will be passionately committed to sharing as glimpsing a truth deeper and wider than the boundaries of a Christian symbolics alone) toward an imaginative reordering in and through which the rediscovery of the world as "home," a habitation fit for human indwelling precisely because it is fit for more than human indwelling alone, might occur. It will be the burden of my final chapter to sketch the contours and landmarks of the world reimagined in this distinctly theological light, as a gift of God's unmerited grace that calls forth from us properly "creative" responses of what I shall dub a "liturgical" and "eucharistic" sort, thereby drawing us—and together with us the whole of creation—into the threefold dynamics of God's own life and being.

The rhetoric of "creation" and "creativity" in particular has enjoyed an ambiguous and uncertain status amidst the decay of modernity and its gradual replacement by less self-assured perspectives. In discourses about the arts, it has for the most part been interrogated, found wanting, and set aside as a language hopelessly wedded to delusory accounts of the status and significance of the human subject and the sorts of "theology" to which these were (albeit often tacitly or unawares) allied. In its turn, this general abandonment of the notion of the creation of the work of art has provoked a vigorous backlash from a vocal minority of theorists much less convinced that the humanist vision can or should be so easily swept aside or that, despite its undoubted difficulties, a strong account of human creativity is not finally needed simply to account for the data of experience. Those willing to advocate such an account, though, are on the whole equally concerned to disentangle it and set it identifiably apart from the other significant form in which talk about human creativity has survived its postmodern deconstruction and denial—namely, the effective democratization and dilution of such language via its metaphorical extension into almost every territory of human endeavor and achievement. Indeed, the conviction that "all of us contain a vast reservoir of untapped creativity"[4] is perhaps more widespread today than either the insistence that acts of a genuinely "creative" sort remain the prerogative of a privileged (or blighted) few or the wholesale eschewal of talk about human creativeness and its apparent implications on the part of some postmodern critics and Christian theologians. The extent to which such varied convictions are actually concerned with the same thing, and thus may be more compatible than first appearances would suggest, is one of the questions which will occupy us in what follows. The point of this chapter and the one that follows, though, is not to extend the necessarily partial and fragmentary narrative sketched in the preceding two. Instead, I will approach the topic by attending synchronically to a series of key moments or elements characteristic of contemporary discussions about creativity and creation (in the arts and more widely), hoping thereby to build up a map of some

---

[4] Jonah Lehrer, *Imagine: How Creativity Works* (Edinburgh: Canongate, 2012), 108.

of the more salient points around which concurrence and contradiction tend naturally to gather. As with most maps there is no obvious point from which to begin sketching, but one strong contender must be the widespread acknowledgment that the creative is bound up in one way or another with the advent of something "new." Beyond this broad point, as we shall see, agreement rapidly fragments into quite different estimates of its significance.

Significant Newness

If *Homo sapiens* is always and as such *Homo faber* too, as my argument thus far has suggested, then as George Steiner notes we are also *Homo quaerens*,[5] the animal that is restless in the mere presence of the given, constantly inquiring about what may yet be, constantly seeking the advent of the new. The possession of the future tense, and of the conditional and subjunctive moods, shapes human existence from first to last and orients it always toward the uncertainty of the possible. Language permits imaginative egress in other directions too, of course, and we are generally just as concerned to situate ourselves in relation to meaningful processes or sequences of events leading up to the present as we are with those which may duly issue forth from or break into it from beyond. This too is basic to the ways in which we situate ourselves in the world and "make sense" of things. For, as Steiner suggests, we cannot "at the level of 'intuitive immediacy' . . . imagine . . . substantive meaning, existence without origination."[6] Only in the abstract imagining of mathematics can we properly conceive of that which has no beginning. In the real world (the "human world," as I have been referring to it), questions of provenance and productive processes therefore spring naturally and quickly to mind, and it is far from being a mere childish conceit even to inquire about the hour before the big bang, the scientific postulate designed finally to silence the relevance of such questioning, at least within science's own sphere of jurisdiction. Yet everything in the deep structures of language and human consciousness strains naturally to travel further in that direction and will not happily let the question go unanswered.

It is undoubtedly one important function of the doctrine of creation to satisfy such questioning, assuring us—while acknowledging to the full the metaphorical sense of the language used—that "before" the beginning (and thus before the created temporality intertwined inexorably with the structures of language itself) there was God, and God alone. Of course, this bold claim in isolation raises rather than answers a whole host of urgent questions about the nature and meaning and moral charge

[5] George Steiner, *Grammars of Creation* (London: Faber & Faber, 2001), 16.
[6] Steiner, *Grammars of Creation*, 14.

attaching to the divine decision to create, and our incessant "chronologi-
cal" curiosity cannot be disentangled from such considerations for long.
But of the new thing arising *within* the flow of creaturely history and
action too, we naturally crave knowledge of its origins and the relevant
conditions of its appearance. Here, at once, we are compelled to acknowledge the many different levels and sorts of "newness" characteristic of different elements in our lived experience.

We need not crave baptism in the river of Heraclitean flux in order to
acknowledge the point that in one sense every moment of our lived experience, every encounter with even the most familiar of things, is possessed
of something irreducibly particular, unique, and in that sense "new."
Repetition of the same is never *mere* repetition but, within the complex
waves and meter of creaturely space-time, arises as something charged
with its own singular significance, should we care to attend to it.[7] And
it is precisely this singularity, this hypostatic nonsubstitutability of every
particular moment in time and every particular object of knowing, that
ethical and aesthetic dispositions in particular are concerned to recognize
and respond to, refusing to move too quickly to classify or subsume under
convenient generalities and asking instead about the special significance
that *this* instance of something may possess, treating the particular, in
Martin Buber's now familiar terms, as *Thou* rather than *It*.[8] The artistic
eye, it seems, often cannot help but notice such radical specificity and
longs to draw our attention to it, adopting various strategies of defamil-
iarization to help to shake us out of our complacent schematizing. And
yet, for both practical and theoretical purposes, we are compelled too in
many contexts to overlook particularity of various sorts, to recognize that
similarity and sameness too have their vital significance in our dealings
with things and our identification of meaningful order in the world. A
world in which *everything* in our experience presented itself for consideration as something radically unique and unfamiliar would, after all, be a
chaotic and bewildering flux rather than an orderly cosmos. Heraclitus'
river may flow through it, but we live in a world in which—in another
sense and for certain important ends, as the biblical author recognized—
there is "nothing new under the sun" (Eccl 1:9). And so, in different life
contexts, it is not newness *as such* but that which presents itself within

---

[7] For an illuminating discussion of this linking the repetition of eucharistic liturgy to
the metrical structure of music in the Western tradition, see Jeremy S. Begbie, *Theology,
Music and Time*, ed. Colin Gunton and Daniel Hardy, Cambridge Studies in Christian
Doctrine (Cambridge: Cambridge University Press, 2000), 155–75.

[8] See Martin Buber, *I and Thou*, trans. Ronald Gregor Smith (Edinburgh: T&T
Clark, 1937).

those contexts as *significantly* new that we tend naturally to notice and to be concerned with.

It is precisely with respect to the provenance of certain instances of such *significant newness*—objects or events that when we encounter them will not submit to convenient classification but insist, as it were, on drawing our attention first to themselves and their peculiar qualities—that the metaphor of "creation" and human "creativity" has been felt by some naturally to commend itself, despite the qualifications and potential misunderstandings attaching to it. If for now we limit our attention to the context of the arts, then, mutatis mutandis, it is often precisely the "eye-catching" nature of the work, its radical particularity and irreducible "thisness," that registers noticeably in our experience and, according to much art theory since Kant, serves to distinguish the contemplative or "aesthetic" gaze from more pragmatic or theoretical dispositions toward it that might otherwise be perfectly proper and helpful (what sort of thing is it, and what might we use it for?). It is this sense of the hypostatic uniqueness of the work, Steiner suggests, that renders the analogy of divine creation most fitting, since here, as at the dawn of the cosmos, we recognize the presence of something particular, contingent, and valuable that, apart from a freely chosen personal act, would and could not exist. "Though material possibility, economic and social circumstance, historical openings bear on aesthetic creation," he writes, "the making of the poem, of the painting, of the sonata remains contingent. In every case, it could *not have been*."[9] The work of art, like the cosmos, is thus doubly haunted by (and in some sense includes within itself) the possibility of its own *nonbeing* and its eventual disappearance or destruction, setting it apart, Steiner suggests, from the objects of mere discovery or invention. (Given the general physical structures and potentialities of the material cosmos, and the pattern of intellectual and practical advancement in human understanding of these, "[h]ad this man or that team not 'made the discovery' . . . another scientist or team would have done so, possibly at almost the same moment."[10] History testifies repeatedly to such heuristic synchronicity in science and technology, but it makes little sense, Steiner insists, to apply it to the nontechnical [genuinely aesthetic] aspects of the poem, the painting, or the play, any more than we can meaningfully posit "progress" as a relevant pattern to apply here, as if Aeschylus' dramas or Dante's poetry, merely by virtue of coming earlier in the passage of time, were inevitably inferior to or less valuable than the works of Shakespeare, Byron, or Eliot. Art, unlike science and technology, Steiner observes, does not in that sense become

[9] Steiner, *Grammars of Creation*, 24 (emphasis in original).
[10] Steiner, *Grammars of Creation*, 24.

"out of date."[11]) As something radically particular, too, Steiner notes, the work of art also bears within it vestiges of nonbeing, of unrealized possibility that might have been, of that which the artist did *not* choose, the imperative "let there be" being wedded necessarily to the corresponding negative, "let there not be,"[12] and creation—as a manifestation of freedom—therefore wedded to election. In all these respects, for Steiner the "gratuity towards being"[13] that marks the activity of the poet, the painter, the composer, the playwright, echoes the primal "negation of negation" effected by God himself and is thus properly to be figured in terms of the language of creation rather than mere "making."

Beyond Déjà Vu

Can there be, then, any absolute *novum* in the sphere of human action and experience? Again, much depends on the roles we permit our terms to play, and of course there is a sense (arguably a reasonable one) in which every moment of our experience is by definition new in relation to all those that have preceded and anticipated it and contains that which is sensu stricto unprecedented and unique rather than unadulterated déjà vu. And yet, if we allow "absolute" to indicate the set of general patterns and possibilities to which scientific investigation of an orderly cosmos bears witness, then the answer would appear necessarily to be in the negative. The contingent "givens" of our material and nonmaterial existence render all manifestations of creaturely newness (even the most considerable among them) relative to themselves and, we suppose, only an interruption or advent from beyond the system of cosmic regulation and what it permits could ever render something *absolutely* new. (It is in precisely this sense, of course, that Christian theology appeals to the "miracles" or "signs" of virginal conception and resurrection as paradigmatic, marking out the territory of the incarnation of the divine Son as a place in space-time where, notwithstanding the continuities of the created order and as in the primordial moment of creation itself, something genuinely and absolutely "new" comes to pass.) Of course, human freedom (unless one subscribes to some version of totalizing determinism) offers a test case of sorts. But few these days are likely to countenance any wholesale voluntarism as adequate to the case (we must reckon with all sorts of influences upon our acting in one way or another—chemical, biological, social, linguistic, as well as material), and even the most determined of voluntarists is compelled to reckon with the fact that we may only choose to do what the material environment permits and not

[11] See, e.g., Steiner, *Grammars of Creation*, 213.
[12] Steiner, *Grammars of Creation*, 108.
[13] Steiner, *Grammars of Creation*, 108.

what it renders (for the moment at least) impossible.[14] "Has any painter invented a new colour?" Steiner asks.[15]

And yet, despite the fact that all "new beginnings" arising within the creaturely sphere, including those generated by the most febrile and fertile acts of the artistic imagination, are by definition relative rather than absolute, bearing the hallmark of their logical posteriority and debt to a world which precedes and in significant measure shapes them, we nonetheless tend to want to draw distinctions and to accord significance in a differentiated rather than a wholesale manner. Insofar as this is bound up with our habitual use of terms, it is possible that many readers might still experience an internal crunch of gears at the suggestion that modern medicine "created" antiretroviral drugs in response to HIV, or Tim Berners-Lee the World Wide Web, despite the undoubted significance of each for the lives of millions of people. Meanwhile, verbs such as "producing," "making," or "inventing" may seem inadequate in the face of the imaginative outputs of Shakespeare, J. S. Bach (though interestingly in music "composing"—despite its formal gesture in the direction of that which preexists and shapes the action—furnishes a respectable alternative), Monet, Eliot, or Joyce. Quite apart from disputed terminology and its appropriate range of application, though, we seem mostly at least to want to reserve a sense of what Steiner calls "primary making" for certain instances or sorts of human *poesis*, even though the line of exclusion may prove impossible to draw with any precision and difficult to draw at all (as circumstances of relativity always are in practice).[16] Some acts of imagining seem significantly to modify the territory of consciousness, opening up and rendering available new worlds, new tracts of possible human experience that would otherwise have remained off limits, perhaps forever; whereas others amount to little more than interesting reconfigurations of or extrapolations from the reservoir of the extant (material, sociolinguistic, and psychological) inventories of the generalities already available in principle (if not yet in practice) to all. All may be genuinely innovative, but while all innovation may be measured according to points on the same scale, not all is of the same magnitude. The point is essentially the same one that we saw made in the last chapter by Coleridge's attempt to distinguish between the outputs of "imagination" and "fancy" respectively, and while the eighteenth-century terminology hardly commends itself for

---

[14] For a brief discussion of views and some of their moral and christological implications, see Trevor Hart, "Sinlessness and Moral Responsibility: A Problem in Christology," *Scottish Journal of Theology* 48, no. 1 (1995): 37–54.

[15] Steiner, *Grammars of Creation*, 19.

[16] Steiner, *Grammars of Creation*, 144.

current use, the thought captured by it, as we shall see, remains central to contemporary efforts to pin down that which distinguishes "creative" novelty from other sorts.[17]

The Advent of the Original

Despite seismic shifts in artistic practice and theory over the past century that have served to challenge the idea, popular presumption still expects the artist in particular to offer something significantly new to his or her public and understands such newness as integral to his or her personal "creative" vision and contribution. One who merely mimics the work, the subject, or even the style of others, we tend to denigrate, instead, as a poor artist "lacking in originality"[18] and even, if the mimicry is done especially well or extensively, guilty of misappropriating "intellectual property" which does not belong to them.[19] All this is a very long way from the Renaissance ideal of mimesis, in which the copying of acknowledged masters was accepted as a tribute to their greatness as well as a necessary pedagogical process. In fact, while great artists through the centuries have no doubt brought something new to their task and thereby modified the parameters and expectations of their particular craft, an emphasis on newness as such and for its own sake is part and parcel of the peculiarly modern understanding of artistry, the advent and early development of which we traced in chapter 9, and bound up closely with the language of artistic creativity itself. Thus it was in the fifteenth century that European painters and sculptors began to sign their work, an indication that they no longer saw themselves as mere craftsmen

[17] See, e.g., the appropriation and reapplication of Coleridge's distinction in David Bohm, *On Creativity*, Routledge Classics ed. (London: Routledge, 2004), 50–75. An analogous thought seems to underlie Berys Gaut's distinction between instances of "originality" arising either from chance or from mere "mechanical procedure" on the one hand and those involving "*flair*" on the part of the maker on the other. See Berys Gaut, "Creativity and Imagination," in *The Creation of Art: New Essays in Philosophical Aesthetics*, ed. Berys Gaut and Paisley Livingston (Cambridge: Cambridge University Press, 2003), 150–51. Since Coleridge's distinction (and Bohm's appropriation of it) clearly include acts of considerable poetic intellection within the category of "fancy" and since "flair" is notoriously difficult to quantify, the relevant line seems likely to be drawn differently, but the desire to draw a line on one side of which genuine "creativity" falls is common.

[18] Even the accomplished artist who admits to working "in the manner of" another artist is at risk of being deemed "second-rate." See Nicholas Delbanco, "In Praise of Imitation," *Harper's Magazine*, July 2002, 59; cited in R. Keith Sawyer, *Explaining Creativity: The Science of Human Innovation* (Oxford: Oxford University Press, 2006), 24.

[19] On the complexities and dangers of this notion in relation to the arts in particular, see Lewis Hyde, *Common as Air: Revolution, Art and Ownership* (London: Union Books, 2010).

transmitting a tradition of skilled making but as individuals with a distinctive vision and contribution to make.[20] And while early Greek practice appears to have understood already that the words of human authors should be quoted rather than stolen[21] and while this notion of the "author" of a meaningful text or utterance was duly adopted as the primary analogue for divine creation in Greek as well as Hebraic and Christian sources, the theological capital of the image was returned with interest added in modernity's account of the artist as one who gives "free, untrammelled expression to his inner self by bringing into existence new realities,"[22] realities springing solely from within, for which he and he alone may thus properly claim credit and over which he exercises legitimate "authorial" right of disposition and control. Here, the "originality" of the artist's work is modeled confidently on the analogy of the divine origination of the cosmos, and the strictly analogical nature of the picture has not always been acknowledged fully or gladly.

An early essay on the subject of original composition[23] is actually quite measured in its claims for the human author, deriding those who merely copy the thoughts and words of other authors (while acknowledging that this may in reality be the necessary fate of most who put pen to paper)[24] but understanding poetic "originality" as secondary in its turn to the realities of nature (here apparently meaning much more than the physical cosmos alone and more "the true nature of things"), to which it is its peculiar gift directly to attend and from which it breaks forth, unmediated by precedent or example, a new account of its glories and its tragedies. This account retains the older associations (captured in the now rare cognate term "originary") according to which an *original* treatment was precisely one returning directly and dutifully to the origins of its vision in some prior reality (nature),[25] as well as promoting the new idea (held in tension with the former) that an original artist must nonetheless be one who is the sole *originator* of her own vision, rather than sharing the fame and the

---

[20] See Sawyer, *Explaining Creativity*, 13.

[21] Steiner notes the existence in seventh- and early sixth-century Greek of a word for plagiarism, *logoklopia*. See Steiner, *Grammars of Creation*, 238.

[22] Nicholas Wolterstorff, *Art in Action: Toward a Christian Aesthetic* (Carlisle, U.K.: Solway, 1997), 51.

[23] Edward Young, "Conjectures on Original Composition," in *English Critical Essays (Sixteenth, Seventeenth and Eighteenth Centuries)*, ed. Edmund D. Jones, 315–64 (London: Oxford University Press, 1922). The "essay" (an extract from a lengthy letter) dates from 1759.

[24] Young, "Conjectures on Original Composition," 333.

[25] "When the term originality was first coined, it meant newness and truth of observation. . . . The most original artists were those who best imitated nature." Sawyer, *Explaining Creativity*, 24.

applause with anyone or anything else.[26] It was the latter rather than the former connotation that duly prevailed, coming to place a huge premium on originality of an unprecedented sort and on the isolated self-consciousness of the artist or "author" as the locus of its virginal conception. No work of art, though, nor the individual "inner vision" that conceives of it, is ever born out of nothing; at best the artist selects from what the matrices of nature and culture together afford her, transforming and recombining elements in some strikingly new way. As Steiner notes, however, "the spaces for innovative transformations are vast and open-ended."[27] Where absolute originality is nonetheless entertained as an ideal, therefore, the nonnegotiable givenness of the world may yet provide the context for a constructive exercise of freedom, accepting and working creatively with and within the finite limits set by the artist's embeddedness in the material and nonmaterial particularities of space and time. But, in more extreme versions of the "cult of originality,"[28] this same aspiration may manifest itself as a "cruel fact" to be railed against and rejected,[29] the denial of a presumed birthright leading to a resentment toward or even a hatred of the given world and a "horror of the object"[30] and to an artistry characterized above all by an exasperated struggle for liberation from limits and constraints of every kind.[31]

Among its more radical modernist proponents, the quest became one for an absolute incipience of *being* rather than meaning, since meaning (and with it the internal structure of self-consciousness) was now increasingly recognized as necessarily wedded rather than prior to language of some sort and thus unhelpfully implicated in a socially mediated rather

---

[26] Young, "Conjectures on Original Composition," 319, 321. Cf. the brief discussion of Young's essay in Rob Pope, *Creativity: Theory, History, Practice* (London: Routledge, 2005), 57–58.

[27] Steiner, *Grammars of Creation*, 118.

[28] Rosalind E. Krauss, *The Originality of the Avant-Garde and Other Modernist Myths* (Cambridge, Mass.: MIT Press, 1986), 155.

[29] Steiner, *Grammars of Creation*, 19.

[30] Wolterstorff suggests helpfully that this dismay at the prospect of the human artist's creativity being constrained or limited by anything prior to itself is a direct echo (because a by-product) of the ancient Christian refusal to suppose that God's own creative act in the beginning was compelled to accommodate the demands of any preexisting "stuff." See Wolterstorff, *Art in Action*, 53.

[31] This is not to deny, of course, that such struggle was born of other strongly felt concerns too, such as a deep disillusionment with the moral and political anemia of many traditional artistic conventions and their perceived complicity in the degenerate bourgeois forms of society that began gradually to collapse under the weight of the 1914–1918 war in Europe.

than an immediate creative activity.[32] The advent of deliberately anarchic initiatives such as Dada or aleatory art forms and practices in which unmediated spontaneity was privileged in a concern to "give chance a chance"[33] and logic reduced to an absolute personal minimum[34] sought precisely to erase the given traces of artistic self-consciousness in the interests of creative originality, resulting in a form of autism the result of which was seemingly much more akin to the primordial chaos of Genesis 1:2 and "the chaotic wind" blowing over the surface of the waters[35] than to the act of authorial sovereign origination and forming on which the early modern artistic ideal and its romantic heirs had been modeled. Thus, in its dogged pursuit of the original, modernity effectively deconstructed itself, giving way duly to the rather different insights, commitments, and expectations of the postmodern, a process which we now consider in more detail.

Artistry at the Gates of Hell

The French sculptor Auguste Rodin (1840–1917) had a somewhat troubled relationship to questions of artistic originality. His own approach to sculpting was, in its day, without doubt highly unconventional, a fact which might be ascribed in part to his repeated failure to gain entry into the École des Beaux-Arts and so be schooled according to the dominant traditions of the Academy,[36] and that seems to have been responsible for his early work being largely shunned by the Salon and other organs of the art establishment.[37] Those who celebrated him, though, did so precisely for his independence of mind and originality of conception, and in an admiring essay first published in 1903 the German poet Rainer Maria Rilke (who served as Rodin's

[32] Modernism's self-appointed paradoxical status as "the tradition of the new" reached a pinnacle in the manifestos of some of the futurists, e.g., who declared all previous art "dead" and deserving only of a decent burial. See Peter Childs, *Modernism* (London: Routledge, 2000), 1, 117.

[33] Wolterstorff, *Art in Action*, 56.

[34] See Tristan Tzara, "Lecture on Dada," in *Theories of Modern Art*, ed. Herschel B. Chipp (Berkeley: University of California Press, 1968), 386. The essay dates originally from 1924.

[35] Tzara, "Lecture on Dada," in Chipp, *Theories of Modern Art*, 386.

[36] See Truman H. Bartlett, "Auguste Rodin, Sculptor," in *Auguste Rodin: Readings on His Life and Work*, ed. Albert Elsen (Eaglewood Cliffs, N.J.: Prentice-Hall, 1965), 18. The essay was originally published in *American Architect and Building News* 25, no. 689 (1889). On Rodin as "essentially self-taught," cf. Frederick V. Grunfeld, *Rodin: A Biography* (New York: Da Capo, 1987), 26–34.

[37] See the accounts in Antoinette Le Normand-Romain, "The Greatest of Living Sculptors," in *Rodin*, ed. Catherine Lampert et al. (London: Royal Academy, 2007); Bartlett, "Auguste Rodin, Sculptor," in Elsen, *Auguste Rodin*, 25–48.

secretary between September 1905 and May 1906) could hardly contain himself, peppering his prose with repeated acknowledgments of prodigious life-giving *newness* in Rodin's work, unable to resist provocative appeal to the divine precedent, so that at one point his acclamation sounds for all the world like the opening chapter of Genesis itself, containing an alliterative fivefold repetition of the emphatic (used here with reference to Rodin rather than God) "He created."[38] Meanwhile, one enthusiastic reviewer of Rodin's bust of the novelist Victor Hugo (exhibited in 1884) had rather damned the man with faint praise by suggesting, "It is not the least of the many felicities of M. Hugo's career that has lived to pass to posterity as the original of what might be an antique bronze."[39] The image, clearly, was here to be preferred to its original.

But what was an "original"? And what was it to be original in art? Rodin himself, after all, concentrated from first to last in his artistic career on exploring the multiple possibilities suggested by the concrete form of the human body, which is, as such, hardly what one typically thinks of as avant-garde. And he himself would have insisted and at times did insist that as an artist he was merely the handmaiden of nature: "[i]t is nature which makes of the artist—when he has understood and translated her—a creator, or rather her sublime copyist."[40] Elsewhere, he concedes that mere "copying" from nature is not really the thing, at least so far as his own work is concerned, pointing instead to the impact and mediating influence of Michelangelo, and more especially the principles of composition that the latter had himself borrowed in turn from the antique marbles of Greece and Rome.[41] Against the conventional assertion that such figures idealized the human form, Rodin insisted instead that the sculptures of ancient Greece were actually the "perfection of realism," the result of eyes and hands untrammelled by artistic convention and liberated by the deep study of an unswerving respect for nature herself.[42] There are, to be sure, awkward juxtapositions of ideas here, but Rodin is quite open and unashamed about his own "borrowing" of principles from an ancient and venerable tradition—again, hardly the thing one might expect from an artist unduly concerned about his profile and reputation as an originator of form or one determined to forge new artistic paths. If, nonetheless, Rodin himself was swept along to some extent by the notion of his own

[38] Rainer Maria Rilke, "Auguste Rodin," in Elsen, *Auguste Rodin*, 138.

[39] W. E. Henley, "Two Busts of Victor Hugo," *Magazine of Art* (1884): 132; cited in Ruth Butler, "Introduction," in *Rodin in Perspective*, ed. Ruth Butler (Eaglewood Cliffs, N.J.: Prentice-Hall, 1980), 4–5.

[40] Elsen, *Auguste Rodin*, 158.

[41] See Bartlett, "Auguste Rodin, Sculptor," in Elsen, *Auguste Rodin*, 31–33.

[42] Bartlett, "Auguste Rodin, Sculptor," in Elsen, *Auguste Rodin*, 88–89.

originality and its significance—as is suggested, perhaps, by the symbolic charge of works such as the *Hand of God* (1896) (see fig. 4 in the appendix), in which the human form is shown being exposed by a divine potter/ sculptor from a lump of clay or stone[43]—it was perhaps in part because he lived with the uncomfortable legacy of having been accused early in his career precisely of "mere copying" or, put at its starkest, of "forging" his way ahead. A reviewer of *The Age of Bronze* (exhibited in Brussels in January 1877), struck by the remarkable lifelikeness of the piece, wondered aloud in print just how much of it had been achieved by taking casts from life—molding rather than sculpting sections of the figure.[44] The accusation and its taint hung over Rodin as the work was eventually translated to Paris and the Salon,[45] and it was to haunt him for the rest of his career, leading him henceforth regularly to fashion figures deliberately larger than life or else in miniature, thus precluding any reiteration of the charge.[46] Significantly, a suggestion that his former friend and colleague Jules Dalou had plagiarized ideas from Rodin's own work, far from being welcomed as the sincerest form of flattery or a natural part of the give and take of artistic collaboration, was instrumental in ending the relationship between the two men.[47] The question of originality, originals, and copies, then, was one that troubled Rodin in one way or another, and his stance on the matter was complex.

That the conception, style, and contribution of Rodin's works was indeed "significantly new"—and, in that sense at least, creative and original—is perhaps something few art historians or critics would wish to deny, whether or not they would follow Rilke and other contemporaries in the direction of presenting him—in good nineteenth-century fashion— variously as elemental spirit or persecuted genius. There was, and has been since, no one quite like Rodin, and his work is certainly widely acknowledged as having significant artistic merit. Beyond that, perhaps, for our purposes we need not go. And yet Rodin's relationship to his own oeuvre was complicated, in part, as Rosalind Krauss has pointed out, because the very nature of the medium in which he worked and the particular ways in

[43] Cf. Grunfeld, *Rodin: A Biography* , 473. See http://www.musee-rodin.fr/en/ collections/sculptures/hand-god (accessed January 13, 2014).

[44] See Ruth Butler, *Rodin: The Shape of Genius* (New Haven, Conn.: Yale University Press, 1993), 99–105.

[45] On the scandal and its impact, see further Normand-Romain, "Greatest of Living Sculptors," in Lampert et al., *Rodin*, 30–31; Bartlett, "Auguste Rodin, Sculptor," in Elsen, *Auguste Rodin*, 39.

[46] See Bartlett, "Auguste Rodin, Sculptor," in Elsen, *Auguste Rodin*, 69.

[47] See Antoinette Le Normand-Romain, "The Gates of Hell: The Crucible," in Lampert et al., *Rodin*, 58.

which he worked that medium had an ambiguity built into them so far as questions of originality and authorship were concerned.[48]

Rodin's greatest work was one he labored over for several decades but never actually completed. *The Gates of Hell* (see fig. 3 in the appendix) was commissioned in 1880, the intention being to provide a vast door for a new museum of decorative arts to be built in Paris. The museum was never built, but the project formed the backdrop to all that Rodin did in the four decades prior to his death in 1917. A piece of work on such a grand scale was hardly likely to be achieved in a spontaneous outburst of creative frenzy, and its conception (inspired by Michelangelo's *Last Judgment* in the Sistine Chapel and perhaps by the vivid characterizations of Dante's *Inferno*[49]) began with plans for a series of compartmentalized bas-reliefs but progressed in due course to something much more unified, with its miniature figures—caught variously in poses of agony and ecstasy—trespassing boldly beyond the space of the doorway itself, as though struggling to escape or, more disturbingly still perhaps, being drawn into the inferno by a force that threatens to suck us in and down with them if we do not take care.[50] The effect is striking, paying its tribute to familiar medieval cameos of final judgment but bringing them quite literally kicking and screaming into a reality much closer to home in its figuration, naked flesh somehow never having looked quite so familiar as this in its fragile solidity. But it was a constantly evolving piece, a work in progress rather than a compositional idée fixe, and it never reached a definitive form in Rodin's studio before he died. Individual figures from the piece were independently cast and displayed in their own right as the years went by (*The Thinker* and *The Kiss* being two familiar instances), and some would eventually be left to fend for themselves, losing their place in later recensions of the larger magnum opus.[51]

[48] Krauss, *Originality of the Avant-Garde*, 151–57.

[49] The latter is less certain, but the resonances between Dante's description and Rodin's depiction are remarkable enough. See Bartlett, "Auguste Rodin, Sculptor," in Elsen, *Auguste Rodin*, 69; Normand-Romain, "Gates of Hell," in Lampert et al., *Rodin*, 55–56; Albert Elsen, *Rodin's Gates of Hell* (Minneapolis: University of Minnesota Press, 1960), 14–63.

[50] For illustration of stages of the work's composition, individual figures set within it, and bronze casting made after Rodin's death, see Antoinette Le Normand-Romain, *Rodin: The Gates of Hell* (Paris: Musée Rodin, 2002); Elsen, *Rodin's Gates of Hell*.

[51] *The Thinker* (originally entitled *The Poet* and depicted pondering the sufferings of humanity in hell) remained central to the tympanum of the door, but *The Kiss*, having been generated by the project, was finally modified to a rather different depiction, *Couple Embracing*, at the bottom of the right pilaster. See Normand-Romain, *Rodin: The Gates of Hell*, 42–43, 66–69.

Cast eventually in bronze, like many of Rodin's works, *The Gates of Hell* was produced by a process entailing the creation of plaster molds from which multiple more or less identical copies might be made.[52] It belonged, in other words, to an art form already thoroughly enmeshed in the techniques of mechanical reproduction, and susceptible to the lines of critical inquiry Walter Benjamin and others would duly pursue.[53] In fact, as Antoinette Le Normand-Romain notes, from an early point in his long career, Rodin had adopted the labor-saving practice of generating multiple identical casts that would then be "reworked and altered . . . to look more spontaneous, and thus original."[54] If, to our modern ears, this seems already to have more than a whiff of something suspect about it, we should remember that, in an earlier age, largely untroubled by the ideology of the original, it would have been a standard practice in the artist-craftsman's workshop, where the "creation" of a work was in any case distributed among a team of artisans and thus an essentially collaborative affair. The final piece may well have borne the master craftsman's hallmark, but no one supposed that its provenance lay in his hands alone. It is significant, therefore, that from the mid-1880s onward Rodin worked increasingly with a "workshop" of collaborators around him and thus, as well as being perfectly happy to "sample" his own work to meet the demands of different projects and contexts, relied in practice on the skill and expertise of others (mold makers, sculptors, and the foundries that cast his works) to turn out the pieces that would nonetheless bear his signature.[55] Catherine Lampert is doubtless correct to suggest that Krauss' reference to the production of "multiple clones" in Rodin's work is unduly provocative,[56] but the circumstances in which his sculptures were crafted nonetheless serve to lift the lid on some deep and difficult questions about the precise nature and status of the "originality" not just of Rodin's work but of any work of art. *The Gates of Hell*, widely acclaimed as Rodin's greatest original "masterpiece," is no exception. Indeed, in the case of this work, the issues are sharpened (or perhaps blurred) even more thoroughly, since not only did the sculpture itself identifiably contain multiples of several figures

[52] See Lampert et al., *Rodin*, 90–91.

[53] See "The Work of Art in the Age of Mechanical Reproduction," in Walter Benjamin, *Illuminations* (London: Pimlico, 1999), 211–44.

[54] Normand-Romain, "Greatest of Living Sculptors," in Lampert et al., *Rodin*, 30.

[55] Normand-Romain, "Gates of Hell," in Lampert et al., *Rodin*, 61–63.

[56] Catherine Lampert, "Introduction: Rodin's Nature," in Lampert et al., *Rodin*, 21. It should be borne in mind, however, that Krauss' point is precisely to move beyond the polarity of a "valorized" originality and a discredited reduplication. See Krauss, *Originality of the Avant-Garde*, 160.

within its larger composition (the work, in effect, "sampling" itself); as we have already noted, it was left unfinished at the time of the artist's death, and, therefore, even in the more widely acknowledged sense, no "original" work exists. The casts made for the work were later taken and a first complete bronze casting made, not by the artist himself, but by others who came after him. A photograph taken by William Elborne in 1887, showing Rodin himself in front of the unfinished work—not directly, but reflected in the frame of a mirror—suggests that the artist was not wholly oblivious to the ambiguity of his relationship to it and maybe even relished it.[57]

Posteriority, Parody, and Pastiche

It was another photograph that perhaps captured most fully the conceit of Rodin the creator, the "crucible of originality."[58] Taken by the American photographer Edward Steichen in 1902, the image presents Rodin in his studio, posed in impressive silhouetted profile together with two of his best-known works, *The Thinker* and *Monument to Victor Hugo*. The chiaroscuro and the suppression of the careful texture of the sculptures suggest the presence of three living forms rather than just one, the artistic progenitor communing with his creatures as it were in their own space.[59] The image accompanied the works themselves (together with several others) to New York in 1903 for Rodin's first individual exhibition in America,[60] no doubt intended to cast the sculptor in the impressive role of the "onlie begetter" of the numerous forms on display, giving the viewer a privileged authentic glimpse of the physical space within which his original ideas were given birth. But there is irony even here. The photographic image itself was not an "original" at all, but rather a composite skillfully patched together from two separate prints by Steichen in order to avoid the visual clutter of Rodin's studio and so achieve the desired effect.[61]

[57] See William Elborne, *August Rodin at the Dépôt des Marbres in Front of "The Gates of Hell," Reflected in a Mirror*, 1887 (albumen print, 16.5 x12 cm), in Lampert et al., *Rodin*, 89. On Rodin's knowing attitude to "the ambiguity in the notion of the original," cf. Lampert, "Introduction," in Lampert et al., *Rodin*, 21.

[58] Krauss, *Originality of the Avant-Garde*, 156.

[59] Cf. the article on http://www.metmuseum.org/toah/works-of-art/2005.100.289 (accessed October 16, 2012). The image can be viewed on this site.

[60] Grunfeld, *Rodin: A Biography*, 445.

[61] See http://www.metmuseum.org/toah/works-of-art/2005.100.289 (accessed October 16, 2012).

Fourteen years after this calculated and apparently successful cultivation of Rodin's "image" for the benefit of New York's art-loving public,[62]
another French artist (now resident in New York) sought to exhibit a piece
anonymously as part of an exhibition of which he was himself one of the
chief organizers. The Society of Independent Artists was established in
New York in 1916 and intended to challenge the constricting and elitist
policies of the art establishment embodied in the National Academy of
Design.[63] The society determined to hold an annual exhibition to which
anyone willing to pay the annual subscription might submit their work.
There was to be no jury, and no prizes were to be awarded. It was a wholesale democratization of the art world. Or so it seemed. Marcel Duchamp
was a member of the society's board of directors, and in April 1917 he
tested its faithfulness to its own founding principles by obtaining a fac-
tory-made urinal, taking it to his studio, where he dated and signed it with
the pseudonym R. MUTT and then entered it for that year's exhibition,
paying the required six-dollar entrance fee and providing the work's title:
Fountain. The test was one the society's board failed. The exhibition was
the largest ever to have been mounted in America, and a majority of the
board's members voted that, despite the self-proclaimed inclusivity of both
the society and its event, the piece could not possibly be exhibited since it
clearly was not serious art and was bound to bring the whole event into dis-
repute. Ironically, so far as posterity is concerned, the work achieved this
precisely by its absence from the galleries. Duchamp promptly resigned
from the board, though the true identity of R. MUTT remained a secret
for several months thereafter.

Fountain was one of a series of so-called readymades that Duchamp
had produced since 1913 when, in an act as much playful as it was ultimately significant, he mounted a bicycle wheel upside down on a kitchen
stool in his studio in Paris.[64] From *Bicycle Wheel* to *Fountain*, the idea
Duchamp was exploring was that, by taking a mass-produced object from
the world of mundane existence and removing it from its accepted context
of use, the artist was requiring us to approach it under a different aspect
and so creating "a new thought for that object."[65] That he or she had not

---

[62] A review of the exhibition in the *New York Times* duly likened the sculptor's work
to the music of that other great self-proclaimed "originator" of form in the nineteenth
century, Richard Wagner. See Grunfeld, *Rodin: A Biography*, 445.

[63] For the following, see Calvin Tomkins, *Duchamp: A Biography* (London: Chatto
& Windus, 1997), 179–86.

[64] See Tomkins, *Duchamp: A Biography*, 133–35.

[65] Tomkins, *Duchamp: A Biography*, 185.

made the object as the work of his or her own hands mattered not a jot. What mattered was the transformation of its significance.

Duchamp's advocacy of the readymade posed more than one fundamental challenge to the presumptions widely entertained both by the makers and by the exhibitors, viewers, and purchasers of art in Europe and North America at the beginning of the twentieth century. It challenged the idea that what made art "art"—and worthy of special consideration and treatment as such—was some quality or capacity embedded in or supervening upon the material object or "work" itself. Instead, what made art "art," it was now suggested, was a particular way of thinking about or treating the object, thereby bestowing upon it special significance and, reciprocally, finding that significance in it. If this meant that more or less any physical artifact could now count as "art" (its status as such depending more or less entirely on the artist's own, the viewer's, or the market's imaginative response to it), then of course the notion of the artist as one uniquely gifted to "create" works possessed of intrinsic power and significance had now to be dispensed with too. After all, no such creative individual "genius" was necessary, since even a factory-produced piece of bathroom equipment might suffice as the essentially arbitrary occasion for the response in question.

Krauss chooses Rodin's *The Gates of Hell* as a focus precisely because his work is situated identifiably, albeit ambiguously, within the era during which the notions of artistic originality and authenticity held huge sway; yet *The Gates of Hell* itself already gestures beyond that age, close examination, as we have seen, revealing it to contain within itself the conditions of its own deconstruction as an "original" masterwork in the generally accepted sense. According to Calvin Tomkins' biography, after a momentous trip to Munich in 1912, Duchamp himself was someone driven by a sense of the need for art constantly to escape its influences, issuing "from nowhere but the artist's imagination."[66] In due course, this same emphasis on freedom from determinative conditions led him to abjure not only traditional materials and methods but "the whole notion of the artist's sensibility as the guiding creative principle," and he began to experiment with aleatory methods, as in *Three Standard Stoppages* (1913)—a piece produced by dropping lengths of white sewing thread onto painted surfaces and then gluing them into positions determined by chance alone.[67] Here, as we noted in chapter 11, the modern pursuit of originality in the arts collapses in upon itself and gives way to a much more postmodern sensibility—the suggestion that it is not the conscious self or the fertile imagination of the

[66] Tomkins, *Duchamp: A Biography*, 93.
[67] Tomkins, *Duchamp: A Biography*, 123.

artist that matters at all, but a larger system of impersonal forces (social, psychological, biological, physical) to which the individual artist, whether he or she realizes it or not, is necessarily subject and which are now understood to be the true generative "source" of his or her "works."

In a rather different way, Duchamp's readymades too presented the art world with a similar suggestion.[68] Forget the idea of the artist as a great individual progenitor emulating the primordial moment of originative creation, they seemed to say, and face the fact that all art, in one way or another, is prefabricated, an objet trouvé—at best a pastiche of inherited elements, its materials and forms already impregnated by prior acts of human conception and construction in a cycle whose true origins are as impossible to trace as granting logical priority to either the fabled chicken or the egg. The parodic conscription and exhibition of a urinal, unmodified save for the addition of an artist's signature, makes the point provocatively by stripping the "creative" contribution of the individual, both inner and outer, to the barest minimum. But the new big idea (if advocacy of a "new big idea" were permitted by the thought itself)—that we inhabit a world in which human originality and creativity are merely the illusions born of romantic hubris and selection, manipulation, and recombination from among a given set of cultural and natural bits and pieces (Coleridge's "Fancy") the most and the best we are humanly capable of—was intended to apply just as surely to the most exalted "creative" outputs of acknowledged masters, placing them decisively on a level with all other products of human "making."

This crisis of origins is one ascribed by much postmodern philosophy, not to artists alone but to us all and thus to artists precisely as those whose acts of *poesis* may serve as a convenient paradigm of human productivity more widely considered. And, inasmuch as the notion of imagination itself is generally bound up with the idea of a productive self capable of bringing forth some distinctive new thing or idea (no matter how trivial), the postmodern denial of origination—eschewing altogether the notion of a "pure" founding reference either in the external world or in the inner world of the self and emptying meaning out instead into an impure and open-ended play of images or signs, each of which, on inspection, can be shown to rely on other equally fragile signs for its significance—tends

---

[68] The link between the two stages, or spheres, of Duchamp's work is suggested in his own claim that *Bicycle Wheel* was itself "the idea of chance" rather than a deliberate new departure. See William A. Camfield, "Marcel Duchamp's *Fountain*: Its History and Aesthetics in the Context of 1917," in *Marcel Duchamp: Artist of the Century*, ed. Rudolf Kuenzli and Francis M. Naumann (Cambridge, Mass.: MIT Press, 1990), 81.

finally to be corrosive of the notion of imagination as such.[69] Instead, as Richard Kearney observes, postmodernism prefers to speak of the "imaginary," displacing or dissolving the conscious and responsible subject with the impersonal effect of "a technologically transmitted sign system over which the individual creative subject has no control."[70] On this view, as we have had reason to note before, in effect language "speaks us" rather than us speaking it.[71]

For postmodern theorists, though, the "language" in question extends beyond the territory of literal speech and inscription to encompass the "sign systems" of mass media audiovisual production, reproduction, and transmission; the saturation of experience by artificially generated and sustained images that shape our expectations and desires and thus our behavior. Just as the artist (on this view) is bound only to produce whatever the multiple images placed at his or her disposal by accident of history already permit and render available as possible permutations (or, more chillingly, to produce precisely and only what the multiple influences operating upon his or her consciousness determine), so too we, in our daily living, are bound to "make of" things and of ourselves something (some "meaning") that is at best a pastiche, a collage made up of semantically unstable bits and pieces coming "readymade" from the social engineers of the popular imaginary, which are in their turn constructed out of other flimsy bits and pieces, pale reflections of pale reflections, with all question of reality and origin constantly deferred, because ultimately unanswerable.

In this endless labyrinth of mirrors, Kearney notes, the presumed distinction and hierarchy between reality and copy, original and imitation, signified and signifier, breaks down, every image turning out to be "an artificial imitation of another equally artificial image."[72] Thus, postmodernism offers its own version of the mimetic paradigm but in a knowing, parodic manner that eschews any attempt to measure or weigh the imitation by appeal to its "original," since it turns out that the "original" itself is not original at all but in its turn merely a construct of other signs. There is no pure presence, no "unproduced" or unedited reality available to us, and thus no critical distance from which to evaluate anything. The work of pop artists such as Andy Warhol and Roy Lichtenstein, by deliberately blurring the boundary between art and everyday objects,[73] compels

[69] So, Richard Kearney, *The Wake of Imagination: Toward a Postmodern Culture* (London: Routledge, 1988), 252–53.

[70] Kearney, *Wake of Imagination*, 251.

[71] See above, e.g., pp. 118–19.

[72] Kearney, *Wake of Imagination*, 254.

[73] Lichtenstein's 'Whaam!', for example, transforms the violence and destruction of

reflection too on the deeper question that postmodernism confronts us with: To what extent can a line be drawn at all between "reality" and the products of human imagining? Is what we take to be "real" itself not shot through with the "artifice" of the image in such a manner that the difference between them cannot meaningfully be demonstrated?

Analyses of things in these terms tend to be offered by postmodern thinkers by way of commentary on the condition of late modernity and the impact of industrialized and technologically advanced societies on the shape of our humanity. But the problem—if indeed it be such—is hardly a new one, even if the media of mass reproduction have exaggerated its dimensions and so drawn it unavoidably to our attention. It was another of the fundamental insights of the work of Ernst Gombrich to notice that our "seeing" of objects and states of affairs in the natural world is never visually innocent but always shaped in some measure by their prior depictions and representations and that artists in particular are prone to view and select from "real life" in accordance with the existing conventions of artistic encoding as well as the concrete realities confronting them.[74] That such preconception is largely tacit makes it all the more significant and all the more inevitable.

In chapters 6 and 7, I suggested that, far from being a peculiarly postmodern pathology, thorough immersion in the economy of signs and images is a proper part of what it means to be a human creature and thus not something we can ever hope to escape from in order to gain an absolute "critical distance" or a "God's eye" point of view on things.[75] But I also argued there (and will rehearse only briefly here) that this conclusion need not lead to the sort of "apocalyptic nihilism" noted by Kearney as the despairing counsel of much postmodern theory.[76] To be embedded in culture and dependent upon its mediations of reality through language, image, and other mechanisms is merely an extension of our logically prior entanglement in the body and our reliance in turn upon its mediation of states of affairs pertaining in the world. Resort to the metaphor of being

---

aerial warfare into a comic book image rendering the viewer's attitude both to the image itself and to the moral realities depicted ambivalent. (See fig. 5 in the appendix.) We are too mature, too refined to permit the adrenalin rush of this sort of thing to configure our perceptions of human conflicts--aren't we? See also the discussion of Warhol's *Brillo Boxes* (1964) in Arthur C. Danto, *Andy Warhol* (New Haven, Conn.: Yale University Press, 2009), 61–64.

[74] See, e.g., Ernst H. Gombrich, *Art and Illusion: A Study in the Psychology of Pictorial Representation*, 5th ed. (London: Phaidon, 1977), 55–78.

[75] See above, pp. 121–25.

[76] Kearney, *Wake of Imagination*, 364.

"trapped," of course, tends to suppose and to encourage the ideas both that "escape" is a theoretical possibility (which I have suggested it is not) and that our immersion in nature and culture respectively is inherently negative, distancing us from "reality" rather than granting us access to its admittedly unfathomable and mysterious depths. But again, this is hardly the case.

That there are better and worse, healthy and unhealthy, ways of constructing and indwelling the world need not and should not be doubted. That we cannot step conveniently outside our humanity in order to gauge with certainty which are which, though, need not be regretted and must not be taken as license either for sinking into the slough of depression or for an ethically disengaged jouissance that reduces everything to the same level of significance. On the contrary, epistemological undecidability (the unavailability of pure presence, unmediated meaning, or absolute certainty) is arguably part of what makes us morally responsible beings at all and calls forth from us imaginative and "creative" responses to situations rather than excusing our failure to engage in initiatives designed to pursue and promote the good, the true, and the beautiful.[77] So, too, epistemological *posteriority* (the fact that every act of human knowing and making comes "after" others upon which it inevitably draws and by which it is in considerable part shaped) need not and should not lead us to conclude that there is no place left for the "creative subject" to make some significant (and ethically accountable) contribution to the world and its history, whether in the arts or elsewhere. As Kearney observes,[78] postmodern explosion of the myth of absolute incipience and of the human subject as "sovereign master" of meaning (and accountable, therefore, only to itself for the antiworlds that it conjures up and opposes to the given world) may perform a helpful and healthy service, not least from a theological perspective.[79] But it need not and must not substitute for this myth another—equally pernicious in ethical terms—according to which the human subject is little more than a mimetic slave, incapable of taking any significant initiative and acting merely in accordance with the dictates of some prior set of determining forces, materially or culturally transmitted. Instead, Kearney recommends, we ought to recognize that it is precisely the "playful" *imagination* that facilitates *curiosity* in the face of the other,

---

[77] For a more fully fledged version of this argument, see Trevor A. Hart, *Faith Thinking: The Dynamics of Christian Theology* (London: SPCK, 1995), passim.

[78] Kearney, *Wake of Imagination*, 363.

[79] I.e., because its "decentering" of the human self restores human action to a more measured place in the scheme of things and leaves God alone (where God is believed in) unopposed as the "onlie begetter" of worlds in this sense.

exploration of different possible constructions that might be placed upon it, *discrimination* between better and worse alterities, and *development* of respectful and life-enhancing strategies of response as distinct from other sorts (though it may, of course, be complicit in those too).[80] Here, again, we find ourselves back in the territory of a dialectic of "give and take" and an understanding of human existence as one caught up constantly in the to-ing and fro-ing of *response* to that which is given to us, whether by nature or culture, by the inheritance of the past or the reality confronting us and calling us to account in the present. In all this, Kearney suggests, "meaning" does not originate from within the depths of the isolated self, but "emerges as a response to the other, as radical interdependence."[81] In this light, in artistry as in life more widely, "coming after," copying, and collaboration (and the accountability that naturally accompanies these) turn out to be the true crucible of human creativity, and not its death knell.

Originality and Creativity Studies

If those concerned with the nature of human creativity in the prestigious and often elitist world of the arts have found themselves forced to reckon seriously with the conditions and status of the original or significantly new, so too have the advocates of a much more egalitarian and broadly based version of the concept. While, for example, proponents of a *creative cognition* approach to human creativity will typically insist upon an inclusive application of the term ("from the young child who refers to cold symptoms as a 'soggy nose' to the development of the theory of relativity"[82]) and upon the biological and psychological basis of creative generativity in "the normative operating characteristics of ordinary minds"[83] rather than exceptional or largely mysterious cognitive capacities, it is nonetheless to instances of significant newness (whether mundane or extraordinary in their scale and

---

[80] See further the discussion of various creaturely "goods" in chap. 13 below.

[81] Kearney, *Wake of Imagination*, 387.

[82] Thomas B. Ward, Steven M. Smith, and Ronald A. Finke, "Creative Cognition," in *Handbook of Creativity*, ed. Robert J. Sternberg (Cambridge: Cambridge University Press, 1999), 190.

[83] Ward, Smith, and Finke, "Creative Cognition," in Sternberg, *Handbook of Creativity*, 190. Runco notes, "Threshold theory suggests that there is a minimum level of intelligence . . . below which the person cannot be creative" without concluding that they are necessarily correlated above a certain level. Rather, "intelligence is necessary but not sufficient for creative achievement." Mark A. Runco, *Creativity: Theories and Theme; Research, Development, and Practice* (London: Academic, 2007), 7. The lower threshold generally deemed necessary in creativity studies, we might observe, seems generous rather than niggardly in its inclusivity.

significance) that they typically point as the "creative" outcomes of these generative processes. Unless there is something significantly new to be observed (and again we should note that the relevant judgment here may be context specific), it seems that discourses about creativity need not be called upon to perform service, other less contentious ways of describing things being perfectly satisfactory. Of course, as a properly scientific field, "creativity studies" is bound to limit the scope of its observations, hypotheses, and experiments to phenomena that it takes to be part of a general and in principle explicable pattern, and it is thus inherently resistant to (though equally incapable of pronouncing with definitive authority upon) appeals to what it may characterize as romantic and even obscurantist notions such as spontaneous inspiration, the muse, creative genius, and unprecedented originality welling up from within. The whole idea of creativity as something special, mysterious, and ultimately inexplicable flies in the face of an approach that takes explication as its forte and raison d'etre and creativity as its chosen subject. Notwithstanding this, though, practitioners in the field are willing—because more or less compelled by the host of available evidence—to acknowledge very high levels of "originality" or significant newness as operative in some examples of creativity, and they are not reduced to defining creativity as the mere (albeit sometimes striking) novel recombination of already extant bits and pieces.[84]

In her extensive work on the theme, Margaret Boden draws attention helpfully to different sorts and levels of newness and creativity that present themselves for consideration.[85] Two particular distinctions that she draws are worth tracing briefly here. First there is the distinction between the psychologically and the historically creative (or *P-creativity* and *H-creativity*).[86] The former refers to ideas in any sphere of human concern that are "surprising, or perhaps even fundamentally novel, with respect to *the individual mind* which had the idea," no matter how many other people may have had the same idea before.[87] An idea that is *H-creative*, meanwhile, is one that, so far as we can tell on the basis of currently available evidence, is novel with respect to *the whole of human history*. Clearly, while the reverse does not obtain, all *H-creative* ideas will also be *P-creative*, since there will typically be a "someone" (an "individual mind") who is the first to "have" them; but here Boden lodges the important caveat that we should not be

---

[84] See Margaret A. Boden, "What Is Creativity?," in *Dimensions of Creativity*, ed. Margaret A. Boden (Cambridge, Mass.: MIT Press, 1996), 75.

[85] See esp. Margaret A. Boden, *The Creative Mind: Myths and Mechanisms*, 2nd ed. (London: Routledge, 2004).

[86] See Boden, "What Is Creativity?" in Boden, *Dimensions of Creativity*, 76–77; Boden, *Creative Mind*, 43–49.

[87] Boden, *Creative Mind*, 43.

misled by this into overlooking the extent to which creativity is also a *social* and thus a collaborative process,[88] a point to which we shall return shortly. We might notice that for Boden creativity is something that occurs first and properly in the realm of ideas or (we might properly say) imagination, the realm in which we "make sense" of things, configuring and reconfiguring them in accordance with some inherited and socially endorsed set of rules and conventions, a "grammar" or "paradigm" relevant to the context and level of our particular engagements with things. This observation is significant for the second distinction she draws—namely, that between mere "first time" novelties (ideas that *could* have arisen before but in fact did not) and "radical originality" (ideas that *could not* have arisen before, whether *P-creative* or *H-creative*). This distinction plays a vital role in Boden's account, since it is only the latter category ("radically original" ideas) that she considers as fully deserving the accolade "creative" at all.[89]

To illustrate the force of this second distinction, Boden draws upon the example of a literal "grammar" and the linguistic constructions and moves that it renders possible. Consider, she says, the following sentence: there are thirty-three blind purple-spotted hedgehogs living in the Tower of London. At the point of her first conceiving of it, and given the striking oddity of what it proposes, it is highly likely that no one had thought of this particular sentence before. Yet it is clearly a sentence that *might* have occurred before, being capable of composition by any competent English speaker with the requisite imaginative bent or even by a computer furnished with adequate vocabulary and grammatical rules.[90] And that is the point, of course; surprising though this sentence is, its novelty is merely a matter of exploring the limits of what is already sayable or thinkable within the constraints provided by a particular schema or set of rules. A radically original or "creative" idea, on the other hand, Boden suggests, is one that does not merely *explore* the conceptual space or generative system within which it arises but rather refuses to be bound by the accepted limits of that space and, in breaking out of its constraints, *transforms* the conceptual space concerned.[91] In language, such rule breaking is to be found in metaphorical predication, a device which (as we have already

[88] Boden, *Creative Mind*, 46.

[89] See Boden, *Creative Mind*, 51. For a slight concession, cf. Boden, "What Is Creativity?" in Boden, *Dimensions of Creativity*, 82.

[90] Boden, *Creative Mind*, 49.

[91] Boden, "What Is Creativity?" in Boden, *Dimensions of Creativity*, 79–84. Again, we might note here the resonances with Coleridge's distinction between "fancy" and "imagination," the latter alone transforming or enlarging experience of reality, rather than merely reorganizing or charting its already familiar territories. See above, pp. 202–4.

noted), since the ways in which we experience the world are so thoroughly intertwined with language, is capable of "reorganizing our perception of things."[92] Boden provides examples from other generative systems to illustrate the point further. The post-Renaissance musical tradition of tonal harmony, she notes, was explored and the reach of its generative possibility thoroughly if not exhaustively mapped in the period up to the end of the nineteenth century, when, by dropping one of its major constraints (the convention of the home key), an entire new dimension of musicality (atonality) was opened up for exploration and enjoyment, and the conceptual space of Western music transformed for good. As Boden observes, the deeper the generative role of the constraint abandoned in the system concerned, the greater the transformation of the relevant space and its impact on the human world is bound to be.[93] Her further example is that of non-Euclidean, or hyperbolic, geometry, which arose from the willingness of mathematicians to think imaginatively and playfully "outside the box" defined by Euclid's axioms, in particular dropping the constraint of Euclid's fifth postulate regarding the meeting of parallel lines at infinity. Again, the relevant conceptual space (and with it the shape of the cosmos itself) was utterly transformed, making possible the sort of physics that we are all familiar with today but that previously had been literally inconceivable.

Paradigm shifts of this sort—whether they occur on the local and psychological level alone, or turn out to be *H-creative* events destined to modify the course of human history—make new thoughts possible by reconfiguring some conceptual space so that such thoughts "make sense" in a way that they did not and could not have before. And in doing so, these creative shifts or transformations make possible new ways of experiencing reality. Several threads here deserve to be teased out further, though, before we move on. First, the sorts of radically original ideas that Boden dubs "creative" are wholly different from the sort of "originality" that declares itself or aspires to be wholly free from constraints of any sort whatever, an act of origination de novo. On the contrary, *P-creative* (and thus *H-creative*) ideas are wedded to constraints in various ways. They typically arise because the constraints of some existing generative system prove incapable of meeting some need or desire or of addressing the complexities of some circumstance, a frustration eventually provoking the creative response that refuses to be hidebound in this manner and

---

[92] Paul Ricoeur, *The Rule of Metaphor: Multidisciplinary Studies of the Creation of Meaning in Language*, trans. R. Czerny and others (Toronto: Toronto University Press, 1977), 236.

[93] Boden, "What Is Creativity?" in Boden, *Dimensions of Creativity*, 82.

either intuits or is willing deliberately to imagine a state of affairs wholly at variance with the set of possibilities permitted by the system itself (and is thus wholly unpredictable in terms of it). Such creative moves are thus themselves precisely generated by and dependent on the initial conceptual space inhabited and can only be understood and defined relative to its constraints. Furthermore, they typically transform some existing generative system by modifying or countermanding one of its key principles (tonal harmony, Euclid's fifth axiom) rather than abandoning the system as a whole or generating an entire new system ab initio (an intellectual feat more or less unimaginable in its demands). In this respect, creativity and constraint exist in equilibrium rather than opposition, and "[c]onstraint is not a barrier to creative thinking, but the context within which creativity can occur."[94] The free and playful improvisations of the jazz saxophonist provide a neat example of the point. They are possible at all only because of long hours over many years spent practicing the scales and arpeggios in terms of which the available aural space is conventionally mapped, and they only work (rather than sounding "bad") because their breaking of the relevant "rules" exists in a positive creative relationship to constraints otherwise laid down by the larger piece being performed. They are not just random sounds, flouting the rules for the sake of it; and if they were, we should quickly lose interest rather than remaining enrapt and blown away by the virtuosity and the new territories of sound and meaning being opened up for our habitation.

Creativity, Value, and Verification

This last observation brings us to our final point about creative newness—namely, that it is never merely perverse. In his study of paradigm shifts in the sciences, Thomas Kuhn describes the manner in which such shifts always outstrip the predictive force of the initial and dominant paradigm ("breaking the rules") and yet, in retrospect, can be seen to make perfectly good sense, retaining identifiable and substantial levels of continuity with the larger shape of that paradigm.[95] And, of course, while the imaginative processes leading to such paradigm shifts may often be quite independent of any relevant experimental process or empirical observation (precisely because those are typically conceived and conducted inside "the box" rather than trespassing outside it), the eventual endorsement of the creative insight

[94] Mike Sharples, *How We Write: Writing as Creative Design* (London: Routledge, 1999), 41; cited in Pope, *Creativity: Theory, History, Practice*, 122.

[95] Thomas Kuhn, *The Structure of Scientific Revolutions*, 3rd ed. (Chicago: University of Chicago Press, 1996).

or intuition and its imaginative elaboration by the wider scientific community rests firmly on an evaluative judgment—namely, that this new way of thinking or approaching things in fact makes *better* sense than the older way or other possible ways alone. In other words, far from being merely capricious or perverse, this rule-breaking initiative opens up reality for us in a new and more satisfactory manner. Work in creativity studies by Boden and others makes an essentially similar point about the nature of creative thinking as a whole. A certain level and sort of newness of thought or approach to things may be held to be a necessary condition of genuine creativity, but novelty as such or for the sake of novelty alone is insufficient and may even be countercreative—resulting in a form of damaging chaos or new order of an identifiably pernicious rather than a beneficent sort. (We balk, naturally, at the suggestion that some highly original method of inflicting torture on prisoners or hacking into computer systems to access confidential information should be considered a "creative" development.) Thus, genuine creativity, it is generally insisted, fuses a certain level of novelty with particular sorts of value, and creative enterprises will thus always be subject to a period of verification by some community, being recognized as "authentic," "effective," or "appropriate" to some shared context and as resulting in good rather than malevolent outcomes.[96]

Even in the arts, where the notion of something undertaken "for its own sake" and with a devil-may-care attitude to the judgments of anyone other than the individual artist him- or herself is de rigueur in certain quarters, in practice, questions of value of one sort or another are shot through the art world and function there, too, as a vital complement to originality where questions about artistic "creativity" are raised and answered. Thus, Berys Gaut observes, "we think of Picasso and Braque as exhibiting creativity, partly because of the originality of their Cubist paintings, but mainly because that originality was exhibited in paintings which, considered apart from their originality, have considerable artistic merit. The production of artworks that have little or no artistic merit, considered apart from their originality, strikes us, in contrast, as empty and not really creative."[97] Such a claim raises more questions than it answers, perhaps, and there will certainly be those who wish to interrogate and deconstruct the notion of artistic merit. For now, though, it

---

[96] So, e.g., Runco, *Creativity: Theories and Themes*, 222, 397; Sternberg, *Handbook of Creativity*, 137; Sawyer, *Explaining Creativity*, 27; Boden, *Creative Mind*, 10, et passim.

[97] Gaut, "Creativity and Imagination," in Gaut and Livingston, *Creation of Art*, 150. Gaut also points out that the combination of originality and value might be achieved inadvertently or mechanically, rather than through the exercise of "flair," and suggests that only in the latter case should the epithet "creative" properly be applied to the output.

serves helpfully to draw attention to the fact that even in the arts, where the term "creative" is deployed, originality alone or for its own sake is in practice rarely in view; generally, there will also be some question of value (whether of an aesthetic, economic, moral, spiritual, practical, or some other sort) at stake too, even if it has been swept discreetly under the rug and so overlooked.

In a discussion of the common concerns of literature and Christian doctrine, Paul Fiddes writes of the tension between freedom and limits, within which distinctly human existence is played out, a tension that generates anxiety and that we all too often seek to resolve by locating our security in some facet or capacity of our own finite being.[98] This inauthentic way, Fiddes suggests, tips over either to one side or to the other of the two poles of our existence: "we either ignore our limits and posture as gods, or we give away our freedom and succumb like animals to the forces that squeeze and determine us."[99] In either event, the result is an alienation from our true being, and a sense of exile or homelessness ensues. It would be hopelessly sweeping to characterize the whole of modernity's aspiration to "creativity" as a symptom of inauthentic or exiled existence in this sense. And yet we have seen that "posturing as gods" or, more properly, aspiring to a sort of freedom that Christians hold to be the prerogative of God alone is certainly an ever-present danger, and sometimes the posturing is deliberate and exile from the world a condition gladly owned and loudly declared. The arrogation of the language of creation and creativity to characterize human *ars* at the Renaissance bore such problematic entailments in its wake, and their influence has been felt more or less powerfully ever since. The artistic quest for absolute originality—eschewing the given starting points afforded by existence in the world and seemingly haunted by the "curse" of posteriority, craving the power to wipe the slate clean and begin over again (deluge-like but seemingly without a rainbow in prospect) and regretting the extent to which this proves impossible—inevitably tends toward posturing of this sort, whatever its ultimate motivations.

We have seen, though, that more measured accounts of creative newness are available, ones that gladly acknowledge its secondary nature as a response to the limits of a given context and that accept constraint of certain sorts as a proper condition of the exercise of creative freedom rather than its natural nemesis. This recognition, accepting rather than railing against the limits of finitude as such, offers an alternative way to resolve the anxiety born of the dialectic of possibility and facticity, through trust that

---

[98] See Paul Fiddes, *Freedom and Limit: A Dialogue between Literature and Christian Doctrine* (Basingstoke, U.K.: Macmillan, 1991), 52–56.

[99] Fiddes, *Freedom and Limit*, 53–54.

the world in which we find ourselves, while far from perfect, is nonetheless even now a home intended for our habitation rather than the blighted wilderness of exile and that, working creatively within its limits and to transform its given conditions, we shall at the last find ourselves fully at home in it, as it is made new not by the work of human hands alone but by the transfiguring act of the God who has purposed and promises to dwell in it together with us. As the manifestation of human freedom and imagination, of course, those "creative" ventures through which originality and value are combined in a transformational manner also resist the collapse into mere animality, which would leave things as they are, abandoning the human world to the play of conditioning influences of genes, inner complexes, social mechanisms, and the rest. By claiming too little rather than too much for the human creature, effectively absolutizing the limits of human existence and proclaiming the sovereignty and triumph of the prefabricated or "ready-made,"[100] such despairing capitulation leaves us trapped in another, equally dangerous form of exile—that of "fancy," or the endless return of the same. The language of "valuable transformation" arising from the creative exercise of freedom within limits, though, draws attention helpfully again to two further features of human creativity widely identified and variously evaluated in the literature (and of particular concern to a theological account of the subject)—namely, its essentially *collaborative* nature and hence its *accountability* in the face of its various collaborators. It is to a consideration of these that we turn in our next chapter.

---

[100] Cf. Steiner, *Grammars of Creation*, 127.

12

Creativity, Collaboration, and Accountability

In chapter 8 we considered the view according to which the artist's chief task and achievement is a *mimetic* one, faithfully reproducing the contours and texture of some reality in the given world. What we found, though, is that there can be no mere "copying" and that, even where this is attempted and seemingly accomplished, in reality the artist is compelled to encode reality in subtle but far-reaching ways in order to solicit the "beholder's share" and so persuade us that we are seeing something that in fact we are not. In one way or another, we concluded, the artistic quest for faithful mimesis necessarily involves the imaginative *transformation* of reality and never its mere reduplication. In chapter 11 we began to see how the converse is also true—namely, that since the conditions for sheer de novo originality are ones unavailable to finite creatures like ourselves, even the most "original" and creative initiatives in the arts and elsewhere are bound to the contingent actualities and possibilities of the given world. They may be *transformative* with respect to the materials and forms drawn from this world, but such transformation can only be attempted and achieved within certain given limits. There is, we might say, a sense in which even the most transformational initiatives are in their measure also mimetic—that is, bound to some extent to reflect and replicate aspects of the world which provides their given starting point. In this chapter our focus will be on some of the elements and implications of this "poetic posteriority." In particular, we shall be concerned to identify some of the collaborators without whose involvement "creative" enterprises of one sort or another could not arise and the questions of accountability that such collaboration throws up in its wake. In the coming sections, we shall attend briefly to some of those with whom the artist must collaborate in making his or her own distinctive contribution.

Collaboration, Tradition, and Particularity

Despite the effective debunking of the myth of the artist as one who works in self-imposed confinement, granting existence to works untouched (in either conception or execution) by human hands other than his or her own, the word "derivative" is still one probably best avoided within earshot of any poet, painter, or sculptor exhibiting his or her work, especially if the latter is still brandishing a chisel. And while books published today on any number of topics tend to be prefaced by self-deprecating lists of "acknowledgments" of ever more sublime proportions, seemingly only ever leaving the remaining errors of fact and judgment to be credited to the author him- or herself, a rapid survey suggests that works of poetry and literary fiction may have developed an immunity to the disease or are at least less susceptible to the unsightly rash accompanying it. It may be true—we have seen that it is true—that there can be no sheer originality where human artistry is concerned, that no art "comes out of nothing";[1] but this does not mean (as some accounts seem to suggest it might) that art is merely the product and the sum of its preexisting ideal, verbal, and material parts. And artists are mostly eager to have this recognized, rather than allowing their personal contribution to be submerged entirely within the impersonal processes and mechanisms in terms of which an account of it might otherwise reasonably be attempted. Art must live with its antecedents, the material and nonmaterial elements and composites from among which alone it is able to select, disintegrate, recombine, and re-present; but, for any but the most thoroughgoing of determinists, the injection of creative freedom into what the artist does here resists its reduction to a mere reorganization of extant bits and pieces, and it compels acknowledgment instead of some valuable addition to the sum of meaning—something significantly new. Thus we may say that artistic creativity arises—in the somewhat unromantic parlance of creativity studies—through "a confluence of environment-centered variables and person-centered variables,"[2] and even though these may be difficult to disentangle from one another in practice, we need not capitulate to any intellectual dogma that would urge us to conflate them.

Freedom and creativity, then, are not variables set necessarily at odds with the many givens of the particular environments in which artists find themselves or to be secured only by seeking imaginative withdrawal from

---

[1] George Steiner, *Grammars of Creation* (London: Faber & Faber, 2001), 19.

[2] Todd I. Lubart, "Creativity across Cultures," in *Handbook of Creativity*, ed. Robert J. Sternberg (Cambridge: Cambridge University Press, 1999), 339.

the limiting trappings of finitude. Rather, receiving those givens in some sense as "gift," creativity arises and flourishes in the form of imaginative response, working gladly, respectfully, and lovingly within the proper limits entailed by them yet making something more of the gift than its given form alone already amounts to and handing it on for reception and response by others in their turn. Of course, considered at a different level, the creative imagination often *refuses* to be bound by what confronts it as limit, constantly transgressing the bounded options presented by a surface reading of things and seeking ever new ways in which trajectories of possibility latent within reality's depths might be opened up and given lease of life. But this is no instance of the untrammeled artistic will triumphing over recalcitrant and inert matter, and it leaves limits of another, more fundamental, sort respected and intact. Indeed, it is precisely a case of imaginative discernment concerning the various sorts of givenness presenting themselves for considered response (what Ruskin refers to as the "penetrative" imagination),[3] seeing deeper than the present surfaces of things alone, and working collaboratively with what is given in order to enable it to become yet more fully and truly itself, realizing goods from among the range of particular possibilities invested in it (and it alone) at the world's creation.

For all its discovery, celebration, and advocacy of the individual and his or her capacities and contributions epistemically, ethically, aesthetically, and otherwise, modernity has, on the whole, had a bone to pick nonetheless with the specificity of our placement as human makers situated in space and time. Try as we might, we cannot transgress the particular place allocated and available to us as embodied and "enhistoricized" beings;[4] but the intellectual projects of the modern age have often been characterized by attempts to do so, aspiring to disembodied and timeless perspectives of a universal and global sort (the so-called God's-eye view of things). Ironically, such aspirations can themselves be treated genetically and shown to be the product of particular (geographically contained and mostly short-lived) combinations of social, cultural, economic, and epistemic factors, even when they have been the occasion of some apparently

---

[3] "[T]he virtue of the Imagination is its reaching, by intuition and intensity of gaze (not by reasoning, but by its authoritative opening and revealing power), a more essential truth than is seen at the surface of things." John Ruskin, *Modern Painters* (London: George Allen, 1904), 2:201.

[4] There is a sense, of course, in which our powers of imagination permit a transgression of precisely this sort; yet on further consideration, the point holds good, since even what is available to us to work with imaginatively is shaped and resourced by our particular context. This, indeed, is the very point this section is intended to establish. Creativity is collaborative in nature and a matter of inheritance as well as inhibition.

genuine advance in our human understanding and handling of the world. Theologically, we might classify even the aspiration itself as suspect, suggesting, as it inevitably does, that our particular situation within the given structures of creaturely space-time is a problem to be overcome, rather than a gift to be celebrated—the gift to each of us by our Creator of our specific place and time in the world, as Karl Barth has it, and thus the nonsubstitutable context for our unique vocation as God's particular creatures.[5] This certainly should not be taken as the premise for a blinkered or passive acceptance of whatever our own context happens to afford us by way of an account of how things stand in the world, let alone as the pretext for an aggressive policy of globalizing the "superior" values and habits that happen to be embedded in our particular culture. Nor, though, does it warrant an ideologically pluralist retreat from serious conversation about differences that, in its attempt to value all perspectives equally, ends up in practice marginalizing and devaluing the particular insights and potential contributions of all but its own.[6] But the doctrine of creation does require us to acknowledge that human life is always "placed" in one way or another. And it encourages the supposition, therefore, that our most responsible personal engagements with created reality will always be ones indebted not just to the given nature of the world which confronts us but equally to the testimony and responses of others who indwell that world together with us and, indeed, to the generations of countless others who have been here before us and upon the distillation of whose wisdom and insight human cultures are founded and continue to develop.

In the theological lexicon, the term lying most readily to hand to describe this collaborative and communitarian aspect of all human knowing and acting is "tradition"—tradition understood now, though, not as the macabre and unwelcome grip upon the present moment of a dead and already decaying past but as the vibrant and dynamic embodiment of particular human vantage points upon the world, through the constantly developing forms of which core beliefs, institutions, and practices are embedded and "handed over" from one time and place to another and

---

[5] See Karl Barth, *Church Dogmatics III/2*, ed. Geoffrey Bromiley and Thomas F. Torrance (Edinburgh: T&T Clark, 1960), 437. There are, of course, difficulties to be faced in this claim. The particular existences "given" to some people may well seem naturally to resist the ascription of the category of "gift." See further Trevor Hart, "Finitude and What Is Withheld: A Critical Comparison of Eschatological Imagining in Karl Barth and John Hick," *Zeitschrift für dialektische Theologie* 18, no. 1 (2002): 9–25; Trevor Hart, *Between the Image and the Word: Theological Engagements with Imagination, Language and Literature* (Farnham, U.K.: Ashgate, 2013), chap. 8.

[6] See Hart, *Between the Image*, chap. 4.

within the terms of which alone, therefore, the fresh insights, innovations, and radical departures contingent upon individual vision and freedom are able to be conceived, given birth, and permitted to grow and to flourish.[7] In recent writing on the subject, this theological category has been borrowed by those reflecting more widely on the nature and development of human cultures and the social realities that structure and perpetuate them. Again, the relevant point to take on board is that, despite the tendency of so much in modernity to suppose otherwise, our individuality as human persons is not to be had *despite* the givenness of our situation within particular human traditions and communities but precisely and only by virtue of it, and our individual perspectives on the world develop and flourish only through a continuous dialectical interplay with the standpoints that our culturally embedded existence as creatures renders available to us.

Artistry and Social Practices

If we are properly to understand artistry, or any other form of human creativity, therefore, it must be in terms consonant with just such an account. The artist, we have already observed (by way of reckoning with the obvious), cannot create anything ab initio, but always first receives something that he or she must then work with and transform. The modern preoccupation with the individual as the essential locus of "creative" activity and responsibility, though, tends to bracket this as an understood qualification, proceeding thereafter unabashed as though (apart from the evident fact that the artist must eventually work with whatever *material* realities lie to hand) the origin of the "work" of art itself nonetheless lay securely within the bounded domain of his or her individual emotive or imaginative life, deserving of adornment by one autograph and one alone, its integrity protected henceforth by the complex conventions of copyright. We will address the purported status of the "work" vis-à-vis its material manifestation duly. Here, without wishing in any way to underestimate the vital contribution of individual artistic vision or compositional ability, what we must reckon with is the countervailing claim that from first to last (and thus even from its "inception" as a twinkle in the artistic mind's eye) the work of art is yet always and inevitably a collaborative venture, embedded identifiably within some tradition of life and practice that already populates and shapes the artist's inner world just as surely as its external and social counterparts. In terms borrowed gratefully from a helpful discussion by Wolterstorff,[8] we

---

[7] See Stephen Holmes, *Listening to the Past: The Place of Tradition in Theology* (Grand Rapids: Baker Academic, 2002), 5–17; Trevor A. Hart, *Faith Thinking: The Dynamics of Christian Theology* (London: SPCK, 1999), 165–80.

[8] Nicholas Wolterstorff, "The Work of Making a Work of Music," in *What Is Music?*

must take fully on board the givenness of the social and cultural as well as the material realities of art and the extent to and ways in which every artist is participant in a set of "social practices" which serve to shape his or her activity in one way or another and from the outset.

Drawing on the work of Alasdair MacIntyre,[9] Wolterstorff defines a social practice as a certain kind of activity that—rather than being something we are capable of from birth or else pick up the ability to do naturally as part of the process of maturation—"requires learned skills and knowledge for its performance."[10] Furthermore, the relevant skills and knowledge are mostly not acquired in isolation but are passed on to us by others, whether by verbal instruction or (more likely) personal example and modeling. So, practices are inherently social in this sense. They involve more than one person. Their transmission from one person and one generation to another, in fact, involves communities of practitioners within which they are sustained and developed, and into which budding participants must duly be inducted by some process of apprenticeship. Learning the relevant skills may depend in significant measure on individual aptitude, and some may progress and excel in performance more quickly and more fully than others ever will; but the social dimension (within which wisdom about techniques, standards of excellence, "rules" of practice, and awareness of wider social expectations are all sedimented) is part and parcel of what it takes to become a practitioner and, perhaps, in due course an instructor or a critic of practice oneself. We can see easily enough how all this constitutes a form of "traditioning," and although in MacIntyre's account it applies to a wide range of socially embedded and communicated forms of life, we can recognize in it too the structure of the craftsman's workshop that we met in earlier chapters. For our purposes here, and in Wolterstorff's treatment of musical composition, the key point is that participation in the arts typically involves social practices in precisely this sense. And, without opening up the relevant can of definitional worms at this point (and inviting the death by a thousand qualifications), we might thus say that—however we understand the relationship between them—artistry typically involves and supervenes upon some carefully learned and socially transmitted "craft" in the first instance, and the work of the individual artist is therefore beholden in one way or another to the

---

An Introduction to the Philosophy of Music, ed. Philip Alperson, 103–29 (University Park: Pennsylvania State University Press, 1987).

[9] For the relevant material, see Alasdair MacIntyre, *After Virtue: A Study in Moral Theory* (London: Duckworth, 1981).

[10] Wolterstorff, "Work of Making a Work," in Alperson, *What Is Music*, 109.

community of practitioners which granted it birth and nurture, wherever its peregrinations may have led it since.

In the greatest and most creative artists, no doubt, all such influences are metabolized and taken up into the development of a quite distinctive personal vision and capacity; but they remain a vital part of the inscape from which any artist's work emerges and are never wholly absent from it, whether their presence is acknowledged and celebrated or not. More obvi-ous, perhaps (though still often unnoticed), are the external features of a social practice that are less easily obscured by personal contribution. Art-ists are born and receive their training at particular times and in particular places, accidents of history which have little to do with their personal choosing but which are determinative in all sorts of concrete ways for the shape and direction their art will duly take. To take music as an exam-ple, a composer must write with the material qualities, possibilities, and limitations of particular instruments or ensembles clearly in mind, and these have varied enormously across time and place. Mozart (1756–1791) is widely celebrated as (among other things) a composer of concertos, and his seventeen "Viennese" concertos for the piano (nos. 11–27) in particu-lar are acknowledged as vital precursors to the inward turn in music (as "the language of the heart") that announced itself more blatantly in the work of Beethoven.[11] So, in one sense this is Mozart at his most avant-garde and cutting edge in musical terms. But Mozart could only write piano concertos at all, of course, thanks to the invention and development of the instrument some seventy years earlier and its gradual adoption as the keyboard of choice in the late eighteenth century. *Sturm und Drang* on the harpsichord is a musical development unlikely ever to have occurred to anyone, no matter how gifted or creative. As Robert Greenberg points out, Mozart's piano concertos bear the musical imprint of the material realities available to him as a composer in other ways too. The *pianoforte* instruments for which he wrote were not today's impressive, metal-harped concert-hall monsters, capable of taking on the combined volume of a symphony orchestra and coming out on top, but much smaller, wooden-framed contraptions, in truth more suited to *piano* than *forte* in their out-put of decibels and easily drowned out, therefore, by the sound of even a smallish chamber ensemble. Accordingly, Greenberg observes, "Mozart accompanies the piano the way he would accompany a very light voiced soprano singer. He never, for example, puts the orchestral strings in the same range as the piano when the piano is playing the theme." Indeed, in

[11] See, e.g., H. C. Robbins Landon, "The Concertos: (2) Their Musical Origin and Development," in *The Mozart Companion*, ed. H. C. Robbins Landon and Donald Mitchell (London: Faber, 1965), 273–78.

general, "[w]hen it comes to orchestral accompaniment, a Mozart piano concerto is about deftness and lightness of touch."[12] Prodigious musical genius he may well have been, but like all artists Mozart was also a product of his time and place, and his creativity was worked out entangled within the constraints of that social matrix rather than by escaping from it. And no matter how uniquely gifted or strong willed, of course, if any composer would have his music performed or heard at all, he is equally beholden to the wider social "language" of music (i.e., not just the contingent range of musical forms but the use, performance, and hearing practices) available in his day.

The Populous Imagination

We ought not, though, to imagine the "creative" phase of artistic composition to be an initial solitary, silent, and antisocial affair, the artist turning to reckon with material and social considerations only at a late stage and once the real "work" is already over and done with. This might be a dangerous inference of "phased" accounts of the creative process that identify a discrete moment of "inspiration" or "invention" logically prior to other activities such as "evaluation" and "selection."[13] I do not mean by this to deny that literal silence (or something close to it) and the sanctum of solitude may well be the conditions under which many artists find that their most creative ideas come to them most readily (though others may find the background noise of a coffee shop or busy airport terminal equally conducive). The point is, rather, that even in solitude we are never entirely alone, even the dialogue of the self with itself being in reality a *polyphonic* exchange, other voices being "present," whether recognized and acknowledged or not. "The ontological aloneness of the creative moment, the 'autism' of the poet and artist," George Steiner writes, "is, one suspects, populous."[14] The inner sanctum of the artistic imagination, therefore, is not "socially oblivious"[15] but is itself in significant measure something socially constituted and thus shaped and guided even in the logically primitive *inventive* phases of

---

[12] Robert Greenberg, *How to Listen to Great Music: A Guide to Its History, Culture and Heart* (New York: Plume, 2011), 165.

[13] Wolterstorff responds critically to theories by Beardsley and Collingwood in this regard. Some alternative attempts to delineate the creative process are less prone to the problem. E.g., the model proposed by Wallace (*The Art of Thought*, 1926) has four stages: preparation, incubation, illumination, verification. Here, the *preparatory* stage might well be accounted for in ways that take fully into account the importance of social realities. See further Mark A. Runco, *Creativity: Theories and Themes; Research, Development, and Practice* (London: Academic, 2007), 19–23.

[14] Steiner, *Grammars of Creation*, 71.

[15] Wolterstorff, "Work of Making a Work," in Alperson, *What Is Music*, 128.

its activity by a tacit awareness of art's material and social realities.[16] And these same realities are duly embodied in art's concrete outputs, being fully implicated in the individual responses or "vision" of the artist herself. And, having shared in the work's origination, they must duly take their share of the credit for its particular qualities.

Of course this does not render the poet or the artist a mere passive recipient and hawker of "preowned" ideas, or an unwitting host whose most original contributions are in truth little more than an evolutionary bid by cultural "memes" to secure their own replication, transmission, and survival.[17] If creativity means anything at all, then it means leaving the habitus of tradition transformed by the particular way in which one indwells and responds to it and leaving it identifiably enhanced and enriched rather than depleted, damaged, or denigrated. Furthermore, a "creative" response to things, theorists tend mostly to agree, is one marked not by significant newness alone but by a surplus that adds value to the existing stock of things in some identifiable manner.[18] Creativity solves problems, meets needs, takes the world as it finds it, but does not leave it as it finds it; intentional creativity, one study concludes, "can help us to construct a better world," whatever its relevant sphere of operation.[19] The Christian theologian will want immediately to challenge the apparent utopianism of such a statement, reminding us of the perpetual propensity of all human initiatives to go awry or "fuck things up," as one recent account of sin puts it in visceral and suitably offensive terms,[20] and insisting that the "making good" of the world lies finally (and therefore reliably) in God's

---

[16] Wolterstorff, "Work of Making a Work," in Alperson, *What Is Music*, 113–14. The images that "come to mind" in moments of artistic "inspiration" are not socially oblivious either but determined in some measure by the realities of the artist's particular time and place.

[17] Cf. the exploration of Richard Dawkins' notion of "memes" (the equivalent at the level of culture of bodily "genes") in Mark Pagel, *Wired for Culture: The Natural History of Human Cooperation* (London: Allen Lane, 2012).

[18] According to the "investment theory" of creativity, "creative people are ones who are willing and able to 'buy low and sell high' in the realm of ideas." Robert J. Sternberg and Todd I. Lubart, "The Concept of Creativity: Prospects and Paradigms," in Sternberg, *Handbook of Creativity*, 10. The image is unduly beholden to certain sorts of economics, no doubt, and needs salting with a good dose of the alternative image of creativity as the receipt and reciprocal giving of "gift" to render it entirely palatable; but its limited appeal here is to make the simple point that value of some sort is added rather than taken away by creative behaviors.

[19] Runco, *Creativity: Theories and Themes*, 412.

[20] Francis Spufford, *Unapologetic: Why, Despite Everything, Christianity Can Still Make Surprising, Emotional Sense* (London: Faber & Faber, 2012), 27.

hands alone as an object of transcendent rather than immanent hope.[21] Nonetheless, an account of human creativity as generating a surplus of value may, I shall suggest duly, be taken up legitimately into a theological vision of it as a responsible priestly participation in God's triune action in the world, earthed in the atoning life, death, and resurrection of Christ and borne up by the undergirding power of the Holy Spirit.

Art as Gift and as Kenosis

To return to my main point here, then, there is little to be gained (and much to be lost) by capitulating to any attempt to account for human action as such (including those behaviors we might reasonably identify as "creative") by appeal to explanatory preconditions—biological, psychological, social-linguistic, or whatever—that leave no space for meaningful talk about human freedom, let alone recognition of a genuinely "creative" contribution issuing unprecedented and unpredictably from particular individual imagining. To hold the artist (or whoever) accountable in his or her imaginative responses to the given world is certainly to presuppose the meaningfulness of such notions. But notions of creative accountability presuppose too that human creativity is never, as it has sometimes been supposed, a matter of "the intense moment / Isolated, with no before and after"—that is, the *wholly* unprecedented outpouring of a vision singular, inexplicable, and answerable only to itself—but always of "a lifetime burning in every moment / And not the lifetime of one man only."[22] In what comes "before and after" the creative response and, as we have seen, "populates" that response itself, there is much that lies beyond the range of the artist's individual determination or choosing and must be accepted not just as "given" but as "gift" if her response is to be a truly creative one and thus a matter of gift in its turn.

No artist chooses the particular context into which she is born and within the constraints and possibilities of which her particular aptitudes, talents, and range of possibilities for development are schooled, directed, and permitted to flourish, or not. The accidents of history have no doubt derailed many a potentially rich creative contribution in the arts or elsewhere, and the remarkable explosion of artistic culture in Renaissance Florence (rather than other larger European cities north of the Alps), for instance, can hardly be made sense of without the serious acknowledgment of propitious societal as well as personal factors.[23] As the recipient of

---

[21] See, e.g., Richard Bauckham and Trevor Hart, *Hope against Hope: Christian Eschatology at the Turn of the Millennium* (Grand Rapids: Eerdmans, 1999), 44–71.

[22] "East Coker" (vv. 21b–24), from *Four Quartets*, in T. S. Eliot, *The Complete Poems and Plays of T. S. Eliot* (London: Book Club Associates, 1977), 182.

[23] "Explaining it requires a consideration of many complex societal factors: the

so much that is given in this way, artistic creativity is always a matter of confluence and collaboration, bearing a debt to its several antecedents and accompaniments, acknowledged or otherwise. Of those to whom much is given and entrusted, of course, much is also expected,[24] and creativity in any sphere of enterprise, far from being the unconstrained outburst of individual feeling or vision, comes with a considerable weight of social accountability and expectation attaching to it. The artist no less than any other has first received freely and is called upon now to give freely in his turn, held accountable for whatever he offers up to be received and responded to by others.

The economy of what comes "after" as well as "before" the artist's creative response is thus also helpfully figured in terms of gift, at least in part, and from at least two angles of consideration. First, the artist gives of his or her creative labors to produce something good, working "with the grain" of its physical and semiotic raw materials to offer back something that transcends the mere demands of its various use-practices, to be and become the best that it can be and whatever it alone can be. Such gratuitous lavishing of care and effort, though, ceases when the "work" in question is reckoned ready for offering up to a wider public. In truth, since the "work" is necessarily composed both of material form and of significance, in some sense it is always offered up *incomplete*, with more meaning as yet to be realized through its reception and the responses of others that will duly greet it. No artist can control or determine in advance the shape or the sum of meaning accruing in this way. As we have already seen, the voice of the "hoped-for listener, spectator or reader" will already be present among many others as a subliminal "accomplice" during the entirety of the creative process itself,[25] and, without the collaboration of such figures once the work is finally unveiled, the artist's individual accomplishment, no matter how great, is bound only to perish in obscurity. As Steiner observes, "Unpublished, unperformed, Shakespeare's *Hamlet* would have died with Shakespeare."[26] Here, therefore, there is more costly giving to be acknowledged, as the artist must now let go of the object on which so much personal attention and care has been lavished and hand it on, thereby risking its completion at the clumsy hands others, a "kenotic" act that is

---

economic and political strength of Florence, the cultural values of the community, the system of patronage that emerged among the wealthy, the apprenticeship systems that were established to train new artists." R. Keith Sawyer, *Explaining Creativity: The Science of Human Innovation* (Oxford: Oxford University Press, 2006), 32.

[24] Luke 12:48.

[25] Steiner, *Grammars of Creation*, 140.

[26] Steiner, *Grammars of Creation*, 140.

at once the act of love, setting the work free to become what it is capable of becoming rather than selfishly clinging to its unfinished and as yet premature form. The umbilical cord must finally be cut (and sooner rather than later) if it is to survive and flourish. These others in their turn—the maker's audience or public—have their own careful and generous role to perform, granting the "work" constant renewal and regeneration across time and place by acts of "reading," interpretation, performance, exhibition, and publication, and so preventing its otherwise ephemeral and unrequited manifestation as an *opus imperfectum*.

Artistry, Works, and Worlds

The acts of reception that grant artistic works ever new leases of life in this way may, of course, be performed well or badly, or even irresponsibly, so that the work suffers loss rather than gain and the creative possibilities invested in it are closed down rather than opened out for wider enjoyment. To put the matter slightly differently, some imaginative responses to the work have the appearance of being naturally felicitous, while others seem only to despoil it and to squander or abuse the imaginative opportunities that it affords.

In a discussion of the status of the "fictional worlds"[27] generated by works of art, Kendall Walton suggests that the "work" produced by an artist generates clusters of fictional truths. Some of these appear to be embedded in the form of the work itself (the sum of these constitutes the imaginative "world" of the work) and will be taken up into any positive reception or interpretation of it. So, to use Walton's own example, in the "world" of Seurat's *La Grand Jatte* it is fictional that a couple is strolling in a park. But much more can and will be done imaginatively with the painting than this by its appreciators, as they use it as a prop in endless games of make-believe. And more than one such game may legitimately be played, affording felicitous rather than deleterious responses to the work and thus enhancing or "completing" the imaginative fragment that it holds out, permitting it to generate ever new worlds of meaning that are far from arbitrary in their shape and substance, but generated directly by impulses within the world of the work itself. Such worlds, Walton insists, are the sum of things "to be imagined" by appreciators of the work[28]—things, that is to say, that,

---

[27] The clusters of "fictional truths" generated by works and our imaginative responses to them. Correspondingly, fictional truths in this sense are propositions that are "true in some fictional world or other." Kendall Walton, *Mimesis as Make-Believe: On the Foundations of the Representational Arts* (Cambridge, Mass.: Harvard University Press, 1990), 35; cf. 62.

[28] Walton, *Mimesis as Make-Believe*, 62.

whether or not they are *actually* imagined by anyone,[29] in some sense properly belong to the worlds of possibility and propriety generated by the artist's original imaginative labor. "Fictional worlds," Walton writes, "like reality, are 'out there,' to be investigated and explored if we choose and to the extent that we are able."[30] In a related discussion, Nicholas Wolterstorff concurs with this. Artists, he suggests, are best thought of neither as the imitators nor as the repudiators of the "real world" but as those who, by composing artifacts, fictionally project a world or worlds *distinct from* the real world.[31] And yet, the "states of affairs" (possible or impossible) proper to these worlds are not ones summoned into being by the sheer will of the artist herself. In some meaningful sense, they preexist her creative appropriation of them, "waiting to become the world of the work."[32]

Insofar as this is true, of course, we are compelled again to acknowledge certain relationships of collaboration and accountability. One who receives the gift of the artist's work generously or faithfully will be one who in some sense collaborates with trajectories of imaginative possibility and potential invested in the work and will offer up readings or performances of it which are warranted or "authorized" by the original creative vision. This certainly does not mean, though, that the artist exercises control over the ways in which his or her work may henceforth be treated or the range of meanings that may legitimately count as "authorized" by it. No human artist, George MacDonald muses, can ever know the sum of meaning lying hidden within his or her own work but only a small part of it. Only God, he suggests, creates something the possible plenitude of which does not exceed the scope of his creative vision and personal authorization.[33] Despite the general tenor of much contemporary "criticism," the role of the good critic, surely, is not to lambast the artist's work or,

---

[29] Walton, *Mimesis as Make-Believe*, 43.

[30] Walton, *Mimesis as Make-Believe*, 42.

[31] See Nicholas Wolterstorff, *Art in Action: Toward a Christian Aesthetic* (Carlisle, U.K.: Solway, 1997), 122–55. For a more thorough consideration of the topic, cf. Nicholas Wolterstorff, *Works and Worlds of Art* (Oxford: Clarendon, 1980). Wolterstorff (122) suggests that pure music and abstract art constitute artistic exceptions to this case of fictional world projection. Music is a difficult case, consideration of which lies far beyond our scope here. Of works of abstract ("nonrepresentational" or "nonfigurative") art such as those by Mondrian, Pollock, and Rothko, though, Walton observes that they might properly be understood as "representations" which encourage us to imagine that certain things are fictionally true—e.g., that a slab of yellow exists in front of a green rectangle, or whatever. See Walton, *Mimesis as Make-Believe*, 54–57.

[32] Wolterstorff, *Art in Action*, 131.

[33] George MacDonald, *A Dish of Orts, Chiefly Papers on the Imagination, and on Shakspere* (London: Sampson Low Marston, 1895), 320.

self-importantly, to suggest ways in which it might better have been done otherwise but precisely to efface himself by gratefully receiving the gift that it holds, and, through his own careful critical responses, to unfold further the worlds of meaning warranted by it.[34] Less optimistic about the capacities, expectations, and likely accomplishments of critical discourse as such, Steiner avers that the best readings of art are themselves art.[35] The insight is a cognate one, though; the best and most faithful reception of a work will itself be participant in the creative breaking open and sharing of the work's stock of imaginative and semantic potential, whatever form that takes. In this, the interpreter's accountability is not to the artist or his or her supposed "intentions" but to the work itself and to the worlds of possible meaning generated and warranted by it—that which is in some sense "'out there,' to be investigated and explored if we choose and to the extent we are able."[36] And again, as with the work of the artist, so too with the work of his or her interpreters—this is hardly a solo effort. What "counts" as a fitting interpretation (and what does not) will also be socially mediated to some extent by conventions and traditions of reading, these being extended and modified in their turn by what are judged to be authentic and valuable renderings of the work.[37]

Whatever we hold the ontological status of the "work" to be, the phenomenology of artistic creativity confirms a sense on the part of many artists themselves that they, too, are accountable to it, or to the "idea," rather than being free, as its absolute Creator and Sovereign, to do with it whatever they will. The dynamics of creativity, it seems, are often difficult to disentangle from those of the discovery, exploration, and charting of something that "comes to" the artist as gift, to be received and worked with and to be made more of before handing it on. Appeals to the muse or to divine mania or to that which bubbles up unsolicited from the depths of the unconscious (individual or shared) are all attempts to bear witness to this awareness—the awareness that the exertions of individual artistic will alone will not suffice but need first freely to receive before they may in turn freely give. But there are appeals, too, to a sense of the form of the work as such being in some sense already out there "waiting to become the world of the work." Michelangelo famously suggested of his sculptures

---

[34] I am indebted to David Baird for this thought.

[35] George Steiner, *Real Presences: Is There Anything in What We Say?* (London: Faber & Faber, 1989), 17.

[36] Walton, *Mimesis as Make-Believe*, 42.

[37] Thus, e.g., "what is fictional in a painting depends not only on splotches of paint on canvas but also on relevant traditions about how to interpret them." Walton, *Mimesis as Make-Believe*, 49.

that "as he worked, figures emerged from the marble. His job was not to carve a statue, but to release forms from within the living stone."[38] This self-perception is reflected in the rough-hewn and unfinished nature of some of his last and greatest pieces, such as the Florentine *Pietà* which, especially viewed from the rear, seems still to be emerging from its petrine state and which Michelangelo himself abandoned, apparently unable to liberate the form he had glimpsed from the stone in which it was securely embedded. MacDonald offers a specifically religious and theological take on the circumstance. The artist, he suggests, is never a Creator nor yet really a Poet or Maker but merely a *trouvère*, a finder, who glimpses things hidden as yet from human view and draws them to our attention—things hidden from the foundation of the world by its true Creator, embedded in the fabric of things for our eventual discovery and delight.[39] In its lopsidedness (ironic from one who was himself a considerable poet, novelist, and fantasist), MacDonald's account deliberately underestimates the extent of the artist's own contribution but captures nicely the wider thought of the work as something "objective" that the artist is privileged to glimpse and then labor creatively to extricate from the surrounding manifold of actuality and possibility, revealing as much of its form as he or she can but leaving much (sometimes more and sometimes less) undetermined and as yet to be explored and revealed by others.

On the whole, one might reckon J. R. R. Tolkien (much indebted to the aforementioned MacDonald) among those whose poetic labors tend to leave less rather than more for his appreciators to "finish off." The nature of true artistry, Tolkien suggested, was precisely to do with the glimpsing of fictional states of affairs and the power to evoke imaginative worlds within which those same states of affairs would properly belong, and granting readers or viewers temporary citizenship of these worlds via the generation of "Secondary Belief."[40] The further removed from "Primary Reality" art takes us, the greater the challenge and skill involved in this feat of imaginative transportation. "Anyone inheriting the fantastic device of human language can say *the green sun*," Tolkien notes. That is merely a matter of rearranging the pieces on the board, redistributing nouns and adjectives in a novel manner. "Many can then imagine or picture it. . . . [But to] make a Secondary World inside which the green sun will be credible, commanding Secondary Belief," is a task of a wholly different order, and

---

[38] Barbara A. Somervill, *Michelangelo: Sculptor and Painter* (Minneapolis: Compass Point Books, 2005), 60.

[39] MacDonald, *Dish of Orts*, 41–42.

[40] J. R. R. Tolkien, *Tree and Leaf: Including the Poem "Mythopoeia"; "The Homecoming of Beorhtnoth Beorhthelm's Son"* (London: HarperCollins, 2001), 37–38.

when it is "attempted and in any degree accomplished then we have a rare achievement of Art."[41] The verb "evoke" rather than "make" seems prudent here, though, since in reality no human artist can ever do more than present for consideration a part of the world he or she has glimpsed and begun to explore. And, while Tolkien probably went further than any before or since to chart and chronicle the landscape—geographic, linguistic, cultural, historical, political, industrial, mythic, and more besides—of the fictional world first glimpsed in the linguistic fragment "*elen síla lúmenn' omentielmo*"[42] and while he was content sometimes to place considerable emphasis on the role of the artistic will in summoning such worlds into presence,[43] he too was haunted by the suspicion that the artist's "subcreative" role was, in the larger scheme of things, merely that of one who stumbles upon something already there, albeit lying hitherto unnoticed, and shares the discovery with others by skillfully laying part of it bare.

Tolkien's personal success in generating Secondary Belief among his readers led to a constant stream of correspondence from people wanting to know much more than he was able to tell them even in the six hundred thousand words and one thousand pages of *The Lord of the Rings*. So, for example, in response to an inquiry about the fate of the horse Shadowfax, he replied, "I think Shadowfax certainly went with Gandalf [across the sea], though this is not stated." The note of caution indicates how Tolkien himself thought about the status of an artistic world. We might suppose that, being the maker of the fictional world of Middle-earth, he was in a position to give an absolute and unequivocal answer. "Yes he did." Or "No he didn't." But Tolkien sensed that he was not the creator of Middle-earth, not in any absolute sense. And so there were lots of things about

---

[41] Tolkien, *Tree and Leaf*, 49.

[42] "Nobody believes me," Tolkien wrote to his son Christopher in February 1958, "when I say that my long book is an attempt to create a world in which a form of language agreeable to my personal aesthetic might seem real. But it is true. . . . [*The Lord of the Rings*] was an effort to create a situation in which a common greeting would be *elen síla lúmenn' omentielmo*, and . . . the phase [*sic*] long antedated the book." Tolkien to Christopher Tolkien, February 28, 1958, in *The Letters of J. R. R. Tolkien*, ed. Humphrey Carpenter (Boston: Houghton Mifflin, 1981), 265 (no. 205). The (Elvish) phrase occurs in bk 1, chap. 3, and translates as "a star shines on the hour of our meeting." The claim reveals how Tolkien's artistry was organically connected to his professional practice as a philologist. Creating a world hospitable to Elvish discourse and "reconstructing" one in order to breathe new life into a surviving fragment of Anglo Saxon poetry are, in the final analysis, essentially similar enterprises, both involving high levels of imaginative work. That the one is unashamedly "fictional" and the other typically granted a more respectable intellectual status was less important to Tolkien than what they shared in common.

[43] So, e.g., "An essential power of Faërie is . . . the power of making immediately effective by the will the visions of 'fantasy.'" Tolkien, *Tree and Leaf*, 23.

this particular literary world, and about any work and world of art, about which the artist was and would never be in any position to declaim with absolute authority. Sometimes the answers are not *available* to him or her, and this is not a sign of the artist's imaginative capacity having failed but of the fact that the "work" (and the attendant "world" evoked by it) always come to the artist first as something given and received, and in one sense, therefore, not "made" by him or her at all.

Tolkien gestured to the same complex relationship between the creative and the heuristic in the literary device employed both in the prefatory note to the second edition of *The Hobbit* in 1951 and in the foreword to the first edition of its massive sequel in 1954. He was, he told his readers, the translator and editor of texts that he had stumbled upon and been privileged to work with. And, in the final analysis, that was how he understood the artist's "sub-creative" labors. The one who "makes" a secondary world and populates it out of his imagination is, viewed from another angle, merely one to whom the secret of this world is unexpectedly opened and who, having begun to explore it himself, delights in introducing its secrets to his friends. One critical inference of this, of course, is that the artist should quite reasonably expect the reader or viewer or whoever now to "discover" all sorts of things in the world of his work that he himself had not found there. For Tolkien, as for MacDonald, such a surplus of meaning and possibility is no accident (and certainly not capitulation to the notion that readers may do whatever they will with texts, abandoning all sense of warrant and placing every reading on the same dubious level of value) but can be traced directly to the ultimate provenance of all human artistry in the primordial plenitude of God's own creative work, which called into being a world not just possessed of objective actuality but pregnant with all manner of possibilities, some but not all of which would duly unfold and enrich its own essential meaning.

The Peculiar Status of the Creative "Idea"

Another critical inference of this sense of an "objective preexistence" of the work and its world is that the artist herself must be held accountable to the work in her efforts to open up a portal to it in the actual world—the artifact or material form of the work, whether painted, written, sculpted, scripted, or whatever. The "work," of course, consists in a perichoretic union of matter and meaning, neither of which can be dispensed with or known apart from the other. Apart from some apprehension of meaning or value, the material artifact appears only as a random concatenation of sensations (since, as we have already seen, even in our perceptual grasping of it as an object it is already laden for us with levels of significance), while, apart from our induction in the peculiar languages of "formed matter" (tactile, kinetic, auditory, visual, olfactory, gustatory), nothing of significance can be shown or apprehended. To refer to something as a work of art at all is thus both to treat it in continuity with all other material entities *and* to insist upon a particular sort of semiotic excess supervening upon its physical form (however this may be understood—e.g., as an object possessed of "aesthetic merit").[44] And, typically, the responsible reception of a work will entail modification and enhancement not of its material presentation (which remains more or less fixed) but of its attendant symbolic or semiotic charge. In the case of the performing arts, the matter is more complex, the enacting of a script or sounding forth of a score being precisely a matter of modifying the material content of a work as well as its meaning or value.

In her acclaimed treatment of the doctrines of creation and trinity in terms of the analogy of human artistry, Dorothy L. Sayers distinguishes three "modes of existence" of the work: the Creative Idea ("passionless, timeless, beholding the whole work at once"), the Creative Activity ("begotten of that idea, working in time . . . with sweat and passion, being incarnate in the bonds of matter"), and the Creative Power ("the meaning of the work and its response in the lively soul").[45] In this creative trinity of modes, the Idea is precisely something that is not itself the product of any deliberate artistic activity but something that "comes to" the artist and "makes its presence felt," already possessed of its own integrity. If it is an idea to be credited to the artist herself in any sense, therefore—insofar as the question "where" it subsists is either relevant or answerable—that credit is clearly only conventionally rather than properly deserved, since the mode in which the work exists in conscious, partial, and gradually realized form in the mind of the maker herself is not that of the Idea at all but already that of the Activity or Energy. This is the glimpse and dawning apprehension on the part of the artist of the shape her work must take ("must," because it must faithfully reflect the Idea, which must therefore

[44] See below, 309–15.

[45] Dorothy L. Sayers, *The Mind of the Maker* (London: Methuen, 1941), 28. The phrase "modes of existence" is mine rather than Sayers' own, but it fits the case perfectly well. The trinitarian structure of every act of human creation was first aired in the concluding speech of the Archangel Michael in Sayers' play *The Zeal of Thy House*, written in 1937. In 1936 G. T. Thompson had published the first English translation of Karl Barth's *Church Dogmatics I/1*, with its articulation of the Godhead in terms of a Trinity of Revealer, Revelation, and Revealedness. Sayers and Barth were already known to one another through his liking for detective fiction, and the parallelism between her description of triunity and Barth's is striking and certainly encourages use of Barth's term *Seinsweisen* to refer to Sayers' three distinct hypostases. Of course Barth would have suffered an apoplexy over her positing of a straightforward analogy between the divine self-giving and that of the human artist.

be distinct from it in order to serve as its rule) and the hard graft of working it out and granting it particular form in "the bonds of matter." Simultaneously, there is also the third mode, the Power that interprets her own Activity to her and so reveals the Idea, proceeding always and only from the Idea and the Activity together.

Here, then, there is a relation of accountability to be reckoned with. What Sayers has in mind is the continual awareness any artist has of having to select the right phrase or the fitting color or the felicitous combination of tones and, until the thing "comes right," knowing that the choice is one that does not yet correspond to a reality only hazily apprehended and still to be worked out in its detail but grasped imaginatively as an integral whole nonetheless.[46] So the artist cannot do whatever she chooses without risk of compromising the integrity of the work and her own integrity as one dedicated to its truthful manifestation. The Energy, Sayers insists, must ever be subdued to the Idea.[47] Or, we might say, the artist's creative freedom must always be exercised in a manner that is accountable to the objective reality of the work itself. Even the characters in her own novels, Sayers acknowledged, while in a perfectly proper sense her own literary "creations" were nonetheless possessed of a freedom and integrity that could not be gainsaid without ruining the story as a whole.[48]

The Work of Art and the Mind of the Maker

As well as an Augustinian and Barthian patterning of the divine Trinity,[49] it is tempting to trace in Sayers' account the influence of the old Neoplatonic notion that the artist creates courtesy of a privileged glimpse of the eternal Forms in the mind of God himself, the form of a work thus being first "in the artist" before it ever enters the material world;[50] and perhaps some version of that notion is indeed compatible with the more open Christian eschatological emphasis (i.e., upon the rich veins of *possible* meaning and value invested

---

[46] She is thus not concerned only with those prodigious instances of artists who claim to "hear" a whole piece at once and must rush to capture it on paper before the audition fades. That she takes something of an analogous sort to be a normal rather than an exceptional part of the creative process becomes apparent from a fleeting reference to Mozart in her correspondence. See Sayers to C. Armstrong Gibbs, January 12, 1942, in *The Letters of Dorothy L. Sayers*, vol. 2, *1937–1943: From Novelist to Playwright*, ed. Barbara Reynolds (Cambridge: Dorothy L. Sayers Society, 1997), 341.

[47] Sayers, *Mind of the Maker*, 58.

[48] Sayers, *Mind of the Maker*, 50–67.

[49] Sayers' debt to the analogical method of Augustine's *On the Trinity* is explicit. Sayers, *Mind of the Maker*, 37. On Barth, see n. 45 above.

[50] Plotinus, *Enneads* 5.8.1. See above, chap. 8.

in the world at its creation) that we have identified in MacDonald and Tolkien. We should note, of course, Sayers' explicit disclaimer that she has a vulgar rather than any philosophical notion of "Idea" in mind;[51] but the term functions in her description nonetheless in a way that Plotinus would have been perfectly content with—namely, to refer to something "objective" yet, at least tacitly, identifiably "in the mind of the maker" and logically (rather than temporally, since temporality is itself already a function of the incarnation of the Idea in the "bonds of matter") prior to its articulation in material form. In fact, there is a further shard of philosophical idealism in Sayers' version of things, though it is one that she gleans from the work of Jacques Maritain and R. G. Collingwood rather than Plotinus. Although she suggests that "the urgent desire of the creative mind is towards expression in material form," Sayers is emphatic in her insistence that "the whole complex relation that I have been trying to describe may remain entirely within the sphere of the imagination, and is there complete."[52] In other words, the work in its threefold simultaneous existence as Idea, Energy/Activity, and Power may in principle exist and remain completely in the mind of the maker, without any need of entanglement in the world of the flesh.

The putative analogy between the structure of the divine Trinity and acts of human artistry was not Sayers' own, though she developed it more completely, duly adding a pneumatology courtesy of Collingwood's aesthetics. The kernel of the analogy, though, is already to be found in Maritain's *Art and Scholasticism*, where—noting that the artist's responsibility is so to deform, reconstruct, and transfigure material appearances as to render them radiant with "the invisible Spirit at play in things"—he indicates nonetheless that "[b]efore the work of art passes by a transitive action from art into matter, the conception of art must itself have taken place within the soul by an immanent and vital action, like the procession of the mental word."[53] This oblique allusion to the patristic distinction between the *logos endiathetos* and the *logos prophorikos*[54] already gestures in the direction of a full-blown analogy between the life of God and the experience and creative activity of the artist, so that Maritain feels bound elsewhere to provide the relevant qualification. When a creaturely mind conceives (and subsequently utters) a word, he acknowledges, there is no new *substance* (hypostasis) brought into being: "[i]n creatures, the mind cannot succeed in producing in facsimile of nature another self, a subsisting person, it does

---

[51] Sayers, *Mind of the Maker*, 28.

[52] Sayers, *Mind of the Maker*, 30–31.

[53] Jacques Maritain, *Art and Scholasticism with Other Essays*, trans. J. F. Scanlon (London: Sheed & Ward, 1930), 63, 64.

[54] I.e., the divine Word eternally present within the Godhead and the "going forth" of that Word in the economies of creation and redemption.

not, properly speaking, engender; it makes an utterance, and that utterance is not an offspring."[55] Yet in God, Maritain notes, this is precisely what happens, as God utters a Word eternally and, in doing so, generates a distinct hypostasis, "giving birth to another self at once substantial and personal, to a Word which shall be truly a Son." It is in the Holy Trinity alone, therefore, he continues, that we see "the coincidence of two functions which everywhere else are separate."[56]

Sayers had certainly read *Art and Scholasticism*, and the influence of such passages on her thinking is already apparent in the 1937 Canterbury drama. What was it, then, that the publication of Collingwood's *The Principles of Art* in 1938 added to the mix? As we have seen, Maritain was content to allude only to one Trinitarian relation of procession, that of the Word or Son from the Father, and his suggestion is that this "Word" (or "work" in terms of the artistic analogy) already subsists and is fully itself prior to its incarnation in the world as "a work at once material and spiritual, like ourselves."[57] Collingwood himself, of course, was not concerned with analogies between divine and human creativity, but his aesthetics served to convince Sayers that the analogy was more than merely felicitous, "the Trinitarian doctrine of Idea, Energy, Power" being "quite literally, what it purports to be: a doctrine of the Creative Mind."[58] For, in his account of the structure of human creativity, what Collingwood had provided was the vital third *hypostasis*.

According to Collingwood the "work of art" must not be confused with the material artifact that the artist produces but is rather an activity of the artist's consciousness. More precisely, it is an activity of imagination in which an inarticulate emotion is expressed in consciousness in such a way that the artist himself becomes conscious of or experiences it fully for the first time. There are thus three discrete but inseparable aspects of a work: the initial "psychic emotion," the activity of expressing it, and the "imaginative emotion" or aesthetic experience that now attends it.[59] This, it should be noted, is for Collingwood the very same process involved in any form of expression, including our everyday use of language, which (consistently enough) he takes to be a form of art,[60] albeit generally a less

---

[55] Maritain, *Art and Scholasticism*, 125–26.

[56] Maritain, *Art and Scholasticism*, 126.

[57] Maritain, *Art and Scholasticism*, 126.

[58] Sayers, *Mind of the Maker*, 102.

[59] R. G. Collingwood, *The Principles of Art* (Oxford: Clarendon, 1938; repr. London: Oxford University Press, 1958), 274. Citations are to the 1958 edition.

[60] "Every utterance and every gesture that each one of us makes is a work of art." Collingwood, *Principles of Art*, 285.

accomplished one than that produced by the poet, the painter, or the composer. Thus, someone who looks at a seascape (say) without painting it or resorting to some explicitly poetic means of expression, insofar as his or her "impressions are transmuted into ideas by the activity of . . . imagination," nonetheless *experiences* the event (rather than it simply happening to them) and does so in a manner consonant with the experience of the artist (i.e., "aesthetically").[61] The experience of looking at the subject and painting it is simply a richer and more adequate one, proportionate to the effort and achievement invested in the performed activity. It is important to notice at this juncture Collingwood's insistence that, while the artist generally puts his artistry "out there" for wider public enjoyment and appreciation, the primary beneficiary of the work is always the artist himself. It is the artist, that is to say, who discovers through the activity of imagination the nature and meaning of the impression made upon him by the initial "psychic emotion," and, since the "work" consists in the imaginative activity of expression itself rather than any material concomitant of this, all three aspects of it (emotion, activity, aesthetic experience) arise in the first instance in the artist's own inner life. The artist is his own target audience, and the meaning of his work dawns on him first, and only as he engages in it. That others may be granted access to the work and to its meaning (to "overhear" the artist's self-expression to himself) may be a good thing, but it is inessential to what he does as an artist.[62]

In her 1944 essay "Towards a Christian Aesthetic," Sayers reveals the extent to which Collingwood's work had shaped her thinking.[63] In particular, she discerns in his patterning of the artist's experience and activity a more adequate template for fusing her account of "creative mind" and the creedal doctrine of God as Trinity. Thus, "the act of the poet in creation is seen to be threefold—a trinity—experience, expression and recognition; the unknowable reality in the experience: the image of that reality known in its expression: and power in the recognition; the whole making up the single and indivisible act of creative mind."[64] The creative act is all about "the *communication of the image in power*," and in it the artist bodies forth and grasps "the in-itself unknowable and unimaginable reality" of her own Idea.[65] Again, though, Sayers is insistent that the Power, this

---

[61] Collingwood, *Principles of Art*, 307.

[62] Collingwood, *Principles of Art*, 300–301. For clarification, see also 308–11.

[63] Dorothy L. Sayers, "Towards a Christian Aesthetic," in *Our Culture, Its Christian Roots and Present Crisis*, ed. V. A. Demant, 50–69 (London: SPCK, 1947). The essay was originally delivered as one of the Edward Alleyn Lectures for 1944. See esp. 50n1.

[64] Sayers, "Towards a Christian Aesthetic," in Demant, *Our Culture*, 64.

[65] Sayers, "Towards a Christian Aesthetic," in Demant, *Our Culture*, 65 (emphasis in original).

all-important third "person" in her trinity, "is the thing which flows back to the writer from his own activity and makes him, as it were, the reader of his own book," whether anyone else ever reads it or not.[66] This being so, she avers, "the creative act . . . does not depend for its fulfilment upon its manifestation in a material creation"; it can subsist wholly and completely, without loss, in the mind of the maker, just as its archetype and counterpart, the triune God, has no need of either creation or incarnation to fulfill his being but subsists as *actus purus*, eternally fulfilled in himself.[67]

Here Sayers both trails her theological petticoat and misreads (or at least departs unannounced from) Collingwood. To begin with, it is now clear that human creativity is for her an analogue not of divine creativity per se but of the divine Trinity that logically precedes creation. Put differently, the analogate for creative mind as we find it in the creature is the *immanent* Trinity, God's triune existence as such, rather than the *economic* Trinity in which God proceeds forth from himself to fashion a material cosmos. To be "creative" is thus, for Sayers, to be made in the image and likeness of God's eternal triune being rather than his economic relation to the world, despite her ostensive starting point in the Genesis narrative.[68] The theological and christological issues here—whether in practice the distinction between Trinity and creation is unhelpfully elided here or whether the notion of a *logos asarkos* who is not eternally bound to take flesh (and thus committed to creation as the condition for incarnation) is feasible—need not concern us at this point beyond noting them.[69] When it comes to Sayers' analogue, though, we should at least note that her appropriation of Collingwood's theory (if this is indeed what she is doing) is insecure. Collingwood's *logos*, we might say, is one much more thoroughly and necessarily entangled in the world of the flesh. So, while he confirms that the aesthetic experience or work of art is "wholly and entirely imaginative"[70] and acknowledges that the artist is his or her own reader or audience, unconcerned in the first instance with granting others access to the work through its incarnation in material form, Collingwood

[66] Sayers, "Towards a Christian Aesthetic," in Demant, *Our Culture*, 31.

[67] Sayers, "Towards a Christian Aesthetic," in Demant, *Our Culture*, 32.

[68] "Looking at man, [the author] sees in him something essentially divine, but when we turn back to see what he says about the original upon which the 'image' of God was modeled, we find only the single assertion, 'God created.' The characteristic common to God and man is apparently that: the desire and the ability to make things." Sayers, "Towards a Christian Aesthetic," in Demant, *Our Culture*, 17.

[69] See further chap. 14 below.

[70] Collingwood, *Principles of Art*, 306.

nonetheless holds that this incarnation is essential rather than merely something to which the work naturally tends, as Sayers maintains.[71]

It is essential in at least two ways. First (as Sayers would certainly concede but does not take adequate account of in this context), while the work has its provenance in the mind (imagination) of the maker, it is, for Collingwood, "not generated out of nothing" but presupposes a corresponding sensuous experience—that is, some feeling state provoked by being in relation to a reality other than itself, typically one situated in the external world. Thus the work of art originates courtesy of the artist's psychophysical engagement with a world and supervenes upon it from first to last. Second, it is precisely and only as the artist labors to express his emotion in material form of one sort or another that the emotion is "communicated in power," first to himself and subsequently to his audience. Only as the painter paints does it become clear to him just what it is that he is painting. Thus, "[t]here is no question of 'externalizing' an inward experience which is complete in itself and by itself."[72] Externalization, incarnation, the "flesh-taking" of the *logos* is precisely the activity in which the emotion (or idea) becomes known to the artist; and, while the material artifact may not be identifiable as "the work," for Collingwood there can be no work without it, for the work (as "imaginative activity") only happens as the artist grants it fleshy form and then again as the audience engages with this same "art object."[73] Revelation is (to borrow a category from Barth) an "event," and one that cannot happen apart from incarnation. If it be observed that Sayers was a writer rather than a painter or a sculptor and thus her "material" was precisely not *material*, we would refer back to Collingwood's own insistence that language, too, participates in the economy of the flesh and of "art," and conversely every material artifact is a sign patient of interpretation.[74] Thus, what occurs in the mind of the maker (whatever her medium of eventual expression) is never independent of her participation in the material world but rather always a result of a collaboration with it, and one in which the artist must therefore always be mindful and respectful of matter itself. Indeed, as Sayers herself insists—in a moment much more fully attuned to the revaluation of the

---

[71] Sayers, "Towards a Christian Aesthetic," in Demant, *Our Culture,* 32.

[72] Collingwood, *Principles of Art,* 304.

[73] On the relationship between the artist's experience of the work and that generated by engagement with the material artifact, see further Collingwood, *Principles of Art,* 308–15.

[74] A parallel case can and should be made for music, often erroneously dubbed the most "spiritual" of the arts but in reality one bound up just as thoroughly with our embodied state and situation as any of the others.

material creation and its significance that belief in the incarnation seems to require—"[t]he business of the creator is not to escape from his material medium or to bully it, but to serve it; but to serve it he must love it. If he does so, he will realise that its service is perfect freedom."[75] This, surely, is an insight oriented much more fully toward a properly "Christian aesthetic" than the suggestion (albeit one compelled by an analogy earthed in Sayers' beloved Athanasian Creed) that, where the artistic *logos* is concerned, flesh taking remains a dispensable option, and one undertaken (albeit gladly) only in the interest of communicating a purely spiritual reality to others in the unfortunate absence of telepathy.

Incarnation in the "Bonds" of Matter

Quite apart from specifically theological considerations, the persistent tendency to dematerialize art—as though the real "work" is something subsisting wholly in the realm of spirit or idea and perhaps (as in some forms of conceptualism) only loosely or arbitrarily connected with any physical object—does not hold water, at least as far as most of what we typically recognize as artistry is concerned. Wolterstorff makes the point succinctly. He writes,

> [A] work of art emerges only when an artist takes chisel in hand and chips away at stone, heats up a furnace and pours bronze, picks up a lump of clay and turns a pot, takes up brush or knife and spreads paint around, takes burin or acid and makes recessions in copper plates, selects from the verbal stock of his language a specific sequence of words, selects from the enormous array of diverse sounds that the instruments at his disposal can produce a sequence of just a few of them, selects from the infinite array of states of affairs just a few to make a story.[76]

Anyone who has ever been in an artist's studio will know just how messily physical the processes of artistic making can actually be, and the ethereal sounds produced by a concert violinist are inexorably wedded to the skilled application of horsehair to strings stopped by calloused fingers. Artistry immerses us in the physicality of the world more fully rather than furnishing an escape from it, and to insist nonetheless on denying this material dimension the status of "art" or limiting the "work" to its imaginative or ideal concomitant or surplus thus seems to reflect a needless prejudice or resentment toward the entailments of our situation as embodied beings. Just as we discover ourselves to be creatures embedded securely both in the physical cosmos and in worlds of meaning and significance distinct but inseparable from our transport in our material environment, so we may

---

[75] Sayers, "Towards a Christian Aesthetic," in Demant, *Our Culture*, 53.
[76] Wolterstorff, *Art in Action*, 91.

reasonably insist that the work of art too is always the union-in-distinction of material and nonmaterial realities, its integrity lost when either dimension is missed, ignored, or separated from the other.[77] In the human world, and in art no less so than anywhere else, in other words, matter matters.

The extent to which all this is so drastically qualifies Sayers' cheerful suggestion that acts of artistic *poesis*, occurring first and foremost in the imagination rather than the external world, represent "the nearest approach we experience to 'creation out of nothing,' and we conceive of the act of absolute creation as being an act analogous to that of the creative artist."[78] Unlike the biblical Creator, the artist must always work with given materials, whether those supplied by her culture or, we now acknowledge, those literal "materials" in which her work takes flesh and takes shape. And, like so much else, the properties and potentialities afforded by physical materials are something given with the materials themselves, and not wholly susceptible to the artistic will. Matter is not "infinitely protean," lending itself to whatever shapes imagination is capable of conjuring up, but it has a nature, itself embedded within the given order of things, rendering matter capable of some things rather than others or better suited to some things than others.[79] This givenness can be experienced by the artist either as a frustration to be resented, railed against, and risen above or as a gift, a set of constraints that, paradoxically, when gladly accepted as such proves to be liberating rather than confining, a generous conversation partner in the creative enterprise rather than a dead weight to be wrestled with reluctantly. Throughout most of history, those recognized as "artists" were craftsmen first, apprenticed not just to a human master but in a genuine sense to their materials too, acquiring through prolonged exposure and hands-on engagement a deep knowledge of its qualities and possibilities—learning first to love, to respect, and to serve it, and only thus to "master" it. Having the well-being of her material at heart, Wolterstorff suggests, the "artist" in this sense will much prefer the superb execution of something well within its capabilities to the tour de force that stretches her material to its uttermost limits, the latter smacking too much of exasperation, hubris, and the will to subjugate matter ruthlessly to an imaginative conception born and nurtured independently of it.[80]

---

[77] See further Trevor Hart, "Through the Arts: Hearing, Seeing and Touching the Truth," in *Beholding the Glory*, ed. Jeremy S. Begbie, 1–26 (London: Darton, Longman & Todd, 2000).

[78] Sayers, *Mind of the Maker*, 23.

[79] See Wolterstorff, *Art in Action*, 92.

[80] Wolterstorff, *Art in Action*, 93. The fact that creativity and craftsmanship remain

Richard Sennett provides some telling examples from the world of modern architecture, where a disconnection of a different sort between head and hand—or in this case more typically between blueprints generated using computer-assisted (or "hands-off") design and "on the ground realities"—resulted in a seriously flawed product, from attractive street cafés rendered largely unusable during the day by the excessive ambient temperature ("simulation is an imperfect substitute for accounting the *sensation* of light, wind and heat on site. The designers would perhaps have done better to sit unprotected in the midday Georgia sun for an hour . . .; physical discomfort would have made them see better") to impressive glass elevators traversing a forty-story hotel atrium and so leaving all the bedroom windows facing out onto a panorama of parking lots.[81] Vital as the purely formal and conceptual elements of imaginative creativity are, they are no substitute for the "embodied knowledge" afforded by a hands-on engagement with the material realities of the world within which both the artist and her work belong fully and properly, and to which the artist cannot help but be accountable. Attempts to compel matter to serve ideas having their independent provenance in a context from which material considerations themselves have deliberately been bracketed out as far as possible (whether the "mind of the maker" or the abstract complexities of some CAD software package) is thus a risky strategy, and one unlikely to succeed in practice in allowing the human world (in which material and nonmaterial realities confront us already united and interpenetrating, and in given configurations) to become more rather than less fully itself.[82]

The base of knowledge and skill in handling materials which develops into a deep respect and love for them typically involves more than our embodied existence in the world alone, being acquired, nurtured, and sustained by our participation in communities of one sort or another. Where the arts are concerned, such knowledge has generally been transmitted, as we have already seen, in some equivalent of the craft workshop, where not just manual skills but larger traditions of practice in which are embedded standards and in which values are inherited as a given habitus to be assumed and responsibly indwelt in the first instance. The artist's accountability to her material, in other words, is bound up from the first

---

distinct and that in the modern period artistry has often proceeded without any necessary training in the latter raises distinctions that will concern us in the next chapter rather than here.

[81] Richard Sennett, *The Craftsman* (London: Penguin, 2008), 39–45. The citation in parenthesis is from pages 42–43.

[82] Cf. Rowan Williams, *Grace and Necessity: Reflections on Art and Love* (Harrisburg, Pa.: Morehouse, 2005), 18.

with her accountability to a wider social matrix, and whatever creative
departures or radical innovations she may duly be inspired to attempt will
remain identifiably earthed in this given inheritance of practical wisdom
and insight concerning the world's flesh and the as yet unrealized goods
to which it naturally inclines or lends itself. Having received much, she
will have much to offer in her turn, both to her materials and to the tradition which has enhanced and intensified her relationship to them. Again,
we find creativity most naturally wedded to and reliant upon patterns of
conversation and collaboration with given partners in relationship, rather
than emerging (as yet socially unscathed) from the autism of a radically
insular imagining.

Workers in Fittingness

Respect for the integrity of the material creation might be reckoned essential to an artistic creativity that enhances rather than defames or defaces
the given world. Christians in particular, it would seem, are without
excuse when they fail in this regard, their very identity being staked on
the value and significance of the flesh that God has not only created but
duly redeemed and assumed into permanent union with his own hypostatic
existence as the Son. It is the enfleshed and not the discarnate Logos of God
who reveals to us the full meaning of our own creatureliness and that of the
world in which we dwell. "Flesh" in the biblical sense, though (Heb., *bāśār*;
Gk., *sarx*), refers not to matter alone but to matter in its integral union
with whatever aspects of our creaturely being we take to transcend mere
physicality—our embeddedness not just in the physical cosmos but in the
"human world" of persons and meanings and values and the rest that we
have already spoken of.[83] To the extent that we take this seriously, of course,
our attempts to steer clear of idealisms of one sort or another will hardly
entail a headlong rush toward any version of materialism. To respect the
material world, to love it and to seek its good, can never mean attending to
its material qualities alone but to those qualities apprehended within a wider
set of relationships, many of which will prove incapable of measurement in
the laboratory. Among these, and especially pertinent to a consideration of
artistic creativity, are those relationships that Wolterstorff refers to as ones
of "fittingness."[84]

---

[83] See E. Schweizer and R. Meyer, "Sarx," in *Theological Dictionary of the New
Testament*, vol. 7, ed. Gerhard Kittel, 98–151 (Grand Rapids: Eerdmans, 1971); N. P.
Bratsiotis, "Bāśār," in *Theological Dictionary of the Old Testament*, vol. 2, ed. G. Johannes
Botterweck and Helmer Ringgren, 317–32 (Grand Rapids: Eerdmans, 1975).

[84] See Wolterstorff, *Art in Action*, 96–121.

Fittingness, Wolterstorff suggests, is a familiar feature of the reality we indwell together as human beings, though we may not typically notice or name it as such. More specifically, fittingness is a matter of relationships between the qualities of things (including nonmaterial things such as feelings or moods or values) and is shot through the whole of that reality, helping to bind it together and grant it overall coherence. In brief, "fittingness" refers to the ways (often surprising and seemingly arbitrary ways) in which the qualities or complexes of qualities of one thing seem to "fit" naturally together with the qualities of other things in some other region or dimension of our experience of reality, so that elements of the world seem naturally to resonate with or to cry out to and answer one another. We might say that they "resemble" one another in some sense, but only in a very odd sense, since, as in the case of metaphor which we have already considered,[85] at first blush it is not the likeness but precisely the unlikeness between the things concerned that strikes us.

In his rather more lengthy treatment of the subject, Wolterstorff resorts frequently to examples to illustrate the sort of thing he has in mind, and one or two may serve helpfully here. The most striking and contentious instance is perhaps the phenomenon we now know as *synesthesia*, where "stimulation in one sense modality produces a sensation or vivid 'image' in a different sense modality,"[86] so that someone hears involuntarily a particular strain of music as "yellow" or "purple," a condition held to have afflicted or blessed many great artists, writers, and composers, including Kandinsky, Nabokov, Liszt, and Messiaen. The neurological capacity to perceive fusions of one sensation with another (or, rather, the incapacity *not* to do so) seems, in other words, to have a high incidence among those we typically think of as "creative" in their engagements with the world.

Less striking, but no less significant, are instances that seem to command much wider assent as involving natural "fits" between ostensibly unconnected qualities of experience. Thus, for example, a jagged black line drawn on a white page seems to "fit" better with restlessness, while an undulating line "fits" better with tranquility. The letter *r* is more likely to suggest "something flowing or moving, and the letter *i* something sharp and bright."[87] In a ping-pong world, ice cream and Siamese cats seem

---

[85] See above, pp. 13–18. Cross-modal fittingness of the sort Wolterstorff describes often furnish the basis for our discernment of apt metaphors, such as the description of Mozart's music as "light" and that of Berlioz as correspondingly "heavy." Cf. Wolterstorff, *Art in Action*, 102.

[86] Wolterstorff, *Art in Action*, 100.

[87] Ernst H. Gombrich, *Art and Illusion: A Study in the Psychology of Pictorial Representation*, 5th ed. (London: Phaidon, 1977), 310.

somehow to fit more closely with the word "ping," while hot soup and elephants naturally incline toward "pong."[88] And we do not need to be synesthetes in the strict sense of the word to feel the irresistible draw of certain pairings between qualities of sound and vision (red = louder, gray = softer) or between music and gustation (a "sweet" melodic line) or mood (sounding the tonic of the scale together with the second or seventh feels "tense" or "unresolved"). Some such correspondences might be accounted for, perhaps, by repeated concomitance in our experience of qualities, but others resist such easy theorizing. "Are wide things generally rough, and narrow things generally smooth?" asks Wolterstorff. "Are sharp things generally red, and dull things generally green?"[89] And why on earth should it be the case, Ernst Gombrich inquires, that, according to so many people when asked, the concept "boulder" should seem to belong on the relevant antonymic scale quite obviously toward the extreme of "sadness" rather than "happiness"?[90]

The research grounding the discussions by Gombrich and Wolterstorff was conducted in the 1950s by Charles E. Osgood and colleagues, and it suggests that particular concepts (qualities or complexes of qualities) are situated in a semantic space helpfully mapped by a series of antonymic bipolar scales (good-bad, clean-dirty, kind-cruel, happy-sad, heavy-light, strong-weak, loud-soft, thick-thin, rough-smooth, fast-slow, hot-cold, active-passive, excitable-calm, and so on), each of which "modes" might in turn be considered in the light of three dispositional dimensions—preferability, potency, and activity. Each concept occupies just one position in the complicated relational web structuring this semantic space, but a particular point may nonetheless correspond to a number of different concepts. These correspondences across modes will tend to be with respect to one or more of the three dimensions. So, for instance, devil, Hitler, and panther might perhaps be situated equally with respect to preferability, potency, and activity, and this would influence their position on various scales of consideration.[91] If we begin with the modalities themselves, taking large-small and loud-soft as our examples, and if we follow Wolterstorff's suggestion that "the relation 'larger than' bears a stronger cross-modal similarity to 'louder than' than it does to 'softer than,' "[92] this

[88] Gombrich, *Art and Illusion*, 314.

[89] Wolterstorff, *Art in Action*, 108.

[90] Gombrich, *Art and Illusion*, 314. Gombrich is referring here to statistical research conducted by Charles E. Osgood and others, on whose work Wolterstorff also draws. See, e.g., Charles E. Osgood, George J. Suci, and Percy H. Tannenbaum, *The Measurement of Meaning* (Urbana: University of Illinois Press, 1957).

[91] This particular example is taken from an early review of *The Measurement of Meaning* by Sol Saporta in *American Anthropologist* 61:1 (1959), 159–60.

resemblance across modes will in its turn be with respect to degree of preferability, potency, and/or activity (PPA). Thus, the resemblance or "fittingness" between a particular concept, quality, or complex of qualities with another in a different mode ("boulder"—perhaps broken down further into "heavy," "gray," etc.—and "sad") will prove, on analysis, to be a matter of cross-modal correspondences measured in terms of PPA.

The research undertaken by Osgood and others was into the quantification of meaning, pertaining first and foremost to the relationships between concepts in "semantic space," rather than the nature of an objective reality presumed to lie behind or beyond our language as such (the qualities of "things" and their relationships to one another). As Wolterstorff notes, though, Osgood's work uncovered remarkable cross-cultural correspondences where the perception of cross-modal similarities is concerned.[93] This might be taken to suggest, of course, that such similarities are either given in the structure of an objective global order (one encompassing both material and supramaterial realities) or else hardwired into our species being as mechanisms of response, rather than arising from the canonizing activity of human cultures and the power of language to structure the human world for its inhabitants.[94] As we have already seen, though, such distinctions are often difficult to draw in any hard and fast manner, and in certain contexts the attempt to do so seems needless. In particular, I have suggested above, in theological terms, where the givenness of structure and order to human experience is concerned, there is no need either to exclude our humanity from the processes whereby the material world is ordered or to exclude God's purposes, presence, and activity from the structuring and enriching capacities of language and culture vis-à-vis the "human world."[95] The more or less global concurrence between cross-modal similarities in human experience is, of course, very significant, and Wolterstorff appeals to it to account for the aesthetic phenomenon of "expressiveness."[96] Not all aesthetic theories prioritize the idea that art is expressive of some state of affairs, either in the world or in the

---

[92] Wolterstorff, *Art in Action*, 99.

[93] Wolterstorff, *Art in Action*, 106.

[94] Osgood himself rather pulled his punches on the question of the objectivity of relations of fittingness, preferring to speak of similarities between our affective responses to the world. Cf. Wolterstorff, *Art in Action*, 108–9.

[95] So David Brown notes, helpfully, that "the natural seldom acts apart from the cultural: apart, i.e., from particular traditions of interpretation. Yet even these should not be confused with the purely human; God can also be active within particular traditions and patterns of interpretation." Brown, *God and Enchantment of Place: Reclaiming Human Experience* (Oxford: Oxford University Press, 2004), 33.

[96] Wolterstorff, *Art in Action*, 110–14.

artist's inner world or (as seems more likely) in the world *as mediated by* the
artist's inner world; but neither must one be a paid-up romantic complete
with oversized white shirt and camp disposition to resonate with the suggestion that a particular poetic image or bodily gesture or composition of
sounds or of color, line, and form *expresses* something (whatever else it may
also be doing at the same time). These relations of expressiveness between
the aesthetic (i.e., material) qualities of objects and the qualities of feeling
or consciousness or whatever are best understood, Wolterstorff argues, in
terms of the relationships of fittingness we have been considering. "Expressiveness," he writes, "is grounded in fittingness"; and so, as well as being a
careful and responsible worker in physical materials, the artist works with
other sorts of materials too, being equally a careful "worker in fittingness,"[97] constrained and liberated in equal measure by the given "grain" of
the universe in this regard too.

From Metaphor to Madness

According to Aristotle "the greatest thing by far is to be a master of metaphor," a capacity that demands "an intuitive perception of the similarity
in dissimilars"[98] or, as Ricoeur has it, for "semantic innovation through
which a previously unnoticed 'proximity' of two ideas is perceived despite
their logical distinction."[99] We might put the matter slightly differently and
say that metaphor involves a transformation of the relevant conceptual or
semantic space, in such a manner that "the novel idea simply could not
have arisen from the generational rules (implicit or explicit)" that already
characterize that space.[100] In his now classic treatment of human creativity,
Arthur Koestler locates at its center a related phenomenon that he dubs the
"bisociation" of distinct matrices or codes, a flash of insight or creative leap
resulting from the collision between two habitually incompatible associative
contexts (or semantic spaces) and the abrupt transfer of a train of thought
from one context to the other, so that some object, event, or idea is perceived

[97] Wolterstorff, *Art in Action*, 112, 114–21. As Wolterstorff observes, natural as well
as humanly made objects can thus be "expressive" in this sense, even though no poet or
artist intends that they should be so. Accordingly, expressiveness, even in works of art, is
not dependent on artistic intention but on the aesthetic qualities of works.

[98] Aristotle, *Poetics* 1459a. See Richard McKeown, ed., *The Basic Works of Aristotle*
(New York: Random House, 2001), 1479.

[99] Paul Ricoeur, *The Rule of Metaphor: Multidisciplinary Studies of the Creation of
Meaning in Language*, trans. R. Czerny and others (Toronto: Toronto University Press,
1977), 6.

[100] Margaret A. Boden, *The Creative Mind: Myths and Mechanisms*, 2nd ed. (London:
Routledge, 2004), 52. See further p. 245 above.

transgressively, in terms of both at once.[101] In the hands of the comedian, such deliberate category errors may generate the fleeting emotional discharge of laughter. In art and poetry, and in science, they have a much more enduring effect, the surprising convergence and transformation of distinct and hitherto independent planes of thought or operation permanently modifying the ways in which we map and experience the world.[102] Koestler's account resonates with the structure of what the American pragmatist philosopher Charles Peirce (1839–1914) had called "abductive" or "retroductive" operations of the mind—forms of logical inference involving inspired guesswork, conjecture, or the following of an intuition, and insight obtained by thus situating something within what is logically neither a necessary nor a probable pattern or gestalt.[103] Other more recent accounts use less precise categories to refer to analogous processes, such as "divergent" and "over-inclusive" thinking[104]—expansive activities of mind or imagination that go beyond ordinary analogical and associative patterns by virtue of their apprehension of some more remote and surprising connection that nonetheless, once grasped and in retrospect (retroductively), appears warranted and even obvious. In each case, what arises—through non-rule-governed imaginative acts that transform the relevant semantic, conceptual, and perceptual landscape—is "novel order . . . which yet makes sense."[105]

Human beings, we have already observed, occupy a peculiar place in the scheme of things, awkwardly straddling and holding together in our own existence two distinct frames of reference at once—that of the body and our participation in the material realm of "nature" on the one hand, and the nonmaterial dimension of meanings, values, persons, feelings, and other supramaterial realities (as we typically suppose them to be) on the other. In many ways this, too, is a fragile, unstable, and apparently incongruous conjunction, albeit a glorious one; and perhaps, we might suppose, it renders us uniquely placed or naturally predisposed among creatures to notice or create "truthful" congruences in the most improbable of places,

---

[101] Arthur Koestler, *The Act of Creation* (London: Hutchinson, 1964), 45, 59, 95, et passim.

[102] Koestler, *Act of Creation*, 94.

[103] See Justus Buchler, ed., *Philosophical Writings of Peirce* (New York: Dover, 1955), 150–56, 302–5. Abduction is thus logically distinct from the movement from general to particular that characterizes deductive reasoning on the one hand and the movement from particular to general that characterizes ordinary inductive reasoning on the other.

[104] Cf. Runco, *Creativity: Theories and Themes*, 1–38; Jonathan A. Plucker and Joseph S. Renzulli, "Psychometric Approaches to the Study of Human Creativity," in Sternberg, *Handbook of Creativity*, 39–40.

[105] Mark Johnson, *The Body in the Mind: The Bodily Basis of Meaning, Imagination and Reason* (Chicago: University of Chicago Press, 1987), 162.

granting us an eye for metaphor, a discernment of fittingness, or a propensity to bisociate and abduce.

Koestler's vision tends in the direction of the democratization of the creative impulse, identifying it in everything from the coarsest of playground puns to the most arresting poetic image or disorienting scientific paradigm shift. Aristotle is more exacting; mastery of metaphor, he insists, is "the one thing that cannot be taught" and a sign of genius, grasping deep connections in the nature of things that otherwise (i.e., to the common eye) remain hidden from view.[106] We should recall that in the classical period notions of *ingenium* were hard to disentangle from those of divinely given inspiration and insight, referring not so much to any wholly immanent or inner human agency as to "a profoundly altered state of consciousness and feeling" contingent upon a peculiar donation or action from the side of the heavens.[107] The characteristic description of the resultant state as "manic" indicates the ambiguity of its perceived status as a grace, though in the *Phaedrus* Socrates insists that (since it is such μανία or madness alone that has its provenance with the gods) sanity (σωφροσύνη)—being of purely human origin—is less to be desired by the poet than "the greatest of blessings." Indeed, "[h]e who without the divine madness comes to the door of the Muses," Socrates continues, "confident that he will be a good poet by art, meets with no success, and the poetry of the sane man vanishes into nothingness before that of the inspired madman."[108] Aristotle too is aware of the typical alter ego of genius, observing that all those who stand out as extraordinary in the fields of philosophy, poetry, and the arts are prone to melancholia, some obviously plagued much more seriously than others by the illnesses associated with "black bile" (μελαίνης χολῆς).[109] Far from connoting unambiguous brilliance of intellect alone, therefore, the classical "genius" was one whose capacity to think outside the box was closely allied to unseemly episodes of ἔκστασις (ecstasy) during which he

---

[106] McKeown, *Basic Works of Aristotle*, 1479.

[107] See, e.g., Martin Kemp, "From 'Mimesis' to 'Fantasia': The Quattrocento Vocabulary of Creation, Inspiration and Genius in the Visual Arts," *Viator: Medieval and Renaissance Studies* 8 (1977): 384. Cf. Kay Redfield Jamison, *Touched with Fire: Manic-Depressive Illness and the Artistic Temperament* (New York: Simon & Schuster, 1993), 50–51.

[108] Plato, *Phaedrus* 244A–245A. See H. N. Fowler, ed., *Plato: Euthyphro, Apology, Crito, Phaedo, Phaedrus*, Loeb Classical Library (London: Heinemann, 1913), 465–69. The distinction between objective and subjective is, of course, typically highly ambiguous in Plato's philosophy and psychology, as his account of the ontological status of the Forms indicates.

[109] Aristotle, *Problems* XXX. See Robert Mayhew and David C. Mirhady, eds., *Aristotle: Problems, Books 20–38; Rhetoric to Alexander*, Loeb Classical Library (Cambridge, Mass.: Harvard University Press, 2011), 277.

would be transported "out of his mind" itself. Apart from the late eighteenth century, when notions of genius became wedded fleetingly to a facility for following the unalloyed dictates of rationality, the suggestion that the poetic spirit, in its most accomplished beneficiaries, is something messy and troubling which holds a person in its grip, rather than being satisfactorily under his or her control, is never far from hand.[110]

Although contested, a close link between artistic temperament and manic-depressive (bipolar) illness remains a significant item on the agenda of modern psychiatric research. So, for example, Kay Redfield Jamison documents plentiful evidential warrant pointing to a significant coincidence of "the molten and amphibious nature of artistic imagination" (its fluctuation between Dionysian and Apollonian impulses) and the extremes of mood typically experienced by bipolar sufferers.[111] Not all artists are bipolar, of course, and not all those who are bipolar are artists; but the expansiveness of vision characteristic of artistic creativity, perceiving or experiencing things on more than one plane or level at once and tracing deep connections and new configurations hidden to the vulgar eye is, she suggests, commensurate with the condition and likely only to be enhanced by it. The statistical data she supplies concerning poets, painters, and others who almost certainly suffered from manic depression (including many who duly succumbed to its darkest regions and committed suicide) is striking to say the least.[112] Shakespeare's oft-cited musing about the impact of "strong imagination" on the lunatic, the lover, and the poet (itself a neat example of abductive reasoning borrowed from the sage of the *Phaedrus*) proves, therefore, to have both considerable mileage and significant warrant.[113]

The hypostatic union of otherwise wholly distinct and incommensurable territories of experience accomplished by artistic expressiveness, metaphor, acts of bisociation, and abduction—supercharged by the fluttering between melancholic and manic states of those blessed with the dubious "gift" of divine mania—succeeds in joining "fittingness to novelty, obviousness to surprise," and so reorganizes our entire perception of things.[114] Ought we to follow Aristotle, therefore, and think of such behaviors as earthed in a privileged glimpse or perception of connections hidden deep

---

[110] Jamison, *Touched with Fire*, 51–56.
[111] See Jamison, *Touched with Fire*, 99. See also Daniel Nettle, *Strong Imagination: Madness, Creativity and Human Nature* (Oxford: Oxford University Press, 2001).
[112] Jamison, *Touched with Fire*, 267–70.
[113] *A Midsummer Night's Dream*, act 5, scene 1, lines 2–22. Socrates ascribes "divine madness" to both lovers and poets alike in his speech. See Plato, *Phaedrus* 245A–B.
[114] Ricoeur, *Rule of Metaphor*, 236, 238.

in the natural texture of things? Or should we think instead of a creative reimagining and redescribing that transforms the semantic spaces canonized by particular cultures and languages, and in effect "makes" the very difference to which it draws our attention in the process of doing so? Again, sharp lines between the territories of nature and culture frequently prove hard, and often needless, to draw. Both together serve to furnish us with the givenness of the human world we indwell together and to which we respond, either creatively or otherwise. And again, therefore, we are compelled to acknowledge with Ricoeur that "the enigma of metaphorical discourse is that it 'invents' in both senses of the word: what it creates, it discovers; and what it finds, it invents." "[R]eality brought to language," he concludes, "unites manifestation and creation."[115] If we have seen anything in this chapter, it is that historical, social, and material realities are not easily peeled apart without damage, because they interpenetrate; for us, at least, there is relatively little reality other than that which has already been "brought to language" in the broadest sense and which is given to and inherited by us as such. The "reality" confronted and received by the artist, as by all of us, is thus always a manifest of many distinct but inseparable layers and levels, and within the plenitude of its "givenness" lie all manner of possibilities for its further unfolding and enrichment by the work of human hands. In theological terms God, the Christian may reasonably suppose, is concerned with and identifiably at work in and through the whole pattern, and not in the initial provision of some putative physical substrate alone. And what God calls for and calls forth from those created in his image are responses which, receiving the world as gift, discover in its givenness opportunities for the exercise of creative freedom as well as constraint and for collaboration with—rather than contradiction of—God's own vision for all that the world may yet be and become. This will be the theme of our final chapter.

---

[115] Ricoeur, *Rule of Metaphor*, 239.

13

Creativity, Gratuity, and Utility

Before drawing together the threads of my argument thus far and setting a positive theological context for the nature and significance of human creativity as manifested in the arts and elsewhere, there are some loose ends still to be tied up. In particular, there are some terms and some implied distinctions to which I have necessarily resorted at points in the preceding chapters but about which I have as yet said relatively little, if anything, as such. So I take the opportunity to do so here, if only for the sake of those whose sense of order and general intellectual hygiene is, like my own, impatient with things left lying around unattended. Again, I shall draw on a range of sources, many of which have no explicit theological concern in view; but again, too, due to the nature of the territory concerned, theology of a sort will not be held at bay for long, and I shall feel free to allude or appeal to its peculiar contributions from time to time, thus anticipating themes and perspectives to be granted free rein and full exposure only in my final chapter.

Gift, Givenness, and Grace

I begin with the seemingly untroubled category of "gift," which has played an extensive role in the Christian doctrine of creation and crops up, inter alia, in various accounts of what is involved in artistic creativity too. The artist, we are likely to be told, is in some identifiable sense always a "gifted" individual, and of the greatest among artists perhaps that they are born with a unique gift, while their creative labors in turn are held to bless those who receive and avail themselves of them with something transformative for which gratitude is the only relevant response. Moving beyond the level of familiar vulgar discourse about the arts and aesthetic experience, though, theories of gift-exchange first developed in anthropology have been appropriated to furnish the basis for an entire aesthetic in works such as Lewis Hyde's widely acclaimed "modern classic" *The Gift*,[1] concerned in particular to disentangle notions of human creativity from the machinations of the market and the dominant spirit of commodification. A gift, Hyde reminds us, is by definition that which must be freely given and equally freely received, not something we can obtain by our own efforts, achievements, volition, or resources (pecuniary or otherwise). It is bestowed upon us unexpectedly, and its "gift" status depends on how we respond and what we duly make of it, degenerating all too easily into pure commodity if we do not respond well. Hyde follows Marcel Mauss in suggesting that a "gift economy" is one characterized by three related obligations—to give, to receive, and to reciprocate.[2] Yet the spirit of giving—if not quite adequately construed as one wholly disinterested—is nonetheless one untainted by any crude expectation of an equivalent or (better still) a profitable "return" on the transaction; and the reciprocal giving generated by genuine gratitude is, as John Milbank (following Pierre Bourdieu) points out, distinguished from any sense of a debt discharged (on terms determined in advance by the formalities of contractual agreement) by the twin features of *delayed return* and *nonidentical repetition*.[3] To give a return gift straight away, let alone an identical gift, misses the point and strips the relationship of its free, unprovoked, and thus authentically "generous" character. Indeed, while the original giver may well receive something in due course (and may reasonably *expect* to do so in a sense as yet to be defined), both Hyde and Milbank draw attention to the fact that the momentum of the gift is often indirect in the first instance, being passed on to a third party in a "non-exact *mimesis*" of the original donation—a mimesis which is, Milbank notes, therefore all the more genuinely exact.[4]

So far, so good, and a gift economy already begins to sound like an attractive and humane prospect by comparison with the Realpolitik of

---

[1] Lewis Hyde, *The Gift: How the Creative Spirit Transforms the World* (Edinburgh: Canongate, 2006). Originally published in 1979 (New York: Random House).

[2] Marcel Mauss, *The Gift: Forms and Functions of Exchange in Archaic Societies*, trans. Ian Cunnison (New York: Norton, 1967). Originally published as "Essai sur le don: Forme et raison de l'échange dans les societes archaïques," in *L'Année Sociologique* (1925).

[3] John Milbank, "Can a Gift Be Given? Prolegomena to a Future Trinitarian Metaphysic," *Modern Theology* 11, no. 1 (1995): 125.

[4] It is part of the complexity of the circumstance, of course, that part of what the original donor receives from having given the gift away may well be the delight of watching it generate further acts of generosity in this manner.

market forces and our habitual resort to indices of "wealth creation" as relevant measures of personal and national success. Sharing or giving away what we have generally attracts less kudos, unless it happens to be wedded to a narrative of prior fortune making or enrichment (in which case, of course, it is precisely the anomaly of someone being willing to part company gratuitously with what society typically encourages us to grab with both hands and hold on to at all costs that is being flagged for attention). In such a milieu, the person of humble means who gives a portion of what little he or she has to others is unlikely to merit much notice. Yet Hyde notes that a gift functions to generate wealth of its own peculiar sort, giving birth to human community in a way that even the most efficient and least exploitative trading of commodities cannot match. Gifts must be received as well as given, and genuinely to receive something as gift is to "suffer gratitude," a condition that inscribes the relevant object with a worth over and above any intrinsic market value it may possess. As gift, it establishes, sustains, and belongs within a personal relationship, and no price can meaningfully be put on it. Part of its worth, though, is that it perpetuates the cycle of giving itself, the pleasure of having received reproducing itself most naturally in the form of a desire to give something away in our turn.[5] All this, it might be suggested, is remarkably consonant with an understanding of creation itself—and the generative plenitude divinely invested in it in the beginning—as possessing the fundamental character of gift, despite the perpetual tendency on the part of the religious imagination to reconfigure (and so misrepresent) it instead in contractual terms. And it corroborates the subtle witness of etymology to a wider, natural, and deep-rooted correlation or overlap between the patterns of the generative and the generous, the concerns of the "creative spirit" (divine or human) and the realities of grace.

But the language of gift and what is "given" has another, ostensibly less attractive connotation too, setting up a suggestive ambiguity upon which I have traded deliberately and repeatedly in earlier chapters. To refer to something as given may not be to evoke the personal matrix of generous initiative and grateful response at all, but instead the seemingly cold, impersonal, and immovable (ungiving) realm of brute objectivity, that which simply "is" the case (*es gibt*) whether we like it or not and which furnishes the given context and constraints within which our personal initiatives and responses alike must take shape. Yet even here the traces of grace have not been wholly erased so as to render an unambiguously negative description. Why, after all, do we persist in borrowing the language

---

[5] Hyde, *Gift*, 48. Cf. André Comte-Sponville, *A Short Treatise on the Great Virtues: The Uses of Philosophy in Everyday Life* (London: William Heinemann, 2002), 132–39.

of positive personal intent to speak of value-neutral occurrences or material accumulations more accurately characterized in purely mathematical terms? Is it not, Milbank muses, that "our language is haunted by the praise of the gods or God, so that we secretly refer all that is to personal givers?"[6] "Blessed are you, O LORD . . . forever and ever. Yours, O LORD, are the greatness, the power, the glory, the victory and the majesty. . . . For all things come from you" (1 Chr 29:10-11, 14). Those sharing David's religious conviction may wish to insist that, far from being a mere unfortunate hangover from an earlier stage in the development of our language, the metaphorical interplay between gift and surd "givenness" in contemporary discourse bears abiding testimony to the truth glimpsed in the doctrine of divine providence. Notwithstanding the demand for a genuinely theological reckoning with the realities of evil and suffering in the world (which may and must not be shirked), the various "givens" of our finite existence (even some of those we struggle with and resent the most) may—if we identify and accept them as "gift" (i.e., as something coming to us from God's hand)—become the occasions for creative response and for the generation of unexpected and unlikely goods in which we "allow the world to become more fully itself." Offered as a theodicy this would be shallow and even blasphemous in the face of some of the worst suffering experienced by human beings, and it is certainly not intended as that. But as an observation and conviction based on the widespread experience and wisdom of many generations of religious believers, it is difficult to gainsay nonetheless. The contingent facts of our circumstance, which we did not choose and might well prefer to be far otherwise, may yet, if we respond to them appropriately, be received and experienced as gift and so become the occasion for the gift of creation itself to be perpetuated and handed on through the exercise of creaturely creativity.

We have already seen some of the ways in which this "gift economy" arises in the arts, which is one of the fields of human endeavor most likely to draw explicitly on the language of donation in one way or another. The artist him- or herself may be said to possess a "natural gift," though this alone will scarcely be sufficient to facilitate the flourishing of his or her work. To account for this, we are compelled to situate the artist within a variety of "given" contexts and streams of life, each of which contributes in some measure (positively or negatively) to the work produced and apart from which it could not be or become what it is. The "work" itself, we have seen, may well be alluded to by the artist as something "given" from beyond his or her own conscious creative activity—a work of invocation as much as one of creation, and demanding a high level of self-giving and

---

[6] Milbank, "Can a Gift Be Given?" 120.

self-forgetfulness in its realization.[7] The artist's gift to the public who duly receives it is notoriously difficult to describe or account for, often provoking resort to flights of poetry of its own, not least, interestingly, those that borrow from the lexicon of theology and liturgy. Thus, for instance, Hyde suggests that the artist's gift is to grant the viewer or reader or listener a moment of suspended disbelief, of communion, of grace, and of transformed being.[8] Skeptics may choose to dismiss such unashamedly metaphysical talk as so much hogwash, but they will do so, of course, on essentially the same grounds that they would dismiss the poetic expressions of faith itself.[9] Indeed, we must not forget Hyde's insistence that the "gift" is not genuinely given at all until it is received and so gains traction within the dynamics of individual lives and sets of personal relationships. To one not drawn in this way into the circle of imaginative response, granting the assent of "secondary belief" to the world of the work he or she now temporarily indwells, the relevant "experiences" (like their religious equivalents) remain by definition unavailable except at second hand and the fittingness or otherwise of the imagery borrowed to make sense of them impossible to discern.[10] Finally, therefore, this life of reception, response, interpretation, and enjoyment is itself an extension of the gift, granting the work existence beyond its inception and ordination at the artist's hands. The artist's role, therefore, is never just creation but always equally (and thereby) conscription, urging upon others the worth and the importance of getting involved in the wider give and take of creativity of which the work is but one concrete manifestation. And, since the logic of giving and that of gratitude here coincide and regenerate one another,

---

[7] Cf. Hyde, *Gift*, 146, 152. The gifted state itself, Hyde notes, is in certain respects one of "poverty," of an emptiness needing to be filled from beyond itself (282). The resonances with theological notions of grace here are palpable.

[8] Hyde, *Gift*, 153.

[9] For a disarmingly humorous yet serious engagement from the side of skepticism, see, e.g., John Carey, *What Good Are the Arts?* (London: Faber & Faber, 2005).

[10] Again, the parallels with theological accounts of what is "given" in God's self-emptying approach to the human person in moments of "revelation" are tantalizing. I am thinking, e.g., of Karl Barth's account of revelation as a Trinitarian "event" in which both an "objective" and a "subjective" pole (faith) may be identified, the latter being anhypostatic and possessing its "hypostasis" only in the generative activity of the Holy Spirit in the believer's heart and mind. See Karl Barth, *Church Dogmatics I/1*, ed. Geoffrey W. Bromiley and Thomas F. Torrance, trans. Geoffrey Bromiley (Edinburgh: T&T Clark, 1975), 295–333. The parallel is one picked up (in a thoroughly un-Barthian way) by Dorothy L. Sayers in her account of the work of art as subsisting in three discrete modes—the Idea, the Activity or Energy, and the Power. See Dorothy L. Sayers, *The Mind of the Maker* (London: Methuen, 1941), 26–34.

artistic creativity is also always a matter too of benediction and dedication, of a response offered gratefully and freely for what has first been freely and gladly received, and one directed toward the gift's source (proximate or ultimate, known or unknown) and in the interest of keeping the gift itself in motion. In a thoroughly secularized age, most contemporary aesthetics has no language available to it to make sense of this, other than the suggestive metaphors of givenness, giftedness, and so forth themselves. This, though, need not deter theologians from detecting in it all a stubborn impulse that (even when it remains confused, anonymous, and inarticulate) might perfectly properly be described as "eucharistic"—a dim but persistent echo in the human spirit and the structures of human language alike of the ancient Hebraic insight, duly taken up into the christologically informed liturgy of the offertory: "All things come from you, and of your own do we give you."

Art and Craft

For reasons that we have already considered, the distinction between art and craft is a modern invention and would have been meaningless to many of those whom art history has retrospectively baptized as "artists" or producers of "works of art." Prior to the Renaissance, the Latin term *ars* (like its Greek equivalent τέκνη) had a wide remit, covering most of what we today would recognize as the product of human craftsmanship, and although much of what we call art today would have qualified as *ars*, quite a lot of it would frankly have struggled to make the cut. The integral connection between art and craft has, in the age of conceptualism and other trends, been severed in theory if not always in practice, reminding us that, as Wolterstorff observes, craft and creativity were never the same thing in any case, even though in the past they often coincided to produce what we now identify as the greatest works of "art."[11] *Ars* meant something identifiably well made or well done, working with given materials and according to accepted canons of skill and technique, whether that be cutlery, carpets, crumhorns, or cathedral interiors. As we have seen in earlier chapters,[12] it connoted a level of care and quality control by communities of practitioners dedicated to accomplishing the best that a given material might render and producing some "masters" whose work would become a hallmark for the material or the process in question.

---

[11] "Of course craftsmanship has nothing much to do with creativity. There are superb craftsmen who have little imagination and superbly imaginative people who display little craftsmanship." Nicholas Wolterstorff, *Art in Action: Toward a Christian Aesthetic* (Carlisle, U.K.: Solway, 1997), 93.

[12] See above, e.g., 23–25.

We need not be unduly sentimental or romanticize the circumstance of the premodern craftsman (many of whose existences were doubtless often far more nasty, brutish, and short than we would ever find tolerable) in order to acknowledge any of this. Our use of the term "craft" today still reflects it, distinguishing certain types of product or ways of working (typically those involving direct manual engagement with materials as distinct from the remoteness of industrialized processes) from the mass of sheer productivity. Indeed, one might argue that it was the impetus provided by the industrial revolution with its new means of mechanical production and reproduction (the cost-efficient capacity to churn out endless identical "widgets" on a "production line") as well as a seismic shift in our notion of "the artist" that, together and from different sides, demanded the sort of theorizing of "craft" available today in a plethora (it is tempting to say an entire industry) of books and journals on the subject. The distinction between craft and industrial (or machine) production must be left in abeyance here, save to observe that most of us intuitively sense the difference in quality between many handmade objects and their factory-produced equivalents, where such comparisons can meaningfully be drawn, and the best products of industry are generally those into which higher rather than lower levels of human craftsmanship have been factored at one stage or another. In the final analysis, there is little substitute for high levels of skill and care taken by human makers where quality is concerned, and, whether it is the concerns of the market (after all, who, if they could afford the price, would not prefer to drive a Rolls Royce with handcrafted leather seats and a walnut dashboard rather than a bottom-of-the-range heap of junk with rattling rivets and all the acceleration of an arthritic tortoise on temazepam?) or those of other more elemental and evolutionary human drives, there will always be a place for what Ellen Dissanayake calls acts of "making special."[13] Such acts, in different ways, characterize the spheres of both art and craft and, as I have just suggested, occasionally invade the territory of industry too; but they are perhaps most characteristic of craft

---

[13] See, e.g., Ellen Dissanayake, *Homo Aestheticus: Where Art Comes from and Why* (Seattle: University of Washington Press, 1995), 53–58. Dissanayake contends that acts of "aesthetic making special" (including the arts but ranging too over other human practices and products, such as many of those typically referred to as "crafted" or "well made") have been evolutionarily, culturally, and socially important to the development and success of the human species, issuing from a biologically endowed need to acknowledge certain aspects of the "human condition" (she lists love, death, memory, suffering, power, fear, loss, desire, and hope as instances) as possessed of extraordinary significance, and to mark this with objects and practices made "special" in a manner that appeals to all aspects of our human capacity for response—perceptual, cognitive, and affective.

and of the arts insofar as they are an extension or offshoot of craft. Yet we can distinguish easily (albeit generally in an intuitive rather than a theorized manner) between craft and mere industrial making. What, then, of the other boundary of contemporary definitions of "craft"—that is, that which distinguishes it neatly from "art" or (more snootily) "Art proper"?

The reader will hardly be surprised to learn that theorists continue to answer this question in various different ways, a fact that already counsels caution about the usefulness of hard and fast application of the categories. Nonetheless, there are some considerations worth taking stock of, and here I will mention just a few examples before making some tentative closing comments.

Sociologist Howard Becker defines craft as "a body of knowledge and skill which can be used to produce useful objects"[14] and concentrates precisely on *utility* as that feature which distinguishes craft most clearly from the products of high or fine art. In short, the products of craft are useful (and, more precisely, useful in ways defined by standards external to "the world constructed around" the object or activity itself—i.e., *practically* useful in "the real world"), while those of art are not. Practitioners of craft may, Becker recognizes, display considerable virtuosity in their handling of materials, and some crafts (he instances the production of stringed instruments by hand) seem to require this; but there are plenty of "ordinary craftsmen" attempting simply to do decent quality work and make a living, with no aspiration or aptitude for elevated "mastery" in their field or the more aesthetic demands of "pure" craftsmanship. Among the virtuosos, though, some, Becker acknowledges, are in addition highly imaginative and creative individuals and, as well as extending the range of technical possibility available to those working within their trade, may also open up new territories or standards of beauty or taste as understood by practitioners and patrons of the relevant craft. These "artist-craftsmen," he observes, while they generally share the same audiences, institutions, and rewards as other craftsmen, nonetheless typically feel some kinship and continuity with those working in the fine arts, and their work, he admits, has some claim to be considered and treated as "art."

We can see easily enough how this way of defining craft presumes and is in turn demanded by the post-Kantian notion of "the arts" as objects and practices essentially divorced from all utility save that singular "use" sanctioned by what Wolterstorff calls the modern institution of high art itself—namely, their fitness as objects or occasions of disinterested

---

[14] Howard S. Becker, "Arts and Crafts," *American Journal of Sociology* 83, no. 4 (1978): 864.

perceptual contemplation leading to aesthetic satisfaction.[15] Thus Becker speaks of the artist-craftsman as in effect accomplishing a skillful negotiation between the potentially competing demands of utility and aesthetic excellence, whereas the practitioner in the fine arts need not be concerned with utility at all, being thus free to follow the dictates of the aesthetic alone. We can see the point. But things are more complex than this. Again we are danger of being blinded by our indebtedness to post-Kantian assumptions and need to obtain some temporary distance from them to see things aright. First, we should remind ourselves again that works of art are embedded securely within a complex mesh of human activity, and although we may choose to exalt one particular use (that of aesthetic contemplation) above others, we cannot extricate the works in question altogether from the surrounding socioeconomic tissue that makes such use possible. The same works are intended to serve the complex purposes of artists, distributors, patrons, curators, critics, and others, as well as the beholder in the moment of aesthetic appreciation; and (as Becker readily admits) while this final "use" may in some identifiable sense be the primary "purpose" of the work in question, the demands attendant on all the other things it is expected to "do" inevitably constrain the artist's creative vision and decisions in the process of making.[16] So, the distinction between utility on the one hand and disinterested "uselessness" on the other can only ever be a relative and not an absolute one. Second, we should recall that Kant himself did not require that objects of aesthetic excellence ("beauty," but let us not get hung up on this troublesome term just now) should by definition be objects possessed of no practical purpose or utility. His point about disinterestedness was, rather, that judgments of an intellectual or practical sort are irrelevant (because different sorts of judgment) to the aesthetic circumstance, which attends to the particular qualities of a specific object and brackets out all other considerations than those of its beauty or aesthetic excellence.[17] Of course, on the whole it is much easier to accomplish such imaginative bracketing out if the object in question *has* no apparent purpose other than that of aesthetic contemplation, but it is not necessary to the circumstance that this be so. Thus, we may reasonably presume that there are plenty of instances of human craft (whose primary purpose lies in their ability efficiently to convey food efficiently from the bowl to the mouth or preserve body heat when used as a coverlet on a cold night) which—because of the virtuosity,

---

[15] Wolterstorff, *Art in Action*, 10–12, 39–46, 158–68.

[16] See Becker, "Arts and Crafts," 866.

[17] See, e.g., Immanuel Kant, *Critique of Judgment*, trans. Werner S. Pluhar (Indianapolis: Hackett, 1987), 163.

imaginative vision, and gratuity of care expended in their making—also
function perfectly well as "art" in the modern sense.[18] This ought hardly
to surprise us, of course, since, third, there always were: Cimabue, Giotto,
and the Gothic architects of Chartres and Reims were, after all, craftsmen first and foremost, notwithstanding our retroactive inclusion of their
works among the annals of art history. Indeed, as Dissanayake observes,
prior to the eighteenth century the sorts of objects that we now typically
identify as "works of art" were almost invariably made with some practical, social, civic, economic, or religious utility primarily in mind, and
rarely if ever for "purely aesthetic" purposes.[19] This means, of course, that
our national museums and galleries are filled to overflowing with objects
once produced for eminently practical purposes, divorced now from their
original *Sitz im Leben* and teleology, and presented for us with a wholly
different sort of use in mind. Not all objects crafted for practical purposes
are well suited to meet the peculiar purposes of the art curator or visitor
to the gallery, of course; but some, it would seem, always have been and
still are, because in addition to and over and above their original utility
they possess whatever qualities we take to be relevant to judgments of *aesthetic excellence*.[20] Again, therefore, the issue of utility as such can hardly
be used straightforwardly as a shibboleth to enable us to disentangle works
of craft from works of art; and were we to do so rigorously, our prized col-
lections would certainly be significantly reduced in both size and scope.
Fourth, and finally, we should acknowledge that, even among those forms
of human artistry typically included within the penumbra of the fine arts,
many (perhaps most) works of art are produced for purposes other than
those dictated by the institutions of the art world itself, and their merits
must be weighed accordingly. So, as Wolterstorff observes, whatever it is
that makes a good concerto will be quite different from whatever it is that
makes a good hymn, and the merits or demerits of background music and
drinking songs will be measured differently again.[21] If time and space permitted (which, fortunately or unfortunately, it does not) we might lift the
lid here too on the hotly contested distinction between the fine and the so-
called popular arts. That such distinctions may and must be drawn seems
reasonable enough; but that the word "art" (or, more probably, "Art")
should be awarded in a privileged manner (". . . but is it *Art* darling?") to
one historically and culturally particular and maverick segment of what is

---

[18] Cf. David Jones' discussion of "Gratuity Ness," intransitivity, and the merely utile.
David Jones, *Epoch and Artist* (London: Faber & Faber, 1959), 148–53, 180–85.
[19] Dissanayake, *Homo Aestheticus*, 39–41.
[20] On this notion, see Wolterstorff, *Art in Action*, 158–68. See below, pp. 307–15.
[21] Wolterstorff, *Art in Action*, 157.

in reality a variegated and complex larger fabric of acts of human making is altogether less obvious, and the burden of proof rests identifiably with those who continue presumptuously to hijack the language in this manner. And, if the boundaries between art of one sort and another are messy and fluid, so too, it seems, are those between art and "craft." We may wish to continue to draw them for one purpose or another, but in doing so we need to be continually aware of the inherent provisionality and fragility of the enterprise.

If the attempt to distinguish craft from art in a wholesale manner by appealing to utility seems bound to die the death of a thousand qualifications, other criteria fare similarly badly if a priori and arbitrary definitions are ruled out of court. Among more recent contributors to scholarly conversation on the subject, Howard Risatti concentrates the functionalist account even more precisely, affording the label "craft" only to those humanly made objects whose practical purpose and function is directly linked to the physiological necessities of our human existence in the body—containing, covering, supporting, and so on. Thus, craft, he suggests, straddles the spheres of culture and nature, being, in fact, "a physical manifestation of human subjectivity in confrontation with nature," whereas "art" is a semiotic phenomenon far removed from universal bodily needs.[22] As well as falling prey to the widespread myopia that generalizes a peculiarly modern and Western aesthetic (i.e., the one I have referred to above for convenience as "post-Kantian"), this approach, while it undoubtedly draws attention in a helpful way to a distinct category of human products, nonetheless does so in a manner that excludes all sorts of things which common or garden discourse would naturally identify as craft, thereby leaving most of them in a peculiar limbo deprived of any identity at all (since many would not typically lay claim to or be granted the accolade "art" either, let alone "Art"). Perhaps the invention of yet further categories is indeed what is required, but nominalist profusion of terms in this particular area seems better suited to the predilections of academic disputation than the practical ends of daily living and ought perhaps to be treated with caution and skepticism. Hobbyists who produce decorative handmade knickknacks for sale in support of church funds can thus almost certainly continue to refer to themselves as purveyors of "craft" with impunity.

A rather different, but no less problematic, account of the difference between art and craft is that provided seventy-five years ago now in R. G. Collingwood's more or less canonical text *The Principles of Art*.[23] For

---

[22] Howard Risatti, *A Theory of Craft: Function and Aesthetic Expression* (Chapel Hill: University of North Carolina Press, 2007), 57, et passim.

Collingwood the defining feature of craft is not its utility but the fact that it is produced by the skilled application of some precise directed action (agreed technique) which imposes form upon raw materials in accordance with a preconceived end, in such a manner that clear criteria of success or failure may be applied. In all this, it is the element of *foreknowledge* that is most decisive, since a work of art, Collingwood insists, can never be preconceived in this way; rather, it involves the expression of an emotion (or idea) the precise nature of which is unknown even to the artist him- or herself until it has been worked out. The artist is involved precisely in an exploratory process, trying to discover what these inner emotions are. Thus, Collingwood writes, "[t]here is certainly here a directed process: an effort, that is, directed upon a certain end; but the end is not something foreseen and preconceived, to which appropriate means can be thought out in the light of our knowledge of its special character. Expression is an activity of which there can be no technique."[24] To clarify still further—it is not absence of planning that defines art as such, since, Collingwood admits, much (and perhaps most of the best) art is based on some craft; but that which sets it apart as "art proper" transcends the level of the craft alone, introducing the element of heuristic expression for the realization of which there can by definition be no blueprint or established technique.[25] So, we can see that Collingwood's argument relies heavily on the sort of insistent idealism according to which the true "work" of art can and must be disentangled thoroughly from its contingent material manifestation, being radically particular and subsisting in the first instance at the level of the artistic mind or imagination alone. Clearly there can be no "technique" prescribed in advance for the material expression of such.

I have already offered some critical observations regarding the (in)adequacy of this way of seeing things from a Christian perspective. Quite apart from specifically theological objections to it, though, one may again inquire whether, absent the sort of imperialistic essentialism in which Collingwood indulges, it is true of all "fine art" that it follows this determinate scheme. I very much doubt it, which means again that much that has been and is treated by the art world as "art proper" would now risk unceremonious exclusion and repatriation were the criterion to be strictly applied (but by whom and on the basis of what sort of evidence?). Perhaps "idealistic expressionism" of this sort tells us something true about the provenance of some art. Maybe its account holds true *to some extent* of

---

[23] See R. G. Collingwood, *The Principles of Art* (Oxford: Clarendon, 1938; rpt. London: Oxford University Press, 1958), 15–41. Citations are to the 1958 edition.

[24] Collingwood, *Principles of Art*, 111. See further the discussion on p. 274 above.

[25] Collingwood, *Principles of Art*, 22.

much art. But beyond that—given Collingwood's own frank admission that the territories of "art proper" and those of other forms of human making overlap and interpenetrate and given some of the considerations we have already listed above—it seems prudent not to press too far, as though hard and fast distinctions of this sort can be drawn with confidence and in a manner that sheds light rather than further fanning the flames of disagreement. Again, we may wish to continue to draw them for one purpose or another, but it may prove more illuminating yet to remind ourselves of what all forms of human making have in common and to refuse to allow any decisive weight to be placed on distinctions born largely of convenience and convention. Or, again, that there is a difference between X and Y as regards their classification according to schemes of "art" and "craft" may well be true and may sometimes even be important; but it may be less important in the final analysis than differences of other sorts, such as that between acts of human making which, by modifying and transforming the given world, may be seen to enhance and add worth to it and those that do so only to its detriment. Questions of "creativity," it might be suggested, are more closely bound up with a distinction of this sort than with attempts to situate artifacts on a putative (in practice constantly shifting) axis between "High" and "Low."

Artistry, Work, and Leisure

The discussion of utility in the previous section suggests a further distinction on which some reflection is called for—namely, that between work and play or labor and leisure. Work, after all, is often linked to notions of utility in one way or another, and leisure with disengagement from it. Thus, for example, after admitting the inherent difficulty of doing so, Miroslav Volf ventures the following purely formal definition of the term: "[w]ork is honest, purposeful, and methodologically specified social activity whose primary goal is the creation of products or states of affairs that can satisfy the needs of working individuals or their co-creatures, or (if primarily an end in itself) activity that is necessary in order for acting individuals to satisfy their needs apart from the need for the activity itself."[26] Work, it seems, while it may not always be bound up with gainful employment, is nonetheless hard to disentangle from that which is useful or needful for those engaged in it or those who benefit from their labors. Art, meanwhile, as we have already seen, is typically thought of in our own society as a leisure pursuit, something the enjoyment of which is deliberately divorced from the hurly-burly

[26] Miroslav Volf, *Work in the Spirit* (New York: Oxford University Press, 1991), 10–11.

of the business and busyness and distractions of living; art is, as it were, essentially useless, our favorite waste of time.

That this will not quite do ought to be obvious from even the briefest consideration of the social realities of the matter. Even in the artificially rarefied atmosphere of the modern world of "High Art," artists themselves, dealers, curators, performers, and the girl selling promotional T-shirts and fridge magnets all rely heavily (albeit more or less directly) on acts of artistry to "make a living," and their modes of engagement with the art itself are not at all those of leisure but increasingly those of big business. Meanwhile, the sweat pouring from the brow of the pianist performing a Rachmaninov concerto, the linseed-spattered overalls of the painter in the studio, and the blunted tools of the sculptor all testify to an easily overlooked fact—namely, that artistry itself is more often than not "hard work," whether of a physical or a mental sort or (again more often than not) probably both. The moment we lift our eyes and broaden the horizons of our definition of "art" even slightly, of course, it becomes apparent that much art, far from being wedded inexorably to leisure, has its beginnings and its end in the conditions and requirements of human work as such. To pick just one example, Wolterstorff notes that "[w]ork and not leisure is needed if weaving songs, spinning songs, etc., are to find their intended public uses."[27] Artistry, then, may well consist and result in something greater than the sum of the labor and utility involved in it, but our enjoyment of it cannot be divorced easily from serious work of some sort done by somebody at some point along the way.

How then, we might wonder, are artistry, *ars*, and creativity more widely to be thought of in relation to distinctions such as that between work and leisure, labor and play, utility and gratuity? Again, some provisional thoughts rather than a carefully developed case must suffice here.

We might begin with the suggestion of Dorothy L. Sayers that work, even of the most mundane and everyday sort, may properly be deemed "creative" and thus from one perspective at least of a piece with what, creatively, the artist does.[28] This may seem odd at first blush, given the tendency we have already observed to associate the creative with some sort of significant newness. Surely, the completion of a routine task is by definition of a different order than the advent of the *novum*? Sayers suggests not, in certain respects at least. "Creativeness," she maintains, "is at the heart both of the cosmos and of our own creaturely being, life itself affording constant opportunities for "making something of" the circumstances that

---

[27] Wolterstorff, *Art in Action*, 26.

[28] See in particular the discussions in Sayers, *Mind of the Maker*, 146–84; Dorothy L. Sayers, *Begin Here: A War-Time Essay* (London: Victor Gollancz, 1940), 11–26, et passim.

confront us as a given starting point.[29] Indeed, she avers, "man is never truly himself except when he is actively creating something,"[30] mere passivity or receptivity with respect to the given being a denial of a human nature created in the image and likeness of a creative God.[31] Thus, even a seemingly uninspired and uninspiring task can become "a sacrament and manifestation of man's creative energy," if only it is approached and undertaken with a clear vision of the intrinsic *worth* of the work (not its economic, political, or social usefulness alone but its value as a creaturely and creative good in its own right, an enhancement of the given world in some manner) and out of a desire and a love that longs only to see it done and done to the highest achievable standard—that it may be all that it is capable of being and becoming. If art can be and often is "work" among other things, then so too, Sayers is suggesting, when undertaken in a more than routine manner—bringing to it the sort of passion and care and concern for its final worth that the artist bestows upon his or her work ("he is in love with his creation for its own sake"[32])—even the most routine task can be *ars*, an embodiment of creativeness that fuses utility and gratuity in the pursuit of a creaturely good. "That the eyes of all workers should behold the integrity of the work," she writes, "is the sole means to make that work good in itself and so good for mankind. This is only another way of saying that the work must be measured by the standard of eternity; or that it must be done for God first and foremost," whether explicitly or unwittingly.[33]

Of course, Sayers readily concedes, there is some work that cannot and could not ever be redeemed in this way and that ought not to be undertaken at all, since no good can possibly come of it[34]—just as, no doubt, there are examples of artistry that we might judge undeserving of the term "creative" on essentially the same grounds, no matter how novel or avant-garde. Furthermore, the advent of industrialization and techniques of mass production—while it has no doubt spoiled the manufacture of many things, turning them into so many characterless clones of one another and robbing human makers of individual enterprise—should

[29] Sayers, *Mind of the Maker*, 156. The notion of "creativeness" is borrowed from Nicholas Berdyaev, *The Destiny of Man*, trans. Natalie Duddington (London: Geoffrey Bles, 1937), which uses this awkward English construction to translate the Russian *tvorchestva* (otherwise "creativity" or "creative act") throughout, and to which Sayers refers repeatedly in *The Mind of the Maker*.

[30] Sayers, *Begin Here*, 23.

[31] Cf. Sayers, *Mind of the Maker*, 17.

[32] Sayers, *Mind of the Maker*, 179.

[33] Sayers, *Mind of the Maker*, 183–84.

[34] Sayers, *Mind of the Maker*, 179.

nonetheless be reckoned a gain when it comes to making certain sorts of goods available cheaply and quickly to the multitude. "We must only see to it," Sayers writes, "that the goods are of a kind suitable to be produced by that means" (she mentions cigarettes, light bulbs, pencils and other examples of things "where standardisation is desirable") "and that the people employed in producing them have other opportunities of developing their creative talents."[35] And, most importantly, we must exercise proper discrimination, deciding which things are best done or made by machine, which by hand, and which things are better not done or made at all, being destructive or demeaning of creation rather than its proper extension and unfolding.[36] It is in the latter, Sayers maintains, whether realized in work or in leisure, that human likeness to God consists.

What, then, should we say of leisure itself? How is it related to work, to artistry, and to creativity more broadly defined? We have seen that creativity need not be excluded from the workplace but may be understood, as by Sayers, as the highest mode in which work is undertaken. We have seen, too, that even artistic creativity can involve hard work and is in fact always tangled up productively with work on someone's part at some point. But while modern Western societies play host to a new set of self-styled "creative industries," enjoyment of or participation in the creative arts will, for most readers of this book, be understood largely as a leisure pursuit, undertaken as we deliberately take time out from our daily labor or routine activity to enjoy making or the fruits of others' making. Insofar as such enjoyment itself involves activity rather than inactivity, we typically characterize this as "play" rather than work, contrasting the two partly in terms of their respective relationship to the utilities that sustain our existence and partly with reference to their respective preferability and our freedom to indulge in them ("play" being typically that which we enjoy, look forward to, and choose to do whenever we can, whereas we "have to" go to work again on Monday morning).

Again, though, the distinctions are not always so easily drawn. There are those today, of course, for whom "play" is little more than a formal definition, since they play for a living (sometimes a very substantial one) as professional athletes or musicians or actors or whatever. And there are others (perhaps many more of them) who have the good fortune to love the particular work that they do and who, given opportunity, enjoy nothing more than allowing it to spill over into their "spare time" (i.e., not cramming in hours of paid overtime in order to maximize their income, but continuing their labor at cost to themselves, from enjoyment of the task itself and the desire to see it completed as fully and as well as possible). For such people the distinction between work (as distinct from employment) and leisure is hard to identify or sustain, and one with little practical function.

Theologically, too, blurring or recasting the distinction may prove fruitful in terms both of our doctrine of God and of our understanding of creaturely creativity. The biblical description of God's creative activity in the beginning as "work" (Gen 2:2) no doubt reflects the Priestly writer's concern to demarcate the first six days from the seventh, thereby bolstering a theological rationale for Sabbath keeping. And no doubt we should indeed picture the creation of a world (whether ex nihilo or by imposing divine order on a formless cosmic chaos) as hard work rather than a sinecure, even for God. As Jürgen Moltmann observes, though, we miss something vital if we picture God as a laborer hard pressed by goals he must achieve and deadlines he must meet, slogging away for six days and looking forward to a day of well-earned rest. To picture creation thus (and this is perhaps the way in which it *is* commonly imagined) is to overlook not just the essential gratuity of God's decision to create at all but the note of sheer wonder, pleasure, and enjoyment that pervades the biblical account. Creation, Moltmann reminds us, has its ground in God's *good will* alone, and thus, while no doubt involving hard work, "the creation is God's play, a play of his groundless and inscrutable wisdom. It is the realm in which God displays his glory."[37] Creating, we might say, is work but work of a sort that comes naturally to this God, that he thoroughly enjoys doing, and to the final end of which (the world) he is passionately committed, whatever it costs him to bring it to completion. Recognition of the biblical portrayal of God as artist/craftsman invites us, perhaps, to hear the reiterated divine "Let there be!" uttered now in a new tone of voice—not so much the strident and authoritative command of a Near Eastern potentate as the excited and enthusiastic suggestion to self of a poet or painter, as a world rich in meaning and possibility unfolds before him in his imagination and through the work of his hands. All that is missing from the text is the occasional "Wow!" after each suggestion is implemented, but it is not hard to supply them imaginatively in a way that makes good sense and persuasive reading. The text itself, of course, is "replete with background"[38] and does not determine our hearing one way or another, while providing reasons for reckoning seriously with both. For this precise reason, though,

[37] Jürgen Moltmann, *Theology and Joy* (London: SCM Press, 1973), 41. Moltmann appropriates Hugo Rahner's definition of "play" as an activity that is meaningful but not necessary. See Hugo Rahner, *Der spielende Mensch* (Einsiedeln, Switz.: Johannes Verlag, 1952), 15.

[38] See Erich Auerbach, *Mimesis: The Representation of Reality in Western Literature*, trans. Willard R. Trask (Princeton, N.J.: Princeton University Press, 1953), 3–23.

it encourages playful and imaginative readings which supply the narrative shortfall and explore different interpretative possibilities. In the final analysis, indeed, there may be no need to choose between the alternatives, each of them capturing imaginatively some important facet of what is involved in the terse biblical and theological claim that "God created."

Reckoning with creation as a form of divine "play" as well as work, though, involves a shift in our thinking about the mood of the seventh day as well as the preceding six, and thus about the theological significance of the Sabbath and of leisure more widely. Rather than a deserved and longed-for respite intended to recharge physical and mental batteries so that we might be fit to return, refreshed, to the drudgery of work in order to earn our keep, Sabbath becomes aligned instead with what God's own day of "rest" so clearly is in the Priestly narrative—that is, an occasion to enjoy the fruits of our labors, to celebrate the goodness of what we have made and are making, and the goodness of its existence alongside us. Viewed thus, Moltmann argues, "leisure" is the creature's basic state, an enjoyment of the goodness of existence itself rooted in God's sheer good-pleasure in our existence alongside him. Discovering that we need not justify our existence but can rest freely in the goodness of God and the promise of the world God has given to us, "work" becomes now, like Adam's laboring in the garden, an extension of festival and celebration, "for the sake of nothing, but to please God only."[39] And leisure, therefore, is the point from which "work" properly begins (as joyful response to see what more we can make of what has first been given to us), rather than its welcome cessation and antithesis.[40]

In theological terms, work and leisure are made sense of here within an economy of grace rather than law, and the boundaries between them are ones naturally blurred by the common disposition of grateful response and thanksgiving, an activity (or relative inactivity) free, gratuitous, spontaneous in its desire to offer back to God nothing but the very best it is capable of being, doing, and becoming. The adage that "joy is peace dancing" and "peace is joy at rest" captures the relationship well. Set free by grace from the compulsive idea (whether imposed externally or welling up unsolicited from within) that we are whatever we produce and are accepted only on the basis of it, the mood and mode even of labor itself, Moltmann suggests, can be transformed into one of playful enjoyment, bathed in the light of celebration and festival and allowing its logic to spill over into the workplace.[41] And it is the logic of worship, too, of a

---

[39] Moltmann, *Theology and Joy*, 67; citing Luther.
[40] Moltmann, *Theology and Joy*, 44.
[41] Moltmann, *Theology and Joy*, 71–74.

eucharistia that joyfully offers back a sacrifice of thanks and praise to the One from whom all things come. So, Josef Pieper argues, the roots of festival (and the genuine enjoyment of leisure) are finally religious and theological, no matter how remote from consciousness the link may have become.[42] Where the link is severed and leisure lacks any discernible trace either of Sabbath peace or the joyful response this engenders in the human soul, leisure dies, to be replaced by the mere interruption of work by periods of inactivity.

Leisure, with its roots sunk deep in Sabbath and liturgical response, is for Pieper the region within which alone "culture" may thrive. He defines culture rather more precisely than we have chosen to do hitherto, as "what goes beyond mere means-to-an-end considerations."[43] This certainly encompasses the arts and artistry in the more precise senses typically ascribed to those terms today; but it includes lots of other things too and might be pressed to embrace any human activity suffused with the spirit of affirmation, gift, and thanksgiving, bringing Pieper's account close to Moltmann's insistence that labor may be undertaken as play and Sayers' desire to bring most if not all human work within the penumbra of a "creative" response to the world. Again, this begs questions of quality—the quality, that is to say, not just of the action concerned and the experience of engaging in it but of its impact upon the world too. What we make of what we have been given—whether in acts of artistry or in our work and leisure more broadly—should be something "worth" making, something that, in adding to the world, enhances rather than spoils it, drawing from its created potential significant new opportunities and occasions for our divinely intended (and divinely shared) delight in it.[44] The peace and joy that characterize Sabbath existence must therefore furnish not just the starting point and accompanying mood for our creative engagements with the world but their end point too, as we look back on what we have done and find ourselves able to enjoy it as something identifiably "good," albeit not perfect.

Goods—Making and Mending the World

In the Old Testament's narration of the world's provenance in the imagination and at the hands of God's himself, the primal divine judgment on the emergent cosmos, reiterated throughout the process of its making and again at its completion, is that it is "very good" (Gen 1:10, 12, 18, 21, 25, 31). This judgment, though, compels consideration of the meaning of the term

---

[42] Josef Pieper, *Leisure: The Basis of Culture*, trans. Gerald Malsbary (South Bend, Ind.: St Augustine's, 1998).

[43] Pieper, *Leisure*, 57.

[44] Cf. Wolterstorff, *Art in Action*, 79–83.

"good" itself in this context. As an empirical judgment, moral goodness can hardly be in view, since the reader is not as yet confronted by the domain where human action is under scrutiny, and in any case the judgment falls equally upon the wider animate and the inanimate creation. So, perhaps we should read it more as an aesthetic judgment, articulating a sense of deep satisfaction obtained through the process and with the outcome of divine making. If, with Barth,[45] we choose instead to interpret the divine utterance as essentially proleptic and teleological, moral goodness at once enters the frame of reference, but it hardly exhausts it. The judgment pertains to the whole creation—that is, to creation as "a whole" and to what it is "good" for each individual part of it to be and to become before God. Where humans are concerned, what we understand by moral goodness is bound to be at the core of this (though even here it does not exhaust it); other creatures will no doubt be judged good on their own terms and in quite distinct ways. Aesthetic goods are likely to be highly relevant too, but unless we use this category in an unhelpfully imprecise manner (one that generates more problems than it solves), it seems that there will be "goods" that are neither obviously moral nor obviously aesthetic to be reckoned with—things, that is to say, that it is good for parts of God's creation to be and to become (and thus in their distinctive manner to "praise God" as the Psalter so often summons them to do) but that fall neither under the aegis of ethics nor aesthetics as generally understood. The language of the Bible, I shall suggest duly, provides us with a category which serves to catch these other creaturely goods, embracing but ranging beyond the limits of the moral and aesthetic alone, and that is "holiness." Although a category defined chiefly by its application to Israel's God, holiness comes to be used analogically to refer to whatever it is good for particular creatures to be within the penumbra of God's presence and so to reflect and to correspond—albeit in their proper creaturely mode and manner—to God's own character.

There is a sense, of course, in which this hardly moves us forward; because what we must now say is that the world is "good" whenever it manifests that being or becoming which God wills for it and for which he has created it and invested it with certain capacities. And, of human acts of making and creativity, we must say (as we already have) that they are to be judged "good" or worthwhile when they permit the world to become more fully itself in this sense—that is, in the sense that God deems and has declared to be good. All this boils down to saying that something is "good" when God judges it to be so and when it accords with God's own holy character, which is hardly the most useful specification, for artists or anyone else, absent some further unpacking and concrete analysis. The tautology itself is inevitable if, as Christian theology holds, the standards

[45] See above, 33–35.

by which any creaturely reality must be measured are themselves a function of creation, rooted in God's eternal character rather than wholly
external to it (either coeternal with God himself or generated by activities
of human consciousness and culture). But it is also useful, for it reminds us
that the question of what it is good for us (or our fellow creatures and our
material environment) to be and to become is one the answer to which is
rooted ultimately and analogically in a reality which transcends our grasp
and resists convenient classification. There is mystery here, and a certain
cautious agnosticism or apophaticism is perhaps a more fitting disposition to answering such questions than has often been acknowledged. We
cannot *know* what it is good for something to be or become, not, at least,
in any full and absolute sense. God alone knows that, and we ought not
to pretend to. There will always be more at stake than we are capable of
apprehending, and our judgments will thus always be partial and provisional. The contested nature of debates in intellectual disciplines such as
ethics and aesthetics bears witness to this and ought not to surprise us.
And yet, of course, our judgments are not for that reason worthless. On
the contrary, the need to make such judgments and to live in accordance
with them, to "make something of" the world in the light of them, is part
of what being created and called to be responsible human creatures is
about. But, as we have already had reason to observe, with responsibility
comes the risk of doing better or worse, and what we make of the world is
undoubtedly sometimes a mess. A more measured approach to our identification and pursuit of creaturely goods—whether of moral, aesthetic, or
other sorts—would seem to be both prudent and likely, perhaps, to result
in more responsible and creative outcomes.

Discussion of creaturely goods and their relationship to human projects of one sort or another has, in the Western intellectual tradition, often
been centered on three of the so-called transcendentals (properties held to
be coextensive with being itself)—namely, goodness, truth, and beauty.
Duly capitalized (Goodness, Truth, and Beauty), these have often been
identified by Christian theologians (following the lead of classical philosophy) as properties of God himself, properties possessed by creatures in a
finite mode precisely by virtue of their analogous resemblance to their Creator. For our particular purposes, the significant theological issues at stake
here (the grounds for positing or denying a so-called *analogia entis*) need
not detain us.[46] We can be content with attending to the supposed creaturely properties as such and to the relationships pertaining among them.

---

[46] For my own discussion of the subject, see Trevor A. Hart, *Regarding Karl Barth:
Essays toward a Reading of His Theology* (Carlisle, U.K.: Paternoster, 1999), 140–51.
Trevor Hart, *Between the Image and the Word: Theological Engagements with Imagination,
Language and Literature* (Farnham, U.K.: Ashgate, 2013), 13–42.

While classical tradition typically held the three categories to be onto-logically one, modern discussion has variously sought to disentangle them, to separate them from one another or, sometimes, to deny their objective reality altogether. So, for example, while Plato and Plotinus held that, wherever beauty was, there too truth and goodness must be acknowledged to be, Kant preferred to treat them serially in his three great critiques,[47] opening the way, for instance, for Oscar Wilde's denial that art has any-thing directly to do with truth and his quip that "[a]n ethical sensibility in an artist is an unpardonable mannerism of style."[48] The artist "is the creator of beautiful things." That is all. The fact that these views are aired, playfully, in the preface to a work of fiction that itself explores some of the deep, underlying ambiguities in the relationship between ostensive beauty and goodness, and some of the deeper truths of the human condi-tion besides, simply adds to the overall sense of irony. Kant's consistent emphasis upon the active role of the human subject in knowing might also be held responsible, at least in part, for the sort of cynicism (already apparent in Nietzsche but far more common today) which holds that, far from goodness, truth, and beauty being the global objects of human desire, aspiration, and delight, engagement with which facilitates our transcendence of particular frameworks of knowing and leads us upward or outward to enjoyment of an ultimate reality greater than ourselves, they are themselves instead the chimerical products of such frameworks. Thus, they promise to lead us nowhere except directly back into the plu-ral, fragmented, and alienated imagining from which they sprang in the first place. The search for beauty, truth, and goodness is, on this account, finally a dark and hopeless one, even if there may be time for some frivo-lous jouissance along the way; for it is a U-shaped quest undertaken by a humanity inexorably *incurvatus in se*.[49]

Whatever we make in metaphysical and epistemic terms of the status of "transcendentals" (and, apart from their despairing collapse to the level of the projects of sheer human imagining, various options remain avail-able to the Christian theologian on this front), the classification of various creaturely "goods" in terms of the qualities of goodness, truth, and beauty

---

[47] *Critique of Pure Reason* (1781), *Critique of Practical Reason* (1788), and *Critique of Judgment* (1790). There is no reason to suppose that Kant himself would ever have encouraged the separation of the three dimensions under which an object or situation might be considered or the sort of "aestheticism" that resulted from doing so.

[48] Oscar Wilde, *The Picture of Dorian Gray*, Penguin Classics ed. (London: Penguin, 1985), 3.

[49] "Curved in upon itself," as Martin Luther's graphic metaphor for the sinful condi-tion has it. See, helpfully, Matt Jenson, *The Gravity of Sin: Augustine, Luther and Barth on Homo Incurvatus in Se* (London: T&T Clark, 2007).

promises to remain a helpful one in terms of which to proceed, initially at least.

Perhaps the first thing to do is to modify the scheme to encompass what Wolterstorff defines as "aesthetic merit" or "aesthetic excellence," a category that is related to but certainly not synonymous with beauty.[50] Beauty is in any case a highly contested and problematic notion, itself deserving of careful theological attention; but even if we rest content for now with the supposition that most of us "know it when we see it," beauty, Wolterstorff observes, is not a necessary feature of the aesthetically good or excellent.[51] Bartók's *Fifth Quartet*, he suggests, is aesthetically excellent, but one would be stretching language beyond its useful range to call it beautiful. Thus, while "the presence of beauty in a thing is sometimes, perhaps always, an aesthetic merit in that thing, its absence is certainly not always an aesthetic defect."[52] That which is aesthetically excellent, Wolterstorff argues, is that which yields satisfaction when submitted to aesthetic contemplation, and "the aesthetic qualities of things are confined to the qualities of the looks and sounds of things under canonical presentations."[53] This means, of course, that aesthetic goods are of a quite distinct sort from intellectual and moral/spiritual goods, or, in the less precise terms of our adopted threefold scheme, beauty is indeed wholly distinct from truth and goodness, and judgments made about them must be capable of drawing the relevant distinctions. So, Wolterstorff observes, the fact that a work of art is (or is not) "true to actuality" is quite irrelevant to questions about its distinctly *aesthetic* merits or defects.

We have already seen that certain approaches to visual and plastic art have traditionally placed great weight on the artist's ability to summon into our perceptual field a convincing likeness of some actual object, person, or place, and corresponding bids to replicate some slice of "reality" may be identified too in other arts such as literature, theater, and film. Of course, the fact that such "likenesses" when they are accomplished are duly recognized to be *artifice*, and thus do not compete with their originals where our responses to them are concerned, is essential in various ways to our appreciation of them as art. The horrendous sufferings depicted on stage in a tragedy, for instance, ought not to provoke the same sorts of response in us that comparable sufferings encountered in "real life" might, and someone incapable of knowing the difference we should rightly suppose emotionally

---

[50] See Wolterstorff, *Art in Action*, 158.

[51] Wolterstorff, *Art in Action*, 161–63.

[52] Wolterstorff, *Art in Action*, 163.

[53] Wolterstorff, *Art in Action*, 159; on the notion of "canonical presentation," cf. 41–43.

pathological and morally confused. To seek to intervene in a murder committed onstage is to have lost the plot in more senses than one, while to stand by and enjoy watching an actual murder take place in the street outside the theater is to have crossed a line in an even more disturbing direction. That this line *is* sometimes crossed, and with terrible consequences, is apparent from the spate of shooting sprees over recent decades, seemingly inspired by and modeled upon the templates of violent films and video games which relish in particular the capacity of their medium to produce highly graphic and "realistic" visual effects.

Fortunately, most of us are perfectly capable of drawing the line between actuality and artifice, and our enjoyment of lifelikeness in the arts when we encounter it relies heavily on this fact, trading on the tension of the metaphorical relation, "it is, and it is not." And, of course, lifelikeness itself comes in all sorts of different shapes and sizes. A "photographic" portrayal of a person in oil paint, for instance, may succeed in capturing less rather than more of their "reality" than one that eschews reliance on surface appearances alone. And even naturalistic realism in the arts is generally wedded to fiction in order to make it interesting or meaningful in a way that the sheer replication of experienced reality would and could not be. (What on earth, we might properly ask ourselves, would that look—or sound or feel or smell or taste—like in any case?) Some process of selection, of editing, of the imposition of narrative or other form is required before it is presented to us for consideration. So, the "worlds" of works of art are often ones that we quite happily accept as shot through with fictional propositions at one level or another.[54] To refer to these as "fictional" rather than "false," of course, is precisely already to have recognized their status as artifice and so to have approached them with a rather different set of expectations than those we bring to bear on realities of other sorts. The demand for lifelikeness, in other words, is never pure or absolute, even where it is granted a significant place. But, as we have seen, not all art grants it a particularly significant place in any case. Some art passes quickly beyond the threshold of mere "fiction" into wholesale fantasy, the intricate imagining of worlds wholly unlike our own in all sorts of basic respects. And much of the art of modernity and postmodernity, we have had occasion to notice, has sought deliberately to part company with the forms and patterns inherited from empirical experience altogether, pursuing abstraction and the avant-garde instead. In truth, even the farthest-flung flights of fantasy and abstraction can have a great deal to teach us, in one way or another, about the primary reality we inhabit and about our own human condition. Whether they do so or not will certainly be

[54] See above, pp. 262–64.

relevant to certain sorts of judgments we may make about them, but it is not relevant to a consideration of their distinctly *aesthetic* merits. Being true or "true to" the primary world is not itself an aesthetic good, and "[a]ctuality does not constitute an aesthetic demand on the artist" in his or her creative endeavors.[55] Truth and beauty, in other words, are not the same thing. We must learn to disentangle them, therefore, in order to ensure that we ask the appropriate sorts of questions.

In a directly parallel vein, Wolterstorff argues, we must take care to disentangle goodness from beauty and to permit it too its own proper space and sphere of concern. So, "[t]he fact that a work of art has desirable effects of one sort or another on those who come into contact with it is not an aesthetic merit in the work, nor is the fact that it has undesirable effects an aesthetic defect. Neither can be a reason for an aesthetic evaluation of the work."[56] One important consideration here, perhaps, is the relativity of such perceived effects to particular individuals. What has an adverse effect on the moral and spiritual habits and commitments of one person, in other words, may leave another wholly unscathed, their inner worlds, resistances, and vulnerabilities being calibrated rather differently. But moral and spiritual judgments may and must finally be drawn about works of art, and it is possible to imagine a work that had an unhealthy impact on any and every beholder, even after a fleeting encounter. Even in such an extreme case, though, questions about its aesthetic merits and demerits would be able to be (and ought to be) asked and answered without reference to such considerations. Again, the reason is that the aesthetic dimension of a thing (and works of art, Wolterstorff notes, participate in many different dimensions of reality at once)[57] is a matter of its material presentation—how it looks and/or sounds—and the capacity of this to stimulate aesthetic satisfaction in one who grants it contemplative attention. What is it, then, about an object (whether a work of human making or one arising in the world of nature) that generates the peculiar sort of satisfaction Wolterstorff has in mind?[58] Can we identify

---

[55] Wolterstorff, *Art in Action*, 159.

[56] Wolterstorff, *Art in Action*, 160.

[57] "Works of art are complex multi-dimensioned objects. They participate in the aesthetic dimension by their configurations of aesthetic aspects, in the economic dimension when being bought and sold, in the psychological dimension when evoking feelings in beholders, in the moral dimension when altering for better or worse the moral character of those who hold commerce with them, in the religious dimension when inducing change in the religious commitments of those who make use of them." Wolterstorff, *Art in Action*, 172.

[58] The satisfaction itself transcends sensory experience but is always grounded in it. Material qualities stimulate an essentially intellectual response. For further discussion, see Wolterstorff, *Art in Action*, 39–46.

some general types of aesthetic merit, some of which are, on the whole, likely to be found in some measure in an object granting someone aesthetic satisfaction?[59] Wolterstorff proposes three aspects for consideration: (1) overall unity of character (whether manifest in the mode of coherence or the mode of completeness), (2) internal richness and complexity, and (3) a high "fittingness intensity" quotient.[60] Since an object may manifest all these without either making any identifiable truth claims or leaving us morally and spiritually the better for our encounter with it, Wolterstorff concludes, cognitive, moral/spiritual, and aesthetic goods must be recognized as distinct and judged accordingly and each on its own terms.

If, though, we pause to consider the place of these various sorts of "goods" in our experience of things, whereas the intrinsic value of cognitive and moral/spiritual goods (i.e., the nature of their "goodness" for us) is more readily appreciated and justified on all sorts of grounds (pragmatic, social, personal, and others), the value of aesthetic contemplation and the satisfaction granted by it is less so, once its association with other goods is stripped away. Why is aesthetic delight a "good" at all, rather than a mere indulgence? And why should we, in our acts of making, pay it heed rather than setting it aside in the interests of the efficient pursuit of more instrumental considerations? Interestingly, at this point Wolterstorff is compelled to return to explicitly religious and theological language, referring us to the conceptuality of eschatological joy and peace (shalom) which concerned us in our earlier discussion of Sabbath rest. It is worth citing him in full.

> Aesthetic delight is a component within and a species of that joy which belongs to the shalom God has ordained as the goal of human existence and which here already, in this broken and fallen world of ours, is to be sought and experienced. That is why you and I are to pursue aesthetic delight, for ourselves and others, along with a multitude of other goals: justice, peace, community. Since it belongs to the shalom that God intends for each of us, it becomes a matter of responsible action to help make available, to ourselves and others, the experience of aesthetic delight. It becomes a norm for action—not, of course, the only norm, but certainly one among them.[61]

The observation that aesthetic goods are but one species and component together with others of that overall good that God desires and intends for his creation points to the need now for some redress for the intellectually

---

[59] On the issue of aesthetic relativism (i.e., the fact that aesthetic tastes differ), see Wolterstorff, *Art in Action*, 163–64.

[60] On "fittingness intensity," see above, p. 281.

[61] Wolterstorff, *Art in Action*, 169.

fruitful disentangling we have performed. What is conveniently dissected for the purposes of analysis is itself a work of human artifice, insofar as it ignores the fact that, in our immediate experience of things, the various qualities, aspects, or parts never arise in isolation but are fused together perichoretically in varying combinations and ratios. It follows that a judgment made about the distinctly aesthetic merits of a painting, a novel, a concerto, or whatever ought not to be confused with larger judgments about its *artistic* merits, the latter being compelled to reckon with all sorts of other aspects of the work in question. Chief among these, Wolterstorff suggests, is the particular purposes or uses for which the object was produced and distributed. Thus, "[a] good hymn is one that serves well the purpose of hymns. A good concerto is one that serves well the purpose of concertos."[62] And so on. In this regard, he insists, works of art are little different from spades, sleeping pills, and automobiles. To this instrumentalist account, though, Wolterstorff adds a qualificatory clause (the "side effect clause") which, from a theological perspective, seems vitally important. The quality of a work of art, he argues, inheres not just in how well it serves the purpose for which it was produced or distributed but also in "how good and satisfying it proves in general to use for the purpose intended."[63] This broadening of perspective permits us to recognize that works of art may accomplish more than one thing at once and that even when used in the manner intended by their maker or distributor may have more than one sort of effect at once. Significantly, it allows us to judge that a work which, be it ever so good at doing what it was made to do, also has an undesirable or deleterious effect on its material, moral, or spiritual environment cannot be judged "generally good and satisfying to use" and thus lacks artistic excellence. Such discrimination will need to be exercised with due caution and care, but if we are to situate an account of artistic creativity (or, indeed, creativity in any sphere of activity) against the backdrop of an account of God's own creative and redemptive purposes for the world, we shall need to be able to exercise it sooner or later. In a fallen and broken world, our encounter with creaturely goods will never be pure, and our choices and judgments in pursuit of them may often be between the lesser of several alloyed evils.

Within the complex mix of things, aesthetic goods are often judged ones likely to be pursued regardless of the potential cost to others, as in Wilde's quip cited above. The dangers are no doubt real, and beauty, or the pursuit of beauty, has consequently acquired a bad name for itself in much contemporary academic discourse, chiefly on ethical and political

[62] Wolterstorff, *Art in Action*, 157.
[63] Wolterstorff, *Art in Action*, 158.

grounds.[64] Before moving on, though, we should pause briefly at least to notice the case argued persuasively by Elaine Scarry that, while aesthetic and moral goods are quite distinct, they are, within the fabric of being, related in such a way that the one calls out naturally for the other.[65] The polysemy of "fairness," Scarry maintains, transcends mere analogy, the presence of aesthetic goods in the world itself serving to exert pressure on us to pursue justice and the interests of that which is other than ourselves. In experiences of beauty, she contends, we undergo a radical decentering, an "unselfing" in which the existence, concerns, and well-being of the other temporarily displace our natural tendency toward selfishness.[66] C. S. Lewis gestures toward the same interruptive capacity of beauty when he allies it naturally with the experiences of raptness in worship, and love.[67] And perhaps this is a more adequate terminology (in theological terms at least) to use: what beauty calls out for and properly engenders in its beholders is goodness, yes—but goodness in the active form of love. Where creativity is concerned, Scarry argues, we should think of it as acting to perpetuate or protect a fragment of beauty already in the world or to supplement it by bringing into being a new object participant in the same goodness. In this sense, she observes, "though human beings have created much of the beauty of the world, they are only collaborators in a much more vast project."[68] Shards of beauty, after all, are "generously present, widely present, to almost all people at all times,"[69] and our creative responses are thus ones of reception and reciprocation, making more of what we have first freely received. In fact, Scarry concludes, the willingness of the beholder "to place himself or herself in the service of bringing new beauty into the world, creating a site of beauty separate from the self," is itself a form of unselfinterestedness.[70] True creativity, in other words, is always a pursuit of the good which renders the self adjacent; it is an act of love.

[64] For a helpful theological reading of this, see E. John Walford, "The Case for Broken Beauty," in *The Beauty of God: Theology and the Arts*, ed. Daniel J. Treier, Mark Husbands, and Roger Lundin (Downers Grove, Ill.: InterVarsity, 2007), 88–109.

[65] Elaine Scarry, *On Beauty and Being Just* (Princeton, N.J.: Princeton University Press, 1999), 57–124.

[66] Scarry, *On Beauty*, 111–14.

[67] C. S. Lewis, *An Experiment in Criticism* (Cambridge: Cambridge University Press, 1961), 141.

[68] Scarry, *On Beauty*, 108.

[69] Scarry, *On Beauty*, 108–9.

[70] Scarry, *On Beauty*, 117.

14

Creativity, Christ, and Correlation

In the body of this work, I have argued that at the heart of the human world and our participation in it there may be traced a constant dialectic of give and take and that our humanity is thus characterized by its capacity and willingness on many different levels to make more of the world than whatever is initially given to it. In this sense, I have suggested, the creative artist—as one who does this self-consciously and with a high level of skill and care—serves not just as a concrete instance but rather as a fruitful paradigm of our human situation more widely. How, then, should we think of this in theological terms? In early chapters I sought to demonstrate the way in which Scripture both links artistry directly to God's own distinctive role as Creator and weaves the figure and the positive contribution of the human artist/craftsman into the warp and weft of the "dwelling place" which stands as anticipation and symbol of the fulfillment of the project of creation itself. Where God and humanity finally dwell at-one, in other words, there will be culture as well as nature to be reckoned with and thus a fully human contribution offered from below as well as a decisive and determinative divine initiative from above. In this final chapter, I want to begin to sketch some of the wider contours of such a claim. In doing so I am aware that this could easily be the point of departure for an entire systematic theology (or at least a series of systematic reflections on different doctrines), and what I offer here cannot aspire to that. The reader will have to await the appearance of companion volumes planned eventually to follow in the wake of this one in order to find some of those reflections worked out more fully. A wide-ranging and necessarily rapid overview of some key horizons and landmarks, therefore, is what I will seek to achieve in what follows. Hopefully this will suffice at least to situate some of the interdisciplinary explorations conducted in earlier chapters within a meaningful theological frame of consideration and indicate clearly why I believe the language of "creativity" and creation is not only appropriate but actually rather important to lay claim to and deploy in theological talk about the arts and other relevant spheres of human action.

Creation and the Character of God

In older manuals of Christian doctrine, the doctrine of creation often appears at the outset or shortly thereafter, reflecting the place of the creation saga in the narrative of Scripture. What this risks overlooking, though, is that the biblical texts themselves already presume (on the part of writer and readers) a thorough familiarity with the one introduced as the key actor in the story. The doctrine of creation, we might say, is and must not be treated as an independent "text" patient of interpretation on its own terms. Properly speaking it is a function of the doctrine of God and bound up from first to last with the character of the God revealed in the canon of Scripture as a whole. This was already true for the authors of the Hebrew account of creation, who wrote, as von Rad reminds us, fully cognizant that the one who "made the heavens and the earth" was none other than Yahweh, the God of election and covenant, and the Holy One of Israel.[1] For Christian readers, the relevant biblical and theological context for interpretation is larger still, and creation theology finds its center of gravity not in protology but in Christology and in the figure of the one who embodies to the full God's character in the world. So the Apostle Paul writes that Jesus "is the image of the invisible God . . . for in him all things in heaven and on earth were created, things visible and invisible . . . all things have been created through him and for him" (Col 1:15-16). And John the evangelist, identifying Jesus with God's own Word who "became flesh" and so pitched his tent in our midst, provides a clear intertextual echo of Genesis 1:1, reminding his readers that this Jesus, who came into the world to make his Father known, is himself the same Word and Son who was "in the beginning," and the world "came into being through him, and without him not one thing came into being" (John 1:1-3, 14, 18). Strictly speaking, therefore, we must go further still and insist that the matrix within which a Christian account of creation must take shape will be a triune one, having something to say of Father, Son, and Holy Spirit, and not of the *Logos incarnatus* alone.

---

[1] See, e.g., Gerhard von Rad, *Genesis: A Commentary*, trans. John H. Marks, 2nd ed. (London: SCM Press, 1963), 43–44.

Nonetheless, it is with Jesus—the pattern of his ministry, death, and resurrection as depicted in the Gospels and the distinctive response of faith that he elicits—that the theological problem to which the doctrine of the Trinity is a considered response arises. And it is the character of God as Jesus reveals it (both in his own disposition toward others and in glimpses of the shape of his relationship to his heavenly Father) that is bound finally to be determinative in a Christian understanding of creation. In his discussion of the matter, Karl Barth concentrates our attention on the biblical motif of covenant as one of the key plotlines straddling the narrative gap between the primordial event of creation and the appearance of God in the flesh, bringing the ancient creative purposes of God to a head if not yet to completion. Thus, Barth insists, as well as creation being the "external basis" of the covenant (providing the stage on which the drama of God's covenantal history is to be played out), the covenant (secure already in the eternal decree of God to be God for us, erupting in history's midst with Abraham and again at Sinai, and fulfilled finally and from both sides in the atoning humanity of Jesus who is both "God for us" and the "true Israel") is the "internal basis" of creation—namely, that in the light of which alone its meaning and purpose may be discerned and understood.[2]

In the history of Israel and its social and religious institutions, although the obligations of the covenant are repeatedly broken by those God has chosen to bear it, God remains constant and faithful to the promises he has made to himself and to Israel. Furthermore, God reiterates those promises through Israel's own eschatological imagining of a time when the reality of her covenanted way of response too will be unfailing—not by her own autonomous efforts or accomplishments but by Yahweh himself, yet not by unilateral fiat from above either but in a surprising initiative erupting in, with, and through the integrity of her own creaturely nature. So drastic and determinative will this adjustment and new beginning to Israel's tenure as the "community of reciprocation" be that it can be reckoned in effect a wholly new covenant, if not supplanting then nonetheless radically regenerating the one made with the patriarchs, and renewed by Moses. And its hallmark will be the spontaneity, integrity, and completeness with which the life of the community is now correlated with God's own life. For

> this is the covenant that I will make with the house of Israel after those days, says the Lord: I will put my law within them, and I will write it on their hearts; and I will be their God and they shall be my people. No longer shall they teach one another, or say to each other, "know the Lord," for they shall all know me,

---

[2] Karl Barth, *Church Dogmatics III/1* (Edinburgh: T&T Clark, 1958), 94–329.

from the least of them to the greatest, says the Lord; for I will forgive their
iniquity, and remember their sin no more. (Jer 31:33-34)

In and through this history of covenant breaking and promise making, as
T. F. Torrance suggests, there is a sense in which the Word is already on
the way to becoming flesh and the hearts and minds and wills of humanity
gradually furnished with appropriate categories of creaturely response and
reciprocation.[3] And at the heart of all this, as institution, as ancient promise,
as (in Christ) interruptive fulfillment, and as still longed-for eschatological expectation, there lies the symbol of the tabernacle—the "place" where
God will at last dwell in the midst of the world he has made, at-one with
his creatures and (in the case of his human creatures through the mediation of the covenant relationship) finding his own holiness reflected back to
him. The words of Jesus from the cross ("It is finished") provide a suggestive
intertextual echo of the immediate prelude both to God's blessing of the
seventh day and his enjoyment of what he has made (Gen 2:1) and to his
"blessing" of the newly completed tabernacle by the effulgence of his glory
(Exod 40:33b), circumstances which, we have already seen, appear to be cast
intentionally in a figurative relationship. But Jesus' words also point beyond
themselves, looking to a time when God will at last be all in all.

While in all this a bilateral pattern of existence and action is consistently presumed (from the side of God and the side of the creature respectively, as God intersects, integrates, and appropriates the material and
spiritual realities of creation),[4] it is nonetheless grounded ultimately in the
unilateral dynamic of divine promising, experienced by the creature in the
form of grace. From the call of Abram out of Haran to the anointing of
Jesus with the Spirit in Jordan, the pattern of election, promise, and expectation begins and continues ever and again with the same unmerited and
unsolicited divine favor and faithfulness. And it is in this—the consistent
testimony to God's grace and goodness and the conviction that this is neither guile nor caprice but rather the authentic manifestation in the works
of the triune God *ad extra* of who this God truly is in himself through
all eternity—that Christian theology seeks the answer to the most fundamental question of all: Why did God create? As Walter Brueggemann
notes, in the Old Testament, "[c]reation, the network of living organisms
that provides a viable context and 'home' for the human community, is an
outcome of Yahweh's generous, sovereign freedom. No reason is given for

[3] See, e.g., Thomas F. Torrance, *The Mediation of Christ*, 2nd ed. (Edinburgh: T&T
Clark, 1992), 22–23.
[4] Cf. Torrance, *Mediation of Christ*, 15.

Yahweh's unutterable act of forming an earth that is viable for life."[5] Set in the wider context of the Christian canon, though, it is natural to name the reason as love and to understand creation as falling within the scope of God's gracious determination of himself in our favor, to be "God with us," and not God without us.

It is for this reason, to be sure, that Christian theology too typically insists that as an act born of God's nature as love (*creatio ex amore Dei*) creation must also be contingent upon God's decision—that is, an act of God's sovereign freedom (*creatio e libertate Dei*). Otherwise, if creation is the result of an impersonal process or something that "happens to" God, as we might say, it loses its quality as gift—for a gift which must necessarily be given is in reality no gift at all. Conversely, if we stress the freedom of God too emphatically and at the same time misconstrue freedom in a voluntarist fashion as freedom from every constraint, then we sail quickly and dangerously back in the direction of a capricious God who decides whether or not to create on the throw of the dice. It is for this reason that Jürgen Moltmann insists that God's resolve (his decision to create), while genuinely free and sovereign, is nonetheless an "essential resolve"—that is, a decision rooted in God's own character and the sort of thing, knowing what we do of this God from other situations, we should suppose to come "naturally" to him rather than being either a random act or one "out of character."[6] Both Barth and Pannenberg confirm this judgment in their own way, each insisting that, while creation is the first act of God's works *ad extra*, it is nonetheless earthed in and anticipated by something true eternally within the triune existence of God himself.[7] Each of the three theologians expresses the matter differently, but for each God's relationship to us as Creator is effectively subsumed within the Father's love for the Son, and the latter is the necessary presupposition for the former.

---

[5] Walter Brueggemann, *Theology of the Old Testament: Testimony, Dispute, Advocacy* (Minneapolis: Fortress, 1997), 528.

[6] Jürgen Moltmann, *God in Creation: An Ecological Doctrine of Creation*, trans. Margaret Kohl (London: SCM Press, 1985), 79–86.

[7] So, for Pannenberg, "[t]he existence of Jesus, like that of all creatures, has its basis in God, the Creator of the world. With his difference and self-distinction from God, however, it is grounded in the self-distinction of the eternal Son from the Father. Hence the eternal Son is the ontic basis of the human existence of Jesus in his relation to God as Father. But if, from all eternity, and thus also in the creation of the world, the Father is not without the Son, the eternal Son is not merely the ontic basis of the existence of Jesus in his self-distinction from the Father as the one God; he is also the basis of the distinction and independent existence of all creaturely reality." Wolfhart Pannenberg, *Systematic Theology* (Edinburgh: T&T Clark, 1994), 2:23. Cf. Barth, *Church Dogmatics III/1*, 97, et passim.

The Father loves us, in other words, with the very same love with which he loves the Son, not just within the context of redemption but already within the context of creation.

The nature of creation itself as gift or grace is further heightened by the doctrine of *creatio ex nihilo*, whether one takes this (as I have suggested one reasonably may)[8] as entailed by the witness of the biblical text or as the "biblical" fruit of later theological interpretation and interrogation of them. For, as Moltmann helpfully makes clear, a God who calls into being something other than himself—when, hitherto, himself is all that has existed—is obliged to "make room" for that existence alongside himself and, in the case of God, to take responsibility for its existence and well-being.[9] Thus, quite apart from the fact that, for an infinite and unlimited God, this can only mean voluntary self-limitation, the case of a God whose holy nature cannot coexist permanently with sin and evil and their consequences presents costs of a quite different order. The eternal decision to create, to be God with us and for us, is thus, Moltmann observes, an inherently costly, self-limiting, and self-emptying enterprise, of which the flesh taking, humiliation, suffering, and death of the incarnation are merely the zenith as distinct from the beginning and the sum.

A number of theological implications follow on quickly from all this. First, existence itself (the fruit of creation) is indeed a gift to be received gladly and gratefully from God's hand, and neither an accident nor something to which we have a right. Second, the understanding of creation itself as a product of God's grace entails an understanding of our creation as a blessing or, as Barth has it, a "benefit" (*Wohltat*).[10] Like the fact of our creation itself,[11] this must always be a matter of faith rather than a conclusion of reason or empirical evidence. For experience (and with it the witness of reason) so often suggests otherwise, that our existence is at best a mixed bag and often apparently marked much more by darkness than light. Faith, though, is called to suppose otherwise and to trust that God's decision to create is justified, if not by empirical experience in the midst of history's turmoil, then by the faithfulness of the One who holds its future in his hands and who has promised to make it good. Third, in the account of creation, the gift of God's love entails the supposition that what God has made matters to God, that creation (as a whole and every part of it) is valuable in his sight.

---

[8] See above, chap. 4.

[9] See Moltmann, *God in Creation*, 86–93.

[10] Barth, *Church Dogmatics III/1*, 330–44.

[11] Cf. Barth, *Church Dogmatics III/1*, 3.

Part of the gift of creation, though, is precisely its contingent otherness from God and, as such, its freedom to be and become what it will. This is difficult territory, to be sure, not least when set in juxtaposition to God's promise to make all things new and to make good on his promises. A full treatment of the subject lies a long way beyond the remit of this volume, but two things in particular are worth drawing attention to. First, in Moltmann's account of the atonement, the godforsaken space of hell and death occasioned by sin is one that God reenters and floods with his presence, not now in the form of the divine Shekinah but by becoming one of us and so identifying with us completely in our godforsakenness, which can no longer separate us from him.[12] This, it seems to me, stimulates helpful resonances in the tabernacle theology to which we have already alluded on numerous occasions. It is in the humanity (or "flesh") of Jesus that God himself tabernacles among us, manifesting his glory as never before (John 1:14). And yet, as in the tabernacle of old, in Christ this is no straightforward matter, the holiness of God being compelled to reckon and to deal graciously with the sin and recalcitrance of our shared nature, bearing it in all its need of redemption into the presence of God's own self and offering it there, uncompromising, in the holy of holies, as an atoning sacrifice to the One who alone can redeem and regenerate it. In the crucifixion, resurrection, and ascension of Jesus, therefore, what we find played out in cosmic miniature is the way in which God must deal, has promised to deal, and in Christ has already dealt with the challenge of sin and evil posed by our "fallen" nature and its capacity to thwart his creative purposes. By himself becoming that in which lies the source of the cosmic problem (as well as its greatest blessing—that is, a creature possessed of its own free will), he both embraces the consequence of that which he now shares with us (and for which he here "takes responsibility") and in his self-substitution for us displaces the power of sin by wrestling with it in the power of the Spirit and emerging triumphant for our sakes. If his death is marked by ambiguity (he is the one who dies "bearing our sins to the tree" and yet precisely because of his own relentless obedience to the Father), his resurrection and ascension mark him out as the one vindicated by God.

Thus it is both as God and humanly (God *hōs anthropos* as the Fathers insist) that Christ prevails, and the atonement (and the fulfillment of the covenant that it represents) is achieved freely from both sides, albeit with a clear Alexandrian gesture toward the determinacy of what God does hypostatically from first to last. This is consonant with the pattern which

---

[12] See Moltmann, *God in Creation*, 90–91; Jürgen Moltmann, *The Crucified God* (London: SCM Press, 1976), passim.

manifests itself from the outset, in which, even in the earliest moments of creation, God does not seize responsibility greedily to himself but constrains himself and shares responsibility for the unfolding and completion of the project (riskily and in a manner that finally proves costly) with the creature. This is part of what Moltmann identifies as the kenotic or self-emptying aspect of God's wider *operationes ad extra*. More precisely, we may argue, it is the function of his love and his desire to draw a creation that is genuinely other than himself into the circle of his eternal triune life of love and communion.

Unfinished Business

On October 7, 1936, Dorothy L. Sayers, a writer as yet acknowledged primarily for a string of successful murder mysteries, had received a letter from the organizers of the Canterbury Festival inviting her to write a play for their forthcoming 1937 event. The invitation came both as a surprise and as an honor—a surprise because, although she was in fact just about to take her first dramatic production to the stage (*Busman's Honeymoon*, cowritten with Muriel St Clare Byrne, was cast and rehearsed in that same month and had its opening night in mid-November),[13] this venture was not widely known about, and Sayers' talent as a playwright was still effectively untried; an honor because her immediate predecessors in writing for the festival were anything but up and coming, let alone unknown and untested. In 1935 the event had been graced by T. S. Eliot's *Murder in the Cathedral*, and in 1936 by Charles Williams' *Thomas Cranmer of Canterbury*.[14] No wonder her response expressed initial caution on the grounds that the project was "rather out of my usual line."[15] Notwithstanding this fact, Sayers accepted the challenge.

In accordance with the festival's theme that year (the celebration of artists and craftsmen) but wishing also to maintain its focus on the history

[13] See Sayers to L. C. Kempson, October 10, 1936, in *The Letters of Dorothy L. Sayers*, vol. 1, *1899–1936: The Making of a Detective Novelist*, ed. Barbara Reynolds (New York: St Martin's, 1995), 401; Sayers to Margaret Babington, November 14, 1936, *Letters of Dorothy L. Sayers*, 1:405.

[14] Williams appears to have suggested Sayers' name as his successor. According to Reynolds' biography, the two had certainly been in contact since 1935 and possibly earlier. As Reynolds notes earlier in her work, Sayers had in fact tried her hand at drama before, incorporating a short mystery play (*The Mocking of Christ*) in her collection *Catholic Tales and Christian Songs* (Oxford: Blackwell, 1918), and a letter written to the *New Witness* in January 1919 reveals that Williams had read this. See Barbara Reynolds, *Dorothy L. Sayers: Her Life and Soul* (London: Hodder & Stoughton, 1993), 98–101, 310.

[15] Sayers to Margaret Babington, October 7, 1936, *Letters of Dorothy L. Sayers*, 1:401.

of the Canterbury Cathedral, Sayers selected for the plot of her drama events surrounding the rebuilding of the church's choir in the late twelfth century.[16] Her protagonist was William of Sens, the French architect duly chosen by the cathedral chapter to undertake this work. Four years into an expensive but thus far successful renovation project, the historical William was seriously injured falling from a cradle he himself had designed to facilitate installation of the keystone to the great arch. His body broken, the master craftsman was compelled to resign his commission, leaving his work unfinished, to be completed by others. Sayers locates the circumstances of this accident at the heart of her play, using it to explore some fundamental questions about the place of human "making" in God's scheme of things. Picking up on fragments of evidence provided by the contemporary chronicler, she characterizes William at first as a man whose spiritual qualifications for building the Lord's house are at best questionable. If, as the cathedral prior suggests, William's avarice, promiscuity, and generous disregard for truth are at least offset by his evident skill and his passion to use it well, it is nonetheless *this* that is the occasion of his quite literal downfall. Immediately before the ascent that will maim him, Sayers places the following words on William's lips:

> We are the master-craftsmen, God and I—
> We understand one another. None, as I can,
> Can creep under the ribs of God, and feel
> His heart beat through those Six Days of Creation . . .
>   since all Heaven was not enough
> To share that triumph, He made His masterpiece,
> Man, that like God can call beauty from dust,
> Order from chaos, and create new worlds
> To praise their maker. Oh, but in making man
> God over-reached Himself and gave away
> His Godhead. He must now depend on man
> For what man's brain, creative and divine
> Can give Him. Man stands equal with Him now,
> Partner and rival.[17]

---

[16] The original choir had burned down in 1174. For the history, see Roslin Mair, "The Choir Capitals of Canterbury Cathedral 1174–84," in *The British Archaeological Association Conference Transactions for the Year 1979*, vol. 5, *Medieval Art and Architecture at Canterbury before 1220* (British Archaeological Association and Kent Archaeological Society, 1982), 56–66.

[17] Dorothy L. Sayers, *The Zeal of Thy House* (London: Harcourt, Brace, 1937), 69–70.

In theological terms, this is a convenient summary of Promethean excess at its worst, and William compounds the tragic hubris further when, to the warning that such blasphemous sentiments may tempt God to strike him down, he responds, "He will not dare; / He knows that I am indispensable / To His work here."[18] This is, of course, a misplaced confidence, and only moments later the sword of the Archangel Michael cuts the rope on which William dangles precariously above the flagstones of the cathedral floor, sending him plunging to his physical ruin but (as it turns out) his spiritual redemption.

Having depicted the folly and outrage of William's theologically informed "aesthetic" and the nature of its outcomes, though, the drama does not proceed, as we might reasonably expect, to eschew the analogy and proposed correlation between divine and human modes of creativity that lies at the heart of it. Instead, it suggests provocatively that God, the great Master Architect of the cosmos (and so William's divine exemplar), has indeed placed himself in a circumstance where he needs human agents to complete the work begun in creation, albeit not quite in the manner that William self-importantly supposes. This, indeed, is the spiritual lesson that William is to learn through his fall and his subsequent inability to complete the masterwork he has begun. His initial proud refusal to relinquish a micromanaging, hands-on oversight of the precise shape "his" work will now take is redeemed when he finally grasps a theological truth lying at the heart of the doctrine of the incarnation—in becoming one of his own creatures, God himself has embraced humiliation, suffering, failure, and death, leaving others behind to pick up his work and carry it forward.[19] Though it is not articulated in the dialogue, close at hand lies the idea we have already identified in Moltmann that, far from being the first moment of kenosis identifiable in God's dealings with the world, the incarnation should be understood as the most acute instance of a wider pattern beginning with the divine decision to create as such.[20] If God

---

[18] Sayers, *Zeal of Thy House*, 70. On William's "blasphemy," cf. Sayers to Laurence Irving, February 26, 1937, in *The Letters of Dorothy L. Sayers*, vol. 2, *1937–1943: From Novelist to Playwright*, ed. Barbara Reynolds (Cambridge: Dorothy L. Sayers Society, 1997), 14.

[19] See Sayers, *Zeal of Thy House*, 99–100: "Not God Himself was indispensable, / For lo! God died—and still His work goes on."

[20] The notion of creation entailing a voluntary self-limitation on God's part is especially prominent in forms of kabbalistic mysticism influenced by Isaac Luria (1534–1572), especially in the distinctive doctrine of *Tsimtsum* or divine concentration/contraction. See Gershom Scholem, *Major Trends in Jewish Mysticism* (New York: Schocken Books, 1941), 260–64.

himself does not jealously exclude but actively conscripts the agency of others in the realization and redemption of his creative project, the drama inquires, how can any human maker be prepared to do less?

There is, of course, another story to be told about the incarnation, and one that it would be very dangerous to lose sight of. According to a soteriological tradition stretching from Irenaeus of Lyons to Karl Barth and beyond, God has, precisely by taking flesh (thereby simultaneously earthing the Trinitarian dynamics of the life of God within the patterns of human history and drawing our humanity redemptively within the penumbra of his own existence), reversed the impact of sin and alienation upon our nature and so established a place within the creaturely sphere where already he dwells together with us in fellowship, so fulfilling by way of prolepsis the purpose of creation itself.[21] Put differently, in Christ, God substitutes his own humanity for ours and thus himself provides the free creaturely response in which creation comes to its intended goal and fulfillment. Nonetheless, the logic of this divine self-substitution is not to displace creaturely action altogether but precisely to create a context in which, understood as a participation in Christ's own action through the Spirit, it may be undertaken freely and without fear of failure or falling short; in the peculiar "already–not yet" modality of human existence situated in between the incarnation and the eschatological consummation of all things, what has been achieved by God for us remains as yet to be worked out in, and with, and through us, and within this context there is much for us still to do and no compromising of the integrity of our actions in doing it.

While, therefore, in William's hubris Sayers shows us the worst and most problematic aspects of the humanism that emerged from the Renaissance, as Nicholas Wolterstorff notes, she does so finally not to damn the project but to seek its redemption by resituating elements of it within a quite different religious and theological perspective.[22] In place of autonomous man, struggling nobly for artistic liberation amidst a rivalry with God, Sayers offers an alternative vision, of human artistry and craftsmanship—understood now in explicitly Christian theological terms—as at the very least a "spiritual" vocation equivalent to others ("William's devoted craftsmanship," she tells a correspondent, has "more of the true

---

[21] This is the central idea of Barth's twofold insistence that the covenant between God and Israel fulfilled once and for all in Jesus Christ is the internal basis of creation, and creation the external basis of the covenant. See Barth, *Church Dogmatics III/1*, 94–329.

[22] See Nicholas Wolterstorff, *Art in Action: Toward a Christian Aesthetic* (Carlisle, U.K.: Solway, 1997), 67–69.

spirit of prayer than . . . self-righteous litanies"[23]) and at best as something much more besides. The play closes with a speech to the audience by the Archangel Michael, and in his words we find the first inkling of a theme to which Sayers would return and that she would work out more fully in her own mind over the next several years. Human making and craftsmanship, it suggests, is not a breach of divine copyright nor is it set in deliberate counterpoise to God's own creative activity; rather, the basic structure of our human ways of engaging with the world "creatively" should be identi-fied as a concrete vestige of and participation in God's own triune being and as such the proper locus of that "image and likeness" of God in which our humanity is itself made: "[f]or every work of creation is threefold, an earthly trinity / to match the heavenly."[24]

Making Good

The idea that God grants humankind a responsible participation in his own creative project is central to the Jewish notion of *tikkun olam*, the mending or perfecting of the world. As Jonathan Sacks notes, this notion has very ancient roots in strands of biblical and Mishnaic teaching but receives its definitive synthesis in the kabbalism of the sixteenth-century mystical rabbi Isaac Luria.[25] The central theme of the doctrine in its various forms is that the world that we inhabit as God's creatures is as yet imperfect (and in and this sense God's creative vision remains unfulfilled or incomplete), and that every Jew, in the radical particularity of his or her circumstance, is called to share actively in the process of "mending," "perfecting," or completing the harmonious whole that God intends his creation to become and to be.[26] In its Lurianic version, as Sacks is at pains to point out, this participation is

---

[23] See Sayers to Father Herbert Kelly, October 4, 1937, *Letters of Dorothy L. Sayers*, 2:47.

[24] Sayers, *Zeal of Thy House*, 110. The play closes with this speech that, although cut from the 1937 production to meet the strictures of prescribed length, was restored in subsequent performances and can be seen in retrospect to be pregnant with the seed that would grow into *The Mind of the Maker* (London: Methuen, 1941).

[25] See Jonathan Sacks, *To Heal a Fractured World: The Ethics of Responsibility* (London: Continuum, 2005), 72–78. For a more extended discussion of the idea, see Scho-lem, *Major Trends in Jewish Mysticism*, 244–86; and Gershom Scholem, *The Messianic Idea in Judaism: And Other Essays on Jewish Spirituality* (New York: Schocken Books, 1995 [1971]), 78–141, 203–27.

[26] Lange notes that in Lurianic kabbalism the despoiling of the world occurs not in a prehistoric fall contingent on human freedom but before or during the act of creation itself. The world is thus always a fractured, imperfect, or incomplete project within which humans are called to act to secure the good. See Nicholas de Lange, *An Introduction to Judaism* (Cambridge: Cambridge University Press, 2000), 206. Cf. Sacks, *To Heal*, 74–75.

understood to be through particular concrete acts of piety and spirituality (and thus chiefly a matter of the soul) rather than by engagement in political initiatives for social justice or efforts to adjust the human impact on our created environment; but in the last hundred years or so the phrase has acquired a more inclusive connotation, all acts designed to avoid evil and do good, specifically religious or otherwise, being understood as a manifestation of *tikkun*.[27] The gist of this participatory vision is summed up neatly by Rabbi Joseph Soloveitchik:

> When God created the world, He provided an opportunity for the work of his hands—man—to participate in His creation. The Creator, as it were, impaired reality in order that mortal man could repair its flaws and perfect it.[28]

Christians are likely to have some legitimate theological concerns and questions about elements of this religious narrative and its linking of divine and human agency so directly in an account of the completion and redemption of the created order. Two concerns in particular stand out and demand some response. First, there is the suggestion that the world was from its inception already flawed or fractured, and received from God's hand, therefore, in a state needful of repair by (among other things) the work of human hands. Any such suggestion compromises the doctrine of creation's primal goodness and flirts dangerously with gnostic notions of a world created not by God himself but by an incompetent demiurge. Christian orthodoxy has always resisted such ideas, insisting that the world is from first to last the work of a Creator the hallmarks of whose character are infinite goodness, wisdom, and love, and accounting for the brokenness and alienation of historical existence by appealing to the radical misuse of freedom and a consequent "fall" of humankind into a condition of sin and death.[29] As Paul Fiddes observes, however, the theological notion of "fall" is not inexorably wedded to a U-shaped narrative in which primal perfection is compromised and lost, to be restored again in due course by a divine salvage operation.[30] The primal goodness of creation can be understood otherwise than this. So, for example, as we have seen, Karl Barth interprets the divine pronouncement in Genesis 1:31 not as a

---

[27] See Sacks, *To Heal*, 78; cf. Lange, *Introduction to Judaism*, 206–8.

[28] Joseph B. Soloveitchik, *Halakhic Man*, trans. Lawrence Kaplan (Philadelphia: Jewish Publication Society of America, 1983), 101; cited in Sacks, *To Heal*, 71.

[29] See, among patristic rejoinders to the idea, Irenaeus, *Against Heresies*; and Augustine, *City of God* 11.17, 11.23, 13.1–3. For discussion, see helpfully John Hick, *Evil and the God of Love* (London: Macmillan, 1966).

[30] Paul Fiddes, *Freedom and Limit: A Dialogue between Literature and Christian Doctrine* (Basingstoke, U.K.: Macmillan, 1991), chap. 3.

valediction but instead as an ordination, proleptic and eschatological in its vision: all that God has made is indeed "very good," given its promised end in the fulfillment of the eternal covenant.[31] And it is true, surely, that the goodness with which Christian faith is finally concerned is not one speculatively posited in a remote prehistoric past but one as yet to come, anticipated decisively in history's midst in the humanity of Jesus, but realized only in the promised future of God when all things shall be made new and God himself will dwell amongst us as "all in all." Thus Fiddes outlines an understanding of fall not as a temporally situated once and for all departure from an original perfection but rather as the continual outcome of a human creatureliness as yet incomplete and imperfect, and therefore caught up in a dialectic between the possibilities of freedom and the limits of finitude, a dialectic constantly resolving itself either in trust and obedience or (more typically) anxiety and idolatry.[32] Such a view does not, of course, view creatureliness and fallenness as the same thing, or ascribe the origination of evil and death to the Creator himself. Sin, and its consequences, remain the result of the creature's free choices. But this sort of view does face squarely the fact that sin arises due to a vulnerability and weakness built into the structure of our finite existence, at least potentially. Doctrines of the fall of the Augustinian sort, which prefer to posit an original human perfection, face a number of significant difficulties of their own. They are, of course, entirely remote from anything in our experience of what it is to be human, and find it notoriously difficult to account for how or why it was that creatures enjoying unalloyed felicitude and imperturbability should choose to set it aside at all.[33] And such doctrines do not finally succeed in their aim of exonerating God of all responsibility for the presence of sin and evil in his world. To the extent that they ascribe ultimate sovereignty to God in creation and in redemption, they are at least compelled to acknowledge that he called into being a world that was, in Milton's phrase, "free to fall"[34] and perhaps even bound finally to do so. Neither understanding of fallenness involves predicating sin and evil as functions of creation itself, or as necessary components of human existence as such; but each in its way finally admits that the *possibility* of

---

[31] Barth, *Church Dogmatics III/1*, 212–13. See above, p. 5.

[32] I.e., seeking security in finite objects and goals and granting these a worth properly due only to God.

[33] See the discussion of this same problem as it arises in Milton's *Paradise Lost* in Trevor Hart, "Poetry and Theology in Milton's *Paradise Lost*," in *Genesis and Christian Theology*, ed. Nathan MacDonald, Mark Elliott, and Grant Macaskill (Grand Rapids: Eerdmans, 2012), 129–39.

[34] See John Milton, *Paradise Lost*, bk 3, line 99.

sin and evil is given in the nature of the world as it comes to us from God's hand. The difference between them, finally, is that one seeks to "justify the ways of God to men" by directing our imaginative gaze backward to a primordial creaturely perfection, whereas the other (granting that the creation itself comes to us as yet incomplete and empirically "imperfect") prefers to direct us to Christ, and to the fulfillment of God's promise in the future of Christ.

The other theological concern likely to trouble Christians in the notion of *tikkun olam* outlined above is the ascription of what is apparently too high a premium to the significance of human actions vis-à-vis the completion or perfection of the world, putting at risk an adequate account of divine transcendence and a theology of grace as the sole source of both our creation and our redemption. That this is indeed a problematic inference of the Lurianic doctrine is suggested by Gershom Scholem, who notes the way in which an organic unity and continuity "between the state of redemption and the state preceding it" tends to characterize some kabbalistic visions, so that redemption "now appears . . . as the logical consequence of the historical process,"[35] with God and humankind functioning effectively as partners (albeit unequal partners) in the enterprise. The specious wedding of process and progress that haunts our culture courtesy of the remaining vestiges of modernity grants such ideas a seductive allure even at the outset of the twenty-first century and makes it all the more urgent that theologians speak clearly and unashamedly of the transcendent nature of Christian hope, vested as it is in God's sovereign otherness and Lordship, and not in any possibilities or potentialities latent within the creaturely (and fallen) order as such.[36] Any indication that the world's redemption might be contingent in some way upon the nature of the actions we perform in the eschatological interim may well seem to compromise this transcendent commitment and to constitute a pernicious form of "works righteousness" inimical to the logic of the Christian Evangel.

As Sacks observes, in Judaism itself there is an unresolved tension at this point, *tikkun olam* functioning both as a principle for ordering human action in the midst of history and as an object of daily prayer and eschatological expectation.[37] It is, paradoxically, *both* something that God will do and must be implored to do (since we cannot), *and* something that

[35] Scholem, *Messianic Idea in Judaism*, 47–48.

[36] See the critical rejoinder to the so-called myth of progress in Richard Bauckham and Trevor Hart, *Hope against Hope: Christian Eschatology at the Turn of the Millennium* (Grand Rapids: Eerdmans, 1999).

[37] It arises at the heart of *Alenu*, the closing prayer of each daily liturgy. See Sacks, *To Heal*, 75–76.

we must do in the here and now and in the nitty-gritty of everyday decisions and actions. The achievement of cosmic harmony thus comes both
"from above" and "from below"—from the side of the creature in faithful
response to the Creator's calling and approach. Within the religious vision
of Judaism, this dual insistence is bound either to remain an unresolved
dialectic or else to resolve itself in some form of religious and ethical synergism likely to place a crushing burden of responsibility on human shoulders. As we have already had occasion to notice, though, Christianity has
a different framework to offer respectfully for consideration, one within
which such seemingly contradictory claims may legitimately be situated
and made sense of, without any confusion arising between them or any
loss of integrity or force attaching to either as a result. In the messianic,
priestly humanity of Christ, the Church discerns and proclaims a fully
human action of *tikkun* corresponding directly to the creative and redemptive purposes and activity of God the Father and energized from first to
last by the activity of the Holy Spirit. Furthermore—and decisively—this
same human action is that undertaken by God himself, substituting his
own humanity for ours at the heart of the covenant he has made with
creation, not in such a manner as to exclude our due response, but rather
to provide a context within which the partial and faltering nature of that
response no longer has the power to crush us, being relativized in significance (though not rendered wholly insignificant) by the response of Christ
made on our behalf.

Within a Trinitarian and incarnational account of atonement, and a
corresponding understanding of human action as a participation in the
priestly human action of Christ, in other words, the "from above" and
"from below" dimensions of *tikkun olam* are able to be correlated and held
together, their whole dynamic situated within the overall triune pattern
of God's activity and life. Only God can finally heal the world and bring
it to completion. But he has chosen to do so not *without* a corresponding
human action but precisely in, with, and through such action, concluded
once and for all in the humanity of his own Son, but participated in and
replicated ever and again in the Spirit-filled lives of others until the time
when God will be all in all. Only God can bring about the "new creation"
to which the apostles and prophets bear poetic witness; but in the meanwhile, we are called already to live in ways that declare this new creation to
be a hidden reality, performing parables of it in the midst of history, and so
conforming historical existence, piece by piece, more fully to its promised
destiny in God's hands. It is this emphasis upon the significance of the
piecemeal and the seemingly inconsequential that is one of the attractions
of the notion of *tikkun olam*. Too often Christians are driven by a utilitarian ethic that supposes things worth doing only if some return can be

identified on the investment, rather than understanding that good actions are worth doing precisely and only because it is good to do them, and that the world is in some sense made better thereby even when no grand strategy is advanced or outcome accomplished in the process. At one level, indeed, acknowledgment of the self-substitution of God's humanity for ours in Christ renders *every* other human action inconsequential; and yet, paradoxically, it simultaneously charges every action with a new significance by situating it within the sphere of action undertaken in union with Christ and thus rendering it either a witness to or a denial of its reality as such. That the healing and completion of the world will not depend finally on my actions or yours is a vital inference of this theological vision; but that we are called, commanded even, to immerse ourselves fully in our own small part of the world and to do all that we can in every sphere of it to "make good" the peculiar claims of faith concerning the world's origin and promised end is an equally vital entailment. And it is, we should recall, precisely *this* world, and not some other, that will be taken up and made new by God in the fullness of time. And in that sense, nothing that we do, no choice that we make or action that we undertake in life, is wholly without eschatological consequence. For it is itself the object of God's redemptive promise.

The Liturgy of Artistry

One of the gains of an adequate theology of the priesthood of Christ is that it liberates us to acknowledge the potential liturgical significance of parts of our identity and action we have hitherto held back or supposed relatively "secular" and lacking in religious merit. The news that the Son of God has laid hold of our humanity in its entirety and offered it back, crucified and risen, to his Father in the power of the Spirit for our sakes compels us in our turn now to offer back to God in joyful thanks nothing less than all that we personally are, and have, and may yet become. As Jonathan Sacks notes, in biblical thought *Homo sapiens* is the one creature that is itself identifiably "creative," capable not just of adapting to its created environment but of making more of that environment than is initially given in it[38]—enhancing, or adding value, to it. Indeed, inasmuch as the world is apprehended as meaningful, it constitutes a distinctly human environment, shot through with significance that transcends its materiality alone, a union of material being and semiotic excess in which "a thing is not just what it is" and its reality takes time to unfold.[39] A distinctly human engagement with or

[38] Sacks, *To Heal*, 79.
[39] Rowan Williams, *Grace and Necessity: Reflections on Art and Love* (Harrisburg, Pa.: Morehouse, 2005), 26.

indwelling of the world is thus inevitably and always one in which we "make something of" the world, rather than functioning as mere passive observers or consumers of it. To live responsibly in this sense, Rowan Williams suggests, is to draw out what is not yet seen or heard in the material environment itself, to "uncover what is generative in the world,"[40] and so, working with the grain of the cosmos, to aid and assist in the imaginative effoliation by which the world approaches more fully what it is capable of being and becoming. In offering our humanity back to God, therefore, we offer back too the world in which we are embedded bodily and culturally and what we have made of it for good or ill.

The sort of creative imagination involved in human artistry, Williams submits, is thus not an eccentric or exclusive sort but precisely an acute form of our wider human engagement with the world, with its distinctive dialectic of imaginative give and take.[41] The premise of artistry is that perception is always incomplete, that truthfulness unfolds as we continue to explore it, that there is always an excess of meaning in what is given to us for consideration.[42] Yet artistry, considered thus, is no mere cataloguing of the world's given forms, no "mimetic" inventory of the extant. Art brings new things into existence and, precisely in doing so, discovers that which it makes. Precisely because significance has no purchase apart from the actions and responses of those who indwell the order of signs, because human acts of signification and sense making are already factored into our apprehension of an orderly and value-laden world (one in which "cosmos" and "ethos" are, as it were, perichoretically related), every act of discovery, of the uncovering or disclosure of new meaning, necessarily entails acts of making too, and every act of making lays bare some latent but hitherto unrecognized semiotic possibility. In art, as in life more generally, our calling is thus, paradoxically, to "change the world into itself,"[43] but we can do so precisely and only by means of imaginative responses which help to make of it more and other than it is as yet. Again, the necessary supposition is that world is in fact not yet "itself" but in some sense unfinished, with much more still to be drawn out of its primordial plenitude and fashioned in accordance with the "generative pulsions" divinely invested and humanly intuited in it.[44] This is not "creativity" of a sort that craves trespass on the soil of divine prerogatives, but it is nonetheless a

[40] Williams, *Grace and Necessity*, 162.
[41] Williams, *Grace and Necessity*, 140.
[42] Williams, *Grace and Necessity*, 135–39.
[43] Williams, *Grace and Necessity*, 18.
[44] Williams, *Grace and Necessity*, 27. Williams borrows the word "pulsions" from Maritain. See Jacques Maritain, *Creative Intuition in Art and Poetry* (London: Harvill, 1953), 302–6.

participation in the unfolding of "creation" and in God's making of new things and making all things new. It is precisely by means of our imaginative and "creative" responses to the given world in the arts and elsewhere, therefore, that the world approaches that fullness of which it is capable (or, conversely, is held back from it).[45]

Having already hosted more than one discussion of the work of Dorothy L. Sayers,[46] it seems fitting to draw this work toward a close by referring to the thought of her direct contemporary and compeer J. R. R. Tolkien. Looking back over his already lengthy career in 1954, Tolkien suggested to a correspondent that the whole of his literary output, imaginative and critical, had from the first really been concerned with exploring a single question—namely, the relationship between divine creation and acts of human making, or "sub-creation," as he preferred to call it.[47] Two poetic texts in particular tackle the issue head-on and in a manner that points to single abiding insight present from his very earliest ruminations on the subject: Primary and Secondary Reality, the world received from God's hand and "what we make of it" in various acts of human *ars*, are not to be too sharply distinguished, since they are both "ultimately of the same stuff,"[48] and our creaturely participation in each demands of us further acts of imaginative response and making. Creation, in other words, always solicits and enables further acts of a "creative" sort rather than jealously guarding its own prerogatives.

The Elvish creation myth "Ainulindalë" was cast in its final form in the 1950s and published only after Tolkien's death more than twenty years

---

[45] Williams, *Grace and Necessity*, 154.

[46] See above, e.g., 268–75.

[47] Tolkien to Peter Hastings, draft, *The Letters of J. R. R. Tolkien*, ed. Humphrey Carpenter (Boston: Houghton Mifflin, 1981), 188 (no. 153). The letter was seemingly never sent. A related suggestion is contained in an earlier letter to Milton Waldman written in 1951: "all this stuff," Tolkien writes (alluding to his entire mythological enterprise), "is mainly concerned with Fall, Mortality, and the Machine" (Tolkien to Milton Waldman, undated 1951, 145 [no. 131]). A footnote to the text reads, "It is, I suppose, fundamentally concerned with the problem of the relation of Art (and Sub-creation) and Primary Reality."

[48] J. R. R. Tolkien, *Tree and Leaf: Including the Poem "Mythopoeia"; "The Homecoming of Beorhtnoth Beorhthelm's Son"* (London: HarperCollins, 2001), 30. The citation is from the essay "On Fairy Stories," first published in 1947. Given the consonance of the idea with those expressed in earlier works and its place in the argument of the essay as a whole, it seems likely that it dates back to the lost original (presumably much shorter) text of the lecture "Fairy Stories" delivered in the University of St Andrews on March 8, 1939. On the history, see Rachel Hart, "Tolkien, St Andrews, and Dragons," in *Tree of Tales: Tolkien, Literature and Theology*, ed. Trevor Hart and Ivan Khovacs (Waco, Tex.: Baylor University Press, 2007), 1–11.

later, but its earliest version belongs to the imaginative genesis of Middle-earth itself in the years immediately following the First World War.[49] It concerns Eru, or Ilúvatar, and his creation of the cosmos not by solo virtuoso performance but by calling into existence creatures themselves capable of sharing in the joyful task of bringing a world to completion. The metaphor in terms of which the myth pictures this creative interplay is itself, appropriately, an artistic one. Ilúvatar propounds a great musical theme and invites the Ainur or Valar (the angelic first-created) to join in the music making, each adorning the main theme with his own, to the end of a great and glorious harmony sounding forth. The creativity of the Ainur, therefore, is at once wholly unlike Ilúvatar's own creative act, while yet constituting an extension of, development of, and participation in it. While each of the angelic creatures is free to fashion his own individual melody, the skill or "art" of the matter lies not in any sheer creativity ex nihilo but precisely in the harmonious development of a theme that Ilúvatar himself has already propounded and that determines, as it were, the form of the overall work. The core image, then, is that of harmonizing by free and spontaneous ornamentation. For his part, we are told, Ilúvatar will "sit and hearken, and be glad that through you great beauty has been wakened into song."[50] Creaturely acts of sub-creation, therefore, are here contingent on a divine self-limitation that, paradoxically, creates the conditions for that which pleases God's heart and satisfies his desire the most—reciprocal acts of a "creative" sort, taking what God has given and offering it back enriched and enhanced in accordance with its original God-given store of possibility. Of course, such kenotic sharing of responsibility opens the emergent cosmos to malign influence, and Tolkien's myth, while hardly a calque on its biblical equivalent, has its own Miltonic Satan figure in Melkor, the most gifted angel of all, in whom sub-creative desire falls away from its proper orientation and manifests itself in the reality-denying wish "to be Lord and God of his own private creation."[51] Melkor's capacity for weaving discord and ruin amidst the primal harmony of the divine design is considerable, and it calls forth from Ilúvatar a deeper and superior artistry in order to redeem it, not (unlike the God of at least one Christian hymn) drowning out "all music but his own"[52] but rather taking

---

[49] See J. R. R. Tolkien, *The Silmarillion*, ed. Christopher Tolkien (London: George Allen & Unwin, 1977), 15–22. On the different rescensions of the myth, see Trevor Hart, "Tolkien, Creation and Creativity," in Hart and Khovacs, *Tree of Tales*, 39–53.

[50] Tolkien, *Silmarillion*, 15.

[51] Tolkien to Milton Waldman, undated 1951, *Letters of J. R. R. Tolkien*, 145 (no. 131).

[52] "Crown Him with Many Crowns," by Matthew Bridges (1800–1894) and Godfrey Thring (1823–1903). The full text may be found in Methodist Conference Office, *The Methodist Hymn Book* (London: Methodist Conference Office, 1933), no. 271.

the offending and destructive noise up skillfully into the pattern of his own music making in such a way that its significance is finally transfigured and made good. The bringing of the creative vision to fulfillment and completion, therefore, is by no means automatic or straightforward; but it *is* contingent on creaturely as well as divine action and response, and, in God's hands, it is finally secure rather than uncertain. In earlier versions of the myth, Tolkien was much more bold in his suggestion of a world given by God only in what amounts to outline form, with empty spaces deliberately left unfilled and adornments unrealized, looking to the "eucharistic" artistry of the Ainur for their due enrichment and completion. Later editions tone this down slightly, as Tolkien perhaps increasingly realized the danger of theological misunderstanding and felt the need to indicate more clearly the distinction he believed must indeed be drawn between that creating which God alone does and is capable of doing, and creaturely "sub-creating" as he had by now dubbed it. For, while the myth is first and foremost a work of the literary imagination, making no obvious claim as such to a truth beyond its own borders, it is also an exploration and daring sketch of the contours of a theological aesthetic—an account not of primordial angelic sub-creating but of that "artistry" to which human beings find themselves called in the very midst of Primary Reality.

The poem "Mythopoeia" had its origins in a now legendary after-dinner conversation between Tolkien, C. S. Lewis, and Hugo Dyson conducted in the grounds of Magdalen College on the evening of September 19, 1931.[53] Among other things, the substance of the conversation touched upon the capacity of myth (and by extension other imaginative and poetic forms) to deal in the stuff of reality and truth, rather than being (in the reported words of Lewis,[54] the "Misomythus" of the poem's cryptic inscription) lies "breathed through silver." In his verse Tolkien playfully drives home his polemical point, that poetry may indeed be a sharp instrument in the hands of truth, helping us to cut the world at its joints, and he decries by comparison the sort of arid rationalism and literalism for which everything is exactly what its label says it is, and nothing is ever found to be more or other than it is. The poetic eye, the poem itself suggests, is thus the one best fitted to explore a world believed to be chock full of deep connections and hidden meanings, rather than exhausted in our measured consideration of its mere surface appearances. Furthermore, such acts of

---

[53] See Humphrey Carpenter, *J. R. R. Tolkien: A Biography* (London: HarperCollins, 2002), 196–99.

[54] The occasion was prior to Lewis' return to Christian faith from the atheism of his early adult years and a significant moment in the narrative of that return. See Carpenter, *J. R. R. Tolkien: A Biography*, 197–98.

poesis are fundamental to the roots of human language and perception themselves ("trees are not 'trees,' until so named and seen— / and never were so named till those had been / who speech's involuted breath unfurled . . ."),[55] and whatever world of meanings and significances we apprehend around us is therefore already in part a product of prior poetic responses to what is divinely given from beyond ourselves—a "refracted light" that has been splintered from its pure white into a glorious array of colors only by being passed first through the prism of our humanity. We experience the world in accordance with the capacities invested in our nature, and, far from being essentially passive and receptive, those capacities turn out to involve us necessarily in acts of construction, interpretation, and "sense making" from the very first. There is, of course, a distinction to be drawn between Primary and Secondary Reality, but it must not be drawn with too thick a pencil, since both are bound up with our peculiar poetic disposition toward things, and the boundaries between them are flexible and permeable:[56] we make, as Tolkien puts it, "in our measure and in our derivative mode," by the law in which we are made—"and not only made, but made in the image and likeness of a Maker."[57]

In the Image and Likeness of Whom?

In this book so far, I have studiously avoided any lengthy treatment of the theme of the creation of human beings "in the image and likeness" of God. I do not exactly intend to remedy that deficit (if such it be) here, but some comment on a notoriously contested and complex subject at least is merited. The omission may seem particularly odd because several treatments of our theme—including those of George MacDonald, and Sayers and Tolkien after him—make great play of the idea. Sayers, for instance, observes that the very first thing the Bible tells us about God is that he is a Creator, one who makes things, only shortly thereafter (and without much else about God having yet been disclosed) asserting that human beings are fashioned by God himself in his own likeness. What else might the reasonable reader conclude, Sayers asks, than that the capacity for creativity lies close to the heart of this "imaging" function, if not entirely exhausting it?[58]

[55] Tolkien, *Tree and Leaf,* 86.

[56] Thus, Tolkien writes, artistic imagination may grant us "[r]ecovery . . . a regaining—regaining of a clear view. I do not say 'seeing things as they are' and involve myself with the philosophers, though I might venture to say 'seeing things as we are (or were) meant to see them.'" Tolkien, *Tree and Leaf,* 57–58. The concession, albeit made in passing, is significant, both including human response already within any accounting of the "real" and suggesting the latter's susceptibility to modification by poetic redescription.

[57] Tolkien, *Tree and Leaf,* 56; cf. 87.

[58] Dorothy L. Sayers, *The Mind of the Maker* (London: Methuen, 1941), 17.

There may, of course, be something in this, not least since, as we have seen, Scripture returns the compliment, picturing God in his creative labors in the guise of a human artist. But on the basis of all that we have said hitherto, it should by now be clear that in the case of this doctrine too (and perhaps above all), the theological center of gravity must lie not in the interpretation of isolated texts (no matter how suggestive in themselves) but in the place where the creation of all things and of humanity in particular is held to come to a head—that is, in the incarnation of the Son of God as a man in our midst. Here, if anywhere, we understand most fully the character of the God in whose image we are said to be fashioned; and here, therefore, the true nature of that image must be supposed to be inscribed on our flesh in unambiguous fashion. Exegesis must be guided and informed by this natural "nodal point" within the text.

As we have seen in earlier chapters, too, it is undeniably the case that the theology of the image had its part to play in some of the less savory developments of early modern aesthetics, in particular fusing ideas of "dominion" in an unhealthy and damaging manner together with new-found confidence and competence in science and technology as well as the arts. We have already seen that such readings of the biblical materials were typically partial and skewed, a theme developed at length in J. Richard Middleton's work on the subject.[59] Having reflected on *why* God creates, Middleton suggests the next relevant question is *how* he does so. What sort of creative power, in other words, does Genesis 1 "rhetorically depict" God as exercising? And what, therefore, would the shape of human creativity be were it genuinely to be modeled on divine precedent? Middleton's answer, based on a close reading of the relevant texts, concurs with the shape of our own forays into this field: namely, even in his sovereign freedom, the God of Scripture constrains himself, exercising creative power "in such a way that we might appropriately describe it as an act of generosity, even of love."[60] More precisely, the relevant texts depict God as "sharing power with his creatures, inviting them to participate (as they are able) in the creative process itself."[61] Middleton's conclusion is worth citing in full:

> While these dimensions of the Genesis 1 creation story are not often noticed, attention to these rhetorical features points us to a God who does not hoard divine creative power, with some desperate need to control, but rather to a God

[59] J. Richard Middleton, *The Liberating Image: The* Imago Dei *in Genesis 1* (Grand Rapids: Brazos, 2005).
[60] Middleton, *Liberating Image*, 278.
[61] Middleton, *Liberating Image*, 287.

who is generous with power, sharing it with creatures, that they might make their own contribution to the harmony and beauty of the world.[62]

The account of the God in whose image and likeness Genesis 1 invites us to suppose that we are created, therefore, is in fact not one of untrammelled power imposing order unilaterally upon the world from above but, as Brueggemann suggests, a "creative use of power which invites, evokes, and permits. There is nothing here of coercive or tyrannical power, either for God or for humankind."[63] The way in which human "creativity" must manifest itself, therefore, is in the image of God's own "dominion," which does not "Lord it over" but always has the good of its fellow creatures set firmly in its sights.

Most typically in recent theologies of creation and in interpretations of the "cultural mandate" (Gen 1:26-30) in particular, this vital adjustment has expressed itself in the form of an alternative reading of dominion as "stewardship." As Thiselton notes, this notion has ancient roots,[64] and, as Richard Bauckham observes, it duly found its place in some of the Renaissance accounts of how humankind was called to produce a "second nature" to improve upon the first, flawed divine effort.[65] But it has received increased profile and recasting recently, when the charge of ecologically detrimental doctrinal underpinning has been laid firmly (if not altogether justifiably) at Christianity's door. In short, on this account of the matter, humanity's role in stewarding creation is to protect and preserve it from the potential predations born of human self-interest, rather than (as in some earlier versions) nature's own self-destructive, harmful, or wasteful impulses. Even this, though, Bauckham suggests, can be unduly interventionist, supposing that nature needs us to do something for it ("playing God" we might say) rather than simply leaving it alone.[66] The challenge for Christian theology today, he suggests, is "whether, now that humans have the power to interfere everywhere on earth (and even beyond), we can learn to care without interfering, simply to keep away and to keep our hands off, and to do so not so that we still have wildernesses to visit as eco-friendly tourists, but actually because God's other creatures have

---

[62] Middleton, *Liberating Image*, 289.

[63] Walter Brueggemann, *Genesis*, Interpretation (Atlanta: John Knox, 1982), 32; cited in Middleton, *Liberating Image*, 297.

[64] See Anthony Thiselton, *The Hermeneutics of Doctrine* (Grand Rapids: Eerdmans, 2007), 229.

[65] Richard Bauckham, *God and the Crisis of Freedom* (Louisville: Westminster John Knox, 2002), 169–71.

[66] So, notions of "stewardship" are "still too freighted with the baggage of the modern project of technological domination of nature." Bauckham, *God and the Crisis*, 172.

their own value for God and for themselves, quite independently of us."[67] This, too, is clearly an area where the discernment of creaturely goods is essential. What is true of wilderness (and what we identify as "wilderness," we should note, is in significant measure a human construct both theoretically and sometimes literally[68]) is hardly true of cancer cells and HIV/ AIDS, both of which, left unchecked by relevant inputs of human wisdom and skill, have devastating consequences.

Bauckham is particularly resistant to the idea that humankind is in some sense exalted above the rest of creation and that the latter needs human "stewarding" in order to fulfill its divinely ordained potential, or to "voice creation's praise." This, he argues, is an idea lacking in any biblical warrant whatever. Humans, he observes, are created on the same "day" as all other animal life forms, and we would be better advised to take into consideration our status as fellow creatures than to permit the ingress of potentially unhelpful (and unbiblical) notions of human superiority, which are difficult finally to disentangle from the elevation of human life to an intermediary status (the very problem we identified among some of the enthusiastic Renaissance theorists). Any such notion, Bauckham insists, "intrudes our inveterate sense of superiority exactly where the Bible will not allow it."[69] The rest of creation is quite capable of praising God in its own distinctive fashion and without human involvement.

This, I think, is a point well made and a legitimate reminder of the proper theological context within which any and every human contribution to the good of God's creation must properly be judged. And yet, as I have argued throughout this book, what it means for humans to praise God entails us in a being and a doing that involves acts of creative *poesis*, in which creaturely goods are realized and so "value" added to (drawn out of) the primordial plenitude given to us. Is this an anthropocentric vision? Yes, and unashamedly so, in the sense that we cannot finally know anything about anything from anywhere other than some distinctly human vantage point. Need it suggest that other parts of God's creation do not matter to God in their own right or that they need human participation to make up some deficit in their distinctive liturgical and eucharistic voice? No, I do not think so. To be sure, my argument has been that, in leaving creation in some sense unfinished and thus open to the energies of

[67] Bauckham, *God and the Crisis*, 172.

[68] See , e.g., discussions of the "wilderness idea" in Michael P. Nelson and J. Baird Caldicott, eds, *The Wilderness Debate Rages On: Continuing the Great New Wilderness Debate* (Athens: University of Georgia Press, 2008).

[69] Bauckham, *God and the Crisis*, 177.

divine-human participation,[70] God solicits our active and "creative" sharing in his own creative project, drawing out particular futures and options
among many that he has rendered possible. But, in light of this claim,
one might say equally that, insofar as such activity is contingent upon
our correlation and "collaboration" not with God alone but equally with
the relevant materials and processes and the potential invested in them by
God himself, other creatures actually enable us to fulfill our distinctive
calling and thus to "voice" our own proper mode of praise. There is no
need to suppose a priori that such materials and processes (our "fellow
creatures" as Bauckham rightly reminds us) are less eucharistic in their
natural state than their humanly modified state (though, again, one can
hardly help wondering whether some, such as the aesthetically impressive
carcinoma, may be so); but humans, without the opportunities afforded
to take and make and offer back something more than they receive or
find to hand, may well be. That which enables the world to "be more fully
itself," in other words, may prove to be a reciprocal rather than a unilateral
movement. And, as such, it will image all the more fully God's own way of
creativity, which does not crush or sideline but engenders and solicits acts
of creativity on the part of others.

Creativity, Christ, and Eucharist

To be participant "in our measure and . . . derivative mode" in God's own
continuing creative engagement with the world and its possibilities of
meaning, drawing it closer by constant small-scale acts of "guerrilla the-
atre"[71] to what, in God's creative vision, it was always intended to be, and
what, through the work of his own hands, it will yet become and be—this,
Tolkien suggests, is not just our right but our distinctive creaturely calling
and charge, whether used or misused.[72] And it is for acts of imaginative sub-
creating that God looks and longs in his human creatures, craving nothing
more than the glimpse of his own creative heart having found purchase and
offered back in joyful thanks from the side of the creature. If, as Rowan
Williams suggests, artistry is indeed but an acute and paradigmatic case of
our wider human disposition to the world, then here the arts, holiness, and
worship promise to fuse in a manner as yet to be fully reckoned with in most
of our churches and with some potentially fruitful implications, perhaps,

---

[70] I.e., a human action that, in its realization of divinely generated possibilities, must
finally submit to the Pauline judgment that credit must be given to "not I, but Christ in
me."

[71] Amos Wilder, *Theopoetic: Theology and the Religious Imagination* (Philadelphia:
Fortress, 1976).

[72] Tolkien, *Tree and Leaf*, 87.

for a newly cast Christology. "Dis-graced" we may well be, Tolkien avers; but neither the right nor the responsibility has decayed. "We make still by the law in which we're made."[73]

There is here, I suggest, a more secure and more fertile doctrinal ground not only for a "Christian aesthetic" but for a meaningful account of human creativity more widely understood than that gestured toward nearly seventy-five years ago by Dorothy L. Sayers. Human sub-creators may or may not "image" the triune God in their creative disposition toward God's world; the jury on that particular theological move is still out. But that our participation in Christ's own Spirit-filled dynamic of enabling our humanity—and with and in and through it the wider creation—to become and to be ever more fully itself is thereby an active participation in God's own (divine and human) completion of his creative project cannot seriously be gainsaid. To understand human "creativity" in this light places a significant premium on it within the creaturely order of things and, at the same time, situates it appropriately as a mode of action wholly subordinate to and dependent upon the prior and accompanying activity of God in his Spirit and his incarnate, crucified, and risen Word. Apart from a grasp of this objective theological context, all agendas to liberate and enable human creativity, no matter how well intended, seem bound sooner or later to go awry, generating only pathetic counterfeits of what God desires for his world. Within such a context, though, the suggestion that human beings are called to be genuinely creative (albeit as created "sub-creators" rather than "co-creators") situates all human response to the world potentially within the field of an action at once eucharistic and eschatological, grounded in the vicarious self-substitution of Christ for us, and opened out by the work of the Spirit of Christ in and through us in the direction of that New Creation promised by the Father.

---

[73] Tolkien, *Tree and Leaf*, 87.

Appendix
Figures

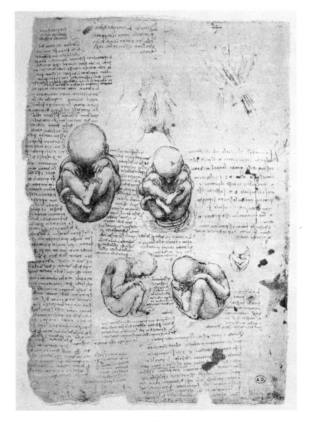

FIGURE 1
Five Views of a Foetus in the Womb, facsimile copy (pen & ink on paper), Leonardo da Vinci (1452–1519) (after) / Bibliotheque des Arts Decoratifs, Paris, France / Archives Charmet / Bridgeman Images

FIGURE 2
Jean-Léon Gérôme (French, 1824–1904), *Bashi-Bazouk Singing* (1868).
Image courtesy of the Walters Art Museum.

FIGURE 3
The Hand of God, 1898 (marble), Auguste Rodin (1840–1917) /
Musée Rodin, Paris, France / Photo © Boltin Picture Library /
Bridgeman Images

FIGURE 4
The Gates of Hell, 1880–1890 (bronze), Auguste Rodin (1840–1917) / Musée Rodin,
Paris, France / Peter Willi / Bridgeman Images

FIGURE 5

Whaam! (1963), Roy Lichtenstein (1923–1997), acrylic paint and oil paint on canvas.
© Estate of Roy Lichtenstein. Photograph © Tate, London 2014.

Bibliography

Abrams, M. H. *The Mirror and the Lamp: Romantic Theory and the Critical Tradition*. Oxford: Oxford University Press, 1953.

Agaësse, P., and A. Solignac, eds. *La Genese au sens littéral en douze livres (VIII–XII)*. Vol. 49 of *Oeuvres de Saint Augustin*. Paris: Desclée de Brouwer, 1972.

Alberti, Leon Battista. *On Painting*. Translated by Cecil Grayson. London: Penguin, 1991.

———. *On Painting*. Translated by John R. Spencer. London: Routledge & Kegan Paul, 1956.

Allen, Scott C. "Gérôme before the Tribunal: The Painter's Early Reception." In Cars, Font-Réaulx, and Papet, *Spectacular Art of Jean-Léon Gérôme*, 89–99.

Ames-Lewis, Francis. *The Intellectual Life of the Early Renaissance Artist*. New Haven, Conn.: Yale University Press, 2000.

Antal, Frederick. *Florentine Painting and Its Social Background*. London: Kegan Paul, 1947.

Aquinas. *See* Thomas Aquinas, Saint.

Aristotle. *Poetics*. Translated by Malcolm Heath. London: Penguin, 1996.

Auerbach, Erich. *Mimesis: The Representation of Reality in Western Literature*. Translated by Willard R. Trask. Princeton, N.J.: Princeton University Press, 1953.

Austin, J. L. *How to Do Things with Words*. 2nd ed. Cambridge, Mass.: Harvard University Press, 1979.

Baillie, John. *The Sense of the Presence of God*. London: Oxford University Press, 1962.

Barbour, Ian G. *Myths, Models and Paradigms: The Nature of Scientific and Religious Language.* London: SCM Press, 1974.

Barr, James. *The Semantics of Biblical Language.* London: Oxford University Press, 1961.

Barrett, C. K. *The Gospel according to St John: An Introduction with Commentary and Notes on the Greek Text.* Philadelphia: Westminster, 1978.

Barth, Karl. *Church Dogmatics I/1.* Translated by Geoffrey Bromiley. Edited by Geoffrey W. Bromiley and Thomas F. Torrance. Edinburgh: T&T Clark, 1975.

———. *Church Dogmatics III/1.* Edited by Geoffrey Bromiley and Thomas F. Torrance. Edinburgh: T&T Clark, 1958.

———. *Church Dogmatics III/2.* Edited by Geoffrey Bromiley and Thomas F. Torrance. Edinburgh: T&T Clark, 1960.

———. *The Epistle to the Romans.* Translated by Edwyn C. Hoskyns. London: Oxford University Press, 1933.

_____. *The Göttingen Dogmatics: Instruction in Christian Religion.* Vol. 1. Translated by Geoffrey Bromiley. Edinburgh: T&T Clark, 1991.

———. *Die kirchliche Dogmatik III/1.* Zollikon-Zürich: Evangelischer Verlag, 1945.

Barthes, Roland. *S/Z.* Translated by Richard Miller. New York: Hill & Wang, 1974.

Bartlett, Truman H. "Auguste Rodin, Sculptor." In Elsen, *Auguste Rodin*, 13–109.

Bauckham, Richard. "Christology Today." *Scriptura* 27 (1988): 20–28.

———. *God and the Crisis of Freedom.* Louisville, Ky.: Westminster John Knox, 2002.

———. "James and the Jerusalem Church." In *The Book of Acts: Palestinian Setting*, edited by Richard Bauckham, 415–80. Grand Rapids: Eerdmans, 1995.

———. *Jesus and the God of Israel: God Crucified and Other Studies on the New Testament's Christology of Divine Identity.* Grand Rapids: Eerdmans, 2008.

———. *The Theology of the Book of Revelation.* New Testament Theology. Cambridge: Cambridge University Press, 1993.

Bauckham, Richard, and Trevor Hart. *Hope against Hope: Christian Eschatology at the Turn of the Millennium.* Grand Rapids: Eerdmans, 1999.

Baudrillard, Jean. *Simulacra and Simulation.* Translated by Sheila Faria Glaser. Ann Arbor: University of Michigan Press, 1994.

Becker, Howard S. "Arts and Crafts." *American Journal of Sociology* 83, no. 4 (1978): 862–89.

Becks-Malorny, Ulrike. *Wassily Kandinsky.* London: Taschen, 2007.

Begbie, Jeremy S. *Theology, Music and Time.* Edited by Colin Gunton and Daniel Hardy. Cambridge Studies in Christian Doctrine. Cambridge: Cambridge University Press, 2000.

Benjamin, Walter. *Illuminations.* London: Pimlico, 1999.

Berdyaev, Nicholas. *The Destiny of Man*. Translated by Natalie Duddington. London: Geoffrey Bles, 1937.

———. *The Meaning of History*. London: Geoffrey Bles, 1936.

Berger, Peter, and Thomas Luckmann. *The Social Construction of Reality: A Treatise in the Sociology of Knowledge*. London: Penguin, 1967.

Berlin, Isaiah. *The Roots of Romanticism*. London: Pimlico, 2000.

Bernhardt, W. "Bara." In *Theological Dictionary of the Old Testament*, vol. 2, edited by G. Johannes Botterweck and Helmer Ringgren, 242–49. Grand Rapids: Eerdmans, 1990.

Berry, Wendell. *The Art of the Commonplace: The Agrarian Essays of Wendell Berry*. Berkeley, Calif.: Counterpoint, 2002.

Blenkinsopp, Joseph. *Isaiah 40–55*. Edited by William Foxwell Albright and David Noel Freedman. The Anchor Bible. New York: Doubleday, 2002.

Blunt, Anthony. *Artistic Theory in Italy 1450–1600*. Oxford: Clarendon, 1962.

Boden, Margaret A. *The Creative Mind: Myths and Mechanisms*. 2nd ed. London: Routledge, 2004.

———, ed. *Dimensions of Creativity*. Cambridge, Mass.: MIT Press, 1996.

———. "What Is Creativity?" In Boden, *Dimensions of Creativity*, 75–117.

Bohm, David. *On Creativity*. Routledge Classics ed. London: Routledge, 2004.

Boorstin, Daniel. *The Image: A Guide to Pseudo-events in America*. New York: Vintage, 1992.

Boyd, Richard. "Metaphor and Theory Change: What Is 'Metaphor' a Metaphor For?" In *Metaphor and Thought*, edited by Andrew Ortony, 481–532. Cambridge: Cambridge University Press, 1993.

Bratsiotis, N. P. "Bāśār." In *Theological Dictionary of the Old Testament*, vol. 2, edited by G. Johannes Botterweck and Helmer Ringgren, 317–32. Grand Rapids: Eerdmans, 1975.

Braun, Herbert. "Plasso, Plasma." In *Theological Dictionary of the New Testament*, vol. 6, edited by Gerhard Friedrich, 254–62. Grand Rapids: Eerdmans, 1968.

Brown, David. *God and Enchantment of Place: Reclaiming Human Experience*. Oxford: Oxford University Press, 2004.

———. *God and Mystery in Words: Experience through Metaphor and Drama*. Oxford: Oxford University Press, 2008.

———. *Tradition and Imagination: Revelation and Change*. Oxford: Oxford University Press, 1999.

Brown, William P. *The Ethos of the Cosmos: The Genesis of Moral Imagination in the Bible*. Grand Rapids: Eerdmans, 1999.

Bruce, F. F. *Commentary on the Book of Acts*. London: Marshall, Morgan & Scott, 1965.

Brueggemann, Walter. *Genesis*. Interpretation. Atlanta: John Knox, 1982.

———. *Theology of the Old Testament: Testimony, Dispute, Advocacy*. Minneapolis: Fortress, 1997.

Buber, Martin. *Good and Evil*. Upper Saddle River, N.J.: Prentice Hall, 1997.

————. *I and Thou*. Translated by Ronald Gregor Smith. Edinburgh: T&T Clark, 1937.

Buchler, Justus, ed. *Philosophical Writings of Peirce*. New York: Dover, 1955.

Butler, Ruth. "Introduction." In *Rodin in Perspective*, edited by Ruth Butler. Eaglewood Cliffs, N.J.: Prentice-Hall, 1980.

————. *Rodin: The Shape of Genius*. New Haven, Conn.: Yale University Press, 1993.

Caird, G. B. *The Language and Imagery of the Bible*. London: Duckworth, 1980.

Calvin, John. *Commentaries on the First Book of Moses Called Genesis*. Vol. 1. Translated by Rev. John King. Edinburgh: Calvin Translation Society, 1848.

————. *Institutes of the Christian Religion*. Edited by John Baillie, John T. McNeill, and Henry P. van Dusen. The Library of Christian Classics 21. Philadelphia: Westminster, 1960.

Camfield, William A. "Marcel Duchamp's *Fountain:* Its History and Aesthetics in the Context of 1917." In *Marcel Duchamp: Artist of the Century*, edited by Rudolf Kuenzli and Francis M. Naumann, 64–94. Cambridge, Mass.: MIT Press, 1990.

Carey, John. *What Good Are the Arts?* London: Faber & Faber, 2005.

Carpenter, Humphrey. *J. R. R. Tolkien: A Biography*. London: HarperCollins, 2002.

Cars, Laurence des. "Gérôme: Painter of Histories." In Cars, Font-Réaulx, and Papet, *Spectacular Art of Jean-Léon Gérôme*, 25–38.

Cars, Laurence des, Dominique de Font-Réaulx, and Édouard Papet, eds. *The Spectacular Art of Jean-Léon Gérôme*. Paris: Skira, 2010.

Cassirer, Ernst. *The Individual and the Cosmos in Renaissance Philosophy*. Mineola, N.Y.: Dover, 2000.

Cennini, Cennino d'Andrea. *The Craftsman's Handbook: "Il Libro dell' Arte."* Translated by Daniel V. Thompson. New York: Dover, 1954.

Chase, Stuart. *The Tyranny of Words*. London: Methuen, 1938.

Childs, Brevard. *Exodus: A Commentary*. Old Testament Library. London: SCM Press, 1974.

Childs, Peter. *Modernism*. London: Routledge, 2000.

Chipp, Herschel B. *Theories of Modern Art*. Berkeley: University of California Press, 1968.

Clark, Tony. *Divine Revelation and Human Practice: Responsive and Imaginative Participation*. Eugene, Ore.: Cascade, 2008.

Cohen Stuart, G. H. *The Struggle in Man between Good and Evil: An Inquiry into the Origin of the Rabbinic Concept of Yeser Hara*. Kampen: Uitgeversmaatschappij J. H. Kok, 1984.

Coleridge, Samuel Taylor. *Biographia Literaria; or, Biographical Sketches of My Literary Life and Opinions*. Edited by James Engell and W. Jackson Bate. Vol. 7 of *The Collected Works of Samuel Taylor Coleridge*. Princeton, N.J.: Princeton University Press, 1983.

Collingwood, R. G. "Plato's Philosophy of Art." *Mind: A Quarterly Review of Philosophy and Psychology* 34 (1925): 154–72.

———. *The Principles of Art*. Oxford: Clarendon, 1938. Reprint, London: Oxford University Press, 1958.

Comte-Sponville, André. *A Short Treatise on the Great Virtues: The Uses of Philosophy in Everyday Life*. London: William Heinemann, 2002.

Conrad, Peter. *Creation: Artists, Gods and Origins*. London: Thames & Hudson, 2007.

Copleston, Frederick. *A History of Philosophy*. Vol. 7. New York: Image Books, 1965.

Cranfield, C. E. B. *A Critical and Exegetical Commentary on the Epistle to the Romans*. Vol. 2. International Critical Commentary. Edinburgh: T&T Clark, 1979.

Culler, Jonathan. *On Deconstruction: Theory and Criticism after Structuralism*. London: Routledge & Kegan Paul, 1983.

Dalferth, Ingolf U. *Becoming Present: An Inquiry into the Christian Sense of the Presence of God*. Leuven: Peeters, 2006.

Danto, Arthur C. *Andy Warhol*. New Haven, Conn.: Yale University Press, 2009.

Delbanco, Nicholas. "In Praise of Imitation." *Harper's Magazine*, July 2002, 57–63.

Derrida, Jacques. *Of Grammatology*. Translated by Gayatri Chakravorty Spivak. Baltimore: Johns Hopkins University Press, 1976.

Dissanayake, Ellen. *Homo Aestheticus: Where Art Comes from and Why*. Seattle: University of Washington Press, 1995.

Dixon, Laurinda. *Bosch*. London: Phaidon, 2003.

Donaldson, J., and A. Roberts, eds. *Ante Nicene Fathers: Translations of the Writings of the Fathers down to AD 325*. Buffalo, N.Y., 1885.

Dunn, James D. G. *Romans 9–16*. Word Biblical Commentary. Dallas: Word Books, 1988.

Durham, John I. *Exodus*. Word Biblical Commentary. Waco, Tex.: Word Books, 1987.

Eagleton, Terry. *Literary Theory: An Introduction*. Oxford: Blackwell, 1983.

Eichrodt, Walther. *Theology of the Old Testament*. Vol. 2. Translated by J. A. Baker. London: SCM Press, 1967.

Eliot, T. S. *The Complete Poems and Plays of T. S. Eliot*. London: Book Club Associates, 1977.

Elsen, Albert, ed. *Auguste Rodin: Readings on His Life and Work*. Eaglewood Cliffs, N.J.: Prentice-Hall, 1965.

———. *Rodin's Gates of Hell*. Minneapolis: University of Minnesota Press, 1960.

Farmer, Herbert H. *The World and God: A Study of Prayer, Providence and Miracle in Christian Experience*. London: Nisbet, 1936.

Feuerbach, Ludwig. *The Essence of Christianity*. Translated by George Eliot. New York: Harper & Row, 1957.

Ficino, Marsilio. "Platonic Theology Books V–VIII." In *Marsilio Ficino: Platonic Theology*, edited by Michael J. B. Allen and James Hankins, 2. Cambridge, Mass.: Harvard University Press, 2002.

———. "Platonic Theology Books XII–XIV." In *Marsilio Ficino: Platonic Theology*, edited by Michael J. B. Allen and James Hankins, 4. Cambridge, Mass.: Harvard University Press, 2004.

Fiddes, Paul. *Freedom and Limit: A Dialogue between Literature and Christian Doctrine*. Basingstoke, U.K.: Macmillan, 1991.

Foerster, Werner. "Ktizo, Ktisis, Ktisma, Ktistes." In *Theological Dictionary of the New Testament*, vol. 3, edited by Gerhard Kittel, 1000–1035. Grand Rapids: Eerdmans, 1965.

Font-Réaulx, Dominique de. "Gérôme and Photography: Accurate Depictions of an Imagined World." In Cars, Font-Réaulx, and Papet, *Spectacular Art of Jean-Léon Gérôme*, 213–21.

Fowler, H. N., ed. *Plato: Euthyphro, Apology, Crito, Phaedo, Phaedrus*. Loeb Classical Library. London: Heinemann, 1913.

Fretheim, Terence. *Exodus*. Interpretation. Louisville, Ky.: John Knox, 1991.

———. *God and World in the Old Testament: A Relational Theology of Creation*. Nashville: Abingdon, 2005.

Fulcher, James. *Capitalism: A Very Short Introduction*. Oxford: Oxford University Press, 2004.

Gardner, W. H., ed. *Poems and Prose of Gerard Manley Hopkins*. London: Penguin, 1953.

Gaut, Berys. "Creativity and Imagination." In *The Creation of Art: New Essays in Philosophical Aesthetics*, edited by Berys Gaut and Paisley Livingston, 148–73. Cambridge: Cambridge University Press, 2003.

Girard, René. *Things Hidden since the Foundation of the World*. Stanford, Calif.: Stanford University Press, 1987.

Gombrich, Ernst H. *Art and Illusion: A Study in the Psychology of Pictorial Representation*. 5th ed. London: Phaidon, 1977.

———. *The Image and the Eye: Further Studies in the Psychology of Pictorial Representation*. London: Phaidon, 1982.

Goodman, Nelson. *Languages of Art: An Approach to a Theory of Symbols*. London: Oxford University Press, 1969.

Green, Garrett. *Imagining God: Theology and the Religious Imagination*. San Francisco: Harper & Row, 1989.

Greenberg, Robert. *How to Listen to Great Music: A Guide to Its History, Culture and Heart*. New York: Plume, 2011.

Grunfeld, Frederick V. *Rodin: A Biography*. New York: Da Capo, 1987.

Gunton, Colin. *The Actuality of Atonement: A Study of Metaphor, Rationality and the Christian Tradition*. Edinburgh: T&T Clark, 1988.

—————. *The Triune Creator: A Historical and Systematic Study*. Grand Rapids: Eerdmans, 1998.

Guyer, Paul. "History of Modern Aesthetics." In *The Oxford Handbook of Aesthetics*, edited by Jerrold Levinson, 25–60. Oxford: Oxford University Press, 2003.

Hamann, Johann Georg. *Writings on Philosophy and Language*. Translated by Kenneth Haynes. Cambridge: Cambridge University Press, 2007.

Hardy, Daniel W. "Coleridge on the Trinity." *Anglican Theological Review* 69 (1988): 145–55.

Harrison, Charles, Paul Wood, and Jason Gaiger, eds. *Art in Theory 1815–1900: An Anthology of Changing Ideas*. Oxford: Blackwell, 1998.

Hart, Kevin. *The Trespass of the Sign: Deconstruction, Theology and Philosophy*. Cambridge: Cambridge University Press, 1989.

Hart, Rachel. "Tolkien, St Andrews, and Dragons." In *Tree of Tales: Tolkien, Literature and Theology*, edited by Trevor Hart and Ivan Khovacs, 1–11. Waco, Tex.: Baylor University Press, 2007.

Hart, Trevor. *Between the Image and the Word: Theological Engagements with Imagination, Language and Literature*. Farnham, U.K.: Ashgate, 2013.

—————. "Complicating Presence: Interdisciplinary Perspectives on a Theological Question." In *Divine Presence and Absence in Exilic and Post-exilic Judaism*, edited by Nathan MacDonald and Izaak J. de Hulster, 1–21. Tübingen: Mohr Siebeck, 2013.

—————. *Faith Thinking: The Dynamics of Christian Theology*. London: SPCK, 1995.

—————. "Sinlessness and Moral Responsibility: A Problem in Christology." *Scottish Journal of Theology* 48, no. 1 (1995): 37–54.

—————. "Finitude and What Is Withheld: A Critical Comparison of Eschatological Imagining in Karl Barth and John Hick." *Zeitschrift für dialektische Theologie* 18, no. 1 (2002): 9–25.

—————. "Poetry and Theology in Milton's *Paradise Lost*." In *Genesis and Christian Theology*, edited by Nathan MacDonald, Mark Elliott, and Grant Macaskill, 129–39. Grand Rapids: Eerdmans, 2012.

—————. "Protestantism and the Arts." In *The Blackwell Companion to Protestantism*, edited by Alister McGrath and Darren Marks, 268–86. Oxford: Blackwell, 2004.

—————. *Regarding Karl Barth: Essays toward a Reading of His Theology*. Carlisle, U.K.: Paternoster, 1999.

—————. "Through the Arts: Hearing, Seeing and Touching the Truth." In *Beholding the Glory*, edited by Jeremy S. Begbie, 1–26. London: Darton, Longman & Todd, 2000.

—————. "Tolkien, Creation and Creativity." In Hart and Khovacs, *Tree of Tales*, 39–53.

—————. "Who Am I? Imagination and the God of *Biographia Literaria*." *Coleridge Bulletin* 38 (2011): 53–66.

Hart, Trevor, and Ivan Khovacs. *Tree of Tales: Tolkien, Literature and Theology*. Waco, Tex.: Baylor University Press, 2007.

Heidegger, Martin. *Being and Time*. Translated by John Macquarrie and Edward Robinson. Oxford: Blackwell, 1962.

Heller, Agnes. *Renaissance Man*. Translated by Richard E. Allen. London: Routledge & Kegan Paul, 1978.

Henley, W. E. "Two Busts of Victor Hugo." *Magazine of Art* (1884).

Hick, John. *Evil and the God of Love*. London: Macmillan, 1966.

Holmes, Richard. *Coleridge: Early Visions*. London: Hodder & Stoughton, 1989.

————, ed. *Samuel Taylor Coleridge: Selected Poems*. London: Penguin, 1996.

Holmes, Stephen. *Listening to the Past: The Place of Tradition in Theology*. Grand Rapids: Baker Academic, 2002.

Holsinger-Friesen, Thomas. *Irenaeus and Genesis: A Study of Competition in Early Christian Hermeneutics*. Journal of Theological Interpretation Supplements. Winona Lake, Ind.: Eisenbrauns, 2009.

Hopkins, Gerard Manlely. "Pied Beauty." In *Poems and Prose of Gerard Manley Hopkins*, edited by W. H. Gardner. London: Penguin, 1953.

Hume, David. *A Treatise of Human Nature*. 2nd ed. Oxford: Clarendon, 1978.

Hyde, Lewis. *Common as Air: Revolution, Art and Ownership*. London: Union Books, 2010.

————. *The Gift: How the Creative Spirit Transforms the World*. Edinburgh: Canongate, 2006.

Jacobi, Jolande, ed. *Paracelsus: Selected Writings*. Translated by Norman Guterman. Princeton, N.J.: Princeton University Press, 1951.

Jamison, Kay Redfield. *Touched with Fire: Manic-Depressive Illness and the Artistic Temperament*. New York: Simon & Schuster, 1993.

Jansen, H. W., and Anthony F. Jansen. *History of Art: The Western Tradition*. Rev. 6th ed. Upper Saddle River, N.J.: Pearson Prentice Hall, 2004.

Jenson, Matt. *The Gravity of Sin: Augustine, Luther and Barth on* Homo Incurvatus in Se. London: T&T Clark, 2007.

Jenson, Robert W. "Aspects of a Doctrine of Creation." In *The Doctrine of Creation: Essays in Dogmatics, History and Philosophy*, edited by Colin E. Gunton, 17–28. London: T&T Clark, 1997.

Johnson, Mark. *The Body in the Mind: The Bodily Basis of Meaning, Imagination and Reason*. Chicago: University of Chicago Press, 1987.

Jones, David. *Epoch and Artist*. London: Faber & Faber, 1959.

Jongh, E. de. *Questions of Meaning: Theme and Motif in Dutch Seventeenth-Century Painting*. Translated by Michael Hoyle. Leiden: Primavera Pers, 1995.

Kandinsky, Wassily. *Concerning the Spiritual in Art*. Translated by M. T. H. Sadler. Mineola, N.Y.: Dover, 1977.

Kant, Immanuel. *Critique of Judgment*. Translated by Werner S. Pluhar. Indianapolis: Hackett, 1987.

————. *Critique of Pure Reason.* Translated by Norman Kemp Smith. London: Macmillan, 1929.

Kaufman, Gordon D. *The Theological Imagination: Constructing the Concept of God.* Philadelphia: Westminster, 1981.

Kearney, Richard. *The Wake of Imagination: Toward a Postmodern Culture.* London: Routledge, 1988.

Keats, John. *The Poetical Works of John Keats.* London: Frederick Warne, 1892.

Kemp, Martin. "From 'Mimesis' to 'Fantasia': The Quattrocento Vocabulary of Creation, Inspiration and Genius in the Visual Arts." *Viator: Medieval and Renaissance Studies* 8 (1977): 347–98.

————. "Leonardo and the Idea of Naturalism: Leonardo's Hypernaturalism." In *Painters of Reality: The Legacy of Leonardo and Caravaggio in Lombardy,* edited by Andrea Bayer, 65–73. New Haven, Conn.: Yale University Press, 2004.

————, ed. *Leonardo on Painting: An Anthology of Writings by Leonardo da Vinci with a Selection of Documents Relating to His Career as an Artist.* New Haven, Conn.: Yale University Press, 1989.

Koch, Hugo. "Zur Lehre vom Urstand und von der Erlösung bei Irenaeus." *Theologische Studien und Kritiken* 96–97 (1925): 183–214.

Koehler, Ludwig, and Walter Baumgartner, eds. *The Hebrew and Aramaic Lexicon of the Old Testament.* Translated by M. E. J. Richardson. Rev. ed. Leiden: Brill, 1994.

Koestler, Arthur. *The Act of Creation.* London: Hutchinson, 1964.

Krauss, Rosalind E. *The Originality of the Avant-Garde and Other Modernist Myths.* Cambridge, Mass.: MIT Press, 1986.

Kristeller, Paul Oskar. *Renaissance Concepts of Man and Other Essays.* New York: Harper & Row, 1972.

Kuhn, Thomas. *The Structure of Scientific Revolutions.* 3rd ed. Chicago: University of Chicago Press, 1996.

Lakoff, George, and Mark Johnson. *Metaphors We Live By.* 2nd ed. Chicago: University of Chicago Press, 2003.

Lamb, W. R. M., ed. *Plato: Lysis, Symposium, Gorgias.* Loeb Classical Library. Cambridge, Mass.: Harvard University Press, 1925.

Lampert, Catherine. "Introduction: Rodin's Nature." In Lampert et al., *Rodin,* 15–25.

Lampert, Catherine, Antoinette Le Normand-Romain, Norman Rosenthal, and MaryAnne Stevens, eds. *Rodin.* London: Royal Academy, 2007.

Lane, William L. *Hebrews 1–8.* Word Biblical Commentary. Dallas: Word Books, 1991.

Lange, Nicholas de. *An Introduction to Judaism.* Cambridge: Cambridge University Press, 2000.

Langer, Susanne K. *Philosophy in a New Key: A Study in the Symbolism of Reason, Rite, and Art.* 3rd ed. Cambridge, Mass.: Harvard University Press, 1956.

Lash, Nicholas. *The Beginning and End of 'Religion.'* Cambridge: Cambridge University Press, 1996.

Lehrer, Jonah. *Imagine: How Creativity Works.* Edinburgh: Canongate, 2012.

Levenson, Jon D. *Creation and the Persistence of Evil: The Jewish Drama of Divine Omnipotence.* 2nd ed. Princeton, N.J.: Princeton University Press, 1994.

Lewis, C. Day. *The Poetic Image.* London: Jonathan Cape, 1947.

Lewis, C. S. *An Experiment in Criticism.* Cambridge: Cambridge University Press, 1961.

Lotman, Yu. M., and B. A. Uspensky. "On the Semiotic Mechanism of Culture." *New Literary History* 9, no. 2 (1978): 211–32.

Lubart, Todd I. "Creativity across Cultures." In Sternberg, *Handbook of Creativity*, 339–50.

Lucie-Smith, Edward. *The Story of Craft: The Craftsman's Role in Society.* Oxford: Phaidon, 1981.

Lundbom, Jack R. *Jeremiah 1–20.* The Anchor Bible. New York: Doubleday, 1999.

MacDonald, George. *A Dish of Orts, Chiefly Papers on the Imagination, and on Shakespeare.* London: Sampson Low Marston, 1895.

MacIntyre, Alasdair. *After Virtue: A Study in Moral Theory.* London: Duckworth, 1981.

Macmurray, John. *Interpreting the Universe.* London: Faber, 1935.

Macquarrie, John. *Existentialism.* London: Penguin, 1973.

Magee, Brian. *The Tristan Chord: Wagner and Philosophy.* New York: Metropolitan Books, 2000.

Mair, Roslin. "The Choir Capitals of Canterbury Cathedral 1174–84." In *The British Archaeological Association Conference Transactions for the Year 1979*, vol. 5, *Medieval Art and Architecture at Canterbury before 1220*. British Archaeological Association and Kent Archaeological Society, 1982.

Makariou, Sophie, and Charlotte Maury. "The Paradox of Realism: Gérôme in the Orient." In Cars, Font-Réaulx, and Papet, *Spectacular Art of Jean-Léon Gérôme*, 259–65.

Malingue, Maurice, ed. *Lettres de Gauguin a sa femme et a ses amis.* Paris: Bernard Grasset, 1946.

Malraux, André. *The Voices of Silence.* Princeton, N.J.: Princeton University Press, 1978.

Manson, William. *The Epistle to the Hebrews: An Historical and Theological Reconsideration; The Baird Lecture, 1949.* London: Hodder & Stoughton, 1951.

Maritain, Jacques. *Art and Scholasticism with Other Essays.* Translated by J. F. Scanlon. London: Sheed & Ward, 1930.

———. *Creative Intuition in Art and Poetry.* London: Harvill, 1953.

———. *True Humanism.* 3rd ed. London: Geoffrey Bles, 1941.

Mauss, Marcel. *The Gift: Forms and Functions of Exchange in Archaic Societies.* Translated by Ian Cunnison. New York: W. W. Norton, 1967.

May, Gerhard. *Creatio ex Nihilo: The Doctrine of "Creation Out of Nothing" in Early Christian Thought*. Edinburgh: T&T Clark, 1994.

Mayhew, Robert, and David C. Mirhady, eds. *Aristotle: Problems, Books 20–38; Rhetoric to Alexander*. Loeb Classical Library. Cambridge, Mass.: Harvard University Press, 2011.

McCormack, Bruce. "Divine Revelation and Human Imagination: Must We Choose between the Two?" *Scottish Journal of Theology* 37, no. 4 (1984): 431–455.

McFague, Sallie. *Metaphorical Theology: Models of God in Religious Language*. Philadelphia: Fortress, 1982.

McKane, William. *A Critical and Exegetical Commentary on Jeremiah*. Vol. 1. International Critical Commentary. Edinburgh: T&T Clark, 1986.

McKeown, Richard, ed. *The Basic Works of Aristotle*. New York: Random House, 2001.

Methodist Conference Office. *The Methodist Hymn Book*. London: Methodist Conference Office, 1933.

Mettinger, Tryggve N. D. *No Graven Image? Israelite Aniconism in Its Ancient Near Eastern Context*. Stockholm: Almqvist & Wiksell, 1995.

Michel, Otto. "Oikos, Oikodomos, Oikodomeo, Etc." In *Theological Dictionary of the New Testament*, vol. 5, edited by Gerhard Friedrich, 119–59. Grand Rapids: Eerdmans, 1967.

Middleton, J. Richard. *The Liberating Image: The* Imago Dei *in Genesis 1*. Grand Rapids: Brazos, 2005.

Milbank, John. "Can a Gift Be Given? Prolegomena to a Future Trinitarian Metaphysic." *Modern Theology* 11, no. 1 (1995): 119–61.

Moltmann, Jürgen. *The Crucified God*. London: SCM Press, 1976.

———. *God in Creation: An Ecological Doctrine of Creation*. Translated by Margaret Kohl. London: SCM Press, 1985.

———. *Theology and Joy*. London: SCM Press, 1973.

Moule, C. F. D. "Sanctuary and Sacrifice in the Church of the New Testament." *Journal of Theological Studies*, n.s. 1 (1950): 29–41.

Murdoch, Iris. *Existentialists and Mystics: Writings on Philosophy and Literature*. London: Penguin, 1999.

———. *Metaphysics as a Guide to Morals*. London: Vintage, 2003.

National Advisory Committee on Creative and Cultural Education (NACCCE). *All Our Futures: Creativity, Culture and Education* (1999). Online.

Nettle, Daniel. *Strong Imagination: Madness, Creativity and Human Nature*. Oxford: Oxford University Press, 2001.

Nichols, Aidan. *Redeeming Beauty: Soundings in Sacral Aesthetics*. Ashgate Studies in Theology, Imagination and the Arts. Aldershot, U.K.: Ashgate, 2007.

Normand-Romain, Antoinette Le. *Rodin: The Gates of Hell*. Paris: Musée Rodin, 2002.

———. "The Gates of Hell: The Crucible." In Lampert et al., *Rodin*, 55–63.

———. "The Greatest of Living Sculptors." In Lampert et al., *Rodin*, 29–38.

O'Hear, Anthony. *The Element of Fire: Science, Art and the Human World*. London: Routledge, 1988.

O'Donovan, Oliver. *Resurrection and Moral Order: An Outline for Evangelical Ethics*. Leicester, U.K.: InterVarsity, 1986.

Osborn, Eric. *Irenaeus of Lyons*. Cambridge: Cambridge University Press, 2001.

Osgood, Charles E., George J. Suci, and Percy H. Tannenbaum. *The Measurement of Meaning*. Urbana: University of Illinois Press, 1957.

Otzen, B. "Yatsar." In *Theological Dictionary of the Old Testament*, vol. 6, edited by G. Johannes Botterweck and Helmer Ringgren, 257–65. Grand Rapids: Eerdmans, 1990.

Pagel, Mark. *Wired for Culture: The Natural History of Human Cooperation*. London: Allen Lane, 2012.

Pannenberg, Wolfhart. *Systematic Theology*. Vol. 2. Edinburgh: T&T Clark, 1994.

Panofsky, Erwin. *Idea: A Concept in Art Theory*. Translated by Joseph J. S. Peake. Columbia: University of South Carolina Press, 1968.

———. *Renaissance and Renascences in Western Art*. New York: Harper & Row, 1972.

Paul, Shalom M. "Creation and Cosmogony in the Bible." In *Encyclopedia Judaica*, vol. 5, edited by Cecil Roth, 1059–63. Jerusalem: Keters, 1971.

Pieper, Josef. *Leisure: The Basis of Culture*. Translated by Gerald Malsbary. South Bend, Ind.: St Augustine's, 1998.

Plato. *The Republic*. Translated by Desmond Lee. London: Penguin, 1974.

———. *Timaeus and Critias*. Translated by Desmond Lee. London: Penguin, 1971.

Pliny. *Natural History: Books 33–35*. Translated by H. Rackham. Cambridge, Mass.: Harvard University Press, 1952.

Plucker, Jonathan A., and Joseph S. Renzulli. "Psychometric Approaches to the Study of Human Creativity." In Sternberg, *Handbook of Creativity*, 35–61.

Polanyi, Michael. *Personal Knowledge: Towards a Post-critical Philosophy*. London: Routledge & Kegan Paul, 1958.

———. *The Tacit Dimension*. London: Routledge and Kegan Paul, 1967.

Pope, Rob. *Creativity: Theory, History, Practice*. London: Routledge, 2005.

Propp, William H. C. *Exodus 19–40*. The Anchor Bible. New York: Doubleday, 2006.

Rahner, Hugo. *Der spielende Mensch*. Einsiedeln, Switz.: Johannes Verlag, 1952.

Renié, Pierre-Lin. "Gérôme: Working in the Era of Industrial Reproduction." In Cars, Font-Réaulx, and Papet, *Spectacular Art of Jean-Léon Gérôme*, 173–78.

Reynolds, Barbara. *Dorothy L. Sayers: Her Life and Soul*. London: Hodder & Stoughton, 1993.

Ricoeur, Paul. *Oneself as Another*. Chicago: University of Chicago Press, 1992.

———. *The Rule of Metaphor: Multidisciplinary Studies of the Creation of Meaning in Language.* Translated by R. Czerny with Kathleen McLaughlin and John Costello, S.J. Toronto: Toronto University Press, 1977.

———. *The Symbolism of Evil.* Boston: Beacon, 1967.

———. *Time and Narrative.* Vol. 1. Translated by Kathleen McLaughlin and David Pellauer. Chicago: University of Chicago Press, 1984.

Ridderbos, Nic. H. "Genesis i 1 und 2." *Oudtestamentische Studien* 12 (1958): 214–60.

Rilke, Rainer Maria. "Auguste Rodin." In Elsen, *Auguste Rodin*, 110–44.

Risatti, Howard. *A Theory of Craft: Function and Aesthetic Expression.* Chapel Hill: University of North Carolina Press, 2007.

Robbins Landon, H. C. "The Concertos: (2) Their Musical Origin and Development." In *The Mozart Companion*, edited by H. C. Robbins Landon and Donald Mitchell, 234–82. London: Faber, 1965.

Ross, David. *Aristotle.* London: Methuen, 1964.

Rothko, Mark. *Writings on Art.* New Haven, Conn.: Yale University Press, 2005.

———. *The Artist's Reality: Philosophies of Art.* New Haven, Conn.: Yale University Press, 2004.

Rousseau, Adelin et al., eds. *Irénée de Lyon Contre Les Hérésies.* In *Sources Chrétiennes.* Paris: Éditions du Cerf, 1965–1982.

Runco, Mark A. *Creativity: Theories and Themes; Research, Development, and Practice.* London: Academic, 2007.

Runco, Mark A., and Steven R. Pritzker, eds. *Encyclopedia of Creativity.* 2 vols. London: Academic, 1999.

Ruskin, John. *Modern Painters.* Vol. 2. London: George Allen, 1904.

———. *Modern Painters.* Vol. 3. London: George Allen, 1904.

———. *The Seven Lamps of Architecture.* Vol. 8 of *The Complete Works of John Ruskin*, edited by E. T. Cook and Alexander Wedderburn. London: George Allen, 1903.

Russell, Bertrand. *What I Believe.* London: Kegan Paul, Trench Trubner, 1925.

Ryken, Leland. *The Liberated Imagination: Thinking Christianly about the Arts.* Eugene, Ore.: Wipf & Stock, 2005.

Sacks, Jonathan. *To Heal a Fractured World: The Ethics of Responsibility.* London: Continuum, 2005.

Saporta, Sol. Review of *The Measurement of Meaning,* by Charles E. Osgood, George J. Suci, and Percy H. Tannenbaum. In *American Anthropologist* 61, no. 1 (1959): 159–60.

Sartre, Jean-Paul. *Existentialism and Humanism.* London: Methuen, 1948.

———. *The Imaginary: A Phenomenological Psychology of the Imagination.* Translated by Jonathan Webber. London: Routledge, 2004.

Sawyer, R. Keith. *Explaining Creativity: The Science of Human Innovation.* Oxford: Oxford University Press, 2006.

Sayers, Dorothy L. *Begin Here: A War-Time Essay*. London: Victor Gollancz, 1940.

———. *Catholic Tales and Christian Songs*. Oxford: Blackwell, 1918.

———. *The Letters of Dorothy L. Sayers*. Vol. 1, *1899–1936: The Making of a Detective Novelist*, edited by Barbara Reynolds. New York: St Martin's, 1995.

_____. *The Letters of Dorothy L. Sayers*. Vol. 2, *1937–1943: From Novelist to Playwright*, edited by Barbara Reynolds. Cambridge: Dorothy L. Sayers Society, 1997.

———. *The Mind of the Maker*. London: Methuen, 1941.

———. "Towards a Christian Aesthetic." In *Our Culture: Its Christian Roots and Present Crisis*, edited by V. A. Demant, 50–69. London: SPCK, 1947.

———. *The Zeal of Thy House*. London: Harcourt, Brace, 1937.

Scarry, Elaine. *On Beauty and Being Just*. Princeton, N.J.: Princeton University Press, 1999.

Schaeffer, Francis. *Art and the Bible*. 2nd ed. Downers Grove, Ill.: InterVarsity, 2007.

Schama, Simon. *Rembrandt's Eyes*. London: Penguin, 1999.

Scholem, Gershom. *Major Trends in Jewish Mysticism*. New York: Schocken Books, 1941.

———. *The Messianic Idea in Judaism: And Other Essays on Jewish Spirituality*. New York: Schocken Books, 1995 [1971].

Schopenhauer, Arthur. *The World as Will and Representation*. Vol. 1. Translated by E. F. J. Payne. New York: Dover, 1966.

———. *The World as Will and Representation*. Vol. 2. Translated by E. F. J. Payne. New York: Dover, 1966.

Schweizer, E., and R. Meyer. "Sarx." In *Theological Dictionary of the New Testament*, vol. 7, edited by Gerhard Kittel, 98–151. Grand Rapids: Eerdmans, 1971.

Searle, Alison. *"The Eyes of Your Heart": Literary and Theological Trajectories of Imagining Biblically*. Milton Keynes, U.K.: Paternoster, 2008.

Seerveld, Calvin. *Rainbows for the Fallen World: Aesthetic Life and Artistic Task*. Toronto: Tuppence Press, 1980.

Sennett, Richard. *The Craftsman*. London: Penguin, 2008.

Sharples, Mike. *How We Write: Writing as Creative Design*. London: Routledge, 1999.

Sidney, Sir Philip. *An Apology for Poetry; or, The Defence of Poesy*. Edited by Geoffrey Shepherd. London: Thomas Nelson & Sons, 1965.

Simon, Marcel. "St Stephen and the Jerusalem Temple." *Journal of Ecclesiastical History* 2, no. 1 (1951): 127–42.

Soloveitchik, Joseph. *Halakhic Man*. Translated by Lawrence Kaplan. Philadelphia: Jewish Publication Society of America, 1983.

Somervill, Barbara A. *Michelangelo: Sculptor and Painter*. Minneapolis: Compass Point Books, 2005.

Sontag, Susan. *On Photography*. London: Penguin, 1979.

Soskice, Janet M. *Metaphor and Religious Language*. Oxford: Clarendon, 1985.

Speiser, E. A. *Genesis*. Edited by William Foxwell Albright and David Noel Freedman. The Anchor Bible. New York: Doubleday, 1964.

Spufford, Francis. *Unapologetic: Why, Despite Everything, Christianity Can Still Make Surprising, Emotional Sense*. London: Faber & Faber, 2012.

Stam, James H. *Inquiries into the Origin of Language: The Fate of a Question*. New York: Harper & Row, 1976.

Steiner, George. *After Babel: Aspects of Language and Translation*. 2nd ed. Oxford: Oxford University Press, 1992.

———. *Grammars of Creation*. London: Faber & Faber, 2001.

———. *Real Presences: Is There Anything in What We Say?* London: Faber & Faber, 1989.

Sternberg, Robert J., ed. *Handbook of Creativity*. Cambridge: Cambridge University Press, 1999.

Sternberg, Robert J., and Todd I. Lubart. "The Concept of Creativity: Prospects and Paradigms." In Sternberg, *Handbook of Creativity*, 3–15.

Strawson, P. F. "Imagination and Perception." In *Experience and Theory*, edited by Lawrence Foster and J. W. Swanson. London: Duckworth, 1970.

Taylor, Charles. *Modern Social Imaginaries*. Durham, N.C.: Duke University Press, 2004.

———. *A Secular Age*. Cambridge, Mass.: Harvard University Press, 2007.

———. *Sources of the Self: The Making of Modern Identity*. Cambridge: Cambridge University Press, 1989.

Thiselton, Anthony. *The Hermeneutics of Doctrine*. Grand Rapids: Eerdmans, 2007.

Thomas Aquinas, Saint. *Summa Theologiae*. Vol. 3, *Knowing and Naming God (1a. 12–13)*. Edited by Herbert McCabe, O.P. London: Blackfriars in conjunction with Eyre and Spottiswoode, 1964.

———. *Summa Theologiae*. Vol. 8, *Creation, Variety, and Evil (1a. 44–49)*. Edited by Thomas Gilby, O.P. London: Blackfriars in conjunction with Eyre & Spottiswoode, 1967.

Tigerstedt, E. N. "The Poet as Creator: Origins of a Metaphor." *Comparative Literature Studies*, no. 5 (1968): 455–88.

Tolkien, J. R. R. *The Letters of J. R. R. Tolkien*. Edited by Humphrey Carpenter. Boston: Houghton Mifflin, 1981.

———. *The Silmarillion*. London: George Allen & Unwin, 1977.

———. *Tree and Leaf: Including the Poem "Mythopoeia"; "The Homecoming of Beorhtnoth Beorhthelm's Son."* London: HarperCollins, 2001.

Tomkins, Calvin. *Duchamp: A Biography*. London: Chatto & Windus, 1997.

Torrance, Thomas F. *God and Rationality*. London: Oxford University Press, 1971.

———. *The Mediation of Christ*. 2nd ed. Edinburgh: T&T Clark, 1992.

———. *Theological Science*. London: Oxford University Press, 1969.

———. *The Trinitarian Faith: An Evangelical Theology of the Ancient Catholic Church*. Edinburgh: T&T Clark, 1988.

Tovey, Donald. *Essays in Musical Analysis*. Vol. 4. London: Oxford University Press, 1936.

Tredennick, Hugh, ed. *Aristotle: The Metaphysics*. Loeb Classical Library. Cambridge, Mass.: Harvard University Press, 1933.

Treier, Daniel J., Mark Husbands, and Roger Lundin, eds. *The Beauty of God: Theology and the Arts*. Downers Grove, Ill.: InterVarsity, 2007.

Trinkhaus, Charles. *In Our Image and Likeness: Humanity and Divinity in Italian Humanist Thought*. 2 vols. Notre Dame, Ind.: University of Notre Dame Press, 1995.

Trossen, P. C. "Erbauen." *Theologie und Glaube* 6 (1914): 804–12.

Tusa, John. *On Creativity: Interviews Exploring the Process*. London: Methuen, 1994.

Tzara, Tristan. "Lecture on Dada." In *Theories of Modern Art*, edited by Herschel B. Chipp, 385–89. Berkeley: University of California Press, 1968.

Vico, Giambattista. *New Science*. Translated by David Marsh. London: Penguin, 2001.

Volf, Miroslav. *Work in the Spirit*. New York: Oxford University Press, 1991.

von Balthasar, Hans Urs. *The Glory of the Lord: A Theological Aesthetics*. Vol. 2, *Studies in Theological Style: Clerical Styles*. Edinburgh: T&T Clark, 1984.

von Rad, Gerhard. *Genesis: A Commentary*. Translated by John H. Marks. 2nd ed. London: SCM Press, 1963.

———. *Old Testament Theology*. Vol. 1, *The Theology of Israel's Historical Traditions*, translated by D. M. G. Stalker. Edinburgh: Oliver & Boyd, 1962.

Walford, E. John. "The Case for Broken Beauty." In Treier, Husbands, and Lundin, *Beauty of God*, 88–109.

Walton, Kendall. *Mimesis as Make-Believe: On the Foundations of the Representational Arts*. Cambridge, Mass.: Harvard University Press, 1990.

Ward, Graham. *Barth, Derrida and the Language of Theology*. Cambridge: Cambridge University Press, 1995.

Ward, Thomas B., Steven M. Smith, and Ronald A. Finke. "Creative Cognition." In Sternberg, *Handbook of Creativity*, 189–212.

Warnke, Carsten-Peter. *Pablo Picasso*. London: Taschen, 2006.

Warnock, Mary. *Imagination*. London: Faber, 1977.

Weiser, Arthur. *The Psalms: A Commentary*. London: SCM Press, 1962.

Weiss, Jeffrey, ed. *Mark Rothko*. New Haven, Conn.: Yale University Press, 1998.

Welker, Michael. *Creation and Reality*. Minneapolis: Fortress, 1999.

Westermann, Claus. *Genesis 1–11: A Commentary*. Translated by John J. Scullion, S.J. London: SPCK, 1984.

White, Lynn. "The Historical Roots of Our Ecological Crisis." *Science* 155 (1967): 1203–7.

Wilde, Oscar. *The Picture of Dorian Gray*. Penguin Classics ed. London: Penguin, 1985.

Wilder, Amos. *Theopoetic: Theology and the Religious Imagination*. Philadelphia: Fortress, 1976.

Williams, Rowan. *Grace and Necessity: Reflections on Art and Love*. Harrisburg, Pa.: Morehouse, 2005.

Wingren, Gustaf. *Man and the Incarnation: A Study in the Biblical Theology of Irenaeus*. Edinburgh: Oliver & Boyd, 1959.

Wink, Walter. *Engaging the Powers: Discernment and Resistance in a World of Domination*. Minneapolis: Augsburg Fortress, 1992.

Winnicott, D. W. *Playing and Reality*. Routledge Classics ed. London: Routledge, 2005.

Wittgenstein, Ludwig. *Philosophical Investigations: The German Text with a Revised English Translation*. Translated by G. E. M. Anscombe. 3rd ed. Oxford: Blackwell, 2001.

Wittkower, Margot, and Rudolf Wittkower. *Born under Saturn: The Character and Conduct of Artists; A Documented History from Antiquity to the French Revolution*. New York: New York Review Books, 2007.

Wolterstorff, Nicholas. *Art in Action: Toward a Christian Aesthetic*. Carlisle, U.K.: Solway, 1997.

———. "The Work of Making a Work of Music." In *What Is Music? An Introduction to the Philosophy of Music*, edited by Philip Alperson, 103–29. University Park: Pennsylvania State University Press, 1987.

———. *Works and Worlds of Art*. Oxford: Clarendon, 1980.

Wybrow, Cameron. *The Bible, Baconianism, and Mastery over Nature: The Old Testament and Its Modern Misreading*. New York: Peter Lang, 1991.

Young, Edward. "Conjectures on Original Composition." In *English Critical Essays (Sixteenth, Seventeenth and Eighteenth Centuries)*, edited by Edmund D. Jones, 315–64. London: Oxford University Press, 1922.

Young, Frances. "'Creatio ex Nihilo': A Context for the Emergence of the Christian Doctrine of Creation." *Scottish Journal of Theology* 44 (1991): 139–51.

Zilsel, Edgar. *Die Entstehung des Geniebegriffes*. Tübingen: J. C. B. Mohr, 1926.

Index of Names